Economic and Societal Impact of Organized Crime:

Policy and Law Enforcement Interventions

Alicia Danielsson
University of Bolton, UK & Hume Institute for Postgraduate Studies, Switzerland

A volume in the Advances in Public Policy and Administration (APPA) Book Series

IGI Global
PUBLISHER of TIMELY KNOWLEDGE

Published in the United States of America by
IGI Global
Information Science Reference (an imprint of IGI Global)
701 E. Chocolate Avenue
Hershey PA, USA 17033
Tel: 717-533-8845
Fax: 717-533-8661
E-mail: cust@igi-global.com
Web site: http://www.igi-global.com

Library of Congress Cataloging-in-Publication Data

Names: Danielsson, Alicia, editor.
Title: Economic and societal impact of organized crime : policy and law enforcement interventions / edited by Alicia Danielsson.
Description: Hershey, PA : Information Science Reference, [2024] | Includes bibliographical references and index. | Summary: "This book, in its exploration of the multifaceted nature of serious and organized crime globally, dedicates a significant portion to examining policy and law enforcement interventions"-- Provided by publisher.
Identifiers: LCCN 2024007178 (print) | LCCN 2024007179 (ebook) | ISBN 9798369303276 (hardcover) | ISBN 9798369303283 (ebook)
Subjects: LCSH: Organized crime. | International crimes. | Human rights.
Classification: LCC HV6441 .E358 2024 (print) | LCC HV6441 (ebook) | DDC 364.106--dc23/eng/20240403
LC record available at https://lccn.loc.gov/2024007178
LC ebook record available at https://lccn.loc.gov/2024007179

This book is published in the IGI Global book series Advances in Public Policy and Administration (APPA) (ISSN: 2475-6644; eISSN: 2475-6652)

British Cataloguing in Publication Data
A Cataloguing in Publication record for this book is available from the British Library.

All work contributed to this book is new, previously-unpublished material.
The views expressed in this book are those of the authors, but not necessarily of the publisher.

For electronic access to this publication, please contact: eresources@igi-global.com.

Advances in Public Policy and Administration (APPA) Book Series

ISSN:2475-6644
EISSN:2475-6652

MISSION

Proper management of the public sphere is necessary in order to maintain order in modern society. Research developments in the field of public policy and administration can assist in uncovering the latest tools, practices, and methodologies for governing societies around the world.

The **Advances in Public Policy and Administration (APPA) Book Series** aims to publish scholarly publications focused on topics pertaining to the governance of the public domain. APPA's focus on timely topics relating to government, public funding, politics, public safety, policy, and law enforcement is particularly relevant to academicians, government officials, and upper-level students seeking the most up-to-date research in their field.

COVERAGE

- Government
- Law Enforcement
- Political Economy
- Politics
- Public Administration
- Public Funding
- Public Policy
- Resource allocation
- Urban Planning

IGI Global is currently accepting manuscripts for publication within this series. To submit a proposal for a volume in this series, please contact our Acquisition Editors at Acquisitions@igi-global.com or visit: http://www.igi-global.com/publish/.

The Advances in Public Policy and Administration (APPA) Book Series (ISSN 2475-6644) is published by IGI Global, 701 E. Chocolate Avenue, Hershey, PA 17033-1240, USA, www.igi-global.com. This series is composed of titles available for purchase individually; each title is edited to be contextually exclusive from any other title within the series. For pricing and ordering information please visit http://www.igi-global.com/book-series/advances-public-policy-administration/97862. Postmaster: Send all address changes to above address.

Titles in this Series

For a list of additional titles in this series, please visit:
http://www.igi-global.com/book-series/advances-public-policy-administration/97862

Regulating Fair Competition Toward Sustainable Development Goals
Siti Fazilah Abdul Shukor (University of Tunku Abdul Rahman, Malaysia) Farahdilah Ghazali (University of Putra Malaysia, Malaysia) Nur Yuhanis Ismon (University of Tun Hussien Onn, Malaysia) and Aerni Isa (Taylor's University, Malaysia)
Information Science Reference • © 2024 • 285pp • H/C (ISBN: 9798369303900) • US $275.00

Analyzing Energy Crises and the Impact of Country Policies on the World
Merve Suna Ozel Ozcan (Kirikkale University, Turkey)
Engineering Science Reference • © 2024 • 283pp • H/C (ISBN: 9798369304402) • US $240.00

Using Crises and Disasters as Opportunities for Innovation and Improvement
Saeed Siyal (School of Economics and Management, Beijing University of Chemical Technology, China)
Information Science Reference • © 2024 • 323pp • H/C (ISBN: 9781668495223) • US $240.00

Cognitive Governance and the Historical Distortion of the Norm of Modern Development A Theory of Political Asymmetry
Renny Rueda (American University in the Emirates, UAE)
Information Science Reference • © 2024 • 254pp • H/C (ISBN: 9781668497944) • US $215.00

Financial Evaluation and Risk Management of Infrastructure Projects
Kleopatra Petroutsatou (Aristotle University of Thessaloniki, Greece) and Constantin Zopounidis (Technical University of Crete, Greece & Audencia Business School, France)
Information Science Reference • © 2024 • 248pp • H/C (ISBN: 9781668477861) • US $225.00

For an entire list of titles in this series, please visit:
http://www.igi-global.com/book-series/advances-public-policy-administration/97862

IGI Global
PUBLISHER of TIMELY KNOWLEDGE

701 East Chocolate Avenue, Hershey, PA 17033, USA
Tel: 717-533-8845 x100 • Fax: 717-533-8661
E-Mail: cust@igi-global.com • www.igi-global.com

Editorial Advisory Board

Table of Contents

Detailed Table of Contents

This chapter critically examines the legal categorization of forced marriage within the context of modern slavery, focusing on the need for legislative reform in England and Wales. It explores the intricate parallels between forced marriage and modern slavery, emphasizing shared elements of coercion, exploitation, and infringement of autonomy and consent. The discussion includes a philosophical analysis of forced marriage, considering feminist theories and the impact of patriarchal norms. By comparing the current legal frameworks of England and Wales with international standards set by the United Nations and the International Labour Organization, the chapter highlights discrepancies and advocates for harmonization. It underscores the importance of recognizing forced marriage as a form of modern slavery to ensure comprehensive legal responses, protection, and support for victims, culminating in a call for legal reform in England and Wales to align with global human rights efforts.

seen as religious sanctioned prostitution in India. Note that, despite the practice being abolished by various state legislations in India, there are approximately more than 48,000 devadasis in the country according to the data by the National Commission for Women, New Delhi. Further, as per the National Human Rights Commission, the state of Andhra Pradesh, India alone had over 25,000 devadasis in 2015 with girls as young as 12 years old who were being pushed into prostitution in the nearby states of Karnataka and Maharashtra. This chapter therefore aims to highlight the reasons behind this social evil considering the broader interconnections between law and religion.

This chapter brings together the various components of organised crime in Ghana and analyses the role of law and law enforcement agencies. It is argued that organised crime in Ghana undermines the emerging fragile democratic institutions in the country. Rooted in transparency, press freedom, rule of law, and free and fair elections, some elected and/or appointed officials who have taken oaths of office to defend the Constitution without fear or favour have largely been compromised to do the bidding of criminal syndicates at the expense of citizens. Despite the improvement in legislation and the coordinated efforts of mandated state agencies, the influence of affluent organised criminal syndicates on some law enforcement agencies has weakened state-agency collaboration. The undermining role of politicians presents a paradox of power subversion that aids and abets organised criminal activities. Sophisticated technology, political preparedness, and individual alertness are crucial in dealing with organised crime in Ghana.

Child pornography on the internet is becoming a more noticeable concern in today's culture. Child pornographers have found an easy arena for spreading terrifying photographs of children being sexually assaulted with the development in home personal computer (PC) usage and more widely available access to the world wide web over the last decade. Detecting and prosecuting cyber child pornographers has also become a difficult task for police and attorneys throughout the world, with a high failure rate of putting culprits behind bars. Law enforcement agents' existing approaches for combating online child pornography might be regarded as archaic and ineffective. In this chapter, the authors will look at the key social and legal difficulties that people, legislators, and police officers face when it comes to online child pornography. This chapter will further focus on providing a solution and suggest innovative approaches to combat online child pornography.

The ultimate goal of society is to maintain social order. This can be attained by restricting the menace of crime. Within crime, there is a category of 'victimless crime' – which may sound oxymoronic. The victimless crimes cover those crimes where victims are not identifiable, or the illegal activity that occurs with the parties' consent. For decades there has been debate on whether victimless activity should be criminalized or not. The argument by the modernized world is in favor of decriminalization due to the lack of harm to others and freedom of the individual. This chapter hypothesizes that 'victimless crimes have victims – society as a whole, hence the term victimless is a façade. The chapter will attempt to establish the correlation between Mill's Harm Principle viz-a-viz modern victimless crimes. Thereafter, the chapter will discuss the various victimless crimes prevalent in India & their impact on the subcontinent. Lastly, the chapter will summarize the arguments with concluding remarks on the criminological aspect of victimless crimes.

The conflicts in Manipur have a long socio-political history. The root causes behind these clashes are diverse and complex, including colonization, governance issues, drug trafficking, discrimination, geopolitics, and militarization. The ethnic groups and governments have failed to reconcile the differences peacefully. Through this chapter, the researcher is trying to provide an overview of the conflict and how this has affected the people of Manipur. The researcher will identify various dimensions of the conflict in Manipur and analyze how drug trafficking, land rights, and illegal migration are linked to ethnic violence between Kukis and Meiteis by highlighting the historical, cultural, and political aspects of the problem. Further, the existing policies and laws are analysed. Finally, the need for peace negotiations, the requirement for the disarmament of the communities, the need for investigation and trial of grave violations, and the necessity for establishing a truth and reconciliation commission will be discussed.

India's constitutional ethos establishes itself to be a secular country, believing in every citizen's right to follow their own religious beliefs. However, in the recent past, the evolution of Hindu nationalistic politics of hate, coupled with a monolithic and myopic viewpoint of construing the nation as a Hindu entity, has fanned the growth of fundamentalistic ideals of cow worship and cow protection. This has significantly led to the rise of non-state actors who employ any or all means possible of strong-arming minorities and the vulnerable sections of society in the name of cow protection. Thus, through this chapter, the author shall at the first instance argue the reasons for the rise of cow-vigilantism in India, situating it in a historical and socio-political context. The author's second argument would be to demonstrate how cow vigilantism has elevated to the status of organised crime in India. Finally, the author shall conclude with arguments suggesting ways to put an end to such heinous incidents of vigilantism and forge a way forward.

This chapter examines the underlying reasons, repercussions, and issues related to organized crime's influence on electricity theft and power infrastructure damage in South Africa in depth. It goes to the incentives that drive organized crime groups as well as the flaws in the power distribution structure that allow such illegal activity. Furthermore, the chapter investigates the socioeconomic effects of these crimes on customers, businesses, and communities, putting light on the broad scope of these illegal acts. As crucial strategies, the chapter advocates stronger security measures, legislative reforms, community engagement, international cooperation, and public-private partnerships. South Africa can alleviate the impact of the ongoing electricity crisis, restore stability to the energy sector, and protect key infrastructure by taking a comprehensive approach. This chapter aims to give useful insights for policymakers, researchers, and practitioners working to prevent organized crime's effect on the nation's energy sector.

Organized crime is a noted facilitator of drugs, weapons, and human trafficking. Overlooked, however, is the involvement of these criminal enterprises regarding flora (i.e., plants) and fauna (i.e., animals) crimes. For example, the trafficking of wildlife and wildlife parts globally. The need to better understand the impact these criminal units is espoused by multiple stakeholders. Subsequently, this chapter will discuss the impact organized crime has on wildlife and the environment through an international lens.

This chapter explores the integral role of taxi and Private Hire Vehicle (PHV) services in combating organized crime, with a specific focus on child sexual exploitation as highlighted by cases like Operation Stovewood. The research scrutinizes the socio-economic impacts of organized crime on individuals and communities, emphasizing the need for a collaborative approach to address these issues. It particularly examines the involvement of the taxi and PHV industry in these crimes and advocates for effective public-private collaboration in tackling organized crime. Organized crime, including activities like human trafficking and extortion, undermines societal stability, fostering violence and eroding public trust in institutions. The chapter presents a disturbing dimension of this crime: the exploitation of certain taxi/PHV drivers in child sexual exploitation scandals, as seen in investigations across cities like Rotherham. This revelation has led to a critical inquiry into taxi and PHV licensing, aiming to address regulatory gaps and ensure the safeguarding of vulnerable individuals. The research adopts a comprehensive methodology, analyzing Operation Stovewood as a case study and reviewing academic and government reports on the effectiveness of policies and legal frameworks governing taxi and PHV licensing. It also explores the ethical and legal responsibilities of regulating taxi and PHV services, balancing safety measures with privacy rights. Key to this discourse is the necessity of public-private collaboration in combating organized crime. The strategic positioning of taxi and PHV drivers as local surveillance agents offers a unique opportunity in this fight. The chapter proposes comprehensive training, legal structures, and ethical guidelines to empower drivers in this role, supplemented by technological advancements like

Preface

Serious and organized crime is a global phenomenon that affects millions of people worldwide. From trafficking in human beings and drug trafficking to cybercrime and money laundering, the impact of these activities is felt by individuals, families, and entire communities (Roth, 2017; Tsuwa, 2023; Lin, 2023; Lallerstedt, 2022; Zabyelina & Thachuk, 2022). Yet what is the human cost of serious and organized crime? What happens to the victims and their families? How do the consequences of serious and organised crime impact the social fabric of our societies? This book started out on a journey, lead by an idea and armed with curiosity and dedication, to look beyond the purely legal, towards organised crime in a broader extent. The idea was to showcase organised crime in its many facets and its different representations across the globe, while at the same time focussing on factors beyond the narrow lens of criminal justice, to include social and economic aspects of serious and organised crime. With contributions from different countries, spread across four continents, the mission has resulted in a collection of research papers that represent the vast and significant diversity of the problem faced not only by law enforcement, but also by the affected communities.

ORGANIZED CRIME: A MULTIFACETED GLOBAL CHALLENGE

Organized crime, as defined by various international and national bodies, presents a complex and dynamic challenge that defies simple categorization. The United Nations, the European Union, and individual nations like the UK have endeavored to provide frameworks and definitions, yet these often struggle to encapsulate the full scope and adaptive nature of organized criminal groups (OCGs). This section aims to explore the various dimensions of organized crime, reflecting on its legal, social, and global characteristics while maintaining coherence with the overarching theme of the book.

At its core, organized crime is characterized by its pursuit of profit and power, frequently at the expense of the community and its members. This pursuit manifests in myriad forms, from traditional rackets like drug trafficking and human smuggling to more modern ventures such as cybercrime and environmental exploitation. The operational structures of OCGs vary significantly, ranging from tightly-knit mafia-style organizations to loose networks of individuals collaborating for specific criminal purposes (Nicaso & Danesi, 2021; Wyatt, van Uhm & Nurse, 2020; Bright & Whelan, 2020; Danielsson, 2023).

The legal definitions provided by entities like the United Nations and the European Union emphasize aspects such as the structured nature of these groups, the seriousness of the offenses committed, and the duration and international or transnational scope of their activities (UN General Assembly, United Nations Convention against Transnational Organized Crime; European Commission, Communication from the Commission to the European Parliament, the Council, the EESC and the Committee of the Regions on the EU Strategy to tackle Organised Crime 2021-2025; Europol. (2017). However, as scholars and practitioners have noted, these definitions often fall short in capturing the fluidity and diversity of modern organized crime. The traditional view of hierarchical, monolithic crime syndicates is increasingly giving way to a recognition of more decentralized and flexible criminal networks. These networks exploit the opportunities afforded by globalization, technological advances, and the interconnectedness of today's world, making them particularly elusive and resilient to conventional law enforcement strategies (Beristain, 2021; Mishra, 2023; Aranega, 2023; Fraser & Van Hellemont, 2020; Çomak, Şeker, Civelek & Bozkuş, 2022; Bøås & Strazzari, 2020).

The social impact of organized crime is profound and far-reaching. It undermines the rule of law, fuels corruption, erodes public trust in institutions, and can destabilize entire communities and economies (Singh, 2022; Manukyan, Stepanyan & Ilyushina, 2023; Pereda, 2022; Rolla, 2022). The most vulnerable segments of society often bear the brunt of these activities. For example, the trade in counterfeit goods and specific frauds against public authorities or large companies, though seemingly benign, can have significant economic and social consequences. These activities not only deprive governments of revenue but also endanger public health and safety (Comolli, 2021; Zabyelina & Thachuk, 2022; Liddick Jr, 2020).

Furthermore, organized crime has a symbiotic relationship with issues of poverty, inequality, and social exclusion. Criminal networks often exploit the vulnerabilities of marginalized groups, drawing them into a cycle of criminality and victimization (Briskey, 2023; Higgins, 2022; Andell, James & Maitra, 2023). The phenomenon of "crime as a service" is also emerging, where criminal skills and services are offered on a contractual basis, mirroring legitimate business practices. This commercialization of crime adds another layer of complexity to the challenge, blurring the lines between the legal and illegal economies (Di Nicola, 2022; Snaphaan & van Ruitenburg, 2024; Kuchalskis, 2020).

The international and transnational aspects of organized crime necessitate a coordinated global response. However, this is often hampered by jurisdictional limitations, differences in legal systems, and varying levels of political and economic stability across countries. The cross-border nature of many organized crime activities, such as cybercrime, human trafficking, and environmental crime, requires innovative and collaborative approaches that transcend national boundaries and legal frameworks (Danielsson, 2023).

This volume recognises that organized crime is a multifaceted phenomenon that cannot be confined to a single definition or framework. Its implications are vast and varied, impacting not just the realms of law enforcement and criminal justice but also social structures, economic systems, and international relations. As this book unfolds, it seeks to provide a holistic understanding of organized crime, drawing on diverse academic perspectives and practical experiences. The aim is to illuminate the complexities of this global challenge and to foster a more comprehensive and nuanced approach to addressing it.

In an era where the branches and roots of organized crime weave ever more convolutedly into the fabric of global society, understanding its multifaceted impacts is not just an academic pursuit but a societal imperative. This edited volume, " Economic and Societal Impact of Organized Crime: Policy and Law Enforcement Interventions," embarks on an incisive exploration of this dark underbelly of human civilization, tracing its manifestations across continents and communities. The chapters within this book are curated to offer a comprehensive view, encompassing a wide range of disciplines and perspectives, from legal analyses and sociological insights to economic ramifications and policy implications.

Organized crime, a phenomenon as old as society itself, has continually evolved, morphing into complex networks that defy traditional borders and legal jurisdictions. Its impact is far-reaching, affecting individuals, institutions, economies, and even the very moral and social fabric of nations. The purpose of this volume is to shed light on these impacts, offering a detailed and nuanced understanding of the various forms of organized crime and their profound effects on society.

The journey begins with a critical examination of the legal categorization of forced marriage within the context of modern slavery in England and Wales. This opening chapter sets the stage by highlighting the intricate interplay between human rights violations and organized crime. It not only scrutinizes existing legal frameworks but also calls for a harmonized global response to these clandestine atrocities.

As the reader progresses through the book, the geographical lens widens, encapsulating diverse national contexts. From the victim protection policies in Tanzania to the challenges faced by law enforcement agencies in Ghana, the chapters offer a rich tapestry of insights into how different societies confront the hydra of organized crime. Each chapter not only delves into the specificities of its focus area but also contributes to a broader understanding of the global landscape of criminal networks.

In a novel approach to combating organized crime, the book explores the potential of community actors, specifically taxi drivers, as allies in this fight. This chapter underscores the necessity of unconventional strategies and the power of grassroots involvement in tackling complex criminal enterprises. The inclusion of such perspectives is indicative of the book's commitment to presenting a holistic view of the battle against organized crime.

The discussion then navigates through the murky waters of religiously sanctioned prostitution in India, the rise of cow vigilantism, and the socio-economic impacts of victimless crimes within the Indian subcontinent. These chapters highlight the unique cultural and societal contexts in which organized crime can flourish and the intricate ways in which it intertwines with traditional practices and beliefs.

Addressing a global concern, the book shifts its focus to cyber child pornography, providing a stark reminder of the evolving nature of criminal activities in the digital age. The discussion on money laundering further expands on the economic dimensions of organized crime, revealing how illicit financial flows can undermine global development and governance.

The chapters on electricity theft and infrastructure vandalism in South Africa, and the exploitation of flora and fauna, serve to illustrate the varied and often overlooked aspects of organized crime, from the tangible damage to critical infrastructure to the less visible but equally devastating environmental impacts.

In sum, this volume offers a comprehensive exploration of the complex web of organized crime. Through its diverse array of chapters, the book not only provides a rich academic resource but also serves as a clarion call for a concerted and multifaceted response to one of the most pressing challenges of our times. As you turn these pages, I invite you to delve deeper into the shadows cast by organized crime, to understand its roots, its branches, and most importantly, the ways we can collectively strive to mitigate its pervasive impact.

THE CHALLENGE

In the realm of criminology and global justice, organized crime stands as a formidable and ever-evolving challenge. It transcends traditional boundaries of law and ethics, weaving complex networks that infiltrate the very core of societies worldwide. This challenge, as reflected in the recent academic discourse, is not only about understanding the vast array of criminal activities but also about comprehending their profound impacts on a global scale.

Recent academic discussions in criminology and sociology have increasingly focused on the fluid and adaptive nature of organized crime (Bright & Whelan, 2020; Nilsson & Ritzén, 2023; Hignett, 2021; Lavorgna, 2020). Scholars like Federico Varese (2011) in his seminal work "Mafias on the Move" have emphasized the transnational aspect of these criminal networks, highlighting how they exploit globalization, technology, and the increasing interconnectedness of the world. The ease with which these organizations adapt and morph presents a significant challenge for law enforcement and policy-makers, who often find themselves playing catch-up in a rapidly evolving landscape.

One of the critical academic debates centers around the definition and scope of organized crime. As argued by scholars such as Letizia Paoli (2008) in "Mafia Brotherhoods," the traditional view of organized crime as strictly hierarchical and structured like mafias has given way to a recognition of more fluid and decentralized networks. This evolution complicates efforts to identify and dismantle these networks, as they often operate within the grey areas of legality, sometimes even under the guise of legitimate businesses.

Furthermore, the impact of organized crime extends far beyond the immediate criminal acts. Recent studies have delved into the socio-economic consequences of these activities, exploring how they undermine state institutions, distort economies, and contribute to political instability. In his work "Illicit," Moisés Naím (2010) has extensively discussed how illicit trade not only fuels criminal enterprises but also has far-reaching implications for global markets and international relations (see also Naím, 2022).

Another area of critical analysis is the intersection of organized crime with issues of human rights and social justice. The exploitative nature of many criminal activities, such as human trafficking, drug trafficking, and cybercrime, raises profound ethical and moral questions (Natarajan, 2019; Comolli, 2018; Roth, 2017; Hingston & Hingston, 2023). Academics like Louise Shelley (2010) in "Human Trafficking: A Global Perspective" have highlighted the human cost of these crimes, arguing for a more victim-centered approach in both policy and academic research.

Moreover, the advent of technology and the internet has given rise to new forms of organized crime, such as cybercrime and online fraud (Di Nicola, 2022; Shulzhenko & Romashkin, 2020; Lavorgna, 2020). Scholars are increasingly focusing on the implications of these digital-age crimes, as highlighted in works like "Cybercrime and Society" by Majid Yar and Kevin Steinmetz (2019). The anonymity and borderless nature of the internet pose unique challenges for detection and prosecution, requiring innovative approaches and international cooperation.

The environmental impact of organized crime is another emerging area of academic interest. The illegal trade in wildlife, timber, and other natural resources has significant ecological consequences, as explored in works like "Green Crimes and Dirty Money" by Toine Spapens et al. (2018). This aspect of organized crime often receives less attention but is crucial for understanding its comprehensive impact on global sustainability and biodiversity.

In light of these academic discussions, this volume presents a multifaceted exploration of organized crime, aiming to bridge the gap between theory and practice. Each chapter contributes to a critical understanding of the different dimensions of organized crime, reflecting the latest academic research and offering insights into effective responses.

The challenge, therefore, is not just to dissect and analyze organized crime as an abstract concept but to understand its real-world implications. The chapters in this book are selected to provide a comprehensive overview of the current state of organized crime, its various manifestations, and its profound effects on societies and economies worldwide. They offer a blend of theoretical exploration and practical insights, drawing on a range of disciplines, including law, economics, sociology, and criminology.

Moreover, the book aims to contribute to the ongoing academic debate by presenting diverse perspectives and case studies from different geographical and cultural contexts. This global approach is essential, as organized crime is a phenomenon that knows no borders, affecting developed and developing countries alike.

While the discourse on organized crime often gravitates towards abstract academic theories and legal frameworks, it is imperative to acknowledge the tangible and often devastating impact it has on the most vulnerable segments of society. Organized crime is not just a topic reserved for the halls of academia or the plotlines of television dramas; it is a stark reality that affects the lives of millions, particularly the poor and the marginalized.

The intersection of organized crime with poverty and vulnerability is a critical area that demands attention. Far from being a distant problem, the effects of organized criminal activities are felt most acutely by those in the lower socio-economic strata. The exploitation inherent in human trafficking, drug trade, and illegal labor practices disproportionately affects those with fewer resources and less access to legal protection. Academics like Alice Hills (2010) in "Policing Africa" have emphasized how the weakest members of society often bear the brunt of the violence and corruption that organized crime engenders. More than a decade later, the issues seem to be more prevalent than ever.

It is a misnomer to perceive organized crime solely through the lens of high-profile criminal syndicates and dramatic law enforcement operations. The reality is much more pervasive and insidious. For instance, the local drug trade can ravage communities, fueling addiction and violence (De Schutter & Duquet, 2023; Steenkamp, 2024; Yusuf & Ojewale, 2023; Ayres, 2020). Illegal logging and fishing practices can destroy livelihoods and ecosystems, directly impacting those who depend on these resources for survival. Such crimes may seem distant to those in more privileged positions, but they have a direct and destructive impact on communities and individuals (Elliott, 2022).

Moreover, the reach of organized crime extends beyond immediate victims and perpetrators. It affects the wider society in more subtle, yet profound ways. Money laundering and corruption, for instance, distort economies and undermine the rule of law, eroding public trust in institutions (Levi & Soudijn, 2020; Korystin, Mihus, Svyrydiuk, Likhovitskyy & Mitina, 2020; Pūraitė, 2020; Remeikienė & Gaspareniene, 2023; Sanz-Levia & Jiménez-Sánchez, 2021). This erosion of trust and the consequent weakening of social and economic structures have a ripple effect, impacting everyone, even those who may feel insulated from the more direct effects of crime.

The pervasiveness of organized crime in everyday life is often underappreciated. Its influence can seep into ordinary transactions, the goods we buy, the services we use, and the integrity of the systems that govern our daily lives. This widespread impact underscores the need for a broader societal engagement with the issue of organized crime. It is not just a matter for law enforcement and policymakers; it is a concern that should resonate with every citizen.

In acknowledging this, the book aims to bridge the gap between the often abstract academic discourse and the on-the-ground realities of organized crime. By presenting a comprehensive view that includes both high-level analysis and personal narratives, the book seeks to illuminate the multifaceted nature of organized crime and its far-reaching implications. It strives to make the issue of organized crime relatable and relevant to a wider audience, emphasizing that it is not just a matter for academic or legal debate but a pressing social issue that impacts us all.

As readers engage with the diverse perspectives and insights presented in this volume, the hope is that they will not only gain a deeper understanding of organized crime in its various forms but also recognize its relevance to their own lives and communities. This recognition is crucial for fostering a more informed and proactive stance towards combating organized crime at all levels of society.

POLICY AND LAW ENFORCEMENT INTERVENTIONS: NAVIGATING THE MULTIFACETED LANDSCAPE OF ORGANIZED CRIME

This book, in its exploration of the multifaceted nature of serious and organized crime globally, dedicates a significant portion to examining policy and law enforcement interventions. By delving into a range of individual policy and enforcement battles from different parts of the world, the book underscores the complexity and diversity of the challenges posed by organized crime. Each chapter presents a unique context, demonstrating that there is no one-size-fits-all solution to this pervasive issue.

The key premise of this section is to showcase how different regions and countries confront organized crime, considering their unique socio-political and economic landscapes. From the dense urban centers of Europe to the sprawling landscapes of Africa and Asia, the nature of organized crime and the responses it elicits vary dramatically. This diversity not only highlights the complexity of the problem but also the necessity for tailored and innovative approaches in both policy and law enforcement.

In examining these varied responses, the book provides insights into the successes and limitations of current strategies. For instance, in some regions, a heavy-handed law enforcement approach, focusing on suppression and punishment, has been the norm. However, this method often fails to address the root causes of organized crime, such as poverty, corruption, and social inequality. In contrast, other regions have adopted more holistic strategies, integrating law enforcement with social policy initiatives aimed at prevention, rehabilitation, and community empowerment.

One of the critical aspects explored is the evolving role of international cooperation in combating organized crime. The transnational nature of many criminal networks necessitates a coordinated global response. Chapters dedicated to this theme discuss the frameworks and mechanisms in place for international collaboration, such as the United Nations Convention against Transnational Organized Crime, and how these are implemented in practice. The successes and challenges of these international efforts provide valuable lessons for future policy development.

Moreover, the book delves into the innovative use of technology and intelligence in law enforcement strategies. With the advent of digital technologies, organized crime groups have adapted, using the internet and advanced communication tools to further their activities. In response, law enforcement agencies have also evolved, employing cutting-edge technologies for surveillance, data analysis, and cybercrime investigation. The ethical and legal implications of these technological advancements are critically examined, highlighting the need for a balance between effective law enforcement and the protection of civil liberties.

Another pivotal theme is the importance of understanding the local context in policy-making and law enforcement. Chapters focusing on specific regions or types of crime illustrate how cultural, historical, and socio-economic factors shape both the nature of organized crime and the effectiveness of interventions. This local perspective is crucial for developing strategies that are not only effective but also sustainable and respectful of community norms and values.

ORGANIZATION OF THE BOOK

The book is organized into twelve chapters. A brief description of each of the chapters follows:

Chapter 1: "Reassessing England and Wales' Approach to Forced Marriage in the Context of Modern Slavery"

This opening chapter critically examines the legal categorization of forced marriage within the context of modern slavery in England and Wales. It explores the parallels between forced marriage and modern slavery, emphasizing elements of coercion, exploitation, and the infringement of autonomy and consent. The chapter includes a philosophical analysis of forced marriage, considering feminist theories and the impact of patriarchal norms. It compares the current legal frameworks in England and Wales with international standards, advocating for legal reform to align with global human rights efforts.

Chapter 2: "A Review of Victim Protection Policy in Tanzania and Recommendations"

Focusing on Tanzania, this chapter addresses human trafficking as a form of organized crime. It reviews Tanzania's approach to combating trafficking, encompassing prevention, prosecution, and protection. The chapter evaluates the effectiveness of these strategies and suggests improvements, considering Tanzania's classification as a Tier 2 country in the U.S. Department of State's Trafficking in Persons Report.

Chapter 3: "Money Laundering and its Reflection on Global Development"

This chapter delves into the complexities of money laundering and its impact on global development. It discusses how illegal funds are integrated into the formal economy and the role of offshore zones in facilitating these activities. The chapter critically examines the global economic implications of money laundering, including its effect on development and governance.

Chapter 4: "Temple Prostitution in India: An Exploitative Practice in the Name of Religion"

Exploring the devadasi system in India, this chapter highlights the exploitation of young girls in the name of religion. It provides an in-depth analysis of how this practice, despite being abolished, continues to affect thousands of girls. The chapter examines the interconnections between law, religion, and organized crime in this context.

Chapter 5: "Organized Crime and the Role of Law and Law Enforcement Agencies in Ghana"

This chapter analyzes the various components of organized crime in Ghana and the role of law enforcement agencies. It discusses how organized crime undermines democratic institutions in Ghana, exploring the paradox of power subversion by politicians and the influence of criminal syndicates on state agencies.

Chapter 6: "Cyber Child Pornography: A Socio-Legal Review"

Addressing the growing concern of child pornography on the internet, this chapter reviews the social and legal challenges posed by online child exploitation. It evaluates the effectiveness of current law enforcement approaches and suggests innovative strategies to combat cyber child pornography.

Chapter 7: "Casual or Casualty: Victimless Crime's Socio-Economic Impact in Indian Context"

This chapter examines the concept of 'victimless crime' in India, analyzing its socio-economic impact. It debates the criminalization of such activities and establishes the correlation between these crimes and societal harm, emphasizing the need for a comprehensive criminological approach.

Chapter 8: "Exploring Reconciliation Prospects Amidst Identity and Governance Crisis in Manipur"

Focusing on the conflicts in Manipur, this chapter provides an overview of the socio-political history and the link between drug trafficking, land rights, and ethnic violence. It discusses the need for peace negotiations and the establishment of a truth and reconciliation commission.

Chapter 9: "In the Name of the Holy Cow!: The Issue of Cow Vigilantism in Contemporary India"

This chapter explores the rise of cow vigilantism in India, situating it in a historical and socio-political context. It demonstrates how cow vigilantism has evolved into a form of organized crime and suggests ways to address this issue.

Chapter 10: "The Influence of Organized Crime on Electricity Theft and Power Infrastructure Vandalism in South Africa"

Examining the impact of organized crime on South Africa's energy sector, this chapter discusses the motivations behind electricity theft and infrastructure vandalism. It advocates for comprehensive strategies involving security measures, legislative reforms, and community engagement.

Chapter 11: "Outside and Out of Mind: Organized Criminal Enterprises and the Fleecing of Flora and Fauna"

This chapter discusses the impact of organized crime on wildlife and the environment through an international lens. It highlights the role of criminal enterprises in the trafficking of wildlife and wildlife parts, emphasizing the need for a global understanding and response.

Chapter 12: "Empowering Community Actors: Training Taxi and Private Hire Vehicle Drivers as Allies in Combating Organized Crime"

The final chapter presents an innovative approach to combating organized crime by involving community actors. It explores the role of taxi drivers in detecting and reporting criminal activities, highlighting the potential of grassroots involvement in the fight against organized crime.

Alicia Danielsson
Bolton University, UK & Hume Institute for Postgraduate Studies, Lausanne, Switzerland

REFERENCES

Andell, P., James, D., & Maitra, D. (2023). County lines and the transformation of middle drug markets within a local organised crime context. In *Understanding Drug Dealing and Illicit Drug Markets* (pp. 245–264). Routledge.

Aranega, A. D. T. (2023). *The Crime-Geopolitics Nexus and Transnational Environmental Crimes in the Amazon Forest* (Doctoral dissertation, PUC-Rio).

Ayres, T. (2020). *The War on Drugs and its invisible collateral damage* (A. Brisman & N. South, Eds.).

Beristain, M. J. O. (2021). Impact of globalization and use of violence within Italian and Mexican criminal groups. *Sapienza Universitá di Roma. Working Paper*, (4).

Bøås, M., & Strazzari, F. (2020). Governance, Fragility and Insurgency in the Sahel: A hybrid political order in the making. *The International Spectator*, *55*(4), 1–17.

Bright, D., & Whelan, C. (2020). *Organised crime and law enforcement: A network perspective*. Routledge.

Briskey, M. (2023). Organized Crime and Penury in Pakistan: The Hybrid Exploitation of the Poor and Powerless. In The Routledge Handbook of Poverty in the Global South (pp. 284-301). Routledge India.

Çomak, H., Şeker, B. Ş., Civelek, Y., & Bozkuş, Ç. A. (Eds.). (2022). *Cyber Environment and International Politics* (Vol. 12). Transnational Press London.

Comolli, V. (2021). Organized crime during and after the pandemic. In *Global Security in Times of Covid-19: Brave New World?* (pp. 245–271). Springer International Publishing.

Comolli, V. (Ed.). (2018). *Organized crime and illicit trade: How to respond to this strategic challenge in old and new domains*. Springer.

Danielsson, A. (2023). Tackling Digital Entrepreneurship Within the Illicit Economy: The Evolving Fight Against Serious and Organized Crime Within a Digitally Facilitated Sex Industry. In Digital Entrepreneurship and Co-Creating Value Through Digital Encounters (pp. 118-144). IGI Global.

De Schutter, A., & Duquet, N. (2023). The nexus between drug markets and gun violence in the European Union.

Di Nicola, A. (2022). Towards digital organized crime and digital sociology of organized crime. *Trends in Organized Crime*, 1–20.

Elliott, L. (2022). Transnational environmental crime and development. In *The Routledge Handbook of Global Development* (pp. 233–244). Routledge.

European Commission, Communication from the Commission to the European Parliament, the Council, the EESC and the Committee of the Regions on the EU Strategy to tackle Organised Crime 2021-2025, COM(2021) 170 final

Europol. (2017). *Defining Serious and Organised Crime*. SOCTA 2017. https://www.europol.europa.eu/socta/2017/defining-serious-an d-organised-crime.html

Fraser, A., & Van Hellemont, E. (2020). Gangs and globalization. In Oxford Research Encyclopedia of Criminology and Criminal Justice.

Higgins, K. C. (2022). *Realness, wrongness, justice exploring criminalization as a mediated politics of vulnerability* (Doctoral dissertation, London School of Economics and Political Science).

Hignett, K. (2021). Transnational organized crime and the global village. In *Routledge handbook of transnational organized crime* (pp. 305–317). Routledge.

Hills, A. (2000). *Policing Africa: internal security and the limits of liberalization.* Lynne Rienner Publishers.

Hingston, C. A., & Hingston, D. (2023). Human Trafficking: A Dark Side of the Cyberspace. In *Cybercrime and Challenges in South Africa* (pp. 177–192). Springer Nature Singapore.

Korystin, O. Y., Mihus, I. P., Svyrydiuk, N. P., Likhovitskyy, Y. O., & Mitina, O. M. (2020). Money laundering: macroeconomic assessment methods and current trend in Ukraine.

Kuchalskis, K. (2020). Organised Crime: New Challenges and Response. *Eur. L. Enf't Rsch. Bull.*, *19*, 95.

Lallerstedt, K. (2022). Global Trade of "Illicit Goods" Its Scale, Consequences, and Addressing the Problem. In *Handbook of Security Science* (pp. 933–954). Springer International Publishing.

Lavorgna, A. (2020). Organized Crime and Cybercrime. The Palgrave Handbook of International Cybercrime and Cyberdeviance, 117-134.

Levi, M., & Soudijn, M. (2020). Understanding the laundering of organized crime money. *Crime and Justice*, *49*(1), 579–631.

Liddick, D. R. Jr. (2020). *Transnational Organized Crime and Natural Resources Trafficking: Funding Conflict and Stealing from the World's Most Vulnerable Citizens*. Lexington Books.

Lin, L. S. (2023). Asian Organized Crime in the United States: Perception, Institutions, and Policy Responses. In *Asian Organized Crime and the Anglosphere* (pp. 43–59). Springer International Publishing.

Manukyan, Y., Stepanyan, A., & Ilyushina, M. (2023). METHODOLOGICAL FOUNDATIONS OF SOCIO-PHILOSOPHICAL AND LEGAL ANALYSIS OF CORRUPTION. *Wisdom*, (2 (26)), 212–222.

Mishra, S. (2023). The Fluidity of World Order and Break from Past: Opportunities and Challenges. *Social Development Issues*, *46*(1).

Naim, M. (2010). *Illicit: How smugglers, traffickers and copycats are hijacking the global economy*. Random House.

Naím, M. (2022). *Ilícito: Cómo traficantes, contrabandistas y piratas están cambiando el mundo/Illicit* (Vol. 18099). Debate.

Natarajan, M. (Ed.). (2019). *International and transnational crime and justice*. Cambridge University Press.

Nicaso, A., & Danesi, M. (2021). *Organized crime: A cultural introduction*. Routledge.

Nilsson, S., & Ritzén, S. (2023). Maneuvering responsive, tactical, and preventive innovation in an innovation ecosystem to address the grand challenge of organized crime. *Creativity and Innovation Management*.

Paoli, L. (2008). *Mafia brotherhoods: Organized crime, Italian style*. Oxford University Press.

Pereda, V. (2022). Why Global North criminology fails to explain organized crime in Mexico. *Theoretical Criminology*, *26*(4), 620–640.

Pūraitė, A. (2020). Economic impact of organised crime to state security. *Проблеми законності*, (149), 185-199.

Remeikienė, R., & Gaspareniene, L. (2023). Effects of Economic and Financial Crime on the Government Budget and the Quality of Public Services. In *Economic and Financial Crime, Sustainability and Good Governance* (pp. 173–204). Springer International Publishing.

Rolla, P. (2022). *The social consequences of organized crime groups* (Doctoral dissertation, University of Sussex).

Roth, M. P. (2017). *Global organized crime: A 21st century approach.* Taylor & Francis.

Sanz-Levia, L., & Jiménez-Sánchez, F. (2021). Breaking democracy: Illegal political finance and organized crime in Guatemala. *Crime, Law, and Social Change*, *75*(1), 21–43.

Shelley, L. (2010). *Human trafficking: A global perspective*. Cambridge University Press.

Shulzhenko, N., & Romashkin, S. (2020). Internet fraud and transnational organized crime. *Juridical Tribune, 10*(1), 162–172.

Singh, D. (2022). The Causes of Police Corruption and Working towards Prevention in Conflict-Stricken States. *Laws, 11*(5), 69.

Snaphaan, T., & van Ruitenburg, T. (2024). Financial Crime Scripting: An Analytical Method to Generate, Organise and Systematise Knowledge on the Financial Aspects of Profit-Driven Crime. *European Journal on Criminal Policy and Research*, 1–21.

Spapens, T., White, R., Van Uhm, D., & Huisman, W. (Eds.). (2018). *Green crimes and dirty money*. Routledge.

Steenkamp, C. (2024). Captagon and conflict: Drugs and war on the border between Jordan and Syria. *Mediterranean Politics*, 1–25.

Tsuwa, J. T. (2023) The Impact of Migration and Transnational Organized Crime on Development in West Africa Rufus Aisedion.

UN General Assembly, *United Nations Convention against Transnational Organized Crime: resolution / adopted by the General Assembly*, 8 January 2001, A/RES/55/25

Varese, F. (2011). *Mafias on the move: How organized crime conquers new territories*. Princeton University Press.

Wyatt, T., van Uhm, D., & Nurse, A. (2020). Differentiating criminal networks in the illegal wildlife trade: Organized, corporate and disorganized crime. *Trends in Organized Crime*, *23*, 350–366.

Yar, M., & Steinmetz, K. F. (2019). *Cybercrime and society*. Sage Publications.

Yusuf, O. L., & Ojewale, O. R. (2023). Implications of urban violence on community security in Ibadan North Local Government Area of Oyo State, Nigeria. *Urban Crime. International Journal (Toronto, Ont.)*, *4*(1), 12–39.

Zabyelina, Y., & Thachuk, K. L. (Eds.). (2022). *The Private Sector and Organized Crime: Criminal Entrepreneurship, Illicit Profits, and Private Sector Security Governance*. Taylor & Francis.

Chapter 1
Reassessing England and Wales' Approach to Forced Marriage in the Context of Modern Slavery

Alicia Danielsson
University of Bolton, UK & Hume Institute for Postgraduate Studies, Switzerland

Junaid Khan
University of Bolton, UK

ABSTRACT

This chapter critically examines the legal categorization of forced marriage within the context of modern slavery, focusing on the need for legislative reform in England and Wales. It explores the intricate parallels between forced marriage and modern slavery, emphasizing shared elements of coercion, exploitation, and infringement of autonomy and consent. The discussion includes a philosophical analysis of forced marriage, considering feminist theories and the impact of patriarchal norms. By comparing the current legal frameworks of England and Wales with international standards set by the United Nations and the International Labour Organization, the chapter highlights discrepancies and advocates for harmonization. It underscores the importance of recognizing forced marriage as a form of modern slavery to ensure comprehensive legal responses, protection, and support for victims, culminating in a call for legal reform in England and Wales to align with global human rights efforts.

DOI: 10.4018/979-8-3693-0327-6.ch001

FORCED MARRIAGE: A GLOBAL CHALLENGE AT THE INTERSECTION WITH MODERN SLAVERY

Forced marriage, a critical and complex global challenge, sits at a unique intersection with modern slavery. This chapter aims to examine the current shift in international law and various jurisdictions across the globe, focusing on the increasing recognition of forced marriage either as a sub-category of modern slavery or as a component of exploitation within it. This shift is not only pivotal but also reflective of the evolving understanding of human rights and the dynamics of exploitation in contemporary society.

The rationale behind this shift is deeply rooted in the recognition of the striking similarities between the characteristics of forced marriage and those of modern slavery. Both phenomena share elements of coercion, exploitation, and a severe infringement on individual freedoms and rights. The analysis of these similarities sheds light on why forced marriage is increasingly viewed through the lens of modern slavery, thereby necessitating a nuanced legal and policy response.

This chapter adopts a predominantly doctrinal research methodology, supported by a comparative approach. The doctrinal aspect involves an in-depth examination of legal texts, international treaties, and judicial decisions to understand the legal principles and frameworks that govern the issue of forced marriage and its intersection with modern slavery. This approach is crucial in comprehensively understanding the legal and theoretical underpinnings that guide international and national responses to forced marriage.

The comparative aspect of this research is vertical rather than horizontal. This means that instead of comparing different national legal systems with each other (horizontal comparison), the focus is on comparing the shifts and approaches in international law and practice with the framework in England and Wales (vertical comparison). England and Wales represent a national system that operates within, yet in some aspects separately from, the international legal framework. This vertical comparative approach is instrumental in highlighting the discrepancies, challenges, and potential avenues for harmonization between national and international legal responses to forced marriage and modern slavery.

The necessity for such a comparative analysis stems from the observation that while there is a growing international consensus on addressing forced marriage within the broader framework of modern slavery, some national jurisdictions, including England and Wales, seem to lag in this global shift. Understanding the reasons behind this lag, and the implications it carries for the effectiveness of legal and policy measures, is critical for advocating for change and alignment with international standards.

Furthermore, this chapter explores the broader implications of this legal shift. Recognizing forced marriage as a form of modern slavery has profound implications for the rights and protections afforded to victims, the responsibilities of states under international law, and the legal remedies available. It also influences the discourse around forced marriage, shifting it from a predominantly cultural or social issue to one firmly rooted in the realm of human rights and legal accountability.

The exploration of this topic is timely and relevant. In an era where human rights issues are increasingly globalized, and the movements of people across borders bring diverse cultural practices into sharper focus, understanding and addressing forced marriage within the modern slavery framework is imperative. This chapter aims to contribute to this understanding by providing a thorough, legally grounded analysis of the current shifts in international law and the comparative study with the legal framework in England and Wales.

By the end of this chapter, readers will gain a deeper understanding of the legal complexities and challenges surrounding forced marriage, its recognition as a form of modern slavery, and the crucial need for a harmonized international and national response to effectively combat this violation of human rights.

Conceptual Reevaluation of Forced Marriage: A Philosophical and Conceptual Analysis

The evolving conceptualization of forced marriage is a reflection of deeper philosophical shifts in understanding human rights, autonomy, and exploitation (Quek, 2018; Horii, 2020; Baumeister, 2018). Traditionally, forced marriage was viewed through a lens that primarily emphasized the violation of individual rights to marry and to consent (McCabe, Stickle, & Baumeister, 2022; Campmajó, 2020; McCabe, & Eglen, 2022). This view, grounded in liberal humanist principles, posits that each individual possesses inherent rights, including the freedom to make personal choices about marriage. However, the expanding discourse around human rights and personal autonomy necessitates a reevaluation of forced marriage, not merely as a breach of individual rights but as a manifestation of broader systemic exploitation and control akin to modern slavery (Freeman, 2020; Montero, 2022; Koretsky, 2021).

The Intersection With Autonomy and Consent

At the core of forced marriage lies the negation of autonomy – a fundamental principle in both moral and political philosophy (Foblets, Graziadei, & Renteln, 2018; Zeweri, 2022; Baumeister, 2018; Muhleisen, 2017). Autonomy, derived from the Greek words 'autos' (self) and 'nomos' (law), refers to the capacity to make an informed, uncoerced decision. It's a concept deeply embedded in Western philosophical thought, particularly in the works of Immanuel Kant, who posited autonomy as central to moral agency (Rossouw, 2012; Otis, 2023; Guyer, 2003; Sensen, (Ed.), 2012; Kant, 1785). In the context of forced marriage, the absence of autonomy is a fundamental and serious issue; individuals are stripped of their capacity to make critical life choices, which is a violation of a core human value (Quek, 2018; Alanen, 2015; Dhaliwal, 2021; Alam, 2021).

Consent, inherently tied to autonomy, is another pivotal concept. Philosophical explorations of consent, ranging from John Locke's social contract theory to contemporary feminist theories, emphasize consent as a cornerstone of legitimacy in relationships and agreements (Hirschmann, 2018; Kirchhoffer, & Richards, (Eds.), 2019; Forgan, 2013; Davies, 2007). In forced marriages, consent is either completely absent or severely compromised by coercion, manipulation, or imbalance of power. This dissonance between the philosophical ideal of consent and the reality of forced marriage necessitates a conceptual shift in how these unions are understood (Tierney, Laurie, Stallworthy, et al., 2019; Horii, 2021).

Forced Marriage as a Reflection of Power Dynamics

The reconceptualization of forced marriage also involves a critical examination of power dynamics and social structures (Erturk, Bredal, Gupta, et. al., 2011; Phillips, 2012; Chantler, Mirza, & Mackenzie, 2022). Michel Foucault's analysis of power and its pervasive nature in societal structures offers a lens through which forced marriage can be viewed as a tool of social and familial control, reflecting broader power imbalances (Anitha & Gill, 2015; Foucault, 1982; Foucault, 2019; Haugaard, 2017). It's not just an infringement on individual rights, but a manifestation of entrenched patriarchal norms, socio-economic pressures, and cultural practices that collectively undermine personal agency (Azim, 2022; Zasha, 2018; Chetty, 2016).

Forced Marriage and Modern Slavery: Conceptual Parallels

The philosophical parallels between forced marriage and modern slavery are increasingly recognized (Patterson & Zhuo, 2018; Davidson, 2015; Quek, 2018; Mende, 2019). Both phenomena involve the severe curtailment of an individual's liberty and autonomy, often for the benefit or under the control of others (Miers, 2004; Patterson & Zhuo, 2018; Warner, 2004; Walker, 2013; Miers, 2017). The concept of modern slavery, extending beyond the traditional notion of chattel slavery, encompasses a range of conditions where individuals are treated as property, exploited, and deprived of their freedom (Miers, 2000; Bales & Robbins, 2001; Davidson, 2015; Scarpa, 2008; Lamas, 2023). This broader understanding of slavery encompasses the dynamics present in many forced marriages – exploitation, control, and the denial of autonomy (Patterson, 2012; Quirk & Rossi, 2022).

The Role of Exploitation in Forced Marriage

Exploitation, a concept extensively discussed in Marxist theories, is central to understanding the shift in the conceptualization of forced marriage (Hartmann, 2020; Baumeister, 2018; Giammarinaro, 2022). In this context, exploitation refers to the use of coercion, deception, or significant power imbalances to benefit from another's vulnerability (Kim, 2010; Jovanovic, 2020). Forced marriage, in many cases, is a form of exploitation where individuals are used for various familial, social, or economic gains (Erturk, Bredal, Gupta, et. al., 2011); Daraz, Naz & Khan, 2014). The exploitative nature of these unions aligns them more closely with practices of modern slavery than mere violations of personal choice.

Gender, Patriarchy, and Forced Marriage

The intersectionality of gender and forced marriage cannot be overlooked in this philosophical discourse (Allwood, 2016; Few-Demo & Allen, 2020; Anitha & Gill, 2017). Feminist theories, particularly those focusing on patriarchal structures and the subjugation of women, provide a critical framework for understanding forced marriages (Hirschmann, 2009; Connelly, Li, MacDonald & Parpart, 2000; Moschetti, 2005; Bimbi, 2014; Ricker, Earn, Das & Greene, 2023). These unions often reinforce traditional gender roles, perpetuate inequalities, and serve as a mechanism for controlling female sexuality and autonomy (Cepan, 2022; Alban, 2020; Bermúdez Figueroa, Dabetić, Yuste & Saeidzadeh, 2023). Viewing forced marriage through a feminist lens reveals its role in sustaining patriarchal systems and the gendered nature of exploitation.

Sub-Conclusion: Towards a Holistic Understanding

In conclusion, the redefinition of forced marriage in philosophical and conceptual terms extends beyond the violation of individual rights to a more profound understanding of autonomy, consent, power dynamics, exploitation, and gender inequality. This shift towards viewing forced marriage as akin to modern slavery is not just a semantic change but reflects deeper philosophical and conceptual transformations in how personal autonomy and systemic exploitation are understood in contemporary society. This holistic understanding is imperative for developing effective responses that address both the individual and structural dimensions of forced marriage.

THE PARALLELS BETWEEN FORCED MARRIAGE AND MODERN SLAVERY

Forced marriage and modern slavery, as acknowledged by the international legal sphere and a growing body of academic research, share distressing parallels that reveal the systemic and interconnected nature of these human rights violations. This section seeks to explore these parallels by discussing selected shared characteristics, including gender-based characteristics, factors of vulnerability, control methods, and the prevalence of violence and exploitation in both forced marriages and modern slavery.

Gender-Based Characteristics of Forced Marriage and Modern Slavery

The examination of forced marriage and modern slavery reveals a stark gender-based dimension, wherein the majority of victims are women and girls (Miriyam, 2023; Hernández Soto, 2023). This parallels broader trends in cases involving trafficking in persons and reflects deeply rooted gender discrimination and unequal power relations that underlie the force, abuse, and exploitation prevalent in both forced marriages and modern slavery (UNODC, 2020).

In forced marriages, gender discrimination often thrives within patriarchal societies, where traditional gender roles persist despite progress towards gender equality (Dahinden & Manser-Egli, 2023; Madut, 2020; True, 2020). Expert interviews and consultations consistently highlight that forced, abusive, and exploitative marriages disproportionately affect women and girls, who are portrayed as dependents and subjected to societal expectations that enable perpetrators and families to exert control over them (UNODC, 2020; Vasil, 2023; Simmons & Wong, 2021).

Harmful practices linked to gender discrimination further exacerbate the vulnerability of women and girls to forced marriages. Child and early marriages perpetuate harmful practices affecting girls' reproductive health and education, with cultural traditions and customs often maintaining their prevalence (Gebre, Hagos, Teklu, Fisseha & Abera, 2020; Idriss, 2022; Abera, Nega, Tefera & Gelagay, 2020). Emphasis on female purity, family honor, and societal values also shapes harmful practices, with the loss of virginity seen as a negative impact on marriage prospects (Kanaan, 2022; Kohno, Techasrivichien, Suguimoto, Dahlui, Nik Farid & Nakayama, 2020; Bhana & Matswetu, 2023).

Financial transactions such as bride prices or dowries, integral to marriage contracts, exacerbate vulnerability, and sometimes lead to abusive practices, as seen in bride kidnapping cases (UNODC, 2020; Islam, 2021; Lundberg, 2021; Casey, Isa, Isumbisho Mazambi, Giuffrida, Jayne Kulkarni, & Perera, 2022). Cultural traditions like ala kachuu in Kyrgyzstan and ukuthwala in South Africa exploit vulnerabilities, generating situations conducive to forced marriages, particularly among young women (UNODC, 2020; Kim, 2022; Becker, Mirkasimov & Steiner, 2017).

While the majority of cases involve female victims, there are instances of forced marriages involving young men, especially among LGBTQ+ individuals coerced into conformity with perceived gender norms (Chantler, 2019; Dauvergne & Millbank, 2010; Anitha & Gill, 2023). Recognizing the unique challenges faced by male victims is essential in crafting inclusive strategies to combat forced marriages and modern slavery comprehensively.

Overall, the gender-based characteristics of forced marriage and modern slavery underscore the urgent need for comprehensive interventions to challenge discriminatory norms and promote gender equality. The vulnerability of women and girls to exploitative practices within marriage requires targeted efforts to dismantle entrenched stereotypes and empower individuals to resist forced unions.

Factors of Vulnerability in Forced Marriage and Modern Slavery

The factors of vulnerability discussed in the context of forced marriages share several commonalities with those contributing to modern slavery, highlighting the interrelatedness of these phenomena (Cameron, Hemingway, Cunningham & Jacquin, 2021; Buscema, 2023).

Poverty is a pervasive factor in both forced marriages and modern slavery (Charnley & Nkhoma, 2020; Such, Laurent, Jaipaul & Salway, 2020). Economic difficulties may drive families to accept marriage offers for their daughters in exchange for financial benefits, while individuals living in poverty are vulnerable to various forms of exploitation, such as forced labor, due to their desperation (Abrego, 2014; Adepoju, 2005; Likoti & Sibanyoni, 2020).

Persons with mental or physical disabilities face heightened vulnerability in both forced marriages and situations of modern slavery (Gledhill, 2021; Barnes, Naser & Aston, 2023; Clawson, Patterson, Fyson & McCarthy, 2020). Families in forced marriages might see marriage as the only option for individuals with disabilities, while individuals with disabilities are often targeted for forced labor due to perceptions of increased manipulability (UNODC, 2020).

Discrimination against minority groups contributes to the prevalence of forced marriages and exposes minorities to exploitation in various forms, including forced labor (Sabbe, Temmerman, Brems & Leye, 2014; Razack, 2004; Longman & Coene, 2016). Limited opportunities for education and employment further compound the vulnerability of these groups in both contexts (Abbas, 2019; Stapleton, Polakowski, 2022).

Forced displacement due to conflicts or attempts to escape forced marriages can render individuals vulnerable to exploitation and trafficking (Bunting, 2012; UNODC, 2020; Karenga, 2022). Similarly, irregular migrants and migrant workers, seeking to regularize their status through various means, may become vulnerable to exploitation, forced labor, or trafficking (Sabates-Wheeler, 2009; Chan, 2018; Triandafyllidou & Bartolini, 2020).

Cross-cutting themes further underscore the interconnected nature of forced marriage and modern slavery. Gender inequality, harmful gender norms, and societal expectations regarding the roles of women and girls influence both phenomena. Financial motives, such as seeking economic benefits through exploitative arrangements, play a critical role in both forced marriages and modern slavery. Manipulation and coercion are recurring elements in both forced marriages and situations of modern slavery, with vulnerable individuals often coerced or manipulated into exploitative situations (Latham-Sprinkle, David, Bryant & Larsen, 2019; Beatson & Hanley, 2017; Jinkang, 2020).

Overall, even a short overview of the common factors of vulnerability make the interrelatedness of forced marriage and modern slavery evident. Addressing these issues requires a comprehensive approach that tackles broader socio-economic challenges, discrimination, and gender inequality to effectively combat these egregious practices.

Control Methods in Forced Marriage and Modern Slavery

Control methods are pervasive in both modern slavery and forced marriages, where women and girls often endure various forms of abuse and manipulation designed to restrict their freedom (Kara, 2017; Jamadar & Pena, 2022; Miriyam, 2023). These control methods contribute to the systemic nature of exploitation in both phenomena. A significant aspect of control in forced marriages manifests through violence, threats, and psychological abuse orchestrated by the groom's family (Aborisade & Olayinka-Aliu, 2023; Haenen, 2014; Nigam, 2019). This coercive behavior extends to encompass financial dependence, accommodation, access to basic necessities, and even residency permits (Conner, 2013; Trask, 2021; Lyneham & Bricknell, 2018; Garreto, Baptista & Mota, 2022; UNODC, 2020). Mothers-in-law play a crucial part in monitoring and guiding the brides, sometimes employing physical and psychological abuse to enforce compliance with expected standards (Jordana, 2016; Muhleisen, 2017; Sharma, 2023).

One particularly disturbing control method involves leveraging the future of the victims' children. Promises of a good life for the offspring are wielded as a mechanism to bind them to forced marriages, making it more challenging for women to escape, as leaving would entail abandoning their offspring (UNODC, 2020).

In some instances, elements of romantic relationships are entangled with control dynamics, as observed by the UNODC in South Africa (2020). Perpetrators may marry their victims and subsequently adopt an authoritarian stance after marriage, asserting dominance with statements like, "I'm your husband now, so I can tell you what to do" (ibid, 37).

Children born within these coercive marriages serve as yet another tool for control (Crossman & Hardesty, 2018; Onwuachi-Willig, 2005; Callaghan, Alexander, Sixsmith & Fellin, 2018). Perpetrators aim to solidify control by ensuring the birth of children, making it more challenging for women to escape, as leaving would entail abandoning their offspring (Chantler & McCarry, 2020; Martin, 2017).

Household work, often considered a normal aspect of marital life, can transform into a form of exploitation when it involves unpaid labor and servitude. Cultural norms may prevent open discussions about such exploitation, making it challenging to address this issue (McCabe & Eglen, 2022; UNODC, 2020). Labor exploitation, both within the family and in outside employment, is noted by experts, where victims are denied access to their wages, further cementing their dependency on their husbands. In some cases, labor exploitation is entangled with financial gains for the family. Forced criminality or begging may also be linked with forced marriages, although it is not as common. Cases have been reported where victims were forced into criminal activities or begging by their spouses, expanding the scope of exploitation beyond the confines of the marriage itself (UNODC, 2020).

Control methods employed in forced marriages and modern slavery exhibit alarming similarities, utilizing a range of tactics from violence and threats to psychological manipulation. Understanding and addressing these control mechanisms are imperative for developing effective interventions to protect the rights and well-being of those ensnared in such exploitative situations.

Prevalence of Violence and Exploitation in Forced Marriage and Modern Slavery

Modern slavery and forced marriages share distressing commonalities when it comes to the prevalence of violence, abuse, and exploitative practices, both within and outside the household (Patterson & Zhuo, 2018; Tikka, 2021). According to experts from various countries, forced marriages are often riddled with instances of physical and sexual violence, creating an environment where exploitation becomes inherent to the marriage itself (UNODC, 2020).

In their issue paper "Interlinkages Between Trafficking in Persons and Marriage", published by the UNODC it is reported that the exploitation is essentially ingrained in the structure of these marriages, further highlighting the ubiquity of the abuse in these circumstances (2020). As such, it is explained in the paper that it is rare to find a forced marriage scenario devoid of exploitation, underscoring the systemic nature of abuse within such unions.

Women and girls ensnared in forced and child marriages routinely encounter psychological, physical, and sexual abuse (McFarlane, Nava, Gilroy & Maddoux, 2016; Seff, Williams, Hussain, Landis, Poulton, Falb & Stark, 2020; Kidman, 2017). This abuse manifests in different forms, including violence, threats, emotional manipulation, isolation, and severe restrictions on freedom (Swegman & Initiative, 2016; Chantler & McCarry, 2020).

Sexual violence, a prevalent form of exploitation in forced marriages linked to human trafficking, encompasses rape, sexual abuse, harassment, and overall infringement on women's rights to sexual self-determination, reproduction, and bodily integrity (Mgidlana, 2020; Mkhize & Vilakazi, 2021; Wilson, 2016). Instances of trafficking for forced marriage have been reported, where women are repeatedly raped and subjected to sexual abuse, further illustrating the harrowing experiences faced by victims (Rajan, 2013; Hauser, 2017; UNODC, 2020).

Reproductive violence is another alarming facet, as women and girls may be coerced into bearing children without control over family planning (Tarzia, Wellington, Marino, & Hegarty, 2019; Hernández & Upton, 2018; Imam, 2005). Pressure to conceive quickly, as seen in Jordan, places additional burdens on child brides, jeopardizing their health and well-being. Access to healthcare is often restricted, with some women requiring permission from their husband or mother-in-law even for essential medical visits during complicated pregnancies (UNODC, 2020).

The exploitation associated with forced marriages extends to instances where individuals are brought into a country through marriage for purposes such as sex work (Quek, 2018; McCabe, Stickle & Baumeister, 2022; Askola, 2018; Palriwala & Uberoi, 2008). What may have started as a consensual marriage can swiftly turn coercive and abusive, leaving victims trapped in exploitative situations (UNODC, 2020).

A particularly troubling manifestation is the phenomenon of temporary marriages, as observed in the early 2000s. Men from certain countries entered into forced marriages with refugee girls, exploiting these marriages for sexual purposes and terminating them when leaving the country, exemplifying the adaptability of exploitative practices within the institution of marriage (Healy, 2015).

Household work, often considered a normal aspect of marital life, can transform into a form of exploitation when it involves unpaid labor and servitude (Quek, 2018; McCabe & Eglen, 2022; Božić, 2017).

Similarly to the findings in the previous section, labor exploitation, both within the family and in outside employment, were noted by experts in the issue paper published by the UNODC in 2020, which is also relevant in relation to violence and exploitation characteristics of formed labor and modern slavery in addition to the control elements. Victims are denied access to their wages, further cementing their dependency on their husbands. Again, these practices link to several aspects of defining characteristics, both in terms of exploitation, but also in relation to control as well as vulnerability.

Forced criminality or begging may also be linked with forced marriages, although it is not as common (Begum, 2016; Leye & Sabbe, 2015; Kim, 2010). Cases have been reported where victims were forced into criminal activities or begging by their spouses, expanding the scope of exploitation beyond the confines of the marriage itself (UNODC, 2020).

In summary, the intertwining of violence, abuse, and exploitation within forced marriages mirrors the insidious nature of modern slavery. Understanding and addressing these parallels are crucial for developing effective interventions to combat both forced marriage and modern slavery comprehensively. In particular, commonalities, such as the links to forced criminality, highlight the significance of a combined approach for both forced marriage and modern slavery more generally. Considering internationally mandated provisions in trafficking legislation (for example in the Directive 2011/36/EU of the European Parliament and of the Council of 5 April 2011 on preventing and combating trafficking in human beings and protecting its victims, and replacing Council Framework Decision 2002/629/JHA) which include provisions for trafficking victims that mandate protection from prosecution or punishment for criminal activities.

As discussed in this section. forced marriage and modern slavery, as acknowledged by the international legal sphere and supported by a growing body of academic research, share alarming parallels that underscore the systemic nature of these human rights violations. Gender-based characteristics, factors of vulnerability, control methods, and the prevalence of violence and exploitation are some of the more prevalent characteristics which intertwine these two phenomena, highlighting the urgent need for comprehensive interventions to address these egregious practices.

To combat forced marriage and modern slavery effectively, it is essential to recognize the interconnectedness of these issues and develop holistic approaches that challenge discriminatory norms, promote gender equality, and address socio-economic challenges. Empowering victims, dismantling control mechanisms, and advocating for legal and policy changes are critical steps towards eradicating these forms of exploitation and ensuring the rights and well-being of all individuals. When the two phenomena are treated separately in national jurisdictions, many of these approaches to combat the abusive and exploitative practices will be undertaken separately as well. Considering the close links between the two phenomena, the international framework, as seen in the previous sections, has moved towards bringing practices together under the same framework. The following section will examine the approach in England and Wales, which still maintains a separate approach, demonstrating some of the conceptual and practical issues which may arise in these circumstances.

LEGAL LANDSCAPE IN ENGLAND AND WALES

The criminalization of forced marriages in England and Wales was a significant step forward in addressing a deeply entrenched problem. The Anti-Social Behaviour and Policing Act 2014, which came into effect on June 14, 2014, brought about a shift in the legal framework surrounding forced marriages. Section 121(1) of the act outlines the current legal provisions regarding forced marriages within these jurisdictions. Under this legislative framework, it is considered an offense to use violence or threats to coerce an individual into a marriage, provided that the perpetrator believes or ought to believe that the marriage lacks the free or full consent of the individual.

This legislation represented a substantial amendment to the Forced Marriage (Civil Protection) Act 2007 and the Family Law Act 1996, introducing a dedicated legal provision specifically addressing forced marriages. One significant transformation was the reclassification of the breach of a Forced Marriage Protection Order, which had previously been a civil remedy under the 2007 act, as a criminal offense. Consequently, compelling someone into marriage can now result in a maximum prison sentence of up to seven years (Anti-social Behaviour, Crime and Policing Act 2014, section 121).

Forced Marriage Protection Orders

The introduction of Forced Marriage Protection Orders into Part 4A of the Family Law Act 1996 was a pivotal development in the legal landscape of England and Wales. These orders serve as a vital legal safeguard for individuals who have been coerced into marriage against their will or are at risk of becoming victims of forced marriages (House of Commons Library, 2015). The court has the authority to issue such an order, which aims to protect the victim or potential victim by imposing restrictions that hinder the progression of the marriage. These restrictions may include measures such as surrendering passports, especially in cases where there is a risk of the victim being transported abroad for marriage (Gaffney-Rhys, R. (2014; Re K (Forced Marriage: Passport Order) [2020] EWCA Civ 190).

What makes Forced Marriage Protection Orders particularly significant is their applicability to situations where individuals have already been forced into marriage, including marriages that have taken place overseas. This provision recognizes the need to safeguard victims even after the coercive act has occurred. Moreover, the application for such an order may be initiated by the at-risk victim or, alternatively, by a relevant third party who can act on behalf of the victim. This provision is particularly crucial in cases involving individuals who may be too young, vulnerable, or lacking the mental capacity to pursue legal remedies independently (SMBC v WMP and Others [2011] EWHC B13 (COP)).

Challenges Within the Current Legal Landscape on Forced Marriages

Despite these legislative advances, forced marriages continue to remain largely concealed and underreported in England and Wales. Since the criminalization of coercive marriage practices in 2014, only a limited number of notable convictions have been recorded (Sheley, 2020; UNODC, UN Women, 2014; European Union Agency for Fundamental Rights (FRA), 2014; Foreign, Commonwealth & Development Office & Home Office, 2023).

However, these convictions represent only a small fraction of the pervasive issue of underreported and concealed forced marriages. The Forced Marriage Protection Unit, a collaborative effort between the Foreign, Commonwealth and Development Office and the Home Office, plays a crucial role in preventing forced marriages among British nationals abroad and providing support to potential victims within the UK. Nevertheless, statistical data shows a gap between the number of cases from 2017 reveal a significant gap between reported cases and convictions, with only two major convictions secured out of 1,196 reported cases to the unit. Since 2018, which saw 1,507 cases in which the Forced Marriage Protection Unit had provided advice, there has been a stark decline, with only 302 cases in which the Forced Marriage Protection Unit had offered advice (Foreign, Commonwealth & Development Office, & Home Office, 2023), while there had been 141 potential offenses that had been reported (Selvarajah, 2023).

This incongruity highlights a consensus among various stakeholders, including charities, law enforcement agencies, and governmental bodies, that the reported figures inadequately represent the actual prevalence of forced marriage. It indicates a substantial gap in awareness, reporting, and the overall effectiveness of the legal framework. What is potentially more concerning is the rapid decline is advice being sought, although there may be many reasons fort this, further research in this area is necessary in order to effectively tackle the issue to ensure that more potential victims have access to support and advice services.

Shift in Legal Definitions: Marriage and Modern Slavery

The legal landscape in England and Wales has seen significant developments, particularly in the definitions governing forced marriages. These shifts reflect a growing recognition of the intricate dynamics and vulnerabilities associated with forced marriages.

One notable change occurred with the enactment of the Marriage and Civil Partnership (Minimum Age) Act 2022, effective since February 27, 2023. This legislation introduced explicit distinctions between forcing a child to marry and forcing an adult to marry. While all circumstances constituting forced marriage in relation to an adult victim continue to apply in the case of a child victim, the new legislation introduced novel circumstances exclusively applicable to child victims (Foreign & Commonwealth Office, Foreign, Commonwealth & Development Office, and Home Office, 2023).

Specifically, it is now considered an offense to engage in any conduct aimed at causing a child to marry before their eighteenth birthday, even in the absence of violence, threats, or coercion. This unequivocally designates the act of causing a child to marry, under any circumstances, as a criminal offense (the Marriage and Civil Partnership (Minimum Age) Act 2022, s. 2).

This legislative alteration abolishes the conventional differentiation between forced and arranged marriages applicable to adults, as any act tantamount to arranging an adult's marriage is now considered forcing a child to marry. This shift in perspective recognizes that children may not be in a position to comprehend the implications of marriage or exercise informed consent. The legislation acknowledges that children are inherently less capable than adults in understanding the complexities of marriage and may face challenges in resisting familial demands (Foreign & Commonwealth Office, Foreign, Commonwealth & Development Office, and Home Office, 2023).

Furthermore, the legislation recognizes the detrimental consequences of child marriages, including early exit from education, limited career prospects, severe physical and mental health challenges, developmental issues for children born to young mothers, and an increased risk of domestic abuse. In alignment with the UN Sustainable Development Goals, the legislation aims to eliminate harmful practices, including child, early, and forced marriages, by 2030 (Cabinet Office, Department for Internatinal Development & the Foreign, Commenwealth and Development Office, 2021).

Additionally, the Marriage and Civil Partnership (Minimum Age) Act 2022 raised the minimum legal age for marriage or entering into a civil partnership to 18 in all circumstances, eliminating the prior provision that allowed marriage for individuals aged 16 or 17 with parental or court approval. While legal marriage alone would render forced marriage legislation unnecessary for children, the legislation recognizes that children, like adults, can engage in unofficial, religious, or customary 'marriages' not recognized by law. Thus, the legislation, effective from February 27, 2023, continues to apply to both official and unofficial marriages (c. 18, sections 1-5).

The critical criterion for enforcement is whether any religious or civil ceremony of marriage, whether legally binding or not, is envisaged or has taken place. This ensures that the legislation covers all scenarios where a child may be subjected to coerced marriage, even if it does not involve a formal legal process (Foreign & Commonwealth Office, Foreign, Commonwealth & Development Office, and Home Office, 2023).

CHALLENGES AND THE NEED FOR A COMPREHENSIVE APPROACH

While these legislative changes represent positive steps in addressing forced marriages, they do not provide a comprehensive solution to the issue. Forced marriages can be complex and deeply ingrained within certain communities, making it difficult to identify and address all instances effectively.

Moreover, the legal framework in England and Wales, despite recognizing the potential vulnerability of young individuals, does not categorize forced marriages as a form of modern slavery under the Modern Slavery Act 2015. The Modern Slavery Act primarily focuses on commercial exploitation through forced labor, omitting the distinct challenges posed by forced marriages (Stoehr & Moeschel, 2019); McGaughey, Voss, Cullen & Davis, 2022; Hodkinson, Lewis, Waite & Dwyer, 2021; McCabe & Eglen, 2022).

The age criteria alone may not suffice in eliminating the problem, especially when forced marriages are disguised as arranged marriages with the legal consent of guardians. The recognition that forced marriages can constitute a form of modern slavery necessitates a more encompassing legislative approach. Forced marriages, often accompanied by psychological, emotional, financial pressure, and threats of violence, can lead to acts of slavery within marriages, including sexual slavery. The acquisition of consent under such coercive circumstances challenges the efficacy of existing legal frameworks (International Labour Organization, 2022; McCabe & Eglen, 2022).

The absence of recognition of forced marriages under the Modern Slavery Act 2015 hampers the effective utilization of the National Referral Mechanism (NRM). Victims of forced marriages, despite political support, are not seamlessly referred to the NRM, which was established in 2009 to identify victims of human trafficking and modern slavery. The NRM's non-support for forced marriage victims leaves them without access to protective measures, potentially endangering those without legal status. In particular the vague and uncertain coverage of forced marriage as a potential component of modern slavery and the lack of any reference to it within most guidance documents from state agencies demonstrates the strong potential for victims of exploitation within the intersections between what is considered modern slavery in England and Wales and what is considered forced marriage (see for example: Home Office & UK Visas and Immigration, 2021; Foreign & Commonwealth Office, Foreign, Commonwealth & Development Office, and Home Office, 2023; Crown Prosecution Service, 2023).

Reforming Legislation for a United Approach

To address the multifaceted issue of forced marriages comprehensively and align with United Nations and International Labour Organization guidelines, the UK must extend its legislative scope beyond age considerations. Forced marriages, often accompanied by psychological, emotional, financial pressure, and threats of violence, can lead to acts of slavery within marriages, including sexual slavery (McCabe, Stickle & Baumeister, 2022; Haenen, 2014; Dauvergne & Millbank, 2010).

The recognition that forced marriages can constitute a form of modern slavery necessitates a more encompassing legislative approach. Notably, the age criteria alone may not suffice, as individuals beyond the defined vulnerable age may still fall victim to coercion. The International Labour Organization's statistics highlight that 88% of forced marriage victims are women, indicating that age is not the sole determinant of vulnerability (International Labour Organization, 2022).

Considering the intricate dynamics involved, it becomes imperative for the UK to extend its legislative scope beyond age considerations. Forced marriages, often accompanied by psychological, emotional, financial pressure, and threats of violence, can lead to acts of slavery within marriages, including sexual slavery. The acquisition of consent under such coercive circumstances challenges the efficacy of existing legal frameworks. In particular, it is generally recognised in law that consent needs to be given freely, which is not the case under coersion (Konow, 2014; Dougherty, 2021; Anitha & Gill, 2017; Gill & Hamed, 2016). Moreover, under various international provisions, it is not legally possible to consent to abuse, which is one of the key reasons why consent within the definition of trafficking in human beings and other forms of modern slavery is often considered irrelevant (Allain, 2014; Clark, 2023; Eriksson, 2013).

The absence of recognition of forced marriages under the Modern Slavery Act 2015 hampers the effective utilization of the National Referral Mechanism (NRM). Victims of forced marriages, despite political support, are not able to be seamlessly referred to the NRM, which was established in 2009 to identify victims of human trafficking and modern slavery. The NRM's non-support for forced marriage victims leaves them without access to the equivalent protective measures, potentially endangering those in particular without legal status.

The International Perspective and United Approach

The United Kingdom's approach to forced marriage, while commendable in some aspects, falls short of a more comprehensive and united approach adopted by some other jurisdictions. Recognizing forced marriage as a form of modern slavery, as some countries have done, could lead to more effective prevention, prosecution, and support for victims (O'Brien, 2016; Hitchens & Daly, 2021; Quek, 2018; Simmons & Wong, 2021).

Australia provides a notable example of a proactive approach in defining forced marriages as a form of slavery within its modern slavery legislation. By including forced marriages within the broader framework of modern slavery, Australia has set a precedent that allows for a more cohesive legal response to the complex issue of forced marriages (Simmons & Wong, 2021).

The inclusion of forced marriages within the Modern Slavery Act 2015 in the United Kingdom would likely lead to increased convictions and empower victims to come forward, protected by a more comprehensive legal framework. It would also facilitate better data collection and reporting, as forced marriages would be recognized as part of the broader modern slavery issue.

Addressing the Overlap With Modern Slavery

The potential for overlooked crossover cases between recognized instances of modern slavery in the UK and forced marriage arises due to the government's limited acknowledgment of the close links and similar characteristics between these two phenomena. The guidance provided by the government on tackling modern slavery exhibits a noteworthy absence of comprehensive information and recognition of the potential for overlaps between modern slavery and forced marriage cases (Foreign & Commonwealth Office, Foreign, Commonwealth & Development Office, and Home Office, 2023).

The government's guidance on tackling modern slavery contains only a brief mention of forced marriage in sections 2.69 to 2.71. While it recognizes forced marriage as a crime and emphasizes the provision of help and support for victims through the Forced Marriage Unit (FMU), it fails to acknowledge the intricate interconnections and shared characteristics between modern slavery and forced marriage. The limited information provided suggests a compartmentalized approach, treating forced marriage as a distinct issue rather than recognizing its potential intersection with modern slavery (Foreign & Commonwealth Office, Foreign, Commonwealth & Development Office, and Home Office, 2023).

The guidance, as illustrated in sections 2.70 and 2.71, outlines the role of the FMU in offering support for victims and those at risk of forced marriage. However, it explicitly states that a forced marriage alone would not necessarily classify a person as a victim of modern slavery. This compartmentalization may lead to cases being narrowly assessed, potentially overlooking situations where elements of both forced marriage and modern slavery coexist.

Furthermore, the guidance acknowledges cases labeled as "unclear" or "sham marriages" (section 2.72) where individuals enter into a marriage or civil partnership for reasons such as immigration advantages, even when no genuine subsisting relationship exists. While recognizing the importance of addressing such situations, the guidance does not delve into the potential complexities where individuals may be forced into marriages under the guise of "sham marriages" for purposes of modern slavery or exploitation (Foreign & Commonwealth Office, Foreign, Commonwealth & Development Office, and Home Office, 2023).

This limited acknowledgment within the guidance highlights the need for a more holistic and integrated approach. By compartmentalizing forced marriage and modern slavery as separate issues, there is a risk of missing cases that involve elements of both, leading to a gap in protection and support for victims.

To address this overlap effectively, it is crucial to expand the guidance and training provided to professionals and frontline workers involved in identifying and assisting victims of modern slavery and forced marriage. Professionals across various sectors, including law enforcement, social services, healthcare, and immigration, should receive comprehensive training that encompasses the interconnected nature of these issues. This training should include guidance on recognizing the signs and indicators of both modern slavery and forced marriage, as well as the potential overlap between the two.

Additionally, there is a need for improved data collection and sharing mechanisms between relevant agencies and organizations. By facilitating the exchange of information, professionals can gain a more comprehensive understanding of individual cases and identify those that involve both forced marriage and modern slavery.

Moreover, a collaborative approach involving multiple agencies and organizations is essential to effectively address the overlap between modern slavery and forced marriage. This includes cooperation between law enforcement, immigration authorities, child protection services, domestic violence support agencies, and organizations specialized in tackling modern slavery and forced marriage.

In summary, recognizing the potential overlap between modern slavery and forced marriage is essential to ensure that victims receive the necessary protection and support. The current compartmentalized approach within the government's guidance on tackling modern slavery and forced marriage in the UK hinders a comprehensive response to cases that involve elements of both. To address this issue effectively, there is a need for expanded guidance, training, improved data sharing, and a collaborative approach among various agencies and organizations. Only through a holistic and integrated approach can the UK better protect and support individuals who may be victims of both modern slavery and forced marriage.

International and Global Implications

The legal approach and framework in England and Wales regarding forced marriage, while progressive in many aspects, require further alignment with international standards and the evolving global understanding of these issues. The current approach primarily focuses on criminalizing forced marriages and providing protection to victims, which is commendable, but it falls short of recognizing the broader international context.

Internationally, there is a growing consensus that forced marriage is not solely a cultural or domestic issue but a human rights violation with global implications (Merry, 2003; Merry, 2009; Harris-Short, 2017; Randall & Venkatesh, 2015; Baumeister, 2018; International Labour Organization, 2022). The United Nations has been at the forefront of addressing forced marriage through various resolutions and conventions, emphasizing the need for a unified and comprehensive response to this issue (UN General Assembly Resolution A/RES/69/156; UNODC, 2020; UN General Assembly, *Protocol to Prevent, Suppress and Punish Trafficking in Persons, Especially Women and Children, Supplementing the United Nations Convention against Transnational Organized Crime*, 15 November 2000; Council of Europe Parliamentary Assembly, Resolution 1468 (2005)).

Failure to align with the international community and other jurisdictions across the globe not only renders the approach in England and Wales outdated but also limits the collective power that comes with a united approach to tackling a global problem. Forced marriage is not confined by national borders; it transcends them. Victims of forced marriage often face challenges that span multiple countries, making it imperative for legal systems to work cohesively on a global scale (Bunting & Ikhimiukor, 2018; McQuade, 2019; Ssenyonjo, 2021).

Additionally, discrepancies in data collection, reporting mechanisms, and legal definitions between jurisdictions can lead to fragmented understandings of the issue and hinder international efforts to combat forced marriage effectively. A unified approach ensures that data and reporting are consistent, enabling a more accurate assessment of the prevalence and scope of forced marriage worldwide (Landman, 2020; Sarich, Olivier & Bales, 2016; Goodey, 2011).

The legal approach and framework in England and Wales regarding forced marriage have made significant progress, but there is a pressing need for further alignment with international standards and a more integrated response that recognizes the overlap with modern slavery. This alignment not only keeps the approach relevant but also strengthens the global impact of efforts to combat forced marriage by fostering cooperation among nations and ensuring consistency in data and reporting. It is crucial for England and Wales to remain at the forefront of this global fight against forced marriage by adapting to evolving international perspectives and standards.

CONCLUSION

The legal landscape concerning forced marriages in England and Wales has undergone substantial reforms, reflecting a commitment to addressing this deeply rooted issue. The implementation of the Anti-Social Behaviour and Policing Act 2014, criminalizing coercive marriage practices, represented a pivotal moment in the fight against forced marriages. This legislative change, coupled with the establishment of Forced Marriage Protection Orders, introduced crucial legal mechanisms to protect both potential and past victims. These measures underscored the recognition of the necessity for pre- and post-marriage safeguards and marked significant progress in the protection of vulnerable individuals.

Despite these advancements, significant challenges persist. Forced marriages remain largely concealed and underreported, leading to only limited convictions. The gap between reported cases and successful prosecutions highlights the need for a more comprehensive and inclusive approach. While the Marriage and Civil Partnership (Minimum Age) Act 2022 introduced important distinctions for child victims, there is an urgent requirement to categorize forced marriages as a form of modern slavery under the Modern Slavery Act 2015. Such recognition would enable a more coherent legal response, enhance data collection and analysis, and offer improved support to victims.

Recognizing the potential overlap between forced marriages and modern slavery is essential to ensure comprehensive protection and assistance for victims. The current compartmentalized approach, where forced marriage and modern slavery are treated as separate issues, may lead to victims being overlooked, particularly in cases where elements of both exist.

To address these multifaceted challenges effectively, a united approach is imperative, both on the domestic and international fronts. England and Wales should align with international standards and collaborate with other nations to combat forced marriages globally. Additionally, comprehensive training for professionals across various sectors, improved data collection and sharing mechanisms, and a collaborative effort among agencies and organizations are essential components of a holistic and integrated response.

In conclusion, while significant strides have been made in the legal landscape of England and Wales regarding forced marriages, further reforms, acknowledgment of the overlap with modern slavery, and alignment with international standards are imperative. By adopting a more comprehensive and united approach, these jurisdictions can provide robust protection and support to victims, ensuring that forced marriages are not only legally prohibited but effectively prevented, prosecuted, and eradicated. This united effort is essential to secure the rights and well-being of vulnerable individuals and to combat forced marriages as a global human rights violation.

REFERENCES

Abbas, T. (2019). *Islamophobia and radicalisation: A vicious cycle*. Oxford University Press. doi:10.1093/oso/9780190083410.001.0001

Abera, M., Nega, A., Tefera, Y., & Gelagay, A. A. (2020). Early marriage and women's empowerment: The case of child-brides in Amhara National Regional State, Ethiopia. *BMC International Health and Human Rights*, *20*(1), 1–16. doi:10.1186/s12914-020-00249-5 PMID:33317540

Aborisade, R. A., & Olayinka-Aliu, D. A. (2023). Marry your rapist! A phenomenological analysis of the experiences of women forced to marry their assaulters in their childhood. *International Review of Victimology*, 02697580231207652. doi:10.1177/02697580231207652

Abrego, L. J. (2014). *Sacrificing families: Navigating laws, labor, and love across borders*. Stanford University Press. doi:10.1515/9780804790574

Adepoju, A. (2005). Review of research and data on human trafficking in sub-Saharan Africa. *International Migration (Geneva, Switzerland)*, *43*(1-2), 75–98. doi:10.1111/j.0020-7985.2005.00313.x

Alam, A. (2021). Marital Consent and the Discourse of 'Women's Freedom'. In Women, Islam and Familial Intimacy in Colonial South Asia (pp. 84-135). Brill.

Alanen, J. (2015). *Custom or crime? Catalysts and consequences of forced marriage*.

Alban, E. (2020). *Marital rape as a violation of women's autonomy and human rights*.

Allain, J. (2014). No effective trafficking definition exists: Domestic implementation of the Palermo Protocol. *Alb. Gov't L. Rev.*, *7*, 111.

Allwood, G. (2016). Gender-based violence against women in contemporary France: Domestic violence and forced marriage policy since the Istanbul Convention. *Modern & Contemporary France*, *24*(4), 377–394. doi:10.1080/09639489.2016.1203886

Anitha, S., & Gill, A. (2017). Coercion, consent and the forced marriage debate in the UK. In *Marital rights* (pp. 133–152). Routledge. doi:10.4324/9781315091464-8

Anitha, S., & Gill, A. K. (2015). A moral panic? The problematization of forced marriage in British newspapers. *Violence Against Women, 21*(9), 1123–1144. doi:10.1177/1077801215590671 PMID:26139693

Anitha, S., & Gill, A. K. (2023). *Understanding Protection and Prevention Responses to Forced Marriage in England and Wales.*

Askola, H. (2018). Responding to vulnerability?: Forced marriage and the law. *The University of New South Wales Law Journal, 41*(3), 977–1002. doi:10.53637/IPTD3484

Azim, T. (2022). *An interpretative phenomenological analysis of the experience of forced marriage for diasporic south Asian women who have left* [Doctoral dissertation, Middlesex University/New School of Psychotherapy and Counselling (NSPC)].

Bales, K., & Robbins, P. T. (2001). "No one shall be held in slavery or servitude": A critical analysis of international slavery agreements and concepts of slavery. *Human Rights Review (Piscataway, N.J.), 2*(2), 18–45. doi:10.1007/s12142-001-1022-6

Barnes, J., Naser, M. M., & Aston, J. (2023). A vulnerability approach to irregular migration and modern slavery in Australia. *Australian Journal of Human Rights, 29*(1), 121–140. doi:10.1080/1323238X.2023.2229619

Baumeister, H. (2018). *Sexualised crimes, armed conflict and the law: The international criminal court and the definitions of rape and forced marriage.* Routledge. doi:10.4324/9781315111490

Beatson, J., Hanley, J., & Ricard-Guay, A. (2017). The intersection of exploitation and coercion in cases of Canadian labour trafficking. *Journal of Law and Social Policy, 26*(1), 137–158. doi:10.60082/0829-3929.1259

Becker, C. M., Mirkasimov, B., & Steiner, S. (2017). Forced marriage and birth outcomes. *Demography, 54*(4), 1401–1423. doi:10.1007/s13524-017-0591-1 PMID:28770502

Begum, P. (2016). *Should 'forced marriage'be criminalised?* Howard League for Penal Reform.

Bermúdez Figueroa, E., Dabetić, V., Yuste, R. P., & Saeidzadeh, Z. (2023). Gender and Structural Inequalities from a Socio-Legal Perspective. In *Gender-Competent Legal Education* (pp. 95–142). Springer International Publishing. doi:10.1007/978-3-031-14360-1_4

Bhana, D., & Matswetu, V. (2023). Girls under surveillance: Engaging Zimbabwean parents on young people's sexual health. *Health Education Journal*, *82*(6), 00178969231176786. doi:10.1177/00178969231176786

Bimbi, F. (2014). Symbolic violence: Reshaping post-patriarchal discourses on gender. In Gendered perspectives on conflict and violence: Part B (pp. 275-301). Emerald Group Publishing Limited.

Božić, V. (2017). Forced marriages of children as a form of exploitation of human trafficking victims. *EU and comparative law issues and challenges series (ECLIC)*, *1*, 48-68.

Bunting, A. (2012). Forced marriage in conflict situations: Researching and prosecuting old harms and new crimes. *Can. J. Hum. Rts.*, *1*, 165.

Bunting, A., & Ikhimiukor, I. K. (2018). The expressive nature of law: What we learn from conjugal slavery to forced marriage in international criminal law. *International Criminal Law Review*, *18*(2), 331–353. doi:10.1163/15718123-01802004

Buscema, L. (2023). A legal analysis of the contributing factors to trafficking in women: points of strength and weakness of the recent developments in Europe. *A legal analysis of the contributing factors to trafficking in women: points of strength and weakness of the recent developments in Europe*, 41-73.

Callaghan, J. E., Alexander, J. H., Sixsmith, J., & Fellin, L. C. (2018). Beyond "witnessing": Children's experiences of coercive control in domestic violence and abuse. *Journal of Interpersonal Violence*, *33*(10), 1551–1581. doi:10.1177/0886260515618946 PMID:26663742

Cameron, E. C., Hemingway, S. L., Cunningham, F. J., & Jacquin, K. M. (2021). Global crises: Gendered vulnerabilities of structural inequality, environmental performance, and modern slavery. *Human Arenas*, *4*(3), 391–412. doi:10.1007/s42087-020-00154-2

Campmajó, M. B. (2020). Forced marriages in Europe: A form of gender-based violence and violation of human rights. *The Age of Human Rights Journal*, (14), 1–18. doi:10.17561/tahrj.v14.5474

Casey, S. E., Isa, G. P., Isumbisho Mazambi, E., Giuffrida, M. M., Jayne Kulkarni, M., & Perera, S. M. (2022). Community perceptions of the impact of war on unintended pregnancy and induced abortion in Protection of Civilian sites in Juba, South Sudan. *Global Public Health: An International Journal for Research, Policy and Practice*, *17*(9), 2176–2189. doi:10.1080/17441692.2021.1959939 PMID:34323171

Cepal, N. (2022). *Child, early and forced marriage and unions: Harmful practices that deepen gender inequality in Latin America and the Caribbean*. Research Gate.

Chan, S. K. L. (2018). Deprivation of citizenship, undocumented labor and human trafficking: Myanmar migrant workers in Thailand. *Regions & Cohesion : the Journal of the Consortium for Comparative Research on Regional Integration and Social Cohesion*, *8*(2), 82–106. doi:10.3167/reco.2018.080205

Chantler, K. (2019). Men's experiences of forced marriage: Ain't I a man? In *Men, masculinities and honour-based abuse* (pp. 60–78). Routledge. doi:10.4324/9780429277726-4

Chantler, K., & McCarry, M. (2020). Forced marriage, coercive control, and conducive contexts: The experiences of women in Scotland. *Violence Against Women*, *26*(1), 89–109. doi:10.1177/1077801219830234 PMID:30822221

Chantler, K., Mirza, N., & Mackenzie, M. (2022). Policy and professional responses to forced marriage in Scotland. *British Journal of Social Work*, *52*(2), 833–849. doi:10.1093/bjsw/bcab068

Charnley, H., & Nkhoma, P. (2020). Moving beyond contemporary discourses: Children, prostitution, modern slavery and human trafficking. *Critical and Radical Social Work*, *8*(2), 205–221. doi:10.1332/204986020X15945756343791

Clawson, R., Patterson, A., Fyson, R., & McCarthy, M. (2020). The demographics of forced marriage of people with learning disabilities: Findings from a national database. *Journal of Adult Protection*, *22*(2), 59–74. doi:10.1108/JAP-09-2019-0029

Connelly, M. P., Li, T. M., MacDonald, M., & Parpart, J. L. (2000). Feminism and development: Theoretical perspectives. *Theoretical perspectives on gender and development*, 51-159.

Conner, D. H. (2013). Financial freedom: Women, money, and domestic abuse. *Wm. & Mary J. Women & L.*, *20*, 339.

Crossman, K. A., & Hardesty, J. L. (2018). Placing coercive control at the center: What are the processes of coercive control and what makes control coercive? *Psychology of Violence*, *8*(2), 196–206. doi:10.1037/vio0000094 PMID:30984466

Crown Prosecution Service. (2023, December 22). *Modern slavery and human trafficking: Offences and defences, including the Section 45 Defence*. The Crown Prosecution Service. https://www.cps.gov.uk/legal-guidance/modern-slavery-and-human-trafficking-offences-and-defences-including-section-45

Dahinden, J., & Manser-Egli, S. (2023). Gendernativism and liberal subjecthood: The cases of forced marriage and the Burqa Ban in Switzerland. *Social Politics*, *30*(1), 140–163. doi:10.1093/sp/jxab053

Daraz, U., Naz, A., & Khan, W. (2014). Early Marriage: A developmental challenge to women in Pakhtun Society. *FWU Journal of Social Sciences*, *8*(1), 91.

Dauvergne, C., & Millbank, J. (2010). Forced marriage as a harm in domestic and international law. *The Modern Law Review*, *73*(1), 57–88. doi:10.1111/j.1468-2230.2009.00784.x

Davidson, J. O. C. (2015). *Modern slavery: The margins of freedom*. Springer. doi:10.1057/9781137297297

Davies, M. (2007). *Property: Meanings, histories, theories*. Routledge. doi:10.4324/9780203937310

Dhaliwal, S. K. (2021). *"So, I Stayed:" Narratives of Agency from Punjabi-Canadian Women in Forced Marriages* [Doctoral dissertation, Carleton University].

Dougherty, T. (2021). Sexual misconduct on a scale: Gravity, coercion, and consent. *Ethics*, *131*(2), 319–344. doi:10.1086/711211

Eriksson, M. (2013). The prevention of human trafficking–regulating domestic criminal legislation through the European Convention on Human Rights. *Nordic Journal of International Law*, *82*(3), 339–368. doi:10.1163/15718107-08203001

Erturk, Y., Bredal, D. A., Gupta, T., Bano, D. S., & Balzani, M. (2011). Forced marriage: Introducing a social justice and human rights perspective. Bloomsbury Publishing.

European Union Agency for Fundamental Rights (FRA). (2014). *Addressing forced marriage in the EU: legal provisions and promising practices*. FRA.

Few-Demo, A. L., & Allen, K. R. (2020). Gender, feminist, and intersectional perspectives on families: A decade in review. *Journal of Marriage and Family*, *82*(1), 326–345. doi:10.1111/jomf.12638

Foblets, M. C., Graziadei, M., & Renteln, A. D. (2018). *Personal autonomy in plural societies: A principle and its paradoxes*. Taylor & Francis.

Foreign, Commonwealth & Development Office, & Home Office. (2023, June 20). *Forced Marriage Unit Statistics 2022*. GOV.UK.

Foucault, M. (1982). The subject and power. *Critical Inquiry*, *8*(4), 777–795. doi:10.1086/448181

Foucault, M. (2019). Power: the essential works of Michel Foucault 1954-1984. Penguin UK.

Freeman, C. P. (2020). *The human animal earthling identity: Shared values unifying human rights, animal rights, and environmental movements*. University of Georgia Press. doi:10.2307/j.ctvxhrmr1

Gaffney-Rhys, R. (2014). The development of the law relating to forced marriage: Does the law reflect the interests of the victim? *Crime Prevention and Community Safety*, *16*(4), 269–293. doi:10.1057/cpcs.2014.11

Garreto, G., Baptista, J. S., & Mota, A. (2022). Characterisation of Contemporary Slavery through the Analysis of Accommodation Conditions. *Social Sciences (Basel, Switzerland)*, *11*(5), 214. doi:10.3390/socsci11050214

Gebre, T., Hagos, F., Teklu, G., Fisseha, M., & Abera, M. (2020). The prevalence of gender-based violence and harmful traditional practices against women in the Tigray Region, Ethiopia. *Journal of Asian and African Studies*, *55*(1), 58–75. doi:10.1177/0021909619867110

Giammarinaro, M. G. (2022). Understanding severe exploitation requires a human rights and gender-sensitive intersectional approach. *Frontiers in Human Dynamics*, *4*, 861600. doi:10.3389/fhumd.2022.861600

Gill, A. K., & Hamed, T. (2016). Muslim women and forced marriages in the UK. *Journal of Muslim Minority Affairs*, *36*(4), 540–560. doi:10.1080/13602004.2016.1260324

Gitlin, M. (Ed.). (2019). *Sexual Consent*. Greenhaven Publishing LLC.

Gledhill, K. (2021). The Committee on the Rights of Persons with Disabilities and the Fight against Human Trafficking. *J. Int'l & Comp. L.*, *8*, 249.

Goodey, J. (2011). Data on Human Trafficking. *Human trafficking: Exploring the international nature, concerns, and complexities*, 39.

Guyer, P. (2003). Kant on the theory and practice of autonomy. *Social Philosophy & Policy*, *20*(2), 70–98. doi:10.1017/S026505250320203X

Haenen, I. (2014). *Force & Marriage: The criminalisation of forced marriage in Dutch, English and international criminal law*.

UN. (2014). *Handbook on Effective Prosecution Responses to Violence against Women and Girls*. UNODC, UN Women. http://www.unodc.org/documents/justice-andprison-reform/14–02565_Ebook_new.pdf

Harris-Short, S. (2017). International human rights law: imperialist, inept and ineffective? Cultural relativism and the UN Convention on the Rights of the Child. In *Children's Rights* (pp. 151-202). Routledge. 10.4324/9781315095769-9

Hartmann, H. (2020). The unhappy marriage of Marxism and feminism: Towards a more progressive union. In *Feminist Theory Reader* (pp. 131–140). Routledge.

Haugaard, M. (2017). Power and meaning. *Journal of Political Power, 10*(1), 1–5. doi:10.1080/2158379X.2017.1287476

Hauser, W. K. (2017). *Invisible Slaves: The Victims and Perpetrators of Modern-Day Slavery*. Hoover Press.

Healy, C. (2015). *Targeting vulnerabilities. the impact of the Syrian War and refugees situation on trafficking in persons. A study of Syria, Turkey, Lebanon, Jordan and Iraq*. Counter Trafficking In Emergencies. https://ctic.iom.int/en/resources/targeting-vulnerabilities-impact-syrian-war-and-refugees-situation-trafficking-persons

Hernández, L. H., & Upton, S. D. L. S. (2018). *Challenging reproductive control and gendered violence in the Américas: Intersectionality, power, and struggles for rights*. Lexington Books.

Hernández Soto, V. (2023). The Marginalization of Slavery in International Criminal Justice: Untapping Its Potential in the Fight Against Modern Slavery. In *Contemporary International Criminal Law Issues: Contributions in Pursuit of Accountability for Africa and the World* (pp. 349–383). TMC Asser Press. doi:10.1007/978-94-6265-555-3_10

Hirschmann, N. J. (2009). *The subject of liberty: Toward a feminist theory of freedom*. Princeton University Press. doi:10.1515/9781400825363

Hirschmann, N. J. (2018). *Rethinking obligation: A feminist method for political theory*. Cornell University Press.

Hitchens, J., & Daly, N. (2021). *Forced marriage law and practice*. Bloomsbury Publishing. doi:10.5040/9781526515988

Hodkinson, S. N., Lewis, H., Waite, L., & Dwyer, P. (2021). Fighting or fuelling forced labour? The Modern Slavery Act 2015, irregular migrants and the vulnerabilising role of the UK's hostile environment. *Critical Social Policy, 41*(1), 68–90. doi:10.1177/0261018320904311

Home Office, & UK Visas and Immigration. (2023, September 21). *National Referral Mechanism Guidance: Adult (England and Wales)*. GOV.UK. [REMOVED HYPERLINK FIELD]

Horii, H. (2020). A blind spot in international human rights framework: A space between tradition and modernity within the child marriage discourse. *International Journal of Human Rights*, *24*(8), 1057–1079. doi:10.1080/13642987.2019.1690468

Horii, H. (2021). *Child Marriage, Rights and Choice: Rethinking Agency in International Human Rights*. Routledge. doi:10.4324/9781003184546

Idriss, M. M. (2022). Abused by the patriarchy: Male victims, masculinity,"honor"-based abuse and forced marriages. *Journal of Interpersonal Violence*, *37*(13-14), NP11905–NP11932. doi:10.1177/0886260521997928 PMID:33631999

Imam, A. M. (2005). Women's Reproductive and Sexual Rights. *Where human rights begin: Health, sexuality, and women in the new millennium*, 65. Research Gate.

IslamS. (2021). Forced Marriage: Law and Practice in Pakistan. *Available at* SSRN 3892076. doi:10.2139/ssrn.3892076

Jamadar, P., & Pena, L. (2022). *Human Trafficking, Forced Labour, and Modern Forms of Slavery: Commonwealth Caribbean Perspectives*. Caribbean Court of Justice.

Jinkang, A. (2020). *Contemporary slavery: the exploitation of migrants in italian agriculture*.

John Chetty, D. (2016). *Mobilising women in the space between education access and socio-economic empowerment: a human rights perspective* [Doctoral dissertation, North-West University (South Africa), Potchefstroom Campus].

Jordana, A. D. (2016). *Situational analysis on child, early and forced marriage in Vietnam*. World Vision.

Jovanovic, M. (2020). The essence of slavery: Exploitation in human rights law. *Human Rights Law Review*, *20*(4), 674–703. doi:10.1093/hrlr/ngaa023

Kanaan, M. (2022). *Virginity Cult and Violent (Dis)*. Honour.

Kant, I. (1785). *Groundwork of the metaphysics of morals*.

Kara, S. (2017). *Modern slavery: A global perspective*. Columbia University Press. doi:10.7312/kara15846

Karenga, P. V. S. (2022). Delimiting the Problem of Trafficking in Persons. In *A West African Model to Address Human Trafficking* (pp. 7–123). Springer International Publishing. doi:10.1007/978-3-030-88120-7_2

Kidman, R. (2017). Child marriage and intimate partner violence: A comparative study of 34 countries. *International Journal of Epidemiology*, *46*(2), 662–675. PMID:27733435

Kim, E. (2022). Competing Discourses in the Child Protection System in Kyrgyzstan: Implications for Redressing Gender Violence Against Girls. *Child Indicators Research*, *15*(4), 1209–1232. doi:10.1007/s12187-021-09900-6

Kim, J. (2010). Trafficked: Domestic violence, exploitation in marriage, and the foreign-bridge industry. *Va. J. Int'l L.*, *51*, 443.

Kirchhoffer, D. G., & Richards, B. J. (Eds.). (2019). *Beyond autonomy: limits and alternatives to informed consent in research ethics and law*. Cambridge University Press. doi:10.1017/9781108649247

Kohno, A., Techasrivichien, T., Suguimoto, S. P., Dahlui, M., Nik Farid, N. D., & Nakayama, T. (2020). Investigation of the key factors that influence the girls to enter into child marriage: A meta-synthesis of qualitative evidence. *PLoS One*, *15*(7), e0235959. doi:10.1371/journal.pone.0235959 PMID:32678862

Konow, J. (2014). Coercion and consent. *Journal of Institutional and Theoretical Economics: JITE*, 49-74.

Koretsky, D. P. (2021). *Death rights: Romantic suicide, race, and the bounds of liberalism*. State University of New York Press.

Lamas, B. (2023). Modern Slavery in the Global Economy. In *The Palgrave Handbook of Global Slavery throughout History* (pp. 661–680). Springer International Publishing. doi:10.1007/978-3-031-13260-5_37

Landman, T. (2020). Measuring modern slavery: Law, human rights, and new forms of data. *Human Rights Quarterly*, *42*(2), 303–331. doi:10.1353/hrq.2020.0019

Latham-Sprinkle, J., David, F., Bryant, K., & Larsen, J. (2019). *Migrants and their vulnerability to human trafficking, modern slavery and forced labour.*

Leye, E., & Sabbe, A. (2015). *Forced marriage in Belgium: an analysis of the current situation.*

Likoti, P. M., & Sibanyoni, E. K. (2020). Children as victims of forced marriages in Lesotho: A question of cultural practice or approval of child exploitation. *International Journal of Criminology and Sociology*, *9*, 723–734. doi:10.6000/1929-4409.2020.09.68

Longman, C., & Coene, G. (2016). Harmful cultural practices and minority women in Europe: From headscarf bans to forced marriages and honour related violence. In *Interrogating Harmful Cultural Practices* (pp. 51–66). Routledge. doi:10.4324/9781315589640-10

Lundberg, A. M. (2021). Prosecuting Bride Kidnapping: The Law Isn't Enough; Aligning Cultural Norms with the Law. *Case W. Res. J. Int'l L.*, *53*, 475.

Lyneham, S., & Bricknell, S. (2018). *When saying no is not an option: Forced marriage in Australia and New Zealand.*

Madut, K. K. (2020). Determinants of early marriage and construction of gender roles in South Sudan. *SAGE Open*, *10*(2), 2158244020922974. doi:10.1177/2158244020922974

Martin, L. V. (2017). Restraining forced marriage. *Nev. LJ*, *18*, 919.

McCabe, H., & Eglen, L. (2022). "I bought you. You are my wife":"Modern Slavery" and Forced Marriage. *Journal of Human Trafficking*, 1–24. doi:10.1080/23322705.2022.2096366

McCabe, H., Stickle, W., & Baumeister, H. (2022). Forced Marriage and Modern Slavery: Analysing Marriage as a "Choiceless Choice". *Journal of Modern Slavery*, *7*(2), 33–57.

McFarlane, J., Nava, A., Gilroy, H., & Maddoux, J. (2016). Child brides, forced marriage, and partner violence in America: Tip of an iceberg revealed. *Obstetrics and Gynecology*, *127*(4), 706–713. doi:10.1097/AOG.0000000000001336 PMID:26959211

McGaughey, F., Voss, H., Cullen, H., & Davis, M. C. (2022). Corporate responses to tackling modern slavery: A comparative analysis of Australia, France and the United Kingdom. *Business and Human Rights Journal*, *7*(2), 249–270. doi:10.1017/bhj.2021.47

McQuade, A. (2019). Modern slavery in global context: ending the political economy of forced labour and slavery. In *The Modern Slavery Agenda* (pp. 29–46). Policy Press. doi:10.2307/j.ctvb1hsm8.6

Mende, J. (2019). The concept of modern slavery: Definition, critique, and the human rights frame. *Human Rights Review (Piscataway, N.J.)*, *20*(2), 229–248. doi:10.1007/s12142-018-0538-y

Merry, S. E. (2003). Constructing a global law-violence against women and the human rights system. *Law & Social Inquiry, 28*(4), 941–977. doi:10.1111/j.1747-4469.2003.tb00828.x

Merry, S. E. (2009). *Human rights and gender violence: Translating international law into local justice*. University of Chicago Press.

Mgidlana, R. H. (2020). *Should South Africa criminalise ukuthwala leading to child and forced marriages?*.

Miers, S. (2000). Contemporary forms of slavery. *Canadian Journal of African Studies/Revue canadienne des études africaines, 34*(3), 714-747.

Miers, S. (2004). Slavery: A question of definition. In Structure of Slavery in Indian Ocean Africa and Asia (pp. 1-15). Routledge.

Miers, S. (2017). Slavery: A question of definition. In Critical Readings on Global Slavery (pp. 184-200). Brill.

Miriyam, T. N. (2023). *An Assessment Of The Global Pattern Of Trafficking Of Minors And Young Adults*.

Mkhize, G., & Vilakazi, F. (2021). Rethinking gender and conduits of control: A feminist review. *Image & Text*, (35), 1–22. doi:10.17159/2617-3255/2021/n35a10

Montero, J. (2022). *Human Rights as Human Independence: A Philosophical and Legal Interpretation*. University of Pennsylvania Press.

Moschetti, C. O. (2005). *Conjugal Wrongs Dont Make Rights: International Feminist Activism, Child Marriage and Sexual Relativism*. University of Melbourne, Political Science Department, Faculty of Arts.

Muhleisen, A. (2017). *Escaping discourse: a critical analysis of fleeing a forced marriage as a journey of personal transformation* [Doctoral dissertation, Swinburne University of Technology].

Nigam, S. (2019). *Women and domestic violence law in India: a quest for justice*. Taylor & Francis.

O'Brien, M. (2016). 'Don't kill them, let's choose them as wives': The development of the crimes of forced marriage, sexual slavery and enforced prostitution in international criminal law. *International Journal of Human Rights, 20*(3), 386–406. doi:10.1080/13642987.2015.1091562

Onwuachi-Willig, A. (2005). The return of the ring: Welfare reform's marriage cure as the revival of post-bellum control. *California Law Review*, 1647–1696.

Otis, W. (2023). *A Decision of One's Own: Understanding Individual Autonomy in Supported Decision-Making* [Doctoral dissertation, University of Otago].

Palriwala, R., & Uberoi, P. (2008). Exploring the links: Gender issues in marriage and migration. *Marriage, migration and gender, 5*, 23-60.

Patterson, O. (2012). Trafficking, gender and slavery: Past and present. *The legal understanding of slavery: From the historical to the contemporary*, 322-359.

Patterson, O., & Zhuo, X. (2018). Modern trafficking, slavery, and other forms of servitude. *Annual Review of Sociology*, *44*(1), 407–439. doi:10.1146/annurev-soc-073117-041147

Phillips, R. (2012). Interventions against forced marriage: Contesting hegemonic narratives and minority practices in Europe. *Gender, Place and Culture*, *19*(1), 21–41. doi:10.1080/0966369X.2011.610093

Quek, K. (2018). *Marriage trafficking: Women in forced wedlock.* Routledge. doi:10.4324/9781315620138

Quirk, J., & Rossi, B. (2022). Slavery and marriage in African societies. *Slavery & Abolition*, *43*(2), 245–284. doi:10.1080/0144039X.2022.2063231

Rajan, I. (2013). *Speaking self out of darkness: The lived experience of sex trafficking survivors in Kolkata.* Pacifica Graduate Institute.

Randall, M., & Venkatesh, V. (2015). The right to no: The crime of marital rape, women's human rights, and international law. *Brook. J. Int'l L.*, *41*, 153.

Rani Selvarajan. (2023). *Violence Against Women and Girls Snapshot Report 2022-23.* End Violence Against Women. https://www.endviolenceagainstwomen.org.uk/wp-content/uploads/2023/02/Snapshot-2022-23-final-140223.pdf

Razack, S. H. (2004). Imperilled Muslim women, dangerous Muslim men and civilised Europeans: Legal and social responses to forced marriages. *Feminist Legal Studies*, *12*(2), 129–174. doi:10.1023/B:FEST.0000043305.66172.92

Ricker, C. L., Earn, S., Das, M., & Greene, M. E. (2023). The Right to Leave: Dissolution of Child, Early, and Forced Marriages and Unions. *Adolescents (Basel, Switzerland)*, *3*(3), 490–507. doi:10.3390/adolescents3030035

Rossouw, T. M. (2012). *Identity, personhood and power: a critical analysis of the principle of respect for autonomy and the idea of informed consent, and their implementation in an androgynous and multicultural society* [Doctoral dissertation, Stellenbosch: Stellenbosch University].

Sabates-Wheeler, R. (2009). *The impact of irregular status on human development outcomes for migrants.*

Sabbe, A., Temmerman, M., Brems, E., & Leye, E. (2014). Forced marriage: An analysis of legislation and political measures in Europe. *Crime, Law, and Social Change, 62*(2), 171–189. doi:10.1007/s10611-014-9534-6

Sarich, J., Olivier, M., & Bales, K. (2016). Forced marriage, slavery, and plural legal systems: An African example. *Human Rights Quarterly, 38*(2), 450–476. doi:10.1353/hrq.2016.0030

Scarpa, S. (2008). *Trafficking in human beings: modern slavery.* Oxford University Press. doi:10.1093/acprof:oso/9780199541904.001.0001

Seff, I., Williams, A., Hussain, F., Landis, D., Poulton, C., Falb, K., & Stark, L. (2020). Forced sex and early marriage: Understanding the linkages and norms in a humanitarian setting. *Violence Against Women, 26*(8), 787–802. doi:10.1177/1077801219845523 PMID:31066342

Sensen, O. (Ed.). (2012). *Kant on moral autonomy.* Cambridge University Press. doi:10.1017/CBO9780511792489

Sheley, E. (2020). Criminalizing Coercive Control Within the Limits of Due Process. *Duke Law Journal, 70,* 1321.

Simmons, F., & Wong, G. (2021). Learning from lived experience: Australia's legal response to forced marriage. *The University of New South Wales Law Journal, 44*(4), 1619–1662. doi:10.53637/YJYS9724

Ssenyonjo, M. (2021). Human Trafficking in the Context of Global Migration: Modern Manifestation of De Facto Slavery, Servitude and Forced or Compulsory Labour. *International Human Rights Law Review, 10*(2), 191–215. doi:10.1163/22131035-10020006

Stapleton, A., Polakowski, M., & Quinn, E. (2022). *The integration of non-EU migrant women in Ireland* (No. 148). Research Series.

Stoehr, M., & Moeschel, M. (2019). *Is the prohibition of modern slavery protecting minors? An analysis of the united kingdom and germany before the backdrop of international human rights law.*

Such, E., Laurent, C., Jaipaul, R., & Salway, S. (2020). Modern slavery and public health: A rapid evidence assessment and an emergent public health approach. *Public Health, 180,* 168–179. doi:10.1016/j.puhe.2019.10.018 PMID:31951910

Swegman, C., & Initiative, T. J. C. F. M. (2016). The intersectionality of forced marriage with other forms of abuse in the United States. *NRCDV Applied Research Paper.* National Resource Center on Domestic Violence.

Tarzia, L., Wellington, M., Marino, J., & Hegarty, K. (2019). "A huge, hidden problem": Australian health practitioners' views and understandings of reproductive coercion. *Qualitative Health Research*, *29*(10), 1395–1407. doi:10.1177/1049732318819839 PMID:30584793

Tierney, S., Laurie, E., Stallworthy, M., Pila, J., Cobley, C., & Lowe, N. (2020). Choice, Culture and the Politics of Belonging: The Emerging Law of Forced and Arranged Marriage. *Miread Enright 331 Constitutional Referendums: A Theoretical Enquiry*.

Tikka, R. M. (2021). *Exploitative Sham Marriages as a Form of Human Trafficking in the European Union* [Doctoral dissertation, Universidade Fernando Pessoa (Portugal)].

Trask, T. (2021). *Child Early Forced Marriage as a Human Rights Violation in International and Domestic Spheres* [Doctoral dissertation, University of Georgia].

Triandafyllidou, A., & Bartolini, L. (2020). Irregular migration and irregular work: A chicken and egg dilemma. *Migrants with Irregular Status in Europe: Evolving Conceptual and Policy Challenges*, 139-163.

True, J. (2020). *Violence against women: what everyone needs to know*. What Everyone Needs to Know.

Vasil, S. (2023). "I Came Here, and it Got Worse Day by Day": Examining the Intersections Between Migrant Precarity and Family Violence Among Women with Insecure Migration Status in Australia. *Violence Against Women*, 10778012231159414. doi:10.1177/10778012231159414 PMID:36913733

Walker, A. (2013). Strange Traffic: Sex, Slavery, and the Freedom Principle. *SSRN*, *46*, 561. doi:10.2139/ssrn.2220879

Warner, E. (2004). Behind the wedding veil: Child marriage as a form of trafficking in girls. *Am. UJ Gender Soc. Pol'y & L.*, *12*, 233.

Wilson, M. S. G. (2016). *Sexual Violence in Armed Conflict Under International Law: The Interplay Between International Humanitarian Law Human Rights Law and International Criminal Law*. University of Pretoria.

Zasha, D. (2018). *Agency and wellbeing in the context of early marriage: A qualitative inquiry into the northern Nigerian context* [Doctoral dissertation, Queen Margaret University, Edinburgh].

Zeweri, H. (2022). Reluctant Disclosure: Epistemic Doubt and Ethical Dilemmas in Australian Forced Marriage Prevention Efforts. *Ethnos*, 1–18. doi:10.1080/00141844.2022.2040564

Chapter 2
Human Trafficking in Tanzania:
A Review of Victim Protection Policy in Tanzania and Recommendations

Godfrey Mpandikizi
Tanzania Anti-Human Trafficking and Legal Initiatives, Tanzania

ABSTRACT

Human trafficking is an issue that affects vulnerable individuals across the world, and Tanzania is no exception. The country has long been a source, transit, and destination for human trafficking, particularly for women and children who are exploited and used for forced labor, sexual exploitation, forced military servitude, and organ trafficking. Despite Tanzania's efforts to combat trafficking in persons in all of its forms, it remains classified as a Tier 2 country by the United States Department of State's Trafficking in Persons (TIP) Report. This classification indicates that while the government has made significant efforts to address human trafficking, it does not fully meet the minimum standards for the elimination of trafficking. In the fight against human trafficking, Tanzania's approach, like many countries globally, focuses on three pillars of combating trafficking in persons: prevention, prosecution, and protection. All three pillars are necessary to help eliminate the sources of trafficking, support survivors, and hold traffickers accountable for their crimes.

DOI: 10.4018/979-8-3693-0327-6.ch002

INTRODUCTION

Human trafficking is a serious abuse of human rights that still happens all over the world. Tanzania is a good example of this problem. The fact that Tanzania is a country that traffics people and is also a transit and destination spot for many of them, especially women and children, shows how hard it is to fight this problem. People are taken advantage of in many ways, such as through forced labour, sexual abuse, military service, and even organ trafficking. The Tanzanian government has made some great efforts, as shown by its Tier 2 ranking in the US Department of State's Trafficking in Persons (TIP) Report. However, there is still a long way to go before they fully meet the basic standards for ending trafficking. This gap is especially clear when it comes to protecting survivors and helping them get back on their feet, which is an area where present strategies are seriously lacking.

The goal of this chapter is to take a close look at this study gap by looking at it through the lens of making victim protections stronger in Tanzania. The Tanzanian strategy, like global strategies, is based on three pillars: prevention, prosecution, and protection. However, the third pillar, protection, needs to be looked at again and strengthened right away. This reevaluation is necessary not only to get rid of the things that lead to trafficking, but also to help survivors more and hold traffickers responsible. The goal of this chapter is to give a full picture of how Tanzania helps survivors of human trafficking by looking at its legal resources, humanitarian aid, and security programmes. It will also look at what has worked and what hasn't in its ongoing fight against human trafficking.

To properly handle survivor protections in Tanzania's human trafficking policy, one must first learn a great deal about the history of trafficking in the country. To do this, Tanzania's present government, extralegal, and international policies against trafficking need to be looked into. This chapter will give these policies a critical review, pointing out their flaws and offering ways to make them better. It will also find ways to improve the measures that have already been tried and tested and suggest them. In the end, this chapter wants to add to the conversation about human trafficking by giving a more detailed view of Tanzania's efforts. This will help policymakers and practitioners make better decisions about how to protect and rehabilitate survivors.

In this chapter, "Human Trafficking in Tanzania: A Review of Victim Protection Policy in Tanzania and Recommendations to Transition from Tier 2 to Tier 1 Under the Trafficking Victims Protection Act Country Standards," Godfrey Mpandikizi offers an in-depth analysis of the challenges and progress in Tanzania's fight against human trafficking. The chapter unfolds as follows:

Background of Human Trafficking in Tanzania: This section delves into the prevalence of human trafficking in various regions of Tanzania, highlighting the multifaceted nature of this issue. It underscores the importance of systematic victim reporting and examines the exacerbating effects of global crises, like the COVID-19 pandemic, on human trafficking.

The Issue of Children Being Trafficked in Tanzania: Focusing on the most vulnerable group, this part discusses the alarming trends in child trafficking in Tanzania. It explores the societal and individual factors that make children, especially girls and those with disabilities, susceptible to trafficking.

Tanzania's Approach to Combating Trafficking in Persons: Here, the chapter scrutinizes Tanzania's current strategies and policies in combating human trafficking. It critically reviews the Anti-trafficking in Persons Act of 2008 and other national and international initiatives Tanzania has adopted or participated in.

Tanzanian Human Trafficking Government Policy and Comparison: This segment offers a comparative analysis of Tanzanian policies with international standards such as the US Trafficking Victims Protection Act and the United Nations Protocol for Human Trafficking. It provides a detailed breakdown of these policies' elements and their effectiveness.

Tanzania's Trafficking In Persons Plan of Action and Comparison: The chapter proceeds to assess Tanzania's National Anti-Trafficking in Persons Plan of Action, comparing it with similar action plans from other countries. It evaluates the practical steps and strategies outlined in these plans.

Review of Tanzania's Trafficking Policy: A thorough examination of Tanzania's policy against human trafficking is presented here. It identifies the strengths and weaknesses in the policy's formulation and implementation, focusing on victim protection.

Comparative Review of Policy and Potential Policy: This part extends the analysis to compare Tanzanian policies with those of the United States and the United Nations, discussing the implications of their differences and similarities.

TVPA Tier Standard: This section contextualizes Tanzania's efforts within the tier system of the Trafficking Victims Protection Act, exploring what it would take for Tanzania to achieve Tier 1 status.

Transitioning from Tier 2 to Tier 1: Here, the author provides specific recommendations for policy improvements, legal reforms, and practical strategies to elevate Tanzania to a Tier 1 country in the fight against human trafficking.

Conclusion: The chapter concludes by summarizing the key findings and recommendations, emphasizing the need for coordinated, multi-sectoral efforts to eradicate human trafficking in Tanzania and to protect and rehabilitate its victims effectively.

BACKGROUND OF HUMAN TRAFFICKING IN TANZANIA

Human trafficking is a problem in the country of Tanzania. According to the Tanzania Human Rights Report, conducted in 2021, there are regions in which human trafficking is common in Tanzania: "Regions where human trafficking is common include Dar es Salaam, Dodoma, Mwanza, Kigoma, Kagera, Geita, Singida, Arusha, Manyara, Shinyanga, Simiyu, Lindi, and Mtwara" (US Department of State, 2023; US Department of State, 2021; Immigration and Refugee Board of Canada; 2023). In Tanzania, there is not a specific region where human trafficking is occurring, but it is happening in different regions throughout the country, showing the importance of having unified protections for victims. An important aspect of protecting victims of human trafficking is reporting. According to the Tanzania Human Rights Report, conducted in 2021, there has been data collecting the number of people being human trafficked: "The most recent police data on human trafficking in Tanzania shows that in the period of 2016 to 2020, a total of 151 incidents of human trafficking were reported. These include 19 incidents reported in 2020, which are one more than those reported in 2019" (Wazambi, Komanya & Henga, 2020). Reporting the human trafficking incidents that have been happening in Tanzania is important for combating human trafficking.

Another important element of protecting victims of human trafficking is understanding the effect that global issues can have on individual countries and the people within, like the COVID-19 pandemic (Wazambi, Komanya & Henga, 2020; US Department of State, 2021; Immigration and Refugee Board of Canada; 2023). The Tanzania Human Rights Report further discusses the impact the COVID-19 pandemic has had on people being human trafficked: "Victims are targeted when they are vulnerable and the Covid19 pandemic has increased vulnerability" (Immigration and Refugee Board of Canada, 2023, 589; US Department of State, 2021). The COVID-19 pandemic has resulted in people finding themselves in vulnerable situations, and perpetrators taking advantage of people being in those positions. In a report conducted by the United Nations Office on Drugs and Crimes (UNODC), there is discussion of how people have become more susceptible to being trafficked since the COVID19 pandemic: "For the victims still in confinement by their traffickers, COVID-19 measures may make their desperate situation even worse. The increased levels of domestic violence reported in many countries is a worrying indicator for the living conditions of many trafficking victims, such as those in domestic servitude or sex slavery, forms of exploitation that disproportionately affect women and girls" (UNODC, 2020).

Global issues, like the COVID-19 pandemic, can make victim's situations worse. Women and girls, who are already systematically disadvantaged in society because of their gender, are at a heightened level of being trafficked. The different socially constructed categories which a person belongs to, interconnected with global issues, can result in people finding themselves in a desperate and vulnerable position.

The Issue of Children Being Trafficked in Tanzania

In Tanzania, children, specifically young girls, are often the victims of human trafficking. According to the Tanzania Human Rights Report, girls make up a large percentage of trafficking victims: "97% of human trafficking in Tanzania is conducted internally, with children in the ages of 12 to 17 being the major victims. Women and girls are the major victims of human trafficking, and child trafficking, particularly child labour trafficking and child sex trafficking, is said to be common. 74% of the victims are girls" (Wazambi, Komanya & Henga, 2020). Most of the human trafficking victims in Tanzania are children and are specifically young girls. Not only can a child's gender make them more susceptible to being human trafficked, but also their disability status. The Human Rights Report discusses how people with disabilities (PWD) can be susceptible to being human trafficked in Tanzania: "Trafficking in PWDs for purposes of begging is becoming a serious human trafficking issue. In July 2021, 15 people in Dar es Salaam, including a businessperson, were accused of trafficking 37 PWDs, including children with disabilities aged 7 to 11 years, from Tabora and Shinyanga Regions and taking them to Dar es Salaam to beg and generate income from them" (Reporter, 2022). The different socially constructed categories which a child belongs to can impact their susceptibility to being human trafficking. Human traffickers can take advantage of a victim's disability, which is why it is crucial that there is awareness to how different people, and the different aspects of their identity, can make them more vulnerable to being trafficked.

There have been efforts to protect children being trafficked in Tanzania. There has been the development of Standard Operating Procedures (SOPS), for Protecting, Assisting and Referring Trafficked Children in Tanzania (Mwalimu, 2016), which are meant to serve as a guiding tool for service providers, policy makers and practitioners from government, non-governmental and international organizations that are providing protection, assistance and referral services to child victims of trafficking in Tanzania (UNHCR, 2009; Mwalimu, 2016). SOPS is an important tool for protecting victims of human trafficking in Tanzania, and ensuring they are getting the resources and support they need.

The Standard Operating Procedures (SOPS), for Protecting, Assisting and Referring Trafficked Children in Tanzania has set out goals and actionable ways to achieve those goals for combating human trafficking in children in Tanzania. According to the Best Interest of Child principle, there is an emphasis on doing what is in the best interest of the individual child who is a victim of trafficking: Ensuring the best interests of the child is a primary consideration in all actions affecting children. This means that when a course of action affecting a child is taken, that course of action should reflect what is best for the child (Mwalimu, 2016). While SOPS has an intended goal of protecting child survivors of human trafficking (UNODC, 2009), that goal is put into action through different protocols like under the quality assurance section which states: "Ensure service provision is carried out by trained and experienced professional service providers" 13 and "Assign a dedicated social worker or case manager for each child victim of trafficking" (Mwalimu, 2016). SOPS provides guidelines to achieve goals for protecting child victims of trafficking in Tanzania.

Investigating the background of human trafficking in Tanzania reveals a system of crime centered around exploiting specific vulnerable populations, namely women and children and those without resources. It is an important mission to combat trafficking in persons in all its forms and in order to effect successful efforts to combat trafficking in persons, our approaches must be catered to the circumstances in which we are operating. Looking into how specific efforts can help these historically exploited populations, and the reasons for this exploitation, will allow us to cater any recommendations or commentary on the steps to increase Tanzania's policy to combat trafficking in persons to the problems that are specific to, even if unfortunately not unique to, Tanzania. Operating to address specific issues will be more effective, more attainable, and more motivating than broad, vague policy suggestions.

TANZANIA'S APPROACH TO COMBATING TRAFFICKING IN PERSONS

Understanding the nature of trafficking in persons in Tanzania, and the populations which suffer most, ultimately informs the focus of our research: what are the strengths and weaknesses of Tanzanian policy to provide protection to survivors and what recommendations can be made

to bring Tanzania to a Tier 1 country? In order to answer these questions, we must follow our background analysis by understanding and reviewing the current policies in place in Tanzania to provide protection to survivors of human trafficking.

Tanzania's historical policy to combat human trafficking is most prominently seen in the country's 2008 policy The Anti-trafficking in Persons Act, 2008 ("the Act"). In short, the policy outlines the definitions of trafficking in persons, what acts constitute trafficking in persons and acts that promote or use an intermediary to traffick, the procedures for investigating and prosecuting trafficking in persons, the rescue, rehabilitation, protection and assistance to victims, and an anti-trafficking fund and committee. While the policy sets out to address all three pillars of human trafficking - prevention, protection, and prosecution - we find it most effective for the purposes of this paper to focus on the sections regarding the protection of victims.

Part IV of The Anti-trafficking in Persons Act, Rescue, Rehabilitation, Protection and Assistance to Victims, is the main section of Tanzania's government policy that addresses protecting survivors of human trafficking (The Anti-trafficking in Persons Act 2008, Part IV). Along with rescue, rehabilitation, and protection, the section outlines the repatriation of survivors and specifically addresses efforts to assist vulnerable populations, like child victims of trafficking (The Anti-trafficking in Persons Act 2008, Part IV, 17-24).

The Act in many ways is similar to the Trafficking Victims Protection Act of 2000 ("TVPA") in America and the United Nations Protocol for Human Trafficking, focusing on strengthening the three Ps and set forward efforts to comprehensively eliminate human trafficking (The Anti-trafficking in Persons Act, 2008, Part IV; Trafficking Victims Protection Act, 2000). Notably, the United States Department of Justice describes the TVPA as a strategy to "mount a comprehensive and coordinated campaign to eliminate modern forms of slavery domestically and internationally" and the Act purports to put in place comprehensive legislation to address all aspects of trafficking in persons (27 USC §7101).

Additionally, both countries, Tanzania and the United States, enacted federal action plans to support the three Ps of trafficking in 2021 (The White House, 2021; Ministry of Home Affairs, 2021).

These action plans chiefly set out to support the three Ps of trafficking by supporting existing policies and structures and putting in place new procedures, policies, and infrastructure to best combat Trafficking (The White House, 2021; Ministry of Home Affairs, 2021). Tanzania's National Anti-Trafficking in Persons Plan of Action ("Tanzania's Action Plan") aims to take an interdisciplinary approach to strengthen the parts of its trafficking policy that have not been effective in protecting survivors (Ministry of Home Affairs, 2021).

Tanzania has also signed on to international agreements, giving guidance and obligations for the country in its fight against trafficking in persons, including the United Nations Office on Drugs and Crime (UNODC) Enhancing Criminal Justice Responses to Trafficking in Persons in Eastern Africa (UN East Africa Response) and the United Nations Transnational Organized Crime (UNTOC) Protocol to Prevent, Suppress and Punish Trafficking in Persons, especially Women and Children (UN Trafficking Suppression Protocol) (2019). These plans set out to give guidelines to signing countries for how to improve their approaches to combating trafficking and set victims at the center of their fight against trafficking in persons (UNODC, 2019; UNTOC, 2000). The UN East Africa response sets out actions to take that are more catered to the specifics of Tanzania's fight and focus largely on how the country can increase its support for victims (UNODC, 2019; UNTOC, 2000). The response also calls for the 13 member states to set out an action plan, taking an approach that aims to compel rather than set forth obligations to be met (UNODC, 2019; UNTOC, 2000). The UN Trafficking Suppression Protocol has three specific articles regarding the protection of victims (UNTOC, 2000). These articles, Articles 6 through 8, obligate countries to provide victims with resources that support their rights, health, living conditions, immigration efforts, educational and employment opportunities, and more (UNTOC, 2000). The protocol, targeting a larger number of states than the UN East Africa Response, is more targeted in its approach (UNTOC, 2000). The UN East Africa Response is just that, a response; the response aims to compel the countries to increase efforts to combat trafficking in ways that it has identified the region has fallen short UNODC, 2019). In contrast, the UN Trafficking Suppression Protocol, enacted in 2000, a time of great increases in efforts to combat trafficking, addresses all the pillars of fighting trafficking specifically with outlined goals for how to begin the fight against trafficking (UNTOC, 2000).

Tanzanian human trafficking government policy and comparison

	US Trafficking Victims Protection Act and T Visa elements	Tanzania Anti-trafficking in Persons Act	United Nations Protocol for Human Trafficking
Date	October 2000	April 2008	Nov 2000
Act	Recruit Harbor Transfer Provide Receive Transport Obtain	Recruit Harbor Transfer Provide Receive Transport Abducts Hires	Recruitment Transportation Transfer Harbouring Receipt
Means	Force Fraud Coercion ● Threats of serious harm or physical restraint ● Scheme, plan, or pattern intended to cause a person to believe that failure to perform an act would result in serious harm to or physical restraint against any person ● Abuse or threatened abuse of legal process	Threat or use of: ● Force ● Fraud ● Deceit ● Violence ● Coercion ● Intimidation "By any means" including: ● Pretext of domestic or overseas employment ● Introduces person to foreign national for marriage ● Offers contract of marriage ● Adoption ● Hiring ● Other contract	Threat or use of: ● Force ● Other forms of coercion ● Abduction ● Fraud ● Deception ● The abuse of power ● A position of vulnerability The giving or receiving of payments or benefits to achieve the consent of a person having control over another person
Purpose	Involuntary servitude Peonage Debt bondage Slavery Commercial sex act	Acquiring, offering, buying, selling, or trading person Prostitution Pornography Forced labor Slavery Involuntary servitude Debt bondage Sexual exploitation Sex tourism Removal or sale of organs Using child or disabled person for armed service	Exploitation ● Sexual ● Prostitution ● Forced labor or services ● Slavery or similar practices ● Servitude ● Removal of organs

Tanzania's trafficking in persons plan of action and comparison

	United States National Action Plan to Combat Human Trafficking	National Anti-Trafficking in Persons Plan of Action
Principle Structure	1) Engaging with victims 2) Safeguarding victims from inappropriate penalization 3) Improving access to immigration benefits and options 4) Expanding and improving victim assistance associated with federal law enforcement 5) Seeking financial remedies for victims 6) Offering or connecting victims to social services	1) Policy, Legislation and Institutional Mechanisms 2) Capacity Building for Skills Enhancement 3) Prevention and Public Awareness Raising 4) Victim and Witness Support and Protection 5) Communication, Coordination and Cooperation 6) Prevention and Public Awareness Raising 7) Monitoring & Evaluation 8) Resource Mobilization
Actions	1) Develop or update, validate, and implement screening forms and protocols 2) Establish protocols and incorporate promising practices regarding victim interviews for law enforcement 3) Regularly train federal law enforcement and service provider agencies on identifying human trafficking 4) Increase access to public awareness materials focused on victim identification, including by displaying those materials in priority locations within 1 year 5) Review and update training, policies, and guidance for federal law enforcement to protect human trafficking victims 6) Provide human trafficking	1) Establish government safe homes for TIP victims 2) Strengthen coordination in implementation of witness protection mechanism 3) Mainstream TIP support services in the existing One Stop Centres 4) Establish transit shelters for TIP Victims in entry and exit border points 5) Provide free legal services to TIP victims 6) Enhance the capacity of safe-house service providers

11
victims protection from removal
7) Provide remedies for victims with inappropriate arrests and criminal records
8) Encourage state, local, tribal, and territorial governments to protect victims from inappropriate punishment for conduct committed as a direct result of being trafficked
9) Modernize immigration program systems connected to human trafficking victims
10) Provide immigration protections to ensure eligible victims are not removed
11) Increase victim assistance personnel
12) Create comprehensive training on restitution
13) Increase access to mental health and other healthcare services
14) Increase access to shelters and safe housing
15) Increase access to employment
16) Increase access to education
17) Increase access to assistance broadly

Tanzania's current international plans and obligations regarding the protection of trafficking survivors and potential future policy

United Nations Office on Drugs and Crime (UNODC)	United Nations Transnation Organized Crime (UNTOC)	African Union (AU)
Enhancing Criminal Justice Responses to Trafficking in Persons in Eastern Africa	*Protocol to Prevent, Suppress and Punish Trafficking in Persons, especially Women and Children*	*Draft Action Plan to Combat Trafficking in Human Beings especially Women and Children*
The response consists of a series of activities implemented in 13 countries in East Africa Based on the United States-funded project Enhancing Effective and Victim-Centred Criminal Justice Responses to Trafficking in Persons in Eastern Africa	The protocol is a United Nations General Assembly Resolution passed in November 2000 for states agreeing to an international approach to eliminating trafficking in persons through the protection of international human rights and transnational cooperation	The drafted action plan was an African Union approach to combating trafficking drafted in 2002. The draft was left unfinished and created with oversight from Sweden/Italy and focuses on international collaboration between members of the African Union and between the African Union and European nations
1. Provide technical assistance to law practitioners and government officials 2. Strengthen national Anti-TIP legislation in line with UNTOC and the supplementary TIP Protocol and national policies 3. Establish a Regional Plan of Action for Member States to strengthen regional cooperation.	1. Shall provide privacy, housing, rights counseling, health support, employment, and educational opportunities (Art 6) 2. Consider legislation to allow victims to remain in the territory (Art 7) 3. Shall assist with repatriation or residence (Art 8)	1. Identify victims of trafficking, rehabilitate them and provide them with appropriate assistance and protection. Account for vulnerabilities and urban/rural divide 2. Adopt specific measures to avoid criminalization of victims of trafficking, as well as risk of re-victimization 3. Provide victims of trafficking with short - and long-term, appropriate, psychological, medical and social assistance

Review of Tanzania's Trafficking Policy

The examination of Tanzania's Anti-Trafficking in Persons Act (2008) against the backdrop of international frameworks like the TVPA and the United Nations Protocol for Human Trafficking reveals both its strengths and limitations. While the Act commendably defines the act, means, and purpose of trafficking, aligning with global standards (The Anti-trafficking in Persons Act, 2008, Part II (6); UNODC, 2019; UNTOC, 2000), its practical application raises questions about efficacy and inclusivity.

Tanzania's commitment to human rights and dignity is evident in its constitutional alignment with the United Nations Convention Against Transnational Crime. The Act's focus on survivor support, prioritizing women and children, and offering comprehensive services including legal counsel and health support is progressive

(The Anti-trafficking in Persons Act, 2008, Part IV). However, the Act's execution does not fully address the nuanced challenges faced by trafficking survivors.

The National Anti-Trafficking in Persons Plan of Action aims to bolster these legislative frameworks, emphasizing interdisciplinary collaboration and resource allocation (The Anti-trafficking in Persons Act, 2008, Part IV). However, its implementation reveals critical areas of concern. Notably, the Plan's focus on witness protection and legal services for survivors underscores a significant effort to provide security and legal redress to victims (Ministry of Home Affairs, 2021). Yet, there is an apparent gap in shielding the identity and information of those cooperating with law enforcement, compromising their safety and the effectiveness of prosecutions.

Furthermore, while the Action Plan articulates six specific actions to augment protections, its effectiveness is hindered by a lack of clear strategies for identifying and supporting trafficking victims, especially among vulnerable populations (US Department of State, 2022). The Plan's prevention-centric approach seems to overlook vital aspects of survivor support, highlighting a disconnection between policy objectives and on-the-ground realities.

A critical shortfall of Tanzania's trafficking policy is its inadequate focus on victim identification. The policy emphasizes procedural adherence for reporting but lacks specificity in implementation, leading to potential underreporting and insufficient protection for vulnerable groups (US Department of State, 2022). The treatment of international victims and those coerced into aiding traffickers also remains a significant concern, with the current approach often leading to the detention and deportation of victims in dire need of support (The Anti-trafficking in Persons Act, 2008; US Department of State, 2022).

Lastly, the Plan's approach to mental and physical health support for survivors appears overly general. It fails to provide detailed resource allocation or specific strategies to address these crucial needs, which are fundamental to the holistic rehabilitation of trafficking survivors (The Anti-trafficking in Persons Act, 2008; US Department of State, 2022).

COMPARATIVE REVIEW OF POLICY AND POTENTIAL POLICY

Tanzania's government policy follows in time the United Nations protocol and the United State's legislation to fight trafficking (The Anti-trafficking in Persons Act, 2008; Trafficking Victims Protection Act of 2000; UNTOC, 2000). Each policy has many similarities, and are comprehensive in their approaches. In comparing each policy, it stands out that Tanzania's policy includes more specificity than the United Nations or the United States. There are pros and cons to this specificity. On one hand, specificity can lead to the underenforcement of trafficking, as if a defendant fits the nature of who the policy intends to prosecute, but their conduct does not conform to the specific acts or motivations set forth in the policy then they often are required to be allowed to walk free. However, with specificity also comes the ability to cater efforts to combat trafficking to the country's own unique situations. Broad sweeping policy often can lead

to higher enforcement generally but can struggle to eliminate the specific vulnerabilities that are exploited in a country that drive the main harms of trafficking for that region. Additionally, a lack of specificity can tackle a broad set of actions, but, especially on the back of international policy, can ignore harms that are not often faced by the international community at large. For example, the United States's policy only covers a few purposes of trafficking, while the United Nations and Tanzania are more specific (The Anti-trafficking in Persons Act, 2008; Trafficking Victims Protection Act of 2000; UNTOC, 2000). While the United States can use broad definitions for these purposes to encompass large swaths of crimes, they can leave unique harms unenforced. Tanzania has taken efforts to cater its approach with specificity. Tanzania's policy, specifically covering the purposes of using children for armed services and taking the organs of trafficked persons, tackles two issues that, largely, the United States does not face (The Anti-trafficking in Persons Act, 2008; Trafficking Victims Protection Act of 2000; UNTOC, 2000). But because these are issues that are prevalent in Tanzania, trafficking in persons cannot effectively be eliminated without these being covered.

The policy of Tanzania, however, is not wholly more specific than those of the United Nations and the United States. Functionally, Tanzania's policy tries to use the benefits of broad language and the benefits of specificity (The Anti-Trafficking in Persons Act, 2008). Specificity can help the country criminalize conduct that is unique and largely unprecedented while broad language can help criminalize a vast range of means. Tanzania's policy defines trafficking to be conducted "by any means," and then gives examples of what this could mean (The Anti-Trafficking in Persons Act, 2008). While this could lead to over-enforcement, Tanzania's policy has calculated that risk and aims to limit it with explanations of what constitutes any means and by being specific about the purposes for which these means must have been used.

Investigation Tanzania's Action Plan comparatively reveals Tanzania's issues with struggling to provide specific protections to victims (Ministry of Home Affairs, 2021). While Tanzania does want to give survivors safe housing, legal services, and increase the protection granted by government officials, it falls short in comprehensively providing opportunity, safety, and privacy. The United States Action Plan outlines 17 specific actions to increase support for survivors while Tanzania chooses to focus on six, three of which address safe houses or shelters (Ministry of

Home Affairs, 2021; The White House, 2021). Moving forward, Tanzania has not identified existing policies that they will support or new policy that will be enacted that will comprehensively provide survivors with safety beyond immediate protection and survivors seem to be without future measures that will offer support for aspects such as immigration support, employment and education opportunities, restitution, and reporting measures (Ministry of Home Affairs, 2021).

Tanzania's approach to combating trafficking does not just rest on government legislation. The country has committed to using international resources for guidance and support. In fact, their government policy itself is based on the United Nations' human trafficking protocol and they have remained connected to the United Nations in their efforts to combat trafficking in persons (UNTOC, 2000). The two main international action plans motivating Tanzania's fight against trafficking set forth comprehensive goals with the aim of eliminating international trafficking and taking a victim-centered approach to combating trafficking (UNTOC, 2000; UNODC, 2019). Combining two such approaches is an effective choice in ensuring that the measures that the government takes to reduce trafficking are effective and do not exacerbate the harms that survivors have already faced.

Utilizing international resources is an effective way to ensure that multiple perspectives are accounted for in the fight against trafficking in persons. However, there are also omplications that can come with international policies such as those put forth by the United Nations. First, the United Nations must cater their action plans to be general and broad (UN General Assembly, Rules of Procedure of the General Assembly (A/520/Rev.19)).

Whether that is global or regional, the United Nations' goal is often to get as many member states to ratify and adopt the measures of their policies as possible. While this is good, as it increases global commitment to collaborating or committing to fight trafficking in persons, it also can leave the plans overbroad, unspecific, and sometimes ineffective (UN General Assembly, Rules of Procedure of the General Assembly (A/520/Rev.19)). Because the United Nations wants its policies adopted, it can make concessions to member states who protest (UN General Assembly, Rules of Procedure of the General Assembly (A/520/Rev.19)). They also can try to use general language to try to be applicable to multiple countries with vastly different atmospheres of trafficking, meaning that a policy that may work for some will not work for others (UN General Assembly, Rules of Procedure of the General Assembly (A/520/Rev.19)). The policies then also can struggle from a lack of specificity, meaning that countries that ratify these protocols will have obligations to follow but these obligations often are lauded for the values they promote rather than setting forth any practical ways for the protocols to be applied within a country (UN General Assembly, Rules of Procedure of the General Assembly (A/520/Rev.19)). The Protocol to Prevent, Suppress and Punish Trafficking in Persons, especially Women and Children is valuable to Tanzania as it sets forth what sort of actions the country can take to protect survivors, but ultimately the plan necessitates further policy to be made as it is up to Tanzania to cater the approach to their own fight and lay out specific actions to meet the goals of the protocol (UNTOC, 2000).

There are benefits and downsides to this approach. Leaving the specifics up to each country can allow the United Nations to write sweeping plans that many states will sign but also can mean that their plans end up largely performative, as countries may sign on as a presentation to the United Nations that they will join the fight, and not put in place further action to do so. A positive of the broad nature of the plans of the United Nations can allow countries to cater approaches to issues that are unique to their country or region. However, as Tanzania works to fight trafficking in persons, many of the issues that arise in their fight are problems that their government policy fails to solve and arise due to the extent to which the vulnerable populations in Tanzania are exploited (US Department of State, 2022).

The African Union Draft Action Plan to Combat Trafficking in Human Beings especially Women and Children (AU Draft), while unfinished, also offers potential roads to increasing the protection of survivors (African Union, 2002). A large strength of the policy is its focus specifically on vulnerable populations, including those who are exploited to large degrees in Tanzania (African Union, 2002). The policy focuses on women and children who are the most exploited populations in Tanzania and offers specifics to protect these populations in particular (African Union, 2002). The AU Draft benefits from its focus on Africa, taking an international policy and catering it to the unique aspects of the region. For example, the policy aims to account for rural/urban divides and aims to stop revictimization (African Union, 2002). Additionally, the AU Draft has efforts that cover some areas in which Tanzania struggles to protect survivors, particularly by offering both short and long-term psychological and physical health support (African Union, 2002). The AU Draft unfortunately is unfinished and unratified but would be beneficial at the least for the fight against trafficking in persons in Tanzania, showing a regional international commitment to defeating trafficking in all of its forms (African Union, 2002).

TVPA Tier Standard

In order for Tanzania to achieve Tier 1 status in its fight against human trafficking, we must look to the standards by which each tier is measured to understand where Tanzania perhaps falls short and what can be done for the country to meet the standards of Tier 1. The tier system is defined by the United States Department of State in their Trafficking in Persons Report ("TIP Report") (US Department of State, 2022, 27 USC §7106(a)(1-4)). The TIP Report defines each tier in light of the TVPA (27 USC §7106(a)(1-4)). Countries in Tier 1 are those whose governments comply with all of the TVPA's minimum standards (US Department of State, 2022). Tier 2 countries are those that are making significant efforts to comply with standards but fall short in some ways (US Department of State, 2022).

Countries on the Tier 2 watchlist are making significant efforts to meet minimum standards but also struggle as either the number of victims in the country is increasing, there is a lack of evidence of efforts to continue to improve, or their Tier 2 designation is based on something like an action plan or other policy that set out future efforts that have not yet been completed (US Department of State, 2022).

When looking at what defines TVPA's minimum standards, there are twelve criteria that are covered that cen be diluted into four approaches (27 USC §7106(b)). First, countries must prohibit severe forms of trafficking and punish those who commit this trafficking (27 USC §7106(b)(3)). Second, countries must give proper punishment to sex traffickers that is proportional to their actions and accounts for the harm caused and the nature of their victims (27 USC §7106(b)(1)). Third, the government's punishment of trafficking must be catered to deter future trafficking (27 USC §7106(b)(3); 27 USC §7106(b)(1)). Fourth, the government must make efforts to eliminate trafficking and these efforts must be sustained (27 USC §7106(b)(3); 27 USC §7106(b)(7-12)). Fifth, whether the government of the country protects victims of severe forms of trafficking in persons and encourages their assistance in the investigation and prosecution of such trafficking (27 USC §7106(b)(2)).

In regards to specifics, the TVPA standards for protecting victims are split into three measures. The TVPA measures whether the country protects survivors and encourages their assistance, has alternatives to removal for those who are in the country because of their trafficking, and ensures survivors are not inappropriately detained or penalized because of illegal actions that they committed as a result of their trafficking (27 USC §7106(b)(2)).

US department of state's trafficking in persons report tier definitions

Tier 1	**Countries whose governments fully comply with the TVPA's minimum standards**
Tier 2	**Countries whose governments do not fully comply with all minimum standards, but are making significant efforts to bring themselves into compliance**
Tier 2 Watchlist	Tier 2 status, but also: ● The absolute number of victims is significantly increasing; or ● There is a failure to provide evidence of increasing efforts from the previous year; or ● The determination that a country is making significant efforts to bring themselves into compliance with minimum standards was based on commitments by the country to take additional future steps over the next year.
Tier 3	Countries whose governments do not fully comply with the minimum standards and are not making significant efforts to do so

TVPA Minimum Standards Referenced by the TIP Report Tiers (US Department of State, 2022)

1. The government of the country should prohibit severe forms of trafficking in persons and punish acts of such trafficking.
2. For the knowing commission of any act of sex trafficking involving force, fraud, coercion, or in which the victim of sex trafficking is a child incapable of giving meaningful consent, or of trafficking which includes rape or kidnapping or which causes a death, the government of the country should prescribe punishment commensurate with that for grave crimes, such as forcible sexual assault.
3. For the knowing commission of any act of a severe form of trafficking in persons, the government of the country should prescribe punishment that is sufficiently stringent to deter and that adequately reflects the heinous nature of the offense.
4. The government of the country should make serious and sustained efforts to eliminate severe forms of trafficking in persons.

   Measures of Serious and Sustained Efforts to Eliminate Severe Forms of Trafficking in Persons in Regards to the Protection of Victims Specifically (US Department of State, 2022) Whether the government of the country:

   1. Protects victims of severe forms of trafficking in persons and encourages their assistance in the investigation and prosecution of such trafficking
   2. Has provisions for legal alternatives to their removal to countries in which they would face retribution or hardship
   3. Ensures that victims are not inappropriately incarcerated, fined, or otherwise penalized solely for unlawful acts as a direct result of being trafficked, including by providing training to law enforcement and immigration officials regarding the identification and treatment of trafficking victims using approaches that focus on the needs of the victims.

Potential Improvements to TVPA Framework Generally

While the TVPA framework for minimum standards addresses all three pillars of combating trafficking in persons, the efforts to combat traffic focus heavily on the prosecution of traffickers. Specifically, given the power disparities inherent to situations of human trafficking, the framework addresses punishments relative to the agency of an actor, or the lack thereof (27 USC §7106(b)(3)). The minimum standards notably include requirements for countries to prohibit their own state actors from participating in and facilitating human trafficking (27 USC §7106(b)(7)). The framework seeks to holistically compel countries to prescribe laws and punishments for participating in trafficking both domestically and internationally, addressing activities from benefitting from existing trafficking, like participating in sex tourism or profiting of off those who are transporting trafficked persons across borders, to directly facilitating trafficking (US Department of State, 2022). The comprehensive aura of

the TVPA's standards to combat trafficking through prosecuting shows that those who use the tier framework for analyzing countries' efforts can provide detailed approaches to ensuring that traffickers are punished and it would be beneficial to the report for the framework to include additional specific approaches to providing protection for survivors that are as similarly detailed as what is discussed regarding prosecution (US Department of State, 2022). The standards for determining tiers ultimately focus largely on the prosecution of traffickers and more weight is given to these efforts than to efforts to protect survivors (US Department of State, 2022; 27 USC §7106(b)).

Transitioning From Tier 2 to Tier 1

Tanzania, currently positioned in Tier 2, has demonstrated a commitment to enhancing the efficacy of its anti-human trafficking initiatives, as evidenced by the nation's Action Plan (US Department of State, 2022). This commitment includes a strategic focus on identifying and addressing the needs of particular vulnerable groups within Tanzania and addressing specific forms of trafficking that may not be universally recognized. To ascend to Tier 1 status, Tanzania must implement certain measures aligned with the TVPA's minimum standards, particularly in terms of victim protection and support.

Analyzing the first criterion, which assesses government protection of victims and their involvement in trafficking investigations and prosecutions, it becomes clear that Tanzania needs to fortify its reporting mechanisms. The discrepancy between the low number of identified victims (165) and estimates suggesting a much higher prevalence of trafficking indicates a significant underreporting issue (US Department of State, 2022). The reliance on NGO-derived data for trafficking statistics suggests that effective victim identification is feasible and that survivors are amenable to reporting their experiences.

A critical shortcoming in Tanzania's approach lies in its over-reliance on NGOs for victim support, often at the expense of formal government procedures and investigations. This practice, while efficient and beneficial in providing immediate resources to survivors, fails to address the root causes of trafficking and does not align with the TVPA's emphasis on government-led victim protection and investigative collaboration.

To address these gaps, the Tanzanian government must establish and adhere to standard operating procedures for all trafficking cases, ensuring formal intake and investigation processes. Additionally, cooperation between NGOs and the government is crucial. NGOs should have protocols to report trafficking cases to the government, allowing for a comprehensive understanding of trafficking trends and more effective countermeasures (US Department of State, 2022).

Regarding privacy concerns, Tanzania's efforts must include comprehensive assessments of survivors' needs while ensuring their privacy and safety, particularly during legal proceedings. This approach is vital in reducing revictimization and encouraging survivors' participation in legal actions against traffickers.

The disconnection between prosecution and protection efforts in Tanzania often leads to the exploitation of survivors as mere instruments in legal processes. To remedy this, a more integrated approach is required, where protection, prosecution, and prevention efforts mutually reinforce each other.

Additionally, the Tanzanian government's intake process should be tailored to comprehend the diverse needs of trafficking survivors. Understanding these needs is essential for effectively allocating resources and guiding survivors to the most appropriate support services, whether governmental or NGO-based (US Department of State, 2022).

The second and third criteria, focusing on legal alternatives to removal and ensuring that victims are not penalized for acts committed as a result of being trafficked, are areas where Tanzania faces challenges. The lack of survivor identification often leads to their treatment as offenders rather than victims. To align with these criteria, Tanzania should provide avenues to prevent detention or deportation of survivors, thereby ensuring their security and cooperation in investigations (US Department of State, 2022).

Lastly, reinforcing Tanzania's efforts in combating trafficking necessitates enhanced training for government officials, adherence to established procedures, and a commitment to the principles underlying the three pillars of anti-trafficking efforts. This holistic approach should permeate all levels of government and NGOs engaged in the fight against human trafficking.

CONCLUSION

In conclusion, the chapter "Human Trafficking in Tanzania: A Review of Victim Protection Policy in Tanzania and Recommendations to Transition from Tier 2 to Tier 1 Under the Trafficking Victims Protection Act Country Standards" by Godfrey

Mpandikizi provides an insightful and comprehensive analysis of Tanzania's efforts and challenges in combating human trafficking. This study aimed to critically evaluate Tanzania's existing policies and strategies, particularly focusing on the protection of trafficking survivors, and to offer targeted recommendations to enhance these efforts.

The findings of this chapter underscore the complexity and pervasiveness of human trafficking in Tanzania, a country grappling with its role as a source, transit, and destination for trafficked individuals, particularly women and children. The exploration of Tanzania's policy landscape, including the Anti-trafficking in Persons Act of 2008 and the National Anti-Trafficking in Persons Plan of Action, highlights both the progress made and the gaps that persist, especially in the area of victim protection.

Crucially, the chapter identifies key areas where Tanzania's policies could be improved to meet the standards set by the Trafficking Victims Protection Act (TVPA) and achieve a Tier 1 status. These areas include enhancing victim identification and reporting mechanisms, strengthening government-led victim support systems, ensuring survivors' privacy and safety during legal processes, and fostering better integration of protection, prosecution, and prevention efforts.

The overarching implications of this work are far-reaching. It not only adds a critical voice to the discourse on human trafficking in Tanzania but also provides a roadmap for policymakers and practitioners. By addressing the identified gaps and implementing the suggested improvements, Tanzania can make significant strides towards more effectively combating human trafficking, providing comprehensive support to survivors, and ultimately, transitioning to a Tier 1 status under the TVPA.

This chapter serves as a call to action for a coordinated, multi-sectoral approach that prioritizes the protection and rehabilitation of victims, while relentlessly pursuing the eradication of human trafficking in Tanzania. The fight against this heinous crime demands not only robust legal frameworks and policies but also a commitment to their effective implementation, ensuring that every individual's rights and dignity are upheld.

REFERENCES

African Union. (2002). Draft Action Plan to Combat Trafficking in Human Beings Especially Women and Children. *AF-EU/MIN.CONF (II)/3.*

Immigration and Refugee Board of Canada. (2023, August 31). *National Documentation Packages*. IRB. https://irb.gc.ca/en/country-information/ndp/Pages/index.aspx?pid=12048

Legal and Human Rights Centre. (2021). *Tanzania Human Rights Report 2021: Calls for Reform of Criminal Justice System to Safeguard Human Rights* (A. Henga, Ed.). Legal and Human Rights Centre.

Ministry of Home Affairs. (2021). *National Anti-Trafficking in Persons Plan of Action 2021 - 2024*. Ministry of Home Affairs.

Mwalimu, H. (2016). Standard Operating Procedures for Protecting, Assisting and Referring Trafficked Children in Tanzania (p. 8). Research Gate.

The Chanzo Reporter. (2022, April 12). LHRC: Option of fine as punishment obstructs efforts against trafficking in persons in Tanzania. *The Chanzo Reporter.* https://thechanzo.com/2022/04/11/lhrc-option-of-fine-as-punishment-obstructs-efforts-against-trafficking-in-persons-in-tanzania/

The White House. (2021). *The National Action Plan to Combat Human Trafficking*. The White House.

United Nations Office on Drugs and Crime. (2020). *Impact of the Covid-19 Pandemic on Trafficking in Persons: Preliminary Findings and Messaging Based on Rapid Stocktaking*. UN.

UNODC. (2009). *International Framework for Action To Implement the Trafficking in Persons Protocol*. UN.

UNODC. (2019). *Enhancing Criminal Justice Responses to Trafficking in Persons in Eastern Africa*. UN.

UNTOC. (2000). *Protocol to Prevent*. Suppress and Punish Trafficking in Persons, Especially Women and Children.

U.S. Department of State. (2021). Tanzania 2021 Human Rights Report. U.S. Department of State.

US Department of State. (2022). *Trafficking in Persons Report*.

U.S. Department of State. (2023, December 7). *Tanzania - United States Department of State*. US DoS. https://www.state.gov/reports/2023-trafficking-in-persons-report/tanzania/

Wazambi, F., Komanya, J., & Henga, A. (2020). *Summary of the Tanzania Human Rights Report 2019: Tanzania Mainland*. Legal and Human Rights Centre.

Chapter 3
Money Laundering and Its Reflection on Global Development

Nika Chitadze
International Black Sea University, Georgia

ABSTRACT

Money laundering — the legalization of cash or other forms of property obtained through illegal means, that is, their transfer from the shadow, informal economy to the formal economy, in order to make it possible to use these funds openly (publicly). In the process of money laundering, the true source of income is concealed by replacing real transactions with formal ones, e.g. By falsifying verification documents, using documents of third parties, etc. In the conditions of economic globalization, offshore zones are often used for money laundering, these are the so-called countries. With a tax haven, where the confidentiality of the beneficiaries is ensured in the banking systems.

INTRODUCTION: DEFINITION OF MONEY LAUNDERING

To ensure the effective protection of human rights, it is necessary to have a legal framework and mechanisms that ensure the effective protection of democratic institutions. Of course, the existence of the above-mentioned circumstances is not enough to protect human rights, but first of all, to prevent the violation of human rights, there is a need for a strongly expressed will to protect and state policy. First of all, the country should create legislation and an appropriate social environment that defines an effective mechanism for the protection of human rights and freedoms. Of

DOI: 10.4018/979-8-3693-0327-6.ch003

course, the Constitution, as the most important law, plays a special role in the protection of human rights, but only at the level of the Constitution, it cannot be protected fundamental human rights, which are important for life. Within the framework of the research on the discussed topic, the threats faced by modern society due to the legalization of illegal income (money laundering) are discussed. Legalization of illegally obtained income is a new type of crime, which, as a separate component, was first included in the legislation of the United States of America in the 80s of the 20th century, and then in other countries. The legalization of illegal income created a special threat to the stability of the financial system of individual countries and the world. The high degree of importance of the problem is determined not only by the number of financial resources involved in circulation but also by the actual and potential results of their origin and circulation. Due to its complexity, economic crimes in the financial sphere are one of the least studied areas from a legal point of view. The legalization of illegal income lays the foundation for the criminal activities of criminal organizations and contributes to widespread corruption, especially in countries with transit economies. "Money laundering" is one of the most common forms of organized crime (UN, 2023). Legalization of illegal income dramatically increases the financial resources of criminal clans, poses a serious threat to the political and economic stability of countries, and hinders their development. It is for this reason that money laundering is considered the most serious crime, and its prevention, in turn, is an important tool in the fight against organized crime. Money laundering is a scheme of fraudulent manipulations through which illegally obtained income acquires a legal appearance, which, in turn, serves to strengthen the criminal community and create a corrupt environment in state structures, banking, and business. Establishing a solid and correct view on money laundering, first of all, contributes to the development of uniform judicial practice. The conclusions of the systematic analysis of the legalization of illegal income create a stable basis for the development of appropriate draft laws. The solution to many normative issues, which are theoretically understood, will have a positive effect on the development of legislation and the purposefulness of law-making activities. Determining the overall picture of money laundering will make it possible to solve comparative legal problems, which will contribute to the introduction of international standards in the legislative and judicial practice of different countries. The description of the legalization of illegal income in criminal law textbooks is not very convincing. The absence of a monographic analysis of the legalization of illegal income hurts the public's attitude to this crime. Knowledge about the legalization of illegal income is needed not only by criminalists but also by the general public. Different layers of the population can objectively evaluate the existing forms of covering illegal income if they have complete information about this crime. Therefore, the study of the legalization of illegal income has not only criminal but also social significance.

Based on the above, the theoretical study of the legalization of illegal income has not only a dogmatic character but also a practical significance.

The literature analysis on money laundering showed us that there is a paucity of works that study the relationship between money laundering, corruption, and foreign direct investment in different countries, which increases the need for research. Thus, a detailed discussion of the mentioned issues will significantly help both supervisory bodies and practicing lawyers in detecting and preventing the facts of the legalization of illegal income. Developing countries, in most cases, suffer more from the consequences of money laundering than developed countries. Money laundering harms the economic situation of the country, reduces the level of economic development, and negatively affects financial institutions and markets. Searching for historical facts reveals all the negative effects that money laundering can bring to the state. In many cases, money laundering is accompanied by a high level of corruption, which also hurts the country's economy, as well as the level of inequality in the distribution of income among the population and the increase in the scale of money laundering. A high level of money laundering often casts doubt on a country's reputation in the international arena, as it reflects a high level of corruption in the country. Anti-money laundering activities should include monitoring banking activities, and tax payments, processing statistical reports, and creating a legal framework that will positively affect the country's economic growth. In other cases, criminals will actively use the loopholes in the legislation of different countries to effectively launder money (US Department of State, 2021).

Legal and criminological literature was used during the research. Some data is taken from mass media. However, the key to a correct view of the problem under consideration is, first of all, in the works of jurists, criminologists, and criminologists, in which economic crime is considered as a whole, in addition to specific issues related to this crime. Also, issues related to crime and punishment, crime investigation, detection, and prevention of causes and circumstances contributing to crime are presented. The analysis of studies devoted to the legalization of illegal income showed that the subsumption issues of the crime in question are deeply multifaceted. ., Ryder N., Stessens G., and others. The main international-legal base of the research is represented by international conventions. Among them are: the 1988 United Nations Convention 7 against Illicit Traffic in Narcotic Drugs and Psychotropic Substances, the 1999 United Nations Convention against the Financing of Terrorism (New York), the 2000 United Nations Convention against Transnational Organized Crime (Palermo), the 2003 United Nations Convention on Corruption v. (Mérida), 1990 Council of Europe Convention on Money Laundering, Tracing, Seizure and Confiscation of the Proceeds of Crime. (Strasbourg), 2005 Council of Europe Convention on the Laundering, Tracing, Seizure and Confiscation of the Proceeds of Crime and the Financing of Terrorism (Warsaw) (Larkin, 2022). Some resolutions of the United

Nations General Assembly, European Commission directives, European Council decisions, FATF (Financial Action Task Force) recommendations, and others were also used while working on the thesis. The normative basis of the research is the existing legal norms of the legalization of illegal income. An important part of the practical base is represented by materials of activities of international organizations (United Nations, Organization for Economic Co-operation and Development OECD, Council of Europe, etc.).

THE ESSENCE OF LEGALIZATION OF ILLEGAL INCOME

A Historical Overview of the Spread of Legalization of Illegal Income in Different Countries

The term "money laundering" was first used by the British newspaper "The Guardian" during the Watergate scandal to denote the illegal financing of Richard Nixon's election campaign. According to reports, this term originated in the USA in the 1920s. In 1934, the leaders of mafia groups established the priority areas of money laundering. It was decided to invest in the US liquor and beverage business, expand into hospitality and food production, establish a foothold in the entertainment industry - first in nightclubs and musicians' unions, and finally take over the gaming business nationwide. Meyer Lansky is considered the "godfather" of money laundering. Al Capone's "companion" concluded that income that was not known to the Internal Revenue Service was not subject to taxation. Taking this postulate as a basis, he began to look for ways to cover illegal money. It was he who became the first discoverer of most of the methods of legalization known today. He was the first to recognize and appreciate the advantages of numbered Swiss bank accounts, Bahamian offshore, and the gambling business. As mentioned, for the first time the term "money laundering" appeared in print media in 1973 in connection with US President Richard Nixon and the "Watergate" scandal. In 1972, to be re-elected to the post of President, Nixon created an election committee under the leadership of George Mitchell. George Mitchell, together with Finance Minister Maurice Stans, began to quietly build a financial base for the upcoming election campaign. Anonymous donations, prohibited by law, poured into the committee. Donations from fictitious committees became known later after the Watergate break-in at the headquarters of the Democratic National Committee. The committee was found to contain laundered money (Ackermann, 2003).

In the 80s of the 20th century, revolutionary changes took place in the world economy. The leading developed countries have moved to a post-industrial economy and an informational method of production. With the development of the Euromarket, new international financial centers "Luxembourg, Singapore, Hong Kong, Panama, Bahamas, etc." were formed (Tretiakov, 2009). Transnational capital was freed from "guardianship" and came out of the jurisdiction of national states. It began to move freely around the world to capture more lucrative markets. If the state could control the national currency market under the conditions of strict financial control, as a result of the liberalization of the financial markets and easing of the currency control, transnational capital had the opportunity to destroy the market of any state. "Practically all transnational financial groups go through the offshores created in the same Herod, today there are about 100 offshore zones in the world, among which the largest are considered to be "Panama (about 400 thousand registered companies) and the British Virgin Islands (with more than 200 thousand registered companies) (Madinger, 2011). Offshores allow transnational capital to avoid taxation of funds. Thus, a unique opportunity in world economic history for the development of the "shadow" economy and the legalization of illegal income has entered the new economic environment. This was immediately taken advantage of by terrorists, drug businesses, and other organized criminal groups. Individual states and the world community had no other solution - they had to radically strengthen control over financial flows and money laundering. That is why in the 90s of the 20th century, quick and decisive measures were taken to prevent the legalization of illegal income, however, in general, the issue of organizing a global crime prevention system remains open. (Asanidze, 2012).

The issue of "money laundering" is not reflected in any single law in US legislation. This is because there is no codified model of criminal law in this country. Unlike the laws of other countries of the world, the laws of the USA are developing in their way. Even today, "money laundering" is given in a broad sense and includes not only the property obtained by criminal means but also the property arising as a result of illegal activities. American science is also developing in this direction (Asanidze, 2012). On October 17, 1931, a jury in a Chicago federal court found one of the leaders of organized crime in the United States, Alphonse Capone, guilty of tax evasion after many hours of deliberation. A court sentenced him to 11 years in prison for tax evasion, which ended his criminal career completely and permanently (Kerner, 1996). Capone's case did not create new legal precedents, but it had a significant impact on legal consciousness. It became clear that the leader of organized crime could be severely punished, not for the crimes he committed, but for tax evasion. The leaders of the criminal world found themselves in a kind of hopeless situation. To pay the tax, it is necessary to show the source of income, which means admitting the crime. A natural solution for criminals was to "launder money", i.e. create the appearance of having legal sources of income, as this allowed them to pay taxes and avoid criminal liability (Quiroz-Gutierrez, 2022).

There are many ways to launder money. They are largely determined by the specifics of national legislation on the control of cash and non-cash money circulation (Scott, 1995). The easiest way is to organize legal enterprises whose activities are related to receiving a significant amount of cash. One of these schemes, which was used by American gangsters during the period of the "dry law", derives the name of the event itself - "money laundering": a network of laundries was opened, under the guise of washing fees in the cash registers Money from the sale of alcohol, the exploitation of prostitutes, and other types of racketeering was brought in by the gangs, which allowed these revenues to be taxed and then used openly (Stessens, 2000). The transnational nature of money laundering led to the need for international cooperation in the fight against such activities, which was expressed both in international agreements and other documents. Initially, the cooperation initiative came from the USA. Some states became undisguisedly rich (and some still are) by creating favorable conditions for money laundering in national banking systems. Currently, the need to fight money laundering is almost universally recognized.

Definition of Illegal Income, Source, and Stages of Receipt

The development of the processes of criminalization of the economy was also facilitated by the thesis of the authors of the program for the transition to the market economy, who argued in the late 80s that the logic of the transition to the market economy envisaged the use of shadow capital for the interests of the entire country's population. Practically, illegal capital was considered a resource guarantee for the reform. In the legislation of many countries, the term "legalization of illegal income" is legally established, and it, according to the laws of many European countries, "on the promotion of prevention of legalization of illegal income" is defined as follows: giving legal form to illegal income (acquisition, use, transfer or other action), as well as its Concealing or disguising true origin, owner or owner and/or property rights, or attempting to do so (Matsne, 2021). By its content, money laundering includes a complex set of operations, the purpose of which is to disguise the source of financial assets in such a way that such assets can be used without compromise. Specialists distinguish several stages of money laundering. Generally, it is accepted to divide into three stages: placement, fragmentation, and integration, however, due to the complexity of the operations, drawing the line between these stages is quite difficult and depends on the intellectual preparation and imagination of the money launderer's person or team. These are illegal business activities, especially large amounts of deliberate evasion of taxes, false business, abuse of official authority, production and storage of large amounts of fake securities for keys, etc.

There are many (although similar) definitions of the legalization of illegal income in science. In 1984, the US President's Commission on Organized Crime defined money laundering as "the process of concealing the illegal origin of proceeds, and of converting and using those proceeds in such a way that they cannot be identified as the proceeds of crime." A slightly different wording is given in Interpol's 1993 newsletters - "In its essence, money laundering is a method whose purpose is to make machinations with money obtained as a result of illegal activities in such a way that the source of their receipt turns out to be legal" (Asanidze, 2012). In international law, the term "legalization of proceeds from criminal activities" was first introduced in the 1988 UN Vienna Convention on Combating Illicit Trafficking in Narcotic Drugs and Psychotropic Substances. According to the convention, the legalization of income refers to the whole complex of actions accompanied by the concealment of the true nature (origin) of property (cash and other property), namely: - "conversion or transfer of property, if it is known that this property was obtained as a result of a crime or crimes or as a result of participation in an offense, to conceal or disguise an illegal source of income, or to assist any person engaged in such offense to avoid responsibility for his actions; - Acquisition, possession or use of property, if at the time of receiving it, it was known that this property was obtained as a result of a crime, or as a result of participation in such a crime." According to the Strasbourg Convention of the Council of Europe of 1990 "On Money Laundering, Search, Seizure, and Confiscation of Proceeds of Crime", the legalization of cash or other property is defined as:

"Conversion or transfer of property, when a person knows that such property is income, to conceal or disguise the illegal origin of the property or assisting any person involved in the commission of the underlying crime to avoid the legal consequences of his actions; - Concealing the true nature, source, location, disposal, movement, rights to or possession of the property, when the relevant person knows that such property is income; - purchase, possession, and use of property, when a person knows at the time of receiving the property that such property represents income; - Participating in the commission of any crime defined following this article, joining a group or conspiring to commit, attempting to commit or assisting in the commission of, inciting, facilitating and giving advice" (Asanidze, 2012). The definition of the legalization of illegal income, which was given in the main international legal acts in the fight against money laundering, was fully reflected in the FATF recommendations. According to these recommendations, money laundering is "the sale or transfer of property, intentionally obtained through criminal means, to cover or hide their illegal origin; For a person who participates in one or more such crimes to evade responsibility for committing the corresponding actions." The analysis of these definitions shows that according to international standards, money laundering is defined as a method of covering an illegal source of income, and the goal is to use this income legally. The views of individual researchers regarding the nature of money laundering are also interesting. A. Kh. Kerner and E. In Dach's research, money laundering means: "all operations carried out to disguise or conceal the receipt of regular income from criminal assets." German author Klaus Kottke refers to money laundering as the process of using the proceeds of general criminal and other crimes. D.A. Brandolini and M. According to Beckner, the term "money laundering" encompasses various methods by which criminals disguise the source, origin, and ownership of illegally obtained money by engaging in transactions that make the money appear to have come from legitimate sources. This is where the term "washing" came from, i.e. Making money clean (legal) and so that it is impossible to trace its origin" (Asanidze, 2012). The definitions of money laundering proposed by individual scientists are also interesting. For example, in the formulation of one part of the experts, it is a "process during which the "black" money obtained as a result of a criminal act, usually in the form of cash, flows through the banking system in such a way that it becomes "clean", that is, it is given an allegedly legal appearance. And it is impossible to determine the person who is the initiator of the transaction, as well as to determine the illegal origin of these funds." The essence of legalization is indeed outlined by the author, but at the same time, its subject and method are artificially narrowed. A large part of this category of crime, related to corruption, fraud, and the use of information technology, is not committed in the field of cash circulation, and the forms and methods of money laundering used by criminals are not limited to operations carried out in the banking field. The second part of specialists defines the legalization of income as "the inclusion of criminally obtained property values in the normal economic circulation to hide their origin." (Solongo, 2004).

For example, in the Law of Georgia "On Promotion of Prevention of Legalization of Illegal Income" legalization of illegal income is defined as "giving illegal income a legal form (acquisition, use, transfer or other action), as well as its true origin, owner or owner and/or property rights Concealing or disguising or attempting to do such acts." (Parliament of Georgia, 2003). In favor of this definition, it should be said that it mostly reflects the requirements of international legal norms. The subject of legalization does not include only criminal income, according to this formulation, the basic social event for money laundering - the legalization of income from other crimes - is also included in the field of legal regulation. In addition, the definition indicates not only the acquisition, use, transfer, or other action of illegal income, but also emphasizes the concealment or disguise of its true source of origin, which in itself is "the basis of evil." Here we offer the following more complete version of this definition: legalization of illegal income ("money laundering") is the deliberate distortion of information about the origin (true) source of property obtained (obtained/purchased) in an illegal way, which is carried out to include (include) them in the legal economic turnover. way, to cover the fact of their illegal receipt (acquisition/purchase) and to ensure the possibility of free disposal of this property. According to the proposed definition, the legalization of illegal income is an intentional act carried out by a person, the subject of money laundering, its method and purpose is outlined, the illegal act is outlined, and its anti-social direction is emphasized. A distinguishing feature of money laundering is giving the appearance of legal origin to funds obtained illegally. It can be discussed about the legalization of illegal income only when the illegal character (nature) of the receipt (source) is disguised, but the fact of their existence is not hidden. This shows the duality of the goal of legalization – to ensure the free use of illegal income and, at the same time, to hide the fact of their illegal acquisition. This makes money laundering different from other crimes where similar methods are used to commit the crime (for example, where the proceeds of crime go beyond the reach of the law for the sole purpose of covering up the crime). In the process of money laundering, the true source of income is concealed by replacing real transactions with formal ones, e.g. By falsifying verification documents, using documents of third parties, etc. In the conditions of economic globalization, offshore zones are often used for money laundering, these are the so-called countries. With a tax haven, where the confidentiality of the beneficiaries is ensured in the banking systems. This type of crime may take place in the banking system to a large extent, the majority of the population in Georgia is suffering from the problem of over-indebtedness. In many cases, since it is not possible to return the debt on time, the debtor does not fully understand what he may be dealing with, because the bank acts within the framework of the contractual relationship and uses all the ways to return the debt. Here most probably are more demands than what the debtor has because the parties are acting within the framework of contractual freedom and the society may often be dealing with a misinterpretation of this right and illegal unsubstantiated income, which of course puts the contracting parties in an unhealthy and disproportionate position and damages and hurts the country. economic stability and development. Within the framework of contractual freedom, the banking sector uses the debtor's immovable and movable property to secure the demand arising from the loan relationship, therefore, when the obligation cannot be fulfilled, it is withdrawn from the secured property.

J. According to Madinger, the ultimate goal of money launderers is the free disposal of illegally obtained income, which is possible through a combination of different methods (Madinger, 2011). J. Treha noted that black money laundering is an attempt to disguise funds, facilitated by the existence of a shadow economy and the influx of investments from other countries with difficult-to-identify sources. He also notes that countries with transit economies are characterized by high levels of money laundering (Theran, 2004). M. According to Milanovic, money laundering is a form of organized crime that cannot be considered a problem in a single country. Adoption of various methods against money laundering for the country, such as blacklisting of money launderers, criminals, organized criminal or terrorist groups and their members, as well as the existence of information by various governmental or international organizations, will help to prevent the mentioned problem (Milanovic, 2015). N. According to Cheng, money laundering is a process in which a joint group tries to hide the real source of income using various methods, although this can be done not only by using individuals but also by using modern technologies. J. Robinson highlighted the essence of black money laundering and highlighted its international importance. According to him, money laundering is a complex of activities that transcend local boundaries (Robinson, 1998). c. Smith and H. According to Volcker, the main essence of black money laundering is obtaining the legal right to use it, which is possible using various methods. In addition, launderers use both bank transactions and cash (Russell, 2010). c. According to Pemberton, there is a problem of money laundering and it is a global problem. Criminals are well aware of money laundering and will use various methods to minimize it (Pemberton, 2000). M. Silkman and V. According to Jovanovic, money laundering is a set of activities aimed at disguising the true nature of the source. In addition, not only criminals are involved in the processes, but also state representatives. Based on the above, it is necessary to study the problem in a complex way and raise the knowledge and qualifications to fight against it. Smith and D. According to Erickson, criminalists will use various methods to disguise real information about an illegal source. For this, both personnel and offshore areas and individuals with different qualifications are used (Smith, 2008). d. According to Jellico's research, black money laundering activities are a group crime, against which it is necessary to strengthen the control bodies, implement, and update financial and other systems and train the internal control bodies to fight the mentioned problem (Zeljkodj, 2011). German author K. Kottke in money laundering refers to the process of using the proceeds of various crimes (Kottke, 1999). A.V. According to Korotkov's definition, legalization of illegal income is "the process of concealing the origin of funds to legally incorporate illegal income into the economic circulation by purchasing movable or immovable property, investing in legal economic activities, and using other methods (Korotkov, 2004) K. According to Hinterseer, the term "money laundering" refers to the various methods by which criminals disguise the source and ownership of illegally obtained black money by engaging in transactions that make the money appear to have come from legitimate sources (Hinterseer, 2001).

Some specific signs of the legalization of criminal income are cited by N. A. According to Lopashenko, "Black money laundering is a process consisting of several stages: sequential actions expressed in the form of financial operations and transactions, the purpose of which is to include criminal funds in non-shadow economic circulation and to give a legal face to the origin of these funds (Lopashenko, 1997). Definitions mostly reflect the main content of the problem. However, less attention is paid to the bleaching process. MN. Zacepin defines the legalization of proceeds as "the inclusion of criminally obtained property values in the legal economic circulation to conceal their origin (Zacepin, 1995). Interestingly, also N. Kepuladze and R. Sulamanidze's paper on "Legalization of Illegal Incomes - Laundering of Black Money". This work emphasizes the role of the state to fight the problem and the need to clarify the term" (Kepuladze, Sulamanidze, 2015). According to E. Asanidze, "legalization of illegally obtained income is a deliberate distortion of information about the source of the property obtained illegally, which is carried out by including it in the legal economic turnover, to cover the fact of their illegal receipt and to ensure the possibility of free disposal of this property" (Asanidze, 2012). Laundered black money is disguised, lost-of-origin funds derived from illegal activities and distributed to multiple accounts using the banking system. In addition, in connection with the mentioned amount, several operations, and transactions were carried out to confuse illegally obtained funds with legal funds (U.S. Congress Office of Technology Assessment, 1995). This definition accurately presents money laundering as a process, however, the focus is only on money laundering and it does not mention that non-money laundering is also possible. V.A. Taran considers the laundering of black money as the procedure, as a result of which black money will pass through banking institutions or other credit-financial areas to give them the appearance of legal income at the final stage (Taran, 2005). The authors do not specify the sectors of economic activity that are used for the legalization of illegally obtained income. M. Levy notes that money laundering is a criminal activity that is carried out using international financial transactions, including currency exchange. Funds are obtained through robbery, corruption, buying and selling drugs, etc. The ultimate goal of money laundering is to transform existing funds into pure money. M. Levy considers only financial operations for the processes of black money laundering, and this is where the deficiency of the mentioned definition is revealed. The group of criminals will use the non-financial sectors as their tools for legalization. S. c. According to Loki, "the process of laundering illegally obtained income involves giving legitimate status to illegal funds using various fields." The author rightly points out that legalization includes the introduction of illegal income into legal economic activities, however, there are no given methods, with the help of which these incomes are included in economic activities and given a legitimate status. V. A. According to Nikulina, the legalization of cash obtained through illegal activities "represents the final stage of obtaining a legal form for assets with material value" (Nikulina, 2000).

Based on the mentioned definition, V. A. Nikulin considers only the last stage of legalization of illegally obtained income, at a time when the process itself is a multi-stage procedure. V. U. Emme believes that "the process of laundering is completed by giving a legal face to the illegally obtained income when it becomes possible to use the obtained illegal income legally" (Emme, 2004). A similar position is based on K. V. Tetiukov also stated that these definitions do not include all stages of giving legal form to illegally obtained income (Tetiukov, 2003). If society is guided by the mentioned definition and does not review the stages of black money laundering, it will be difficult to bring responsibility to the offender during the investigation of the mentioned process. In 1984, the Presidential Commission on Organized Crime in the USA used the following wording: "Money laundering is the process of concealing its nature, illegal origin, or using illegal proceeds to disguise illegally obtained proceeds so that they are finally given a legal origin." (Schroeder, 2001).

Purposes of Using the Proceeds of Crime

Proceeds obtained through crime can be used for the following purposes: 1) covering the current costs of criminals and their entourage (expenses incurred on the organization and consumption of crimes); 2) accumulation (of cash, jewelry, other luxury items, etc.); 3) development of criminal activity (expansion of the main type of activity and its diversification); 4) Investments in the legal economy (placement on the financial market, purchase of the real estate, etc.) (Chain analysis, 2022). It is clear that in the process of realization of the specified goals, the criminal income undergoes certain changes - it becomes the object of the operations during which these incomes more or less fall into the sphere of activity of the legal financial system. If such proceeds are received in the form of cash (for example, through the street sale of drugs) and are planned to be used to finance further criminal activities (purchase of a new batch of drugs), to facilitate further financial operations, it is usually necessary to exchange banknotes (exchange of a small denomination for a larger one). or placing them in a banking institution. Illegally obtained property may be used to seize power. Such events are typical for countries where there is no legal framework, strategy, or desire to fight such crime.

The issue of criminal responsibility for the legalization of illegal income on an international scale.

International policy against the legalization of illegal income, international standards for combating crime.

Such authoritative international organizations such as the United Nations, the Organization for Economic Cooperation and Development, the European Union, and the Organization of American States actively fight against money laundering. A powerful and strict instrument of international cooperation in the fight against money laundering is the Financial Action Task Force (FATF) established by the G7 in 1989. It not only actively gives recommendations on issues of combating money laundering and regularly checks the extent to which the laws and policies of the participating countries comply with these recommendations (on the results of which it regularly prepares reports) but also actively encourages cooperation with those states that do not participate in its work. A powerful tool in such activities of the FATF is the production of a "black list" of countries that do not cooperate with it in the fight against "money laundering". In Europe, the criminalization of money laundering started in the second half of the 80s of the 20th century, when relevant laws were adopted in Denmark, Great Britain, France, and Norway. European norms on money laundering are distinguished by a significantly higher degree of generalization than American ones. The term (or size) of punishment for the said crime is reduced to a reasonable maximum under US law and does not exceed 10 years of imprisonment; Fines are also widely used. An exception is Article 162 of the Norwegian Criminal Code, which, like the US federal law, provides for up to 20 years in prison, and in Great Britain in 1986, money laundering was punishable by up to 14 years in prison (Asanidze, 2012). The development of norms on money laundering in Europe was greatly influenced by the Strasbourg Convention of November 8, 1990, on the "Tracing, Seizure and Confiscation of Money Laundering, Proceeds of Crime" (Strasbourg Convention). Many European states have criminalized money laundering, although not following the natural development of national legal consciousness (Mitsilegas, 1971). One clear example of a norm on money laundering ("lavado de dinero") that is less compatible with the concept of national legislation is Article 301 of the Spanish Penal Code (comp. 301 and Articles 298, 240 of the same Code) Articles 242) (Shashiashvili, 2015). Paragraph 261 of the Criminal Code of the Federal Republic of Germany provides for liability for "money laundering; This illegally obtained article was included in the Criminal Code by the Law of July 15, 1993, on the fight against the illegal drug trade and other forms of manifestation of organized crime. The administrative mechanism for combating money laundering in the Federal Republic of Germany is based on the law of 25 October 1993 on the disclosure of the proceeds of serious crimes. Paragraph 1 of paragraph 261 prescribes a sentence of 3 months to 5 years of imprisonment for 1) concealing objects, 2) disguising the origin of objects ("verschleiern"), 3) creating obstacles to establishing the origin of objects, their discovery, detection, confiscation or confiscation. According to paragraph 2 of paragraph 261, the person who acquires, keeps, or uses the specified objects for himself or a third person, if he knew about its origin at the time of acquisition of the property, is also punished. In the presence of aggravating circumstances (committing a crime in the form of activity (craft) by a member of a gang created for repeated money laundering, other particularly serious cases), the commission of actions provided for in paragraphs 1 and 2 of paragraph 261 is punishable by imprisonment from 6 months to 10 years (Asanidze, 2012). One of the most recent norms on money laundering in Europe was introduced in France by Law No. 96-392 of May 13, 1996, after the implementation of the Criminal Code. In France, the criminal responsibility for laundering the proceeds from the drug business was established for the first time by the law of December

31, 1987. This norm (with subsequent amendments) is given in Article 222.38 of the Criminal Code. The law of May 13, 1996, did not cancel this norm - it retains its independent meaning (in connection with the fact that more stringent procedural rules are used in the laundering of proceeds from the drug business). A special norm on the laundering of income obtained from the exploitation of prostitutes is provided by Article 225.6 of the Criminal Code (Asanidze, 2012). Article 324.1 of the French Penal Code defines "laundering" (le blanchiment) as "facilitating, by any means, the false justification (justification) of the origin of property or income for a participant in a crime or misdemeanor who directly or indirectly benefits from it ". "Laundering" is also considered to be the facilitation of an operation to place, conceal or disguise, directly or indirectly, the proceeds of crime or misconduct. Thus, in the first case, the prosecution must prove that the criminal was aware that he was helping the perpetrator of the illegal act to launder the proceeds of the crime (Asanidze, 2012). In the second case, it is not necessary, but it is necessary to prove the fact that the person was aware that this or that valuable was the proceeds of a crime, and, at the same time, facilitated the operation of placing, hiding, or disguising such proceeds. "Laundering" is punishable by imprisonment for up to 5 years and a fine of up to 2.5 million francs, and in the presence of aggravating circumstances (Article 324.2 - when it is committed systematically or by using the opportunities that a person has in connection with the exercise of professional activity, or it is committed by an organized gang) - 10 Up to a year in prison and a fine of up to 5 million francs. The amount of the fine can be increased by the court to half of the value of the laundered assets (Asanidze, 2012). Article 299 of the Polish Criminal Code can be cited as an example of a typical European norm on money laundering. The subject of the crime is cash, securities, and other property, in the broadest sense of the word (including property rights), received by another person as a result of the commission of a bribery crime, in particular, as a result of the commission of crimes related to the illegal circulation of drugs and psychotropic substances, smuggling, counterfeiting Money laundering, robbery, or large amounts of cash and other property obtained from the illegal circulation of weapons, ammunition, explosives, or explosives (Asanidze, 2012).

Among the documents created regarding actions against money laundering, the 1988 UN Convention on Combating Illicit Traffic in Narcotic Drugs and Psychotropic Substances (Vienna Convention) is fundamental. The Vienna Convention established the principles of the UN's global approach to the organization of actions against money laundering, defining the concept of "money laundering" (Shashiashvili, 2015). According to the Vienna Convention, "laundering of illegal proceeds" means the conversion or transfer of property and proceeds, concealing the true nature, sources of origin, methods of disposal of property, and proceeds obtained as a result of crimes related to drug trafficking. Here, the definition of what should be considered illegal income is of particular importance. According to the first article of the Vienna Convention, illegal proceeds are any property received or acquired directly or indirectly as a result of the commission of a crime, i.e.Any asset, tangible or intangible, immovable or movable, as well as legal documents or deeds evidencing the right to or interest in such assets (UN, 2004).

"Freeze" or "seizure" means the temporary prohibition of the transfer, conversion, placement, or movement of property or the temporary seizure or control of property under an order issued by a court or other competent authority. "Confiscation" means removal, e. i. Seizure of property by a court or other competent authority. Following Article 5 of the Vienna Convention, appropriate measures must be taken to identify and "freeze" or confiscate income, property, funds, or any other thing related to the commission of crimes within the scope of the Convention. In case the proceeds are converted or converted into other property, the specified measures shall be taken in respect of such property and not the proceeds. If the proceeds are attached to property obtained from lawful sources, such property shall, without prejudice to any powers relating to seizure or "freezing", be subject to confiscation to the extent corresponding to the value of such attached proceeds. It is clear from the cited provisions that the Vienna Convention defined the basic concepts for the organization of the system of actions against money laundering, as well as the actions that are the basis of the fight against money laundering (seizure, confiscation). It should be noted that the convention refers to the laundering of the proceeds of crimes related to illegal drug trafficking, but the standards for combating the legalization of "dirty" money established in it can also be used to combat the legalization of proceeds from other criminal activities (UNOC, 2023). The Vienna Convention established various norms, which can be called norms-principles for organizing the international fight against money laundering. For the first time in international law, concepts such as "criminal proceeds", their "freezing" and "removal", as well as the principle that the removal of such proceeds is necessary, even if they have been converted into other property or mixed with legal assets, have been defined as mandatory provisions for all countries participating in the Convention. In the theory of international public law, actions directed against the laundering of criminal proceeds are one of the forms of combating international crime and at the same time are considered as a method through which the funds obtained through criminal means can be seized and withdrawn. Not only laundered funds but also any other valuables whose criminal origin is proven are subject to confiscation. The specificity of the composition of the laundering of criminal proceeds is such that any financial operation related to them will be their laundering (provided that the amount of the laundered property is sufficient from the point of view of the objective side of the composition of the crime). Since it is possible to take the proceeds of crime abroad, including in cashless form, only by carrying out one or another financial operation related to them, any asset subject to confiscation following the international rules in question becomes a subject of money laundering. A new step in the development of a system of actions against money laundering was the Model Law on Drug Money Laundering adopted by the United Nations in November 1993, which is based on the laws of different countries and contains recommendations for the prevention of money laundering, the detection of similar activities and the corresponding actions (Hart, 2010).

On establishing sanctions. It provides that the following are liable for the crimes related to money laundering derived from illegal drug trafficking: 1) persons who convert or transfer funds or property directly or indirectly obtained from the illegal trafficking of narcotic drugs, psychotropic substances, or precursors, to cover the illegal source of such property or funds or for concealment or to provide assistance to any person participating in the commission of one of the crimes, so that he can avoid responsibility for his actions; 2) Persons who contribute to concealment or concealment of the nature, source, location, disposal, mode of movement or real rights of funds, property or rights related to them, which are obtained directly or indirectly from the illegal circulation of narcotic drugs, psychotropic substances or precursors, most often in a criminal way The proceeds are used by organized crime groups. At the same time, criminal groups need to obtain a solid income that will justify the risks associated with criminal activities. In practice, the incomes of organized criminal groups, which, for example, carry out activities in the field of illegal drug and arms trafficking, human trafficking, and exploitation of prostitutes, are significantly higher than the average rate of profit in the legal business. Such revenues not only cover the running costs of criminal groups but also allow them to expand their criminal activities and establish control over the legal sector of the economy (UNOC, 2023).

CONCLUSION

Money laundering is the legalization of illegal income so that the owner can use it openly and openly. This type of money laundering happens all over the world every day. Billions of dollars are laundered every year through various financial institutions. A continuous flow of cash flows across the world every moment in both real and virtual space. Where and when did the term "money laundering" appear? How does the mechanism of this financial machination work? What are the methods of money laundering and who launders money?

When and Why Did the Term "Money Laundering" Appear?

There is a legend according to which the term "money laundering" appeared in the USA during Prohibition. At that time, the Chicago mafia made very high profits from the illegal trade in spirits and other sources. According to the report, it was then that a scheme was developed, according to which this amount was officially recorded as the income of the laundry chain. Back then, laundry services were paid in cash, so it was impossible to know how many people used this service. This allowed the gangsters to turn criminal money into legal profits from the laundries. Thanks to this association, illegal money was called "washed", or "laundered" (money laundering). However, this is more of a myth than a fact.

The Mafia's interest in money laundering arose after Al Capone was caught for income tax evasion in 1931.

Law enforcement authorities were able to prove that his real and official income did not match. Thinking about this, the second big mafioso, Meyer Lensky, came up with a scheme to launder the illegally obtained money.

Initially, money was laundered through casinos. Later, the same Lensky came up with a scheme that would work through the banking system. He opened anonymous accounts in Swiss banks where he deposited large sums of money. Then he received loans from the same banks and named them as the source of his money. It was in this way that dirty money became clean and legal through the bank.

Anyway, for the first time the term "money laundering" was recorded in the press in 1973 in the British publication The Guardian in an article about the Watergate scandal. In legal practice, this term was used for the first time in 1982. As part of this case, it was established that Sonal, an American company owned by several Colombians, was transferring the proceeds from the sale of drugs to its account at Capital Bank (Miami, USA) and was laundering money in this way.

After September 11, 2001, US law enforcement agencies pay particular attention to the money with which charitable, religious, and non-governmental organizations manage to finance terrorism through an underground quasi-banking system (for example, Hawala) (UNOC, 2023).

What Are the Methods of Money Laundering?

One method of money laundering is the Colombian black market, where money from the drug trade is exchanged for Colombian pesos. With this state currency, they then buy various expensive goods, which are finally sold in dollars. This is one of the most popular methods of money laundering in the Western Hemisphere.

Another way to launder money is to divide a large amount of money into smaller parts and deposit it in different banks at different intervals. For example, in the case of a one-time deposit of more than 10,000 dollars into an account in the USA, the bank is obliged to notify the federal government about this operation.

The third method of money laundering is the shadow (underground) banking system. At this time, the illegal income is transferred to an offshore account in a country where the bank secrecy law applies. In other words, in such states, it is allowed to open a bank account anonymously. Banks of Cayman and Bahamas, Panama, Bahrain, Singapore, and Hong Kong are mainly used for this purpose. In Asia, some banks have a legal alternative system that allows the client to carry out any transaction without any documentation, leaving no chance for investigation.

Another way of money laundering is when a deposit is opened in the name of a fake company, then this money is invested in a legitimate business with fake invoices and accounting balances. Such companies are created by criminals to launder money. However, it may also be a legitimate business in which "investments" are made. For example, a brokerage firm, a casino, a bar, or a strip club. Such institutions are usually associated with a large flow of money, which is a good means of laundering illegal money (UNOC, 2023).

What is the Process of Money Laundering?

The first step is to place the dirty money as a bank deposit in a legitimate financial institution. After that, through electronic transactions, money is transferred to different accounts or transferred to another currency, with which they then buy expensive things to change the monetary form. In the final stage, the laundered money begins to circulate through a legitimate bank transfer to the account of the company used to launder the money or with the expensive items purchased in the second stage.

Who Launders Money?

Money is laundered by drug dealers, fraudsters, corrupt politicians, officials, bandits, terrorists, etc.

Why do They Launder Money?

The money has to be "clean" because criminals don't want to leave a trace. Members of the mafia and terrorist groups do not spare money for this financial machination. They know very well that if the criminal activity is fully exposed, the punishment will be much harsher than it would be for money laundering alone.

What Are Examples of Money Laundering?

In the late 1980s, the famous economist Franklin Jurado laundered money for the Colombian drug lord Jose-Santa Cruz London. He deposited the money he received from the sale of drugs in the USA into a bank account in Panama. After that, the money was deposited in more than 100 European banks. The amount of each financial operation did not exceed 10,000 dollars. Already from here, money was transferred to Colombia, where Jose-Santacruz Londono could finance his drug business with this money. Before he was caught and sentenced to seven and a half years, Jurado managed to launder more than $36,000,000 (England, 2022).

Money laundering is often masked by the love of art because the buyer of this or that expensive painting has the right to remain anonymous. In 1982, Brazilian banker Edemar Cid Ferreira showed up at John F. Kennedy Airport in New York with a painting worth $100. Law enforcement authorities soon found out that it was a masterpiece worth 8 million dollars, which belonged to an American artist. Thanks to a criminal scheme disguised as an interest in art, Edemar laundered more than 50 million dollars and created a collection of 12 thousand paintings. In 2006, Ferreira was sentenced to 21 years for fraud, tax evasion, and money laundering.

The New York Times conducted a journalistic investigation in 2015, which revealed that the majority of elite real estate in the US is owned by name-based companies that do not disclose the identity of the buyer. The seller is not interested in the origin of the money, because the law does not require it. As a result of a journalistic investigation, 37% of the elite apartments in the multifunctional complex Time Warner Center (New York) belong to foreigners. Among them are citizens of Russia, China, Colombia, and Mexico (England, 2022).

Can Money Laundering be Controlled?

Controlling money laundering is very difficult, as any country's financial institutions are used for this purpose. Experts consider this a serious problem and believe that to overcome it, the efforts of the whole world are necessary. However, the fight against money laundering has a serious barrier, which is created by the bank secrecy rules in some countries. That is why it becomes almost impossible to control money taken abroad.

REFERENCES

Ackermann, J. B. (2003). *Money laundering*. Open Science. https://openscience.ge/bitstream/1/497/1/samagistro%20gurguchiani.pdf

Alexander, K. (2000). The Legalization of the International Anti-money Laundering Regime: The Role of the Financial Action Task Force. *Centre for Business Research. C- 8.*

Anti-money laundering unit. (2004). *An overview of the UN conventions and the international standards concerning anti-money laundering legislation.* NGLP. http://www.nplg.gov.ge/dlibrary/collect/0002/000828/Dis.Shashiashvili%20G.pdf

Asanidze, S. (2012). *Criminological characterization of legalization of illegal income (money laundering).* Grigol Robakidze University. http://www.nplg.gov.ge/dlibrary/collect/0002/000576/Asanidze%20S%2B.pdf

Chernikova, L. (2012). *The role of the banking sector in the fight against money laundering: domestic and foreign experience - National interests: priorities and security.* Aspect Press.

England, A. (2022). Financial crimes watchdog puts UAE on 'grey list. *The Financial Times.*

FATF. (1996). *VII Annual Report (1995-1996).* NPLG. http://www.nplg.gov.ge/dlibrary/collect/0002/000828/Dis.Shashiashvili%20G.pdf

Hart. (2010). Criminal infiltration of financial institutions: a penetration test case study – *Journal of Money Laundering Control, 13*(1).

Kepuladze, N., & Sulamanidze, R. (2015). *Legalization of illegal income – money laundering.* NPLG. http://www.nplg.gov.ge/dlibrary/collect/0002/000828/Dis.Shashiashvili%20G.pdf

Kerner, X., & Dax, E. (1996). Money laundering. Guide to Current Legislation and Legal Practice. *International Relations.*

Kiselev, I. (2009). *Dirty Money.* Jurisprudence.

Larkin, C., Pearce, N., & Shannon, N. (2022). Criminality and cryptocurrencies: Enforcement and policy responses – Part II. In S. Corbet (Ed.), *Understanding Cryptocurrency Fraud. The challenges and headwinds to regulate digital currencies.* De Gruyter. https://www.degruyter.com/document/doi/10.1515/9783110718485-010/html?lang=

Larry,, B. (1996). Underground Banking and National Security. *Journal of Contemporary Criminal Justice.*

Lopashenko, A. (1997). *Crimes in the Sphere of Economic Activity.* Aspect Press.

Madinger, J. (2011). *Money Laundering: A Guide for Criminal Investigators* (3rd ed.). Shodh. http://shodh.inflibnet.ac.in/bitstream/123456789/3140/3/03_literature%20 review.pdf doi:10.1201/b11845

Matsne. (2021). *Law of Georgia - Regarding making changes to the Law of Georgia On Facilitating Prevention of Money Laundering and Financing of Terrorism.* MATSNE. https://matsne.gov.ge/ka/document/view/5137611?publication=0

Mitsilegas, V. (1971). *Money laundering counter-measures in the European Union: a new paradigm of security governance versus fundamental legal principle*. Kluwer Law International. p.

Norwegian Ministry of Justice Legislation Department. (2006). *The General Civil Penal Code.* Wipolex. https://wipolex-res.wipo.int/edocs/lexdocs/laws/en/no/no122en.html

Quiroz-Gutierrez, M. (2022). *A handful of NFT users are making big money off of a stealth scam. Here's how 'wash trading' works*. Fortune.

Ryder, N. (2012). *Title Money laundering – an endless cycle: a comparative analysis of the anti-money laundering policies in the United States of America, the United Kingdom, Australia, and Canada. London*. Routledge. doi:10.4324/9780203126783

Scott, D. (1995). *Money Laundering and International Efforts to Fight It –The World Bank*. Public Policy for the Private Sector.

Shashiashvili, B., & Taran, B. (2005). *World Economy and World Finance System*. International Finance Control.

Shashiashvili, T. (2015). *Legalization of illegal income as a criminal justice problem*. Grigol Robakidze University. http://www.nplg.gov.ge/dlibrary/collect/0002/000828/Dis.Shashiashvili%20G.pdf

Smith, S. L. & And Ericson D. (2008). *Money Laundering Monitor*. U.S. Department Of Justice, Criminal Division, Asset Forfeiture & Money Laundering Section.

Solongo D. (2004). Russian Capitalism and Money-Laundering. *Global Program against Money Laundering*.

Stessens, G. (2000). *Money laundering: a new international law enforcement model*. Cambridge University. doi:10.1017/CBO9780511494567

Trehan, J. (2004). *Crime and Money Laundering: The Indian Perspective*. Shodh. http://shodh.inflibnet.ac.in/bitstream/123456789/3140/3/03_literature%20review.pdf

Tretiakov, V. (2009). *Organized Crime and Legalization of Criminal Incomes*. Nekeri.

UNOC. (2023). *Money Laundering, Proceeds of Crime and the Financing of Terrorism*. UN. https://www.unodc.org/unodc/en/money-laundering/index.html

U.S. Congress Office of Technology Assessment. (1995). Information Technologies for Control of Money Laundering. Washington, Dc: U.S. Government Printing Office.

U.S. Department of State. (2021). 2021 International Narcotics Control Strategy Report (INCSR). USDoS. https://www.state.gov/2021-international-narcotics-control-strategy-report/

Zatsepin, M. (1995). *Security of Entrepreneurship: Criminological and Criminal Law Issues*. Aspect Press.

KEY TERMS AND DEFINITIONS

Anti-Money Laundering Laws: The web of laws, regulations, and procedures aimed at uncovering efforts to disguise illicit funds as legitimate income. Money laundering seeks to conceal crimes ranging from small-time tax evasion and drug trafficking to public corruption and the financing of groups designated as terrorist organizations.

Dirty Money: Money earned in an illegal activity.

Extortion: The practice of obtaining benefit through coercion. In most jurisdictions it is likely to constitute a criminal offense; the bulk of this article deals with such cases. Robbery is the simplest and most common form of extortion, although making unfounded threats to obtain an unfair business advantage is also a form of extortion.

Financial Action Task Force on Money Laundering: Also known by its French name, ***Groupe d'action financière*** (**GAFI**), is an intergovernmental organization founded in 1989 on the initiative of the G7 to develop policies to combat money laundering. In 2001, its mandate was expanded to include terrorism financing.

Illegal Gambling: The making, placing, or receipt of any bet or wager in the Commonwealth of money or another thing of value, made in exchange for a chance to win a prize, stake, or other consideration or thing of value, dependent upon the result of any game, contest or any other event the outcome of which is uncertain or a matter of chance, whether such game, contest or event occurs or is to occur inside or outside the limits of the Commonwealth.

Insider Trading: Involves trading in a public company's stock by someone who has non-public, material information about that stock for any reason. Insider trading can be either illegal or legal depending on when the insider makes the trade.

Law Enforcement Agencies: Any government agency responsible for the enforcement of the laws.

Money Laundering: The process of concealing the origin of money, obtained from illicit activities such as drug trafficking, corruption, embezzlement, or gambling, by converting it into a legitimate source. It is a crime in many jurisdictions with varying definitions. It is usually a key operation of organized crime.

Trade-Based Laundering: The process of disguising the proceeds of crime and moving value through the use of trade transactions in an attempt to legitimize their illicit origins.

Chapter 4
Temple Prostitution in India:
An Exploitative Practice in the Name of Religion

Amit Anand
https://orcid.org/0000-0002-9219-5858
REVA University, India

ABSTRACT

The practice of 'marrying' young girls of lower castes to gods and goddesses is one of the oldest cultural practices in India. This practice is called the devadasi system in which minor girls belonging to the Scheduled Castes are sexually exploited by temple priests and other high caste men in the name of religion. The term 'devadasi' is a Sanskrit word which means 'female slave of God.' The devadasi system is also seen as religious sanctioned prostitution in India. Note that, despite the practice being abolished by various state legislations in India, there are approximately more than 48,000 devadasis in the country according to the data by the National Commission for Women, New Delhi. Further, as per the National Human Rights Commission, the state of Andhra Pradesh, India alone had over 25,000 devadasis in 2015 with girls as young as 12 years old who were being pushed into prostitution in the nearby states of Karnataka and Maharashtra. This chapter therefore aims to highlight the reasons behind this social evil considering the broader interconnections between law and religion.

DOI: 10.4018/979-8-3693-0327-6.ch004

INTRODUCTION

Indian society, similar to other patriarchal societies in the world, is governed by a system where men control and dominate women socially, politically and economically (Behl, 2019). Patriarchal values and beliefs subjugate women at every stage of their lives. For instance, young girls are constantly pressured to remain within the confines of their homes and are taught to behave in an 'appropriate' manner, they are often not allowed to pursue education after a particular age, they are also discouraged from taking up high paying jobs or continue to work post marriage (Jacobsen, 2015). It is even possible to argue that societies which believe in male superiority and favour practices that place male authority at the centre of the family structure are the ones more prone to violence against women (Kalra and Bhugra, 2013). This particular line of argument is supported by the constant control and restrain over women's thoughts and movements in male-centred societies that do not leave any scope for dissent and punishes those women who either question the 'status quo' or try to break free from their stereotyped roles (Gangoli, 2007). As noted by Dagar (2014),

'Violence against women and girls was not the pathological behavior of a few 'sick' men; rather it was an extension of a system of practices and laws which sanctioned men's rights to regard women as their property and therefore keep them under their control.'

Violence against women is not new to India, one example is the disproportionate gender ratio resulting from female infanticide. As per the 2011 Census of India, the sex ratio stands at 940 females per 1000 males (Chandramouli, 2011). The recent National Family Health Survey (NFHS), 2020 also revealed a decline in the sex ratio. This decline was recorded in states which had shown gains in previous years (Tandon, 2020). In India, violence against women appears to have been largely accepted as normal and is often justified. This is mainly because of society's own understanding of violence against young girls and women and how it chooses to respond to it (Johnson and Johnson, 2001). One example is the Delhi gang rape case of 2012, wherein a 23 year old woman was raped by six men and brutally assaulted when she was returning home after watching a movie with a male friend. When the incident came to light, people in the national capital came out on the streets demanding stringent laws to protect women in the country. As a result, amendments were brought especially to the offence of rape under the Indian Penal Code (IPC), 1860 with new crimes also being added to the list such as stalking and acid attack.

Despite the amendments to the IPC in the aftermath of the Delhi gang rape, violent crimes against young girls and women have not stopped in India. As per the data released by the National Crime Records Bureau (NCRB), the Indian agency responsible for collecting data on crime, a rape was reported every 16 minutes on an average in 2019 in the country (*One Rape Every 16 Minutes in India, NCRB Data Highlights Country's Deteriorated Law & Order*, 2020). Another important observation that can be drawn from the Delhi gang rape in relation to violence against women is with respect to the selective outrage of the general public to such crimes. Note that, there are no nation-wide protests for every rape victim or for every form of violence against women in India. As noted (*December 16th 2012: A Rape, a Murder and a Movement | Gunda-Werner-Institut | Heinrich-Böll-Stiftung*, 2014),

'In most societies, women who have had to face rape, are often stigmatized, as if they are the guilty ones. While this cuts across the board, it is true that certain kinds of rape, or the rape of certain women evokes more outrage than that of others. Caste rape, for example, where Dalit women are particularly targeted by upper caste men, is so naturalized in Indian culture, that it evokes very little outrage, and even the legal machinery sees it as something that is a part of our society.'

This is the case because, there are a host of factors such as family, community, social norms, religion that directly or indirectly are responsible for violence against women and these factors also play an important role in society's understanding of what acts constitute as violence against women and what should be society's reaction to such acts (Ministry of Women and Child Development New Delhi Vol 1, 2015).

In light of the above, this paper brings to attention the wider lack of focus on violence against women in India through the study of the devadasis system (or temple prostitution), considering how gender based violent practices often go unnoticed and unpunished because they seem to be justified in the name of custom, culture, religion etc. This paper is important in the sense that it addresses the lack of focus to violence against women in India by highlighting the neglected violent practice of the devadasi system in the backdrop of social-cultural norms. Furthermore, as shown in the discussion below, the existing research on the devadasi system neither completely acknowledges the social-cultural reality of India nor examines this practice within the framework of violence against women.

The devadasi system is a social and religious practice of dedicating young girls to Hindu temples in India (Shingal, 2015). Girls belonging to the dalit community are married to a Hindu deity and are asked to serve a temple. Once a girl becomes a devadasi she cannot remarry because of being married to a deity but anyone in the community is allowed to have sexual relations with her. As a result, these girls are sexually exploited by temple priests and people belonging to dominant castes (Shingal, 2015). After a certain age when these girls are not considered 'ideal' for temple service they are abandoned to lead a life of humiliation. These former devadasis are left with no other choice but to turn to prostitution to earn their living as no one else either marries or economically supports them (Orchard, 2007). The devadasi practice, unfortunately, has also become a means for poor dalit families to unburden themselves of their daughters. Due to social-economic pressures, families dedicate young girls as devadasis and after a certain period those devadasis dedicate their own daughters thereby making the entire practice an inter-generational cycle (Harishankar and Priyamvadha, 2016).

Most of the available literature on devadasis focuses mainly on providing information about the origin of this social practice and giving a detailed account of the customs and rituals surrounding the dedication of young girls to local deities (Tarachand, 1992). Further, in most such writings, authors have often blamed the loss of religious sanctity of the customs and rituals surrounding the dedication process for the present-day downfall of the devadasis (Panjrath and Ralhan, 2000). Several writings also tend to over emphasize the 'glorious past' of the devadasi system by highlighting the so-called high social and economic status of devadasis (it is said that devadasis used to receive gifts such as land by kings and other prominent persons in the society for their services and were more respected than 'normal' women because of their 'marital' status) during the Medieval period (500CE - 1500CE) in India (Jordan, 2003). But, the literature is not clear whether every devadasi was treated similarly during this period. Further, regardless of the 'glorious past' of devadasis, this was and still remains a practice which pushes young dalit girls into sexual slavery which the existing literature fails to properly acknowledge. The devadasi system is an exploitative social practice that targets the most vulnerable section of women in the Indian society, i.e., dalit women. Because of this practice, young dalit girls are sexually abused, exploited, and later forced in life to involve themselves in commercial sexual activity. This practice forces them to live a degraded life in the name of tradition and culture. The literature on devadasis does not effectively reflect upon the question of why in the name of tradition and culture dalit women are forced into perennial oppression. Though, the literature mentions factors such as caste, poverty, societal pressure that are responsible for the continuity of the practice despite prohibitory legislation, there is, however, a failure to see the practice entirely as caste-based violence against women. Recognizing the devadasi practice as caste-based abuse is important as it reflects the complexities of the Hindu social order along with the status of women. Further, the literature does not engage either with the effectiveness of the existing legal mechanisms that abolishes the practice or suggest measures to support victims of this practice.

In this backdrop, the following sections will address some of the key aspects (namely the definition of devadasis, origin of the devadasis system, the intersection of caste and gender with the devadasi system, analysis of the legislative framework relating to prevention of dedication of young girls) of the devadasi system in India.

DEFINING THE DEVADASIS

The devadasi system is a social-cultural practice that exists mostly in the southern states of India such as Maharashtra, Karnataka, Andhra Pradesh, Telangana, Tamil Nadu and is believed to have been first reported between 6th and 7th century CE. However, there is no concrete answer available on when the system first originated in India (Orr, 2000). The term 'devadasi' means 'female slave of god' (Tarachand, 1992). It is said that devadasis served gods and later men (kings), as their slaves and considered it an honour (Vishwanathan, 2008).

The practice of dedicating young girls to local deities differs in different regions and therefore, the term 'devadasi' is often used as an umbrella term for a general understanding of this practice. In different regions in India 'devadasis' are known by several names such as *jogini*, *mathammas* (Tarachand, 1992). According to Farquhar (1997),

'Every well-appointed Hindu temple aims at being an earthly reproduction of the paradise of the god in whose honour it was built...The Gandharvas (celestial musicians in Hindu mythology) are represented by the Temple-band, the Apsaras (celestial dancers in Hindu mythology) by the courtesans who sing and dance in the service. These are dedicated to the service of the god; but they give their favours to his worshippers. They are usually called Devadasis, handmaidens of the god...'

Altekar (1959) defines the devadasi system as follows:

'When temples of Hindu gods came to be built and endowed on a magnificent scale, some people began to feel in course of time that there should be singing girls attached to shrines to play music on the occasions of the different services and worships of the day...The introduction of dancing girls in temples tended to lower their moral and spiritual atmosphere. Some people began to visit shrines not so much to pay their respects to deities, as to carry on their love intrigues with the singing girls employed there.'

Despite the devadasi system having a long history in India, the general understanding about devadasis and how the practice came into being is limited in nature mostly due to scarcity of historical accounts. Nonetheless, ethnographic accounts of late nineteenth and early twentieth century along with the social movements in South India and the legislative debates that took place during that period throw sufficient light on the influence of religion, role of women in society and how the devadasi practice came into being.

Another important aspect worth noting is with respect to the exact number of devadasis in the Indian states where the practice still exists. The lack of official data has been identified by many scholars as a major hindrance in understanding and prohibiting the practice in the first place (Parker, 2016). However, in an affidavit before the Supreme Court of India in 2015, the National Commission for Women (NCW) said that there were 250,000 dalit girls dedicated to various temples along the Karnataka-Maharashtra border alone. The NCW affidavit was in response to a public interest litigation filed by an NGO to immediately stop a dedication ceremony in the state of Karnataka (Tripathi, 2015). An officer of the NCW also acknowledged in the same affidavit that despite the state of Karnataka having passed a legislation, The Karnataka Devadasi (Prohibition of Dedication) Act, 1982 to prohibit temple dedication, there had been no study undertaken either on the status of devadasis or on the implementation of the said legislation since its inception (Tripathi, 2015). In addition, in the states of Andhra Pradesh and Telangana, there were about 80,000 devadasis as per a report submitted by former Justice Raghunath Rao in 2015 (Vadlapatla, 2015).

ORIGIN OF THE DEVADASI SYSTEM

The dedication of young girls to Hindu temples varies from region to region in India and is composed of different local traditions, however, all variations generally share certain common features associated with the devadasis (Black, 2007). The common features consists of the following: dedication of a young dalit girl by 'marrying' her to the deity; her deflowering immediately after the dedication ceremony or at puberty either by the temple priest or a high caste person and her subsequent availability to all for sexual use (Black, 2007).

With respect to the question on the origin of the devadasi system, though, several scholars have referred to this issue either through mythology or ancient literature, yet, there is no final answer available regarding the same (Mishra and Rao, 2005). As mentioned earlier, the devadasi practice is believed to have been first reported sometime in the 6th century CE, but, there are some indications that the practice might also have existed in the 2nd century BCE. The famous bronze dancing girl figurine found in the city of Mohenjo-daro (one of the largest cities of the Indus-Valley civilization) is often associated with the devadasis, but there is no evidence to corroborate the same (Mishra and Rao, 2005). The Vedic literature too has references of courtesans who frequented places of gambling and of slave girls who were gifted to kings to serve them (Vishwanathan, 2008). During the Medieval period (500CE - 1500CE), kings kept courtesans to promote dance, music etc. The performer of these arts were mostly young women and sometimes they were used to provide hospitality to other kings who visited the royal court. There are also references to courtesans being subjugated when a kingdom was captured, and it is believed that the subjugation of courtesans later also gave rise to organized prostitution in society (Prasad, 1999). Note that, since, there is no mention of the term 'devadasi' per se prior to 6th and 7th century CE in any literature, most scholars have tried to analyze the devadasi system either by associating it with the keeping of courtesans by kings or by the practice of prostitution prevalent at the time (Panjrath and Ralhan, 2000).

Furthermore, during the early Medieval period, art as a knowledge was under the exclusive domain of the Brahmans who were priests in Hindu temples and controlled all the activities associated with it. It is believed that, the Brahmans would have wanted courtesans who were young and beautiful girls in their temple courts and therefore, they encouraged local families to dedicate their girls to the services of the temple. Later, when temples began to spread, the dedication process also increased and young girls who once were the courtesans of royal courts became devadasis dedicated to the gods (Panjrath and Ralhan, 2000). During the Medieval period, temples began getting huge donations first from kings and later from landlords and as a result, they gradually assumed the status of social-financial institutions (Mishra and Rao, 2005). With increase in economic resources, temples were now in a position to perform more rituals. However, they soon were in need of a lot of servants to manage the vast property. This led to temples recruiting many young girls as servants. Besides working as labourers in temples, girls were also being employed to sing and dance on festivals and other religious occasions.

As noted by, Mishra and Rao (2005), apart from recruiting labour for the maintenance of temples, there was also a religious sentiment attached to dedicating young girls during the Medieval period.

'It was said and believed that the dedication of dance or song by young girls became more meritorious than other offerings like flowers and food; it helped fulfilling all desires and equalled in virtues to the performance of a sacrifice. Since the chastity of a virgin was considered to be of incomparable value, sacrificing one's chastity to the god as a devadasi was also taken as one of the highest virtues. Due to these beliefs, girls were sacrificed to temples; the kings and nobles often appointed or presented well-trained girls to the temples and made rich endowments. The rich class devotees even purchased the girls from the poor class parents and offered them for the service of the gods.'

As far as the ritual of dedication is concerned, several authors highlight that it was necessary that the girl who was to be dedicated belonged to the family of an existing devadasi. The dedication ritual generally took place between the age of six and nine. Usually, a senior devadasi or the mother of the girl recommended the name of the girl to the temple for dedication. But, often young girls were purchased by high caste individuals and dedicated to temples. The dedication ritual was followed by ceremonies that lasted two to three days resembling a Hindu marriage. The expenses for the dedication ritual was usually borne by a rich high caste individual or the head priest who later claimed first rights over the girl.

INTERSECTION OF CASTE AND GENDER WITH THE DEVADASI SYSTEM

As noted previously, most devadasis are dalit women and the caste factor is an essential feature of this practice. Additionally, according to a report by the Ministry of Women and Child Development, New Delhi, the social and religious custom of devadasi victimizes dalit women in India (Ministry of Women and Child Development, 2015).

Gender as a concept has often been used in traditional societies to construct identities, dictate relationships and establish principles to govern various aspects of social life such as sexuality, marriage and property. Most social practices in traditional societies are even tailored around a certain perception of gender (Torri, 2009).

In the Indian context, social practices that are condemned by feminist scholars as oppressive in nature, demonstrate how gender is used to build hierarchies and clearly mark out the difference in power relations between men and women (Torri, 2009). But, this distortion of gender either remains hidden or is ignored despite repeated incidents of violence against women that are carried out in the name of social-cultural norms. Further, neglecting to recognize the intersection of other social markers such as caste, and class with gender has brought the fight against gender inequality in India to almost a standstill. As explained by Torri (2009),

'Feminist scholars have persuasively argued for the analysis of race, class and gender as intersecting and interlocking systems of oppression. Focusing on the mechanisms of intersection across caste and gender allows for exploring how individuals negotiate, resist, and struggle against inequalities. In the Indian context, the caste system is an important aspect of the social sphere. The hierarchy and characteristics that govern the caste system constrain life changes gained through acquiring skills. Intersection of caste and gender lead to women having less prestige and respect compared with the men even within the same caste.'

According to the data released as part of India's annual economic survey 2017-18, 'there are 63 million women "missing" from India's population, with 2 million more from every age group going "missing" every year because the desire for sons has given rise to sex-selective abortions, and girls suffer disproportionately from disease, neglect, or inadequate nutrition (Ministry of Finance Department of Economic Affairs, 2018).' For instance, in the state of Andhra Pradesh, girls are dedicated because they are considered an economic burden in the absence of sons in the family. By dedicating their daughters to temples, families avoid giving dowry and hope that their daughters can support the family like a son through their temple earnings (Harishankar and Priyamvadha, 2016). Though gender is used as a primary tool for organizing social relations in most societies, in India, caste also plays a significant role in 'determining both the social division of labour as well as the sexual division (Torri, 2009).' For instance, under the devadasi system, young girls belonging to the dalit community are 'married' to a Hindu deity and then sexually exploited by temple priests and members of the higher caste. As noted by Torri (2009),

'The dedication usually occurs before the girl reaches puberty and requires the girl to become sexually available for community members. Traditionally, it is believed that these girls are "serving" society as "ordained" by the goddess. In other words, "the devadasis are courtesans in God's court". Due to her sacred condition and her belonging to the divinity, a devadasi cannot be married to one particular man. Instead, she is a property of a divinity that benevolently concedes her to the whole community. This concept is well summarized by a saying that: "a devadasi is servant of God but wife of the whole town."'

Caste in India is a social, political and economic reality and the dalit community are placed at its bottom. As a result, the dalit community has been denied opportunities in every sphere of life such as education, employment, healthcare. Moreover, there are numerous instances of caste based violence against dalits in the form of murder and rape being reported on a daily basis (Thorat, 2002). As rightly mentioned by Ghose (2003), 'the idea of the polluted bonded servant is so ingrained in the subcontinental mind that the dalit remains at the bottom of the intellectual and emotional landscape of contemporary India, however far he may advance in a public career and agitate for change.' Majority of dalits today still live in rural areas and continue to face discrimination. Since, large sections of the dalit population live below the poverty line and have no access to jobs they are forced to either work as bonded labourers or take up caste-designated occupations such as manual scavenging (Shah, 2002).

The discrimination faced by dalit women is closely associated with the Hindu religion which has a significant role in the subjugation of women in India. Controlling female movement and their sexuality is crucial to maintaining the patriarchal ideology and caste hierarchy under the Hindu religion. This control is also exercised rigidly on upper caste women. As far as dalit women are concerned, under the Hindu religion, they have always been portrayed as opposites to the 'virtuous' upper caste women. While upper caste women were shown to be of high moral character, dalit women were depicted as loud, unfaithful and immoral (Gupta 2008). As noted by Gupta (2008),

'Dalit women were said to live in temporary marriages, have questionable sexual morals and experience frequent divorces and desertions. They were seen as sex objects by the high-caste men...the Dalit female body, while represented as 'unfeminine', was also perceived as lustful. She was unattractive but alluring. Her body was both at the same time-repulsive and desirable, untouchable and available, reproductive and productive, ugly and beautiful. Sexual exploitation of Dalit women was an everyday fact, which was often expressed in terms of the alleged 'loose' character of the Dalit women themselves.'

Because of socially created notions of gender, dalit women often find themselves in a hostile environment which normalizes discrimination through force and coercion. According to data collected by an NGO as part of its report to the International Labour Organization (ILO) in 2015, it was found that almost 85 per cent of devadasis belonged to the dalit community within the sample that was taken for study (Harishankar and Priyamvadha, 2016). Further, as part of its report, the NGO also took interviews of devadasis from the states of Karnataka, Maharashtra and Telangana. The following is an excerpt from one of the interviews showing how devadasis often belong to the dalit community:

'Rathnakka, Devadasi from Belagavi, Karnataka stated: I belong to Scheduled Caste. I am the third child for my parents after two elder brothers. I used to fall ill often, and my parents would take me to all the nearby temples but finally my parents felt that offering me to the Goddess was their only option and that is how I am dedicated to the Yellamma (Goddess). I was made devadasi at the age of 8 (Harishankar and Priyamvadha, 2016).'

The devadasi practice can be better understood as an outcome of the use of both caste and gender to bind dalit women and their families in the perpetual cycle of discrimination in the name of social and religious custom (Harishankar and Priyamvadha, 2016). But, the discourse on gender-caste and its implications on the present position of devadasis in India seems to be missing. Devadasis themselves are also unaware of the root cause of the practice and at present there are no other agencies barring a few NGOs which are able to shed light on the genesis and current growth of the devadasi system.

Superstition is also closely associated with dedication of girls in Andhra Pradesh, wherein, lack of knowledge on health issues significantly affects the decision of a family. For example, health issues such as cough, dehydration, malnutrition, mental illness are interpreted as work of 'evil' or are seen as a sign of godly displeasure and as a result, families dedicate their daughters as devadasis to ward off any further danger or harm to the family (Lalou, 1995). Poverty is another key factor responsible for dedication of young girls to temples. Religion too plays a crucial role apart from caste, gender and economic compulsion in explaining the dedication of young girls as devadasis (Ramberg, 2011). Majority of the dalit community in India, strongly believe in the power of gods/goddesses and the possible harm they can cause if displeased. This strong belief usually leads to blind faith and superstition due to lack of education resulting in dedicating young girls for ensuring either well-being of the family or a male heir. As noted by Lalou (1995), dedication is often done to please local gods/goddesses out of fear of any repercussion and also to ask for favours.

Hereditary practice and societal pressure are two other reasons responsible for keeping the devadasi practice alive. The practice is hereditary in nature as most girls become devadasis because either their mother or grandmother had been dedicated. Often the practice of dedication is also carried forward because of pressure from within the family as well as from dominant castes in the village (Harishankar and Priyamvadha, 2016). Upper caste men often force families to dedicate their daughters as devadasis. As noted by Harishankar and Priyamvadha (2016),

'Most often it is the upper class men who have first sexual intercourse with these girls. Likewise, the temple priest who has a hold on the community will give "religious sanction" to families to dedicate their girls. Once a girl is dedicated, she should offer sexual service to the upper class men, priests and other men of power and money. The upper class people encourage the lower class people to practice the system in order to get access to the desirable women to fulfil their extra marital sexual needs.'

Addressing the practice of dedicating young girls to Hindu temples requires an analysis through a combination of concepts of gender, sexuality, caste and religion (Parker, 2016). Though one factor may take precedence over the other for a particular family, it needs to be understood that all the above mentioned factors are interlinked with one another and contribute towards the continuity of the devadasi practice within the dalit community.

DOMESTIC LEGISLATIONS ON PREVENTION OF DEDICATION OF YOUNG GIRLS

States where the devadasi practice is prevalent have brought in legislations to prohibit dedication but, this step has only led to dedications getting hidden from the eyes of the authorities (Harishankar and Priyamvadha, 2016). One of the important reasons behind the prevalence of this practice despite legislations is the lack of accurate data on the number of devadasis. The National Commission for Women (NCW) in its Annual Report (2017-18) also acknowledged that there exists no official statistics on the number of devadasis in India. The lack of official data on devadasis is also a big hindrance in the proper implementation of the various state legislations against this social evil.

The devadasi system exists mainly in the Indian states of Maharashtra, Karnataka, Andhra Pradesh, Telangana and Tamil Nadu. The state of Karnataka passed The Karnataka Devadasis (Prohibition of Dedication) Act in 1982. Under section 3, of the Act, the dedication of young girls as devadasis is unlawful.

'Notwithstanding any custom or law to the contrary, the dedication of a woman as a devadasi, whether before or after the commencement of this Act and whether she has consented to such dedication or not, is hereby declared unlawful, void and to be of no effect and any woman so dedicated shall not thereby be deemed to have become incapable of entering into a valid marriage.'

Under section 5 of the Act, the penalty prescribed for a person who 'performs, permits, takes part or abets the performance of any ceremony or act of dedication' is imprisonment of up to three years and a fine of two thousand rupees. The proviso to section 5 states that, if the person mentioned under this section happens to be the parent or guardian or any relative of the woman so dedicated then such person will be liable to be punished with imprisonment of five years and a fine of five thousand rupees. Further, section 7 of the Act gives power to the state of Karnataka to make rules for carrying out the purpose of the Act. The rules under this section may provide a) for the manner of investigation of offences under this Act and b) for custody, care, protection, welfare and rehabilitation of devadasis. However, the state government has not framed any rules for the implementation of the Act. Note that, there is no data available in the public domain with respect to the number of cases filed, the number of convictions or the number of acquittals under the 1982 Act.

In addition to the 1982 Act, there are various welfare schemes introduced by the Karnataka government for the upliftment of the devadasis. Under the 'Devadasi Rehabilitation Programme', the government is providing counselling services, involving the devadasis in income generating activities, providing shelter homes, subsidies, loans through banks and also giving them pensions (Kothari et al., 2019). As per a report prepared by The Centre for Child and Law (CCL), National Law School of India University, Bengaluru in 2018, the Karnataka State Women's Development Corporation is responsible to provide rehabilitation and pension schemes to devadasis. But, when information was sought from the department under The Right to Information Act, 2005 regarding the number of devadasis availing such benefits under the different schemes in the last five years preceding 2018, there was no response given by the corporation (Wilson, Giliyal and Raman, 2018). CCL in its report also highlighted that when devadasis where asked (via interviews) about the various schemes provided by the government (though, 80 per cent of them knew about either one or two schemes) only 4 per cent of them said that they were getting benefits (Wilson, Giliyal and Raman, 2018). Another important issue highlighted in the report is with respect to the lack of implementation of the scheme mostly because of corrupt officials at the local level who despite taking bribes from these women do not put their names under the beneficiary list so that they can avail benefits. Further as per Wilson, Giliyal and Raman (2018),

'The community is also aware of the schemes available for Devadasis. They are aware of the documents required to avail the schemes like requirement of age-proof, ID proof etc. They are mostly aware of the pension scheme and the presence of middlemen to facilitate this process. They know that Devadasi women below the age of 35 are not availing pension and most of them feel that they need pension as they have to take care of their children without support from their partners. Even though the community is aware of the schemes available to the Devadasis, they do not help them to avail the benefit under the schemes, due to fear of being identified as a locality where Devadasi dedication persists and repercussion from the law enforcement agencies for permitting dedication within their village.'

Additionally, due to the age limit of 45 years, many younger devadasis are also barred from benefiting from the pension scheme. Because women below the age of 45 years are also asked to leave the temple premises as they are no longer considered 'fit' for service, devadasis have been demanding that the age limit be brought down to 25 years for availing the pension benefits.

The state of Tamil Nadu passed The Tamil Nadu Devadasis (Prevention of Dedication) Act in 1947. Note that, this legislation has not been reviewed or amended since. Under section 3 of this Act, the dedication of a woman as devadasi irrespective of her consent is declared unlawful. However, under section 4 of this Act, any woman who is dedicated as a devadasi and is of sixteen years of age can be punished for dancing with imprisonment of up to six months and a fine of five hundred rupees. It is interesting that, though section 3 of the Act acknowledges that a woman can be dedicated without her consent, under section 4, any woman who is a devadasi and is of sixteen years of age can be punished if she dances in the temple premises even to this day. Section 4 does not take into account the fact that devadasis are dedicated at a young age often without their consent and therefore, even when they are of sixteen years of age or more they continue to dance and serve the temple as they have no choice in the matter mostly because they continue to be bound to the goddess.

The provisions under The Andhra Pradesh Devadasis (Prohibition of Dedicated) Act, 1988 are similar to the provisions under The Karnataka Devadasis (Prohibition of Dedication) Act, 1982 in relation to penalties. Also, under section 5 of the Andhra Pradesh Act, devadasis are exempted from punishment. The Maharashtra Devadasi System (Abolition) Act, 2005 is also similar to the above mentioned legislations.

Due to the non-implementation of the above-mentioned legislations, the Ministry of Home Affairs, India, in 2015, issued an advisory to states where this practice persists to initiate special drive to identify all victims and suitably rehabilitate them by providing proper counselling, medical treatment, guidance, support and motivation to lead a dignified life. But, despite the advisory, there has been no improvement in the implementation of laws. This is also evident from the 2016 ruling of the Supreme Court in the case of *S.L. Foundation*. In *S.L. Foundation v Union of India*, the Supreme Court held that the dedication of dalit girls in a temple in the Bellary district of Karnataka was unconstitutional and in violation of several articles of the Constitution including article 21 which guarantees the right to life. The court in this case also passed the following directions:

'(a) complaints can be filed in specific instances of violation of the provisions of the Acts which have been brought into force in the States of Karnataka, Tamil Nadu, Andhra Pradesh, Telangana, Maharashtra as well as in any other States before the police authorities or by bringing it to the notice of the concerned Secretary of the State who is in charge of Women Development and it will be incumbent upon them to invoke the statutory provisions prevailing in the respective States and proceed against the culprits in accordance with law; (b) The Union of India is at liberty to approach the Court if its Advisory dated 22nd December, 2015 to all the States as well as Union Territories to stop the Devadasi practice was not implemented and (c) The court also allowed any future petitions to be filed against the concerned State Government for extending the rehabilitation measures to such victims in the event of any such instances being brought to the notice of the respective States Governments/ Union Territories with specific details and State Governments to take appropriate steps for their rehabilitation by providing all supportive rehabilitation measures.'

Therefore, the devadasi system continues to prevail in the Indian society mostly because legislations that were brought in to put an end to the practice have failed to address the primary reasons behind the existence of such practice in the first place.

CONCLUSION

This paper has shown how the devadasis who belong to the dalit community coming from extremely poor family backgrounds are dedicated to temples at very young age mostly at the behest of upper caste men. Young dalit girls after their dedication are made sexually available to everyone in the name of religion and after a certain age are left with no choice but to take up prostitution to earn their livelihood.

Today, the devadasi practice exists merely to satiate the sexual needs of the dominant castes and to ensure the continuity of caste hierarchy in the society. As noted in this paper, factors such as poverty, illiteracy, religious beliefs also play an important role in the continuation of the practice of dedication. More importantly, these factors contribute towards strengthening of the caste hegemony through the practice of dedication. The devadasi practice also shows that both superstition and religious beliefs are deep rooted in the Hindu society and dalits themselves firmly believe in them. Devadasis consider the rituals of dedication as sacrosanct and therefore, once the ritual is over, they feel obligated to serve as devadasis for the rest of their lives. This firm belief in many ways is also the result of societal pressure which forces dalits to conform to the practice of dedication.

Note that, in India, violence against women is carried out in the name of caste, gender, religion, family values, tradition etc. Women suffer from this violence right from their childhood in various forms. In short, in a patriarchal society like India, a host of issues are responsible for the subordination of women. But, violence against women in India is not equated with or seen as the outcome of structural violence. Structural inequalities created as a result of social-cultural factors which lead to normalization of certain practices that are detrimental to rights of women, are not considered important in the discourse on violence against women. The discussions in this paper has shown that factors such as caste, gender, religion, family values, community beliefs are responsible for violence against women in India because they are not only deep rooted in society but also affect the real-life experiences of women. More importantly, these factors form part of a larger structure which reproduces violence by normalizing gender based discrimination.

For instance, as noted in this paper, with respect to the devadasi system, there are a host of factors that intersect with each other to contribute towards the oppression of young dalit girls. The devadasi system, in particular, is also another form of structural violence wherein the entire practice is tailored mostly around caste and gender. Caste and gender are used not only to label a particular section of women as devadasis but to dictate their day to day relations with the society at large. The focus on devadasi system has shown how religion and religious beliefs play a significant role in the continuity of this practice. The devadasi system represents a form of social control exercised by the upper castes over dalits in India. The practice of dedication strengthens the caste hierarchy and further marginalizes the dalit community. In short, both caste and gender dynamics are used to supress dalit women by making them victims of structural violence through the devadasi institution.

To summarize, social-cultural norms are used to embolden patriarchal values in the Indian society and the practice of devadasi system is the end result of not one but multiple factors interlocking with each other forming part of structural violence against women in India. This paper also highlights how in order to exercise control over women and their sexuality, social, cultural and religious reasons are often advanced by family and society. More importantly, the paper emphasizes upon the importance of identifying some of the structural reasons responsible behind the violent crime of temple prostitution which are vital in understanding why there exists a denial of violence against women in India in the first place or why such a crime against women is seen as normal practice and sincere efforts are not made to either strengthen anti-devadasi legislations or treat this practice as an offence under the Immoral Traffic Prevention Act, 1956.

REFERENCES

Altekar, A. S. (1959, January 1). *The Position of Women in Hindu Civilization.* Motilal Banarsidass Indological Publishers.

Behl, N. (2019, July 3). *Gendered Citizenship.* Oxford University Press.

Black, M. (2007). *Women in Ritual Slavery: Devadasi, Jogini and Mathamma in Karnataka and Andhra Pradesh, Southern India.* Anti-Slavery International. http://idsn.org/wp-content/uploads/user_folder/pdf/New_files/Key_Issues/Dalit_Women/WomeninRitualSlavery.pdf

Chandramouli, C. (2011). *Census of India 2011: Provisional Population Totals Paper 1 of 2011 India Series 1.* Office of the Registrar General & Census Commissioner. https://censusindia.gov.in/2011-prov-results/data_files/india/Final_PPT_2011_chapter5.pdf

Dagar, R. (2014). *Gender, Identity and Violence.* Routledge.

Gunda-Werner-Institut. (2014). *December 16th 2012: A Rape, A Murder and A Movement.* Gunda-Werner-Institut, Heinrich-Böll-Stiftung. https://www.gwi-boell.de/en/2014/04/02/december-16th-2012-rape-murder-and-movement

Farquhar, J. N. (1977). *Modern Religious Movements in India.* Munshiram Manoharial Publishers.

Gangoli, G. (2007). *Indian Feminisms: Law, Patriarchies and Violence in India*. Routledge.

Ghose, S. (2003). The Dalit in India. *Social Research*, *70*(1), 83–109. doi:10.1353/sor.2003.0032

Gupta, C. (2008). (MIS) Representing the Dalit Woman: Reification of Caste and Gender Stereotypes in the Hindi Didactic Literature of Colonial India. *The Indian Historical Review*, *35*(2), 101–124. doi:10.1177/037698360803500206

Harishankar, V. B., & Priyamvadha, M. (2016). *Exploitation of Women as Devadasis and its Associated Evils*. National Commission for Women New Delhi. http://ncwapps.nic.in/pdfReports/Exploitation_of_Women_as_Devadasis_and_its_Associated_Evils_Report.pdf

India, T. (2020, December 13). *Worrying sex ratio trend in eight states*. Tribune India News Service. https://www.tribuneindia.com/news/nation/worrying-sex-ratio-trend-in-eight-states-184002

Jacobsen, K. A. (2015, August 11). *Routledge Handbook of Contemporary India*. Routledge.

Johnson, P. S., & Johnson, J. A. (2001, September). The Oppression of Women in India. *Violence Against Women*, *7*(9), 1051–1068. doi:10.1177/10778010122182893

Jordan, K. K. (2003, January 1). *From Sacred Servant to Profane Prostitute*. Manohar Publishers.

Kalra, G., & Bhugra, D. (2013). Sexual violence against women: Understanding cross-cultural intersections. *Indian Journal of Psychiatry*, *55*(3), 244–249. doi:10.4103/0019-5545.117139 PMID:24082244

Kothari, J., Ganesan, D., Jayalakshmi, I. R., Sharma, R., & S, A. (2019). *Intersections of Caste and Gender: Implementation of Devadasi Prohibition Laws*. Centre for Law and Policy Research Bangalore. https://clpr.org.in/wp-content/uploads/2019/11/Policy-Brief-on-Devadasi-Legislations.pdf

Lalou, C. (1995). What future for the Devadasis and their children? *International Journal of Children's Rights*, *3*(1), 19–50. doi:10.1163/157181895X00348

Ministry of Finance Department of Economic Affairs. (2018, January). *Economic Survey 2017-18*. The Hindu Center. https://www.thehinducentre.com/multimedia/archive/03223/Economic_Survey_20_3223793a.pdf

Ministry of Women and Child Development New Delhi. (2015, June). *Report of the High Level Committee on the Status of Women in India*. NIC. https://wcd.nic.in/sites/default/files/Vol%203.compressed.pdf

Ministry of Women and Child Development New Delhi. (2015, June). *Report of the High Level Committee on the Status of Women in India*. NIC. https://wcd.nic.in/sites/default/files/Vol%203.compressed.pdf

Mishra, K. K., & Rao, K. K. (2005). Evolution and Devolution of the Devadasi System in India: A Socio-Historical Analysis. *Journal of the Indian Anthropological Society*, *40*(1), 31–49.

Nirbhaya case: Four Indian men executed for 2012 Delhi bus rape and murder. (2020, March 20). BBC News. https://www.bbc.co.uk/news/world-asia-india-51969961

One Rape Every 16 Minutes in India, NCRB Data Highlights Country's Deteriorated Law & Order. (2020, October 2). India.Com. https://www.india.com/news/india/no-country-for-women-one-rape-every-16-minutes-in-india-ncrb-data-highlights-countrys-deteriorated-law-order-4159540/

Orchard, T. R. (2007, June). Girl, woman, lover, mother: Towards a new understanding of child prostitution among young Devadasis in rural Karnataka, India. *Social Science & Medicine*, *64*(12), 2379–2390. doi:10.1016/j.socscimed.2007.02.031 PMID:17412471

Orr, L. C. (2000, March 9). *Donors, Devotees, and Daughters of God*. Oxford University Press.

Panjrath, S., & Ralhan, O. P. (2000, January 1). *Devadasi System in India*. OM Publishers.

Parker, E. R. (2016). *Theologising with the Sacred "prostitutes" of South India*.

Prasad, A. K. (1999). Origin of the Devadasi System. *Proceedings of the Indian History Congress, 60*, 129-136.

Ramberg, L. (2011). When the Devi Is Your Husband: Sacred Marriage and Sexual Economy in South India. *Feminist Studies*, *37*(1), 28–60. doi:10.1353/fem.2011.0014

Shah, G. (2002, January 1). *Dalits and the State*. Concept Publishing Company.

Shingal, A. (2015). THE DEVADASI SYSTEM: Temple Prostitution in India. *UCLA Women's Law Journal*, *22*(1). doi:10.5070/L3221026367

Tarachand, K. C. (1991, January 1). *Dēvadāsi Custom*. Reliance Publishers.

Thorat, S. (2002). Oppression and Denial: Dalit Discrimination in the 1990s. *Economic and Political Weekly*, *37*(6).

Torri, M. C. (2009). Abuse of Lower Castes in South India: The Institution of Devadasi. *Journal of International Women's Studies*, *11*(2).

Tripathi, A. (2015, January 24). *NCW to study actual status of "devadasi" system*. Deccan Herald. https://www.deccanherald.com/content/455398/ncw-study-actual-status-devadasi.html

Vadlapatla, S. (2015, February 23). Devadasi system still exists in Telangana, AP, says report. *The Times of India*. https://timesofindia.indiatimes.com/india/Devadasi-system-still-exists-in-Telangana-AP-says-report/articleshow/46337859.cms

Vishwanathan, L. (2008, January 1). *Women of Pride*. Roli Books.

Wilson, B., Giliyal, A., & Raman, S. (2018). *A Qualitative Study of The Legal Dimensions of Devadasi Dedication Phenomenon*. Centre for Child and the Law-National Law School of India University Bengaluru. https://www.researchgate.net/publication/332141651_A_QUALITATIVE_STUDY_OF_THE_LEGAL_DIMENSIONS_OF_'DEVADASI'_DEDICATION_PHENOMENON

Chapter 5
Organised Crime and the Role of Law and Law Enforcement Agencies in Ghana

Elijah Tukwariba Yin
https://orcid.org/0000-0003-2757-092X
University of Cape Coast, Ghana

ABSTRACT

This chapter brings together the various components of organised crime in Ghana and analyses the role of law and law enforcement agencies. It is argued that organised crime in Ghana undermines the emerging fragile democratic institutions in the country. Rooted in transparency, press freedom, rule of law, and free and fair elections, some elected and/or appointed officials who have taken oaths of office to defend the Constitution without fear or favour have largely been compromised to do the bidding of criminal syndicates at the expense of citizens. Despite the improvement in legislation and the coordinated efforts of mandated state agencies, the influence of affluent organised criminal syndicates on some law enforcement agencies has weakened state-agency collaboration. The undermining role of politicians presents a paradox of power subversion that aids and abets organised criminal activities. Sophisticated technology, political preparedness, and individual alertness are crucial in dealing with organised crime in Ghana.

DOI: 10.4018/979-8-3693-0327-6.ch005

INTRODUCTION

Organized crime is a structured, centralised, and sustained criminal enterprise that rationally engages in illicit profitable activities (Catino, 2020; Wright, 2013; Miraglia, Ochoa, & Briscoe, 2012), mirroring otherwise a formal capitalist enterprise. Such criminal enterprises engage in various forms of crime including financial fraud, human trafficking, drug trade, etc. (Kar, & Spanjers, 2017). In its pursuit of markets and maximization of profit, organize crime disregards national and international boundaries (Livey, 2017; Wright, 2013).

The roots of organised crime in Ghana can be traced to the colonial era (Ellis, 2016). The engagement in illegal gold, diamond, and other natural resources trade was prevalent. There were other forms of unauthorized trade such as the smuggling of food produce to neighbouring countries for high prices. Additionally, trade in human beings for the slave market in the Americas also constituted organised crime in the colonial period (Wannenburg, 2005). The British colonialists in Ghana used law and order as a tool of manipulation, perpetuation, and preservation of organised criminal activities (Killingray, 1986). Following British colonial rule in Ghana, the government under Dr. Kwame Nkrumah inherited the governance structure, cultural makeup, and the associated criminal practices of the colonial regime. The post-colonial era, from the first republic to the present-day fourth republic, still witnesses varied forms of organised crime.

Besides the colonial consequences, the strategic location of Ghana along the Gulf of Guinea, as well as its status as a key transit point for drug trafficking and other illegal operations, has made it a rich target for criminal networks (Ogunniyi, & Akpu, 2019; Brown, 2013). The coastlines and borders of Ghana are generally porous. The Navy and Coast Guard lack the necessary patrol boats, planes, surveillance drones, and radar to track suspicious ships and individuals. This makes it easy for Latin American drug traffickers to use Ghana's coastlines and borders as transportation points to Europe (see Figure 1 on cocaine flows and seizures). The involvement of external actors reveals the role of international criminal networks in the growth of organised crime in the country.

Figure 1. Cocaine flows and seizures
(African Union, 2014)

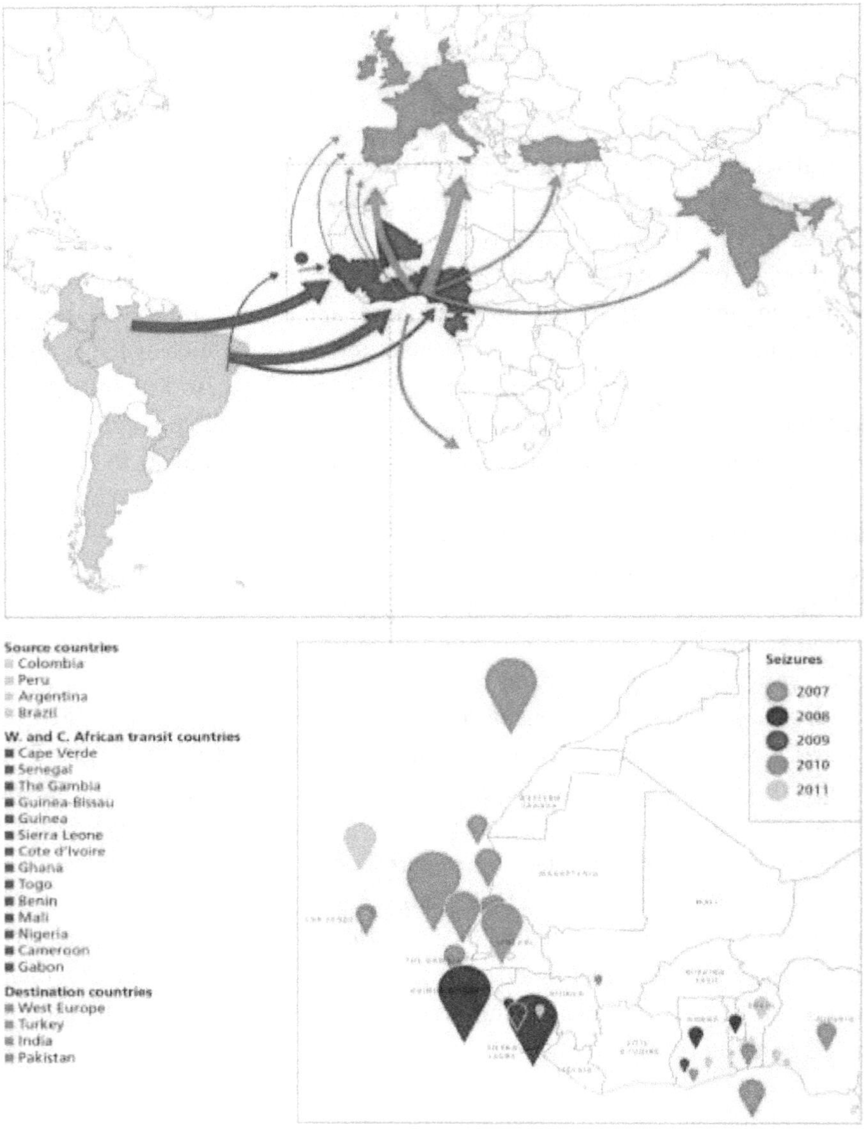

In addition to the porousness of Ghana's coastlines and borders, socio-cultural and economic conditions such as poverty, high unemployment rates, and corruption have further fueled the growth of organised crime in Ghana (Mohammed, 2022; Dukku, & Yunusa, 2022; Jonathan, et al., 2021). There is evidence to the effect that subaltern and disadvantaged groups, particularly young people, in many development settings are more likely to be lured into criminal groups due to the prestigious, beneficial social network, and the material and financial gains that one may derive from such affiliation. Living and working in the 'underworld' offers social status where legitimate opportunities for advancement and mobility are scarce (Schultze-Kraft, 2016). As crime becomes more embedded in social life, the lure of quick money is all-pervading, making young women and men vulnerable (Siegel, 2014). Although a few, women in organised crime are at risk of being victims of gender-based violence (Arsovska & Allum, 2014). In parts of West Africa, participation in drug trafficking, pharmaceutical counterfeiting, and gun running, especially if it generates substantial financial gains is not viewed as criminal per se, but rather elicits envy and jealousy by neighbours. In some communities, such illicit practices are seen and interpreted as a "decent" way to earn a living (Schultze-Kraft, 2014). This social acceptance of illegal and criminal actions by sections of society can be seen in the development of what is known as a 'culture of lawlessness' (Williams, 2009). All these suggest that some prevailing socio-cultural and economic ambiances serve to promote the activities of organised crime in Ghana.

The pervasiveness of organised crime has had a significant impact on various aspects of Ghanaian society (Schultze-Kraft, 2016; Sotande, 2016). One of the most visible results has been a decline in public trust in government institutions and the legal system. The involvement of corrupt officials and law enforcement personnel in criminal activities has undermined the rule of law and created a sense of impunity among criminals (Yeh, 2022). The participation of corrupt officials is evidenced in the arrest of former Ghana's Member of Parliament for Nkoranza North and his accomplice in New York in 2005 for drug trafficking (Bonsu, 2011). The active participation of some state officials in organised crime has further perpetuated a cycle of crime and corruption, making it difficult for the government to effectively combat organised crime. Moreover, the influence of criminal networks extends beyond traditional illicit activities, as they have also infiltrated sectors such as politics, business, media, and the criminal justice system (Duijn, Kashirin, & Sloot, 2014). In respect of the latter, there are cases where criminal syndicates are arrested and subjected to the justice system, yet the case drags on for years, less often without any significant and satisfactory outcome. It is as though the prosecuting agencies drag out the case till it fades out of public consciousness (Yin & Seiwoh, 2021). This infiltration allows criminal organisations to exert control and influence over key decision-making processes, enabling them to protect their illicit activities and expand their networks. Any attempt to expose these criminal entities could lead to unforeseen consequences for the whistleblowers. In some circumstances, the whistleblowers rather become deviantised and at a disadvantage, as they are unable to compete with the power and resources of these criminal networks (Yin, 2021).

This not only undermines the principles of democracy and the rule of law but also hinders economic growth and development.

As stated above, organised crime has implications for economic growth and supply chains in Ghana and Africa. Using the fishing industry as an example, the fish business worldwide generated over US$164 billion in exports, with 60% of that amount coming from developing nations in 2018. Unreported, unregulated, and illegal fishing accounts for a sizable chunk of the world economy. A reasonable estimate places the annual value of illegal fish imports from Africa into the European Union at €1.1 billion, or 500,000 tonnes (Enact Observer, n.d.). In Ghana, according to ADF (2023), nearly 50 tons of fish were dumped by Chinese trawlers over about 45 days at sea in 2022. For decades, some Chinese trawlers, in collaboration with some Ghanaians, have engaged in illegal fishing in Ghana and other countries in West Africa. Ghana's small pelagic fish stocks, specifically sardinella, have declined by 80% over the previous two decades as a result of overfishing and various illicit activities. This practice has detrimental repercussions for the sea economy, as it reduces fish stocks, biodiversity, damages ecosystems, and jeopardises food security. The Environmental Justice Foundation, through the Guardian, reports that Ghana loses $81 million yearly due to illegal fishing. This amount is true when such fish are sold at port but reduces to $50 million when sold at sea (Hodal, 2019). This reveals how organised crime depletes the country's finances which otherwise could be used to boost developmental projects for economic development. Beyond the economic challenges are human rights abuses.

The consequences of organised crime on human rights could be discussed under four themes: violence, and civil and political rights; economic, social and cultural rights; repressive state responses to organized crime; and access to justice and redress, and impunity. Organized crime and state actors' involvement in violence undermines citizens' civil and political rights, particularly for minority and structurally vulnerable groups. According to the UN (2023), homicide rates are higher in criminal groups than in conflict zones, with approximately 60,000 murders annually linked to organized crime and gang violence between 2000-2017 (UNODC, 2019). Organized crime does not only hinder civil and political rights but also states' economic, social, and cultural rights. The resources allocated to fight organised crime could be better used to address social needs, particularly for young people, as inequality gaps create opportunities for organized crime (Oliveira, 2023). Regarding repressive state actions against organised crime and their impact on human rights, it is important to note that highly securitized crackdowns and specific investigative techniques employed to combat crime may result in abuses of human rights. An illustration of a repressive state's reaction is evident in the anti-drug campaign in the Philippines, wherein deliberate measures were taken against individuals involved in the distribution and consumption of drugs, leading to a significant number of extrajudicial deaths (Kennert & Eligh, 2019; Oliveira, 2023). Also, according to unofficial reports, President Rodrigo Duterte's regime killed an estimated 6,200 alleged drug users or dealers (Robertson, 2022). Finally, the victims of organised crime are often characterised by their lack of rights to seek redress and access to justice. This is especially apparent in relation to the entitlement to legal remedies in criminal cases. The inability of victims to utilise such avenues for seeking justice, particularly in situations where criminal elements have gained control over the criminal justice system or where state agents collaborate with criminals, and where there is a lack of support for victims and survivors in coping with trauma, is identified as a factor that fosters a feeling of helplessness and abuse of victims' rights (Oliveira, 2023).

The widespread effects of organised crime on governance, economic growth, and human rights suggest the importance of the subject matter in academic literature. Scholarly works (Dziwornu, 2021; Owusu et al., 2016; Adam & Adongo, 2016; Appiahene-Gyamfi, 2003, etc.) related to Ghana suggest that scholars have paid much attention to the issue of crime in general. The focus of the existing literature reveals scanty attention to organised crime and the role of law and law enforcement agencies in Ghana. The very few writings (Duho et al., 2022; Appiahene-Gyamfi, 2021; Boakye, 2020; Ennin & Mensah, 2019; Overdevest, & Zeitlin, 2018; Agyapong, Asiamah, & Addo-Danquah, 2016; Aning, 2007) on organised crime and law enforcement are fragmented. This chapter brings together the various components of organised crime in Ghana and analyses the role of law and law enforcement agencies. In this chapter, I argue that organized crime in Ghana undermines the emerging fragile democratic institutions in the country. Based on principles of openness, press freedom, rule of law, and democratic elections, certain elected and/or appointed officials who have sworn to uphold the Constitution impartially have, to a great extent, been influenced to serve the interests of criminal organisations, disregarding the well-being of the citizens. Examining law enforcement and organised crime in Ghana is crucial to tackling the widespread problem of criminal networks and corruption. Like many other countries, Ghana is grappling with the detrimental effects of organised crime, which not only threatens the safety and security of its citizens but also undermines the foundations of economic growth and a just and democratic society. By understanding the dynamics of organised crime and the strategies employed by criminal networks, law enforcement agencies can better equip themselves to combat these illicit activities and safeguard the interests of the nation. Furthermore, studying organised crime can shed light on the etiology and the compromising situations that engender its growth.

This chapter is divided into eight sections. The first section delineates the topic, aim and scholarly justification of the study. The second section delves into the definition and characteristics of organised crime while the third section gives an overview of organised crime in the world and Africa. The fourth section zooms into the nature of organised crime in Ghana, focusing on illicit drugs, trade, people/ human trafficking, cyber fraud and financial crimes, and the environment. The fifth section looks at the actors of organised crime while the sixth section also looks at the role of law and law enforcement agencies in dealing with organised crime. The seventh section pays attention to the challenges associated with fighting organised crime in Ghana. The final section presents the conclusion of the chapter.

DEFINITION AND CHARACTERISTICS OF ORGANISED CRIME

To understand organised crime, it is critical to define crime broadly and demonstrate how organised crime differs from other types of criminal activity. Crime is defined as any human behaviour that violates a criminal law of a country and is subject to punishment, whether imprisonment, fine, and/or pardon (Adler, Mueller, & Laufer, 2013). In Amand v Home Secretary and Minister of Defence of Royal Netherlands Government [1943] AC 147, the House of Lords indicated that a cause or matter is criminal in nature if it is one which if carried to its conclusion might result in the conviction of a person. This approach to crime is a purist legal view. According to Siegel (2001) "crime is a violation of societal rules of behaviour as interpreted and expressed by a criminal legal code created by people holding social and political power". Organised crime is also a form of crime as it violates the criminal law of a country, however, what distinguishes it from other forms of criminal activities is that organised crime is planned and executed. It emphasises rational actions that demonstrate the collective efforts of individuals (UNODC, 2018). The UNODC (2018) defines organised crime as "a continuing criminal enterprise that rationally works to profit from illicit activities that are often in great public demand. Its continuing existence is maintained through corruption of public officials and the use of intimidation, threats or force to protect its operations." It is useful to note that the nature and form of organised crime varies across countries and regions, hence a universal application of the definition may be limited in some respect.

Considering the limitation associated with having a common definition of organised crime, the United Nations Convention against Transnational Organized Crime (UNTOC) (2003), instead defines an "organised criminal group". Under Article 2a of the Convention an "organized criminal group" is considered to have four criteria. The first of such criteria is that it is a structured group of three or more persons. This structured group may not require a formal hierarchy or membership continuity. This concept encompasses a wide range of groups that are loosely connected and lack specific roles for their members or a well-established structure. The second criterion is longevity or lifespan. Although some groups may exist for a while, others may be temporal due to mass arrests, in-fighting, and killings resulting in their dissolution. The third and fourth criteria of an organised criminal group are that it acts in concert to commit at least one serious crime; and to obtain, directly or indirectly, a financial or other material benefit. The defining characteristics of these groups are the gravity of the crimes they perpetrate and their profit-oriented motives (UNODC, 2018).

The academic works of Albanese (2023; 2021; 2016), Calderoni et al. (2022), and Finckenauer (2005) reveal the common characteristics of organised crime. One of these traits is that organised crime exists primarily to make money off of crime. These forms of crime mostly serve to meet public demand for services. Corruption is identified as serving as a facilitator that shields and supports the activities of organised criminal enterprises. To safeguard those operations, intimidation, threats, and/or force may occasionally be required. All these components make up organised crime as a persistent illegal business. The work of Gomes and Cervini (1997) also identifies the following as characteristics of organised crime: the desire to amass wealth; a hierarchical structure; "businesslike" planning; advanced technology; a functional division of activities; a structural relationship with public authorities; the provision of social services; the division of illegal activities geographically; a serious power of intimidation; a diffuse capacity for deception; and local or international organisations. The findings of Albanese (2016), Finckenauer (2005), Gomes and Cervini (1997 cited in Lucas, 2007) are not much different from those of Oliveira (2004) and Mingardin (1996). According to Oliveira (2004) and Casas-Zamora (2013), organised criminal groups maintain their influence by utilizing actual or threatened violence, collusion with corrupt public officials, extortion, or corruption. Mingardin (1996 cited in Lucas, 2007) identified fifteen characteristics: engaging in illegal activity; covert operations; hierarchical organisation; profit-driven pursuits; labour division; resort to violence; symbiosis with the State; illicit goods; corporate strategy; use of coercion; sale of illicit services; favouritism; law of silence; monopoly of violence; and territorial control. Common among these enumerated characteristics are profit-making, offering services based on demand, connection between criminal organisations, violence/intimidation, corruption, hierarchy of authority, planned purpose, and division of labour. All these features give us an idea of the nature of organised criminal groups and their operations. The next section looks at an overview of organised crime on the global stage and in Africa.

OVERVIEW OF ORGANISED CRIME IN THE WORLD AND AFRICA

According to the Global Organised Crime Index (GOCI) (2023), 83% of people worldwide live in high-crime environments, demonstrating the ongoing global rise of organised crime. On the other hand, the proportion of individuals worldwide who live in environments with little resilience to organised crime has drastically decreased, from 79.4% in 2021 to 62% currently. Although the number of individuals residing in highly resilient nations has increased, the data indicates that global resilience has not kept pace with the growing prevalence of criminal activities. Response structures have proven inadequate in addressing the danger posed by organised crime. The increasing disparity between organised crime and the collective efforts of various governments to resist it emphasises the pressing necessity for well-informed and practical solutions to combat organised crime on a worldwide scale.

The major findings of the Index indicate that the disparity between criminality and resilience is increasing. Currently, a staggering 83% of the global population resides in nations characterised by high crime rates, marking a notable rise from the 79% recorded in 2021. In contrast, when examining resilience over the past two years, it is evident that the global average has been rather consistent, scoring 4.81 out of 10. The influence of non-state actors as agents of resilience has significantly diminished. These players, particularly investigative journalists, play a crucial role in ensuring governmental institutions are held accountable and serve as essential elements in communities impacted by organised crime (GOCI, 2023).

The Index reveals that political shifts and economic hardships have fueled organized crime, with financial crimes ranking among the top three illicit economies globally in 2022 excluding the Americas, where it is one of the top five. The next three most significant illegal markets were those for weapons, marijuana, and human trafficking. It is important to note that the biggest factor influencing organised crime is still the state's involvement in criminal activity. Conflict also provides an opportunity for criminals to profit from the emergent chaos. Many of the countries with the worst crime rates in 2022, including Afghanistan, Iraq, Myanmar, Ethiopia, and, most recently, Ukraine, have been plagued by conflict and instability for decades (GOCI, 2023).

Based on a comparative review of the data from 2020, Southern Asia, Western Asia, South-Eastern Asia, Central Asia and Eastern Asia and the Caucasus, show the highest levels of organized crime of all the continents. Due to the addition of financial and cybercrimes to the index, Europe has had the largest growth in continental criminality. However, there has also been a rise in drug, environmental, and human trafficking. While 10 criminal markets showed rise in Africa between 2020 and 2022, the continent as a whole saw the least increase in criminality. In

2022, financial offences like embezzlement and fraud overtook human trafficking as the most common illegal economy. However, since 2020, there has also been an upsurge in human trafficking. Notably, Eastern and Central Asia as well as West and Central Africa experienced a decline in total crime (GOCI, 2023).

The Organized Crime Index shows Africa is second only to Asia in terms of criminality, with human and arms trafficking being the most prevalent. Eritrea and South Sudan have the highest scores globally for human trafficking. The Index also shows that financial crimes are prevalent in Africa, with North Africa being the highest-scoring region. Globally, the number of people living in countries with high levels of organized crime has increased, with 83% of the global population living in such countries (GOCI, 2023). The next section focuses on organised crime in Ghana.

ORGANISED CRIME IN GHANA

According to the Organised Global Crime Index report (2023), Ghana's criminality score is 5.8 with a resilience score of 5.46. The criminal markets for organised crime include drugs, people/human trafficking, trade in illicit goods, environment, cyber-fraud and financial crimes. These will be discussed in turn.

Drugs

Ghana is a major transit and destination country for heroin trafficking, primarily originating from Afghanistan. Ghanaian drug trafficking groups, along with Nigerian counterparts, have expanded the global heroin trade and illicit drug markets across West Africa (Atta-Asamoah, 2014; Brown, 2013; GOCI, 2023). Inbound heroin seizures mainly involve East African nationals, while outbound heroin seizures mainly involve Ghanaian nationals. Corrupted officials facilitate heroin trafficking through Ghanaian seaports and airports. Ghana is also a major player in the global cocaine trade, with organized criminal groups at the forefront (Sandor, 2016; Bonsu, 2011). Cocaine seizures have declined in Ghana, and this could be attributed to the change in regime posture to rigorously prosecute arrested criminals. In other words, it could also be stated that criminal syndicates operate unnoticed because the press, enforcement agencies, and government officials have colluded to facilitate the illicit market. Ghana has also emerged as a prominent cannabis cultivation area, with the UK being the primary destination for cannabis exports (Agboli, 2023 Chouvy, 2019; GOCI, 2023). The synthetic drug trade is prevalent, with Tramadol being a prominent drug (GOCI, 2023).

People/Human Trafficking

Human trafficking is a significant issue in Ghana, involving forced labour, sexual exploitation, and child trafficking (Okyere, 2017). The country serves as a transit point for West Africans, often destined for sex trafficking in Europe (Bello, & Olutola, 2020; GOCI, 2023). Major cities like Accra, Kumasi, and Takoradi are hotspots for this crime, with traffickers embedded in various sectors of the economy. Unwitting parents offer their children to traffickers who promise them schooling and a better life. An NGO called "Free the Slaves" carried out a baseline survey in 20 communities in the Volta and Central Regions in August 2016, and the results show that some of these areas serve as both the source and the destination of human trafficking. There were limited reports of early and forced marriage (1%), with children who had been victims of human trafficking and principally exploited in the fishing business (18%) and domestic servitude (10%) making up 35.2% of households throughout all 20 communities. Villages differed greatly in their incidence rates; every household reported having experienced trafficking at some point in the past or present. There were multiple child trafficking cases in over 20% of the households surveyed (GOCI, 2023).

Foreign nationals also experience forced labour, with Cuban medical professionals and Chinese nationals subjected to bonded labour in the mining and fishing sectors. Transnational Ghanaian smugglers play a pivotal role in the development of West Africa's human smuggling industry. The production of fake travel documents and counterfeit American and European visas in Ghana facilitates the work of traffickers. In 2016, the State Department reported the existence of a fake U.S. Embassy in Ghana which has been operated for decades by both Ghanaian and Turkish organized crime rings (Yeebo, 2017; Kennedy, 2016). Figure 2 shows the fake US embassy. The operators of this fake U.S. Embassy extorted money from gullible customers. Extortion and protection racketeering in Ghana are both individual and organized crime group activities.

Figure 2. Fake US embassy in Ghana
(The Guardian/Yeebo, 2017)

Trade in Illicit Goods

Ghana is a source of commercial explosives and arms trafficking (Small Arms Survey, 2023; GOCI, 2023). Arms trafficking is a growing issue in Ghana, with Kumasi and Accra being key markets for illegal weapons. Figure 3 depicts Tudu in Accra as a major hub for arms trading. Kumasi is known for its skilled craftsmen and affordable raw materials, making gun manufacturing profitable. The production cost of a homemade firearm in Ghana amounts to a mere $9. Gunsmiths manufacture over 200,000 illicit firearms annually, retailing them for prices ranging from US$90 to US$150, contingent upon the weapon's nature and technological features. These weapons are utilised by criminals in 90% of the nation's residential robberies, as well as in acts of banditry, trafficking, and retaliatory assaults (Azure, 2009). Between September 2022 and April 2023, a total of 30 homicides involving craft firearms in 12 distinct occurrences in north-east Ghana were reported. The demand for illicit arms extends beyond traditional communities to urban and rural areas, where rising crime rates threaten safety and livelihoods. Criminal networks target international traders and local purchasers of highly prized items such as diamonds and gold (GOCI, 2023).

Figure 3. Small arms flows, trading hubs, and current conflict flashpoints (African Union, 2014)

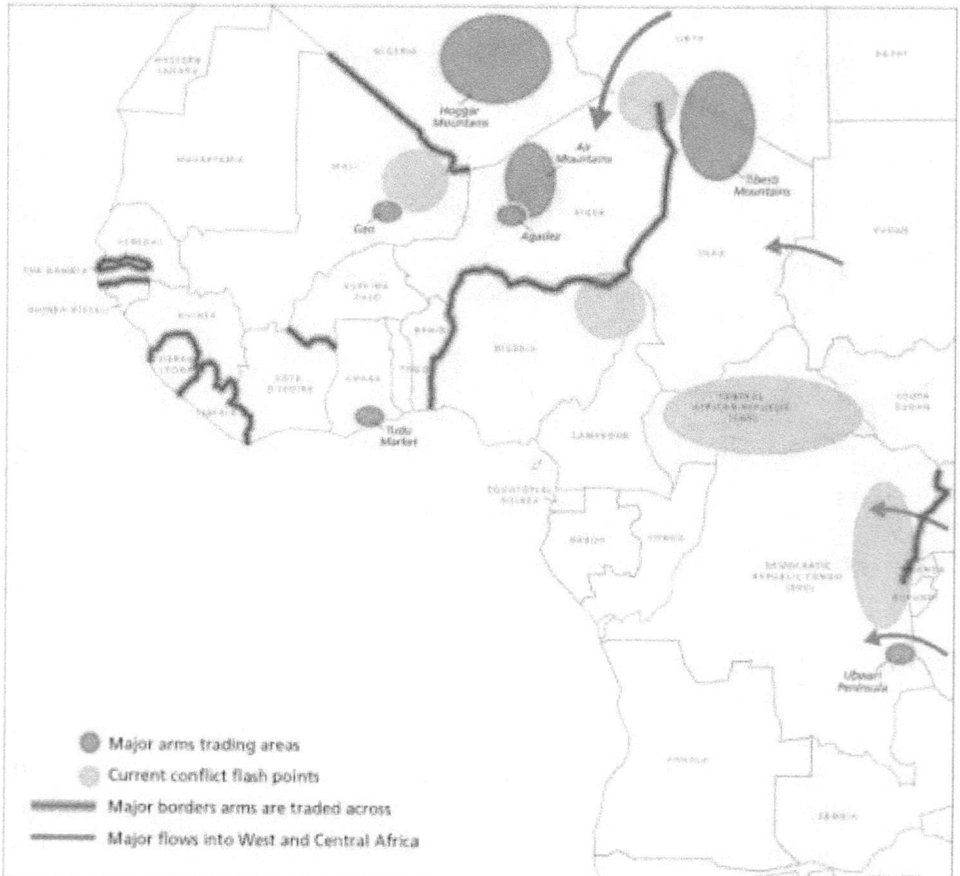

While some criminal syndicates deal in firearms in Ghana, the country is also a source for other criminal enterprises interested in gold. The National Security Secretariat in Accra apprehended two Chinese nationals and one Ghanaian in 2021 in connection with the transportation of twenty-one gold bars from Gbane, located in the Talensi District of the Upper East Region. These Chinese nationals unlawfully mined in a concession owned by a small-scale miner, circumvented Ghanaian mining regulations, and were apprehended while transporting the gold for their international trading partners (Daily Statesman, 2023).

Other criminal syndicates also rob and trade stolen cars in Ghana. Between July 2022 and January 2023, the Ghana Police Service arrested 12 persons suspected of having engaged in various forms of organised robbery across Ghana. Upon the arrest of these suspects, the police retrieved 10 snatched vehicles and a cash sum of GH¢10,010 (Ghanaweb, 2023).

Counterfeit goods, such as electrical products and medicines, are prevalent in Accra. Over 25% of cigarette packs sold in Ghana's Tobacco market are thought to be illegal. Figure 4 shows the smuggling routes of illegal cigarettes of which Ghana is a major point. The facilitation of this commerce is primarily enabled by the existence of permeable borders and a lack of awareness of stakeholders. Civil society organizations are addressing these issues through awareness campaigns (GOCI, 2023).

Figure 4. Smuggling routes of illicit cigarettes
(African Union, 2014)

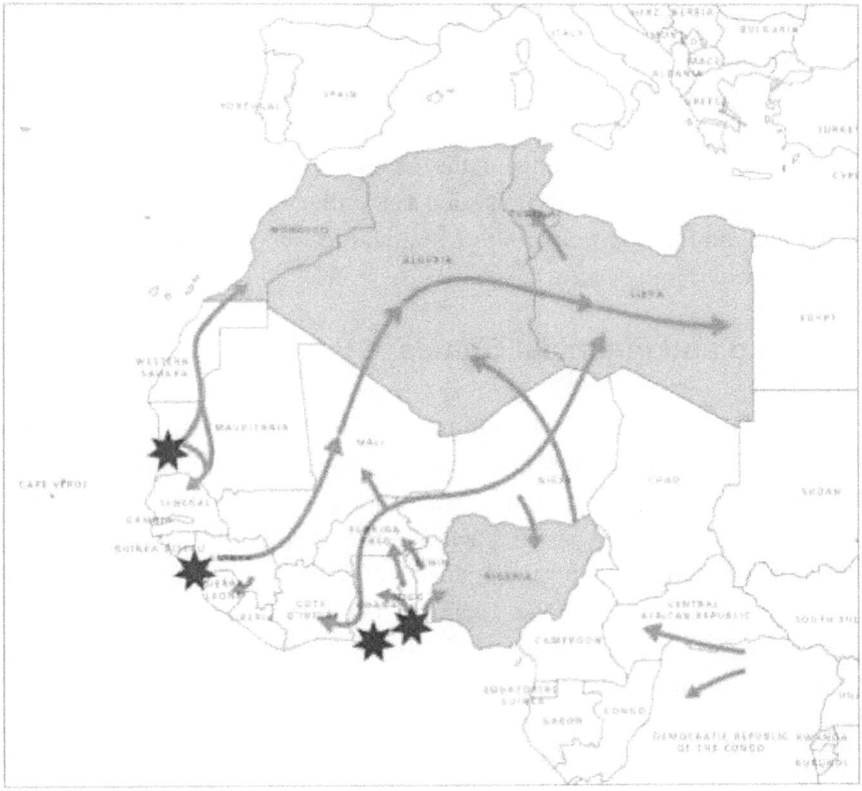

Environment

Ghana has witnessed substantial deforestation over the last twenty years, primarily caused by illicit logging activities, especially in the Bono, Ahafo, and Western North areas (Peprah, 2022; Agariga, Abugre, & Appiah, 2021; Atampugre et al., 2022). The evidence available indicates a rise in criminal syndicates engaged in unlawful deforestation activities, with Ghana playing a significant role as a primary source of illicit rosewood that is smuggled to Asia (Kansanga et al., 2021; GOCI, 2023). Illegal rosewood harvesting and exports persist despite sporadic bans, primarily due to the prevalence of bribery and corruption. In November 2021, illicit rosewood shipments with a value above $2 million were transported from Ghana to China, in violation of the existing restriction on harvesting. According to the Environmental Information Agency, almost 50% of Ghana's rosewood exports to China occurred during periods of prohibition, facilitated by bribery and forged documentation (GOCI, 2023). Illicit logging is widespread in the Savannah Region, where corrupt officials are manipulated, and rosewood is smuggled out through land borders and ports (Peprah, 2022; Agariga, Abugre, & Appiah, 2021; Atampugre et al., 2022). This shows that government agents at various ranks aid and abet organised criminals instead of ensuring their arrest, prosecution and imprisonment.

The illicit trafficking of pangolins, elephants, and birds poses a significant risk to the country's wildlife (GOCI, 2023; Ibanga, 2017). As a result of the decline in elephant poaching, some criminals have turned their attention to avian species (Merem et al., 2023). According to the Index report, in Ghana, nonrenewable resource crimes encompass activities such as the illegal trading of gold, smuggling of oil and fuel, and the participation of political leaders, through their proxies, in the artisanal gold mining sector.

Cyber Fraud and Financial Crimes

Cybercrime in Ghana has significantly impacted individuals and businesses, especially during the COVID-19 pandemic (Duho, 2022). Criminals exploit vulnerabilities and insecurities, using malware programs to steal money (Broadhurst, 2017). Botnet and cryptocurrency miner attacks have impacted Ghanaian enterprises at an above-average rate, affecting economic progress and causing concerns for international companies (GOCI, 2023). In 2019 and 2020, Ghana lost millions of dollars to cyber fraud. According to a news outlet in Ghana, in 2020, the country lost $19,800,000 through fraud and other criminal activities, as against $11 million in 2019. This information was presented by the Director of the Child Protection Digital Forensic Laboratory and Cybercrime Unit of the Ghana Police Service (Ghanaian Times, 2021).

Ghana is facing a surge in financial crimes, including money laundering, fraud and tax evasion, affecting various industries like banking, real estate, and gold mining (Wayo, 2023). On February 16, 2022, a New York-based Ghanaian, Fred Asante, was imposed with a sentence of 108 months. Asante was the principal money launderer based in the United States for a criminal organisation originating from Ghana, which perpetrated fraudulent schemes involving the theft of tens of millions of dollars from victims throughout the United States. Among these fraud schemes were those involving business email hacks, romance scams aimed at elderly victims, and COVID-19-related fraud schemes. Upon arrest, it was revealed that Asante had opened 19 bank accounts at over 10 different banks in order to carry out his money laundering scheme. Over 4.5 years from September 2016 to January 2021, these bank accounts received deposits totaling about $36.4 million, which included fraud proceeds from over 80 confirmed victims (US Attorney's Office, 2022). Reports of internet Ponzi schemes and banking fraud have led to accusations of betrayal and bribery (Akelola, 2012). Tax evasion cases have resulted in significant damage to businesses (Amponsah, Isshaq, & Agyapong, 2019). The misappropriation of funds for COVID-19 as revealed by the 2022 Auditor-Generals report also culminates into financial crimes by state officials (Africanews, 2023). The rise of financially motivated cybercrimes, particularly online romance scams, highlights the endemic nature of cyber fraud and financial crimes and the need for more robust policing tactics.

ORGANISED CRIME PERPETRATORS IN GHANA

Ghana's governmental administration is plagued by pervasive corruption, which significantly hampers the country's legislative capacity and processes. Government officials working in security and intelligence services, such as customs, tax, and immigration administrations, as well as certain sections or units of the Ghana Police Service, are involved in aiding drug and gun smuggling, illegal mining, and other forms of organised crime. Politicians are accused of accumulating fortune by participating in drug trafficking. Political parties have allegedly received financial support from individuals involved in the drug trade. Additionally, the country's housing boom is said to have been funded by money obtained from drug-related activities by the elite (GOCI, 2023).

Government officials in collaboration with private individuals engage in crimes against the state. What is most insidious and paradoxical about crimes against the state is the fact that the duly elected and/or appointed officials are the culprits. Insidious because, as guardians of the state agencies, they operate in their interest, and in collaboration with organized criminals in the context of their normal functions. Their strategic positions enable them to pillage and plunder the coffers of the state. Tasked with public projects, these elected and appointed officials invent schemes by which to squander public funds with impunity. Paradoxically, these state officials subvert the power vested in them to collaborate with criminal syndicates to award fraudulent contracts, arrange kickback schemes, inflate prices, overpay for procurements, and other wasteful spending.

Individuals from China and Nigeria, who are foreign criminals, have had a notable impact on several illegal activities in Ghana. Chinese criminals have established themselves in illegal gold mining activities, gaining significant economic control over the market for non-renewable resource crimes in the country (Kumah, 2022). Nigerian criminals exhibit a notable presence in the illicit trade of drugs, particularly in the southern areas surrounding Accra (Targba, 2023). They actively engage in the illegal transportation of methamphetamine. It is suspected that criminal individuals from Mali, Burkina Faso, Ivory Coast, and Niger are currently engaged in illegal activities inside Ghana's gold mining and forest industries (GOCI, 2023).

Secretive criminal organisations in Ghana operate discreetly, however, confrontations between competing factions have sometimes resulted in the apprehension of their leaders and several associates. In Ghana, smaller informal criminal networks are involved in a range of unlawful activities, including drug trafficking, arms trafficking, human trafficking, computer crimes, and vehicle theft. The proliferation of illicit and legitimate networks has become prevalent, rendering it arduous to differentiate between them.

THE ROLE OF LAW AND LAW ENFORCEMENT AGENCIES IN DEALING WITH ORGANISED CRIME IN GHANA

The spate of organised crime and its consequences on the socio-economic development of Ghana has resulted in the introduction of new legislation as well as the strengthening of the already existing ones. Ghana adopted the UNTOC as part of its instruments in the fight against organised crime at the transnational level. The three protocols that underpin the operation of UNTOC are the ones against the illicit manufacturing and trafficking of firearms, their parts and components, and ammunition, the Protocol to Prevent, Suppress, and Punish Trafficking in Persons, especially Women and Children, and the Protocol against the Smuggling of Migrants by Land, Sea, and Air. Ghana has also amended the Narcotics Drugs (Control, Enforcement and Sanctions Law)/PNDC Law 236, Criminal Offences Amendment Acts 2012 (Act 849), Ghana Human Trafficking Act 2005 (Act 694), and the Anti-Money Laundering Act, 2008 (Act 749) as a way of strengthening its fight against organised crime. To protect the integrity of accounting books, records, and financial statements about public revenue and spending, Ghana has put in place an electronic integrated financial management system. This system aims to prevent the falsification of such documents. This is in accordance with the Anti-Money Laundering Act of 2008. As a member of the Intergovernmental Action Group against Money Laundering in West Africa, Ghana has come up with strategies to counter the financing of terrorism and money laundering to deal with the shortcomings of its legislative framework. With the Mutual Assistance Act 2010 (Act 807), the Office of the Special Prosecutor Act 2017 (Act 959), and the Economic and Organized Crime Office Act 2010 (Act 804), properties acquired through criminal means can be confiscated (Duho et al., 2022).

The adoption of the Public Financial Management Act in 2016 and the passage of the Right to Information Bill into law in 2019 (Right to Information Act, Act 989) have aimed to strengthen transparency and public sector accountability. The latter mandates government agencies to make available upon demand specified information requested by members of the public. Individuals who are suspicious of government contracts and share that such contracts could be an act of organised crime by this law can apply for the details of such contracts. Despite the relevance of this Act, the lack of awareness has led to its low usage. The bureaucratic challenges and the limited knowledge of the appeal and internal review mechanisms have created many uncertainties (Media Foundation for West Africa, 2021).

The Ghanaian government has implemented several policies, legislation, and programs to combat human trafficking. The Human Trafficking Act, 2005 (Act 694) provides a legal framework to prevent and suppress trafficking, punish complicit persons, and promote victim protection. The Human Trafficking Secretariat (HTS) aims to provide public sensitization, reduce trafficking instances, and accelerate national development by eliminating trafficking-related issues. Other initiatives include the Anti-Human Trafficking Unit (AHTU) of the Ghana Police Service and the Anti-Human Smuggling and Trafficking in Persons Unit (AHSTIP) of the Ghana Immigration Service. In 2015, the Ghana government and the US signed the Child Protection Compact (CPC) Partnership to strengthen the government's capacity to identify and prosecute child trafficking cases. The Human Trafficking Prohibition Regulations were passed in 2015 to aid the Act's implementation. In 2016, Ghana and La Cote d'Ivoire signed an agreement to combat cross-border child trafficking and child labor. These efforts aim to address the root causes of trafficking and promote inclusive approaches to tackling trafficking in Ghana (Ministry of Gender, Children and Social Protection, 2022).

Ghana established the Economic and Organized Crime Office (EOCO) in 2010 (EOCO ACT 804). The office investigates, prosecutes, recovers crime proceeds, monitors activities, disseminates information, and cooperates with law enforcement and international agencies to uphold the Act. In a report by the Daily Graphic, EOCO retrieved GH¢50 million/$4.2 million from crime proceeds in 2022 and GH¢79 million/$6.6 million by June 2023 (Daily Graphic, 2022/2023). In the same report, EOCO has a five-year strategic plan with an aim to recover and manage proceeds of crime worth GH¢350 million by June 2028. Apart from these proceeds, EOCO has also arrested people alleged to be involved in organised crime. For example, in 2012 EOCO arrested 12 people suspected to be part of the Ghana Youth Employment and Entrepreneurial Development Agency (GYEEDA) corruption scandal. In 2018, it was reported by Graphic Online that Abuga Pele – a former member of Parliament, and a businessman, Philip Akpeena Assibit, have been sentenced to a total of 18 years in prison for their involvement in the GH¢4.1 million GYEEDA scandal (Graphic Online, 2018). However, upon serving 3 years in prison, Abuga Pele was given a presidential pardon (Ghanaweb, 2022). This shows the institutional efforts of EOCO and the undermining role of political agents.

The Narcotics Control Board (NACOB), established in 1990 under PNDC Law 236, s55, is responsible for reducing narcotic drugs in Ghana. It enforces and controls government policies, aiming to use multidisciplinary measures against cultivators, traffickers, peddlers, and users. The Board collaborates with government and non-governmental organizations to address illicit drug trafficking and psychotropic substances. The Board also aims to educate the general public, particularly youth, workers, parents, and law enforcement personnel, on the harmful effects of drug abuse and its dangers. In 2018, NACOB was reported to have seized and burnt marijuana worth GH¢600,000/$50,000 from a group of people engaged in the drug trade (Graphic Online, 2018). The fight against the illegal drug trade is still ongoing.

In terms of coordination, the Board collaborates with various organizations to combat drug abuse, adhering to the United Nations Comprehensive Multi-Disciplinary Outline (CMO), aiming for a common objective. As a way of showing its international commitment to dealing with illegal use and trade in drugs, Ghana is a signatory to the following United Nations Conventions and Protocols on drugs: the 1971 Convention on Psychotropic Substances, the 1961 Single Convention on Narcotic Drugs, the 1988 Convention Against Illicit Trafficking of Narcotic Drugs and Psychotropic Substances, and the 1972 Protocol Amending the 1961 Single Convention. NACOB has cooperated with international agencies such as the International Narcotics Control Board, the United Nations Development Program, and the World Customs Organization in its quest to curb the drug menace. At the local level, NACOB coordinates with law enforcement and control organisations such as the National Investigation Bureau, Ghana Immigration Service, Defence Intelligence, National Security Council, Ghana Police Service, and Ghana Airport Company Ltd. To this end, NACOB is best seen as a coalition of all the governmental agencies to combat the illicit drug problem in Ghana (Ministry of Defence, n.d.).

The Ghana Police Service through its Narcotic Unit of the Criminal Investigation Department is principally in charge of looking into drug trafficking offences in Ghana.

It is also in charge of managing cases involving both domestic and foreign drug trafficking. From time to time, the team conducts operations in Ghana to combat drug misuse and trafficking. In addition, it works with other national security agencies, the Narcotics Control Board of Ghana, and the Drug Enforcement Authority (DEA) of the United States of America to apprehend, prosecute, and even extradite drug traffickers who are on the run. The Narcotics Unit is an essential component of Ghanaian law enforcement, much like other sections within the Criminal Investigations Department of the Ghana Police Service. In 2011, the US embassy in Ghana collaborated with the unit to apprehend notorious drug dealers, Edward McCauley, Frank Ehiobu, Fred Oppong Brobbey, and Matilda Antwi, who were extradited to the US and sentenced to various prison terms. Also, Mustaapha Issaka, a fugitive drug dealer, was apprehended in Accra on June 18, 2012, by the Unit, and extradited to the US, where he was sentenced to a term of imprisonment. The statistics available reveal that, from January to June 2023, the Unit received 65 cases involving 77 suspects. Out of the 65 cases, 55 cases involving 64 suspects have been taken to court with the remaining 10 involving 13 suspects under investigation. Out of the 55 taken to court, 20 suspects associated with 20 cases have been convicted with the remaining cases still on trial. The cases concern narcotic drugs such as cocaine (13,2688g), heroin (3,0616g), and cannabis (35,073.1536g) (Ghana Police Service, n.d.).

The Cyber Crime Unit of the Ghana Police plays a crucial role in detecting and investigating organised crimes whereby digital device(s), or the internet space are used. As earlier stated, Ghana lost $11,000,000 and $19,800,000 to cyber fraud and other criminal activities in 2019 and 2020 respectively. According to the Ghanaian Times (2021), the Cyber Crime Unit arrested 241 fraudsters, recovered six cars, $101,000, and three plots of land bought with proceeds of fraud. The data shows that the Unit is instrumental in fighting organised crime, however, there is much-needed improvement.

The Ghana Police Service has also been instrumental in dealing with human trafficking. On March 11, 2008, the Ghana Police Service established the Anti-Human Trafficking Unit (AHTU), which operates under the jurisdiction of the Criminal Investigation Department (CID). The Unit collaborates with stakeholders to prevent human trafficking, investigates and prosecutes offenders under the Human Trafficking Act, 2005 (Act 694), and collaborates with various units such as Interpol/Ghana and the Domestic Violence and Victims Support Units (DOVVSU) to provide prompt responses to cases and collect information for the National Crime Statistic Database. As part of the achievement of the AHTU, in 2009, seven Chinese nationals were arrested for trafficking 14 Chinese individuals for sexual exploitation. They were found guilty and sentenced to 5-10 years each. These Chinese nationals have since been repatriated to China. A case is also reported of the 10-year sentence of Elizabeth Inaba Love for trafficking 8 victims from Nigeria to Ghana for prostitution in 2011. In a very recent case in 2018, the Unit arrested two persons by the name Emmanuel Obeng Sintim and Angelina Danso for trafficking their victim to Kuwait without proper documentation. They were sentenced to 7 years each. Also, Ella Peter, a 20-year-old individual, was found guilty by an Accra Circuit Court on July 3rd, 2018 for the acts of recruiting and trafficking two victims from Nigeria to Ghana to engage in prostitution. All these cases show how the unit has responded to human trafficking over the period (Ghana Police Service, n.d.).

Aside from the roles played by the state actors, non-state actors such as Civil Society Organisations (CSOs) also play a crucial role in community awareness against transnational crime (Phale, 2021). Ghana Integrity Initiative (GII) of Transparency International, for example, awakens public awareness of corruption through its annual ranking of state institutions. The CSOs also engage governments to enforce extant laws (Anheier, Lang, & Toepler, 2019). The Revenue Administration (Amendment) Act and the Whistleblower Act are examples of laws that anti-corruption agencies keep putting pressure on the government to enforce.

In recent times, some media outlets in Ghana, especially the ones engaged in investigative journalism, have taken center stage in exposing organised crime. In an article published by the New Crusading Guide on February 25, 2010, the renowned journalist Anas Aremeyaw Anas uncovered fraud and bribery at the Tema Port that involved personnel from the Customs, Exercise, and Preventive Service (CEPS). Also, in 2012, the same journalist uncovered massive rot leading to the loss of millions of Ghana Cedis at the Electricity Company of Ghana. Manasseh Azure Awuni's investigation exposed how GYEEDA colluded with private persons to steal money from the state through fraudulent contracts. In 2014, the Deputy Attorney General announced the retrieval of GHc14.5 million from the GYEEDA contractors. Some actors in this corrupt contract have since been sentenced to serve a term of imprisonment.

CHALLENGES ASSOCIATED WITH LAW ENFORCEMENT AGAINST ORGANISED CRIME

Ghana has made progress in addressing governance malfeasance but lacks the political determination to combat organized crime and illegal proceeds (Abdulai, 2009). The bribery act of affluent criminal syndicates undermines collaboration efforts between authorities. Efforts to address human trafficking and oversee the logging industry are hindered by corruption in the police service, lack of government support, resource allocation, and public influence (Singh, 2022).

Ghana is grappling with widespread corruption in government agencies. There are even allegations of embezzlement of COVID-19 funds by the Ministry of

Health and the Ministry of Information (Africanews, 2023; Ghanaian Times, 2023). Despite a robust legal framework, enforcement is challenging, and anti-corruption organizations have insufficient resources to fight corruption (Badet et al., 2016). Political parties are mandated to provide financial statements, yet frequently neglect to fulfill this obligation, resulting in a feeling of obscurity and elevated degrees of corruption among the general populace (GOCI, 2023).

The insurmountable obstacle confronting the criminal justice system is the lack of specialized staff with the technical know-how to tackle information technology-related crimes. Unwittingly, the already overcapacity prisons have become boot camps for inmates with the technical know-how to share their technology and social media-based crimes. With easy access to mobile phones, inmates liaise with collaborators outside the prison to scam innocent citizens of their money – romance scam (Yin, 2018; 2020; 2021; 2021).

The prevalence of police corruption is extensive, leading to the erosion of public trust. The police force struggles with personnel shortages (Amoah, 2020; Oppong, 2010) as well as inadequate logistics (Hoggett et al., 2019). The police-to-population ratio falls short of the UN's recommended level. Despite efforts by the government to enhance anti-money laundering legislation, deficiencies in implementation persist. The industries most commonly associated with money laundering are illicit drug trade, arms proliferation, human trafficking, environmental destruction, fraud, corruption, and romantic schemes. A substantial proportion of the populace lacks access to formal financial services in light of the economic regulatory environment, which offers both prospects and obstacles. Corrupt practices and a substantial informal economy impede the government's endeavours to foster private sector development.

CONCLUSION

This chapter consolidates the many elements of organised crime in Ghana and examines the function of law and law enforcement authorities. It is argued that organized crime in Ghana undermines the emerging fragile democratic institutions in the country. Despite Ghana's democratic credentials, certain elected and/or appointed officials who have sworn to uphold the Constitution impartially have been largely influenced by criminal syndicates, prioritizing their interests at the expense of the citizens. Organised crime is a complex continuing criminal enterprise that is based on rational planning to engage in criminal activities for profit. Ghana is not immune to organised crime as the country serves as a transit point for human trafficking, illegal trade, and drug deals. Cyber and financial crimes are also common with state officials' involvement. The actors of organised crime as shown are government officials in sectors such as custom officers, Ghana Revenue Authority, Ghana

Immigration Service, Ghana Police Service, political parties, and private individuals from within and outside the jurisdiction of Ghana.

Ghana has introduced various legislation to deal with organised crime. Such legislation includes but is not limited to the following: Narcotics Drugs (Control, Enforcement and Sanctions Law)/PNDC Law 236; Criminal Offences Amendment Acts 2012 (Act 849); Ghana Human Trafficking Act 2005 (Act 694); the Anti-Money Laundering Act, 2008 (Act 749); Public Financial Management Act in 2016; and the Right to Information Act, 2019 (Act 989). The complementary efforts of state agencies in the implementation of these laws are commendable, however, not without challenges. The influence of affluent organized criminal syndicates on some law enforcement agencies has led to weak collaboration between state agencies. The undermining role of Politicians in power against the efforts of law enforcement agencies fighting organised crime is a huge challenge. This presents a paradox of power subversion by state officials to aid and abet criminal syndicates. Despite these challenges, the role of law and law enforcement institutions cannot be understated. The role of non-state actors such as Civil Society Organizations, whistleblowers, and investigative journalists' persistence in exposing crimes by politicians is noteworthy. The use of sophisticated technology to track down actors of organised crime is crucial. Political preparedness, rapid response by responsible state agencies, good socio-economic conditions, and individual alertness are warranted for a successful fight against organised crime.

REFERENCES

Abdulai, A. G. (2009). Political will in combating corruption in developing and transition economies: A comparative study of Singapore, Hong Kong and Ghana. *Journal of Financial Crime*, *16*(4), 387–417. doi:10.1108/13590790910993753

Adam, I., & Adongo, C. A. (2016). Do backpackers suffer crime? An empirical investigation of crime perpetrated against backpackers in Ghana. *Journal of Hospitality and Tourism Management*, *27*, 60–67. doi:10.1016/j.jhtm.2016.03.003

ADF. (2023). *Illegal Fish Dumping by Chinese Trawlers Rising in Ghana*. ADF. https://adf-magazine.com/2023/03/illegal-fish-dumping-by-chinese-trawlers-rising-in-ghana/#:~:text=Chinese%20trawlers%20have%20committed%20acts,in%20the%20past%20two%20decades

Adler, F., Mueller, G. O. W., & Laufer, W. S. (2013). Criminology, (8th Edition). New York.

Africanews. (2023). Ghana Auditor General reveals violations in use of Covid 19 funds. *Africa News*. https://www.africanews.com/2023/01/23/ghana-auditor-general-reveals-violations-in-use-of-covid-19-funds//

Agariga, F., Abugre, S., & Appiah, M. (2021). Spatio-temporal changes in land use and forest cover in the Asutifi North District of Ahafo Region of Ghana,(1986–2020). *Environmental Challenges*, *5*, 100209. doi:10.1016/j.envc.2021.100209

Agboli, J. M. (2023). Implications of legalisation of cannabis cultivation in Ghana: A critical review. *Drugs, Habits and Social Policy*. doi:10.1108/DHS-06-2023-0023

Agyapong, D., Asiamah, M., & Addo-Danquah, M. (2016). Organised Crime, Foreing Direct Investment and Economic Growth in Ghana. *British Journal of Economics. Management & Trade*, *15*(4), 1–12.

Akelola, S. (2012). *Fraud in the banking industry: A case study of Kenya*. Nottingham Trent University.

Albanese, J. S. (2021). Organized crime as financial crime: The nature of organized crime as reflected in prosecutions and research. *Victims & Offenders*, *16*(3), 431–443. doi:10.1080/15564886.2020.1823543

Albanese, J. S. (2023). Development and Surges of Organized Crime: An Application of Enterprise Theory. In *Organized Crime in the 21st Century: Motivations, Opportunities, and Constraints* (pp. 11–24). Springer International Publishing. doi:10.1007/978-3-031-21576-6_2

Amoah, R. (2020). *Public Perceptions of Human Rights Abuses of the Ghana Police Service in the Jomoro Municipality* [Doctoral dissertation, University of Cape Coast].

Amponsah, S., Isshaq, Z., & Agyapong, D. (2019). Determinants of tax stamp evasion in rural districts in Ghana: A case of Twifu Atti-Morkwa and Hemang lower Denkyira districts. *International Journal of Law and Management*, *61*(1), 73–90. doi:10.1108/IJLMA-08-2017-0190

Anheier, H. K., Lang, M., & Toepler, S. (2019). Civil society in times of change: Shrinking, changing and expanding spaces and the need for new regulatory approaches. *Economics*, *13*(1), 20190008. doi:10.5018/economics-ejournal.ja.2019-8

Aning, K. (2007). Are there emerging West African criminal networks? The case of Ghana. *Global Crime*, *8*(3), 193–212. doi:10.1080/17440570701507729

Appiahene-Gyamfi, J. (2003). Urban crime trends and patterns in Ghana: The case of Accra. *Journal of Criminal Justice*, *31*(1), 13–23. doi:10.1016/S0047-2352(02)00196-4

Appiahene-Gyamfi, J. (2021). Policing in Ghana. *Global Perspectives in Policing and Law Enforcement, 1*.

Arskova, J., & Allum, F. (2014). Introduction: Women and transnational organized crime. *Trends in Organized Crime, 17*(1-2), 1–15. doi:10.1007/s12117-014-9223-y

Atampugre, G., Mensah, E., Boateng, E., Mabhaudhi, T., & Cofie, O. O. (2022). *Situational analysis of a social-ecological landscape in the Ahafo Ano Southwest District of Ghana*. Research Gate.

Atta-Asamoah, A. (2014). *Transnational security challenges and statehood in Africa: A case study of drug trafficking in Ghana*. Research Gate.

AU. (2014). *Comprehensive Assessment of Drug Trafficking and Organised Crime in West and Central Africa*. AU. https://au.int/sites/default/files/documents/30220-doc-organized_crime_in_west_and_central_africa_-_july_2014_-_abridged_summary_english.pdf

Azure, J. F. (2009). *The customs excise and preventive service and cross border crimes management: a case study of the eastern frontier of Ghana* [Doctoral dissertation, Kwame Nkrumah University of Science and Technology].

Badet, G., Damiba, L., Engueléguélé, S. B., Gaima, E., Iwuamadi, C. K., Ndiaye, S., & Williams, S. (2016). *Effectiveness of anti-corruption agencies in West Africa*. Open Society Foundations.

Bello, P. O., & Olutola, A. A. (2020). The conundrum of human trafficking in Africa. *Modern slavery and human trafficking*, 15-27.

Boakye, J. (2020). Enforcement of logging regulations in Ghana: Perspectives of frontline regulatory officers. *Forest Policy and Economics, 115*, 102138. doi:10.1016/j.forpol.2020.102138

Bonsu, P. (2011). *The effect of the distribution of illicit drugs on a transit country-a case study of Ghana* [Master's thesis, Institutt for statsvitenskap].

Broadhurst, R. (2017). Cybercrime: Thieves, Swindlers, Bandits, and Privateers in Cyberspace. In The Oxford Handbook of Cyber Security. Oxford Press.

Brown, D. E. (2013). *The challenge of drug trafficking to democratic governance and human security in West Africa* (Vol. 8). Army War College Press.

Calderoni, F., Comunale, T., Campedelli, G. M., Marchesi, M., Manzi, D., & Frualdo, N. (2022). Organized crime groups: A systematic review of individual-level risk factors related to recruitment. *Campbell Systematic Reviews*, *18*(1), e1218. doi:10.1002/cl2.1218 PMID:36913220

Casas-Zamora, K. (Ed.). (2013). *Dangerous liaisons: Organized crime and political finance in Latin America and beyond*. Brookings Institution Press.

Catino, M. (2020). Italian organized crime since 1950. *Crime and Justice*, *49*(1), 69–140. doi:10.1086/707319

Chouvy, P. A. (2019). Cannabis cultivation in the world: Heritages, trends and challenges. *EchoGéo*, (48), 48. doi:10.4000/echogeo.17591

Daily Statesman. (2023). Criminal gold syndicate busted over $2.7m deal. *Daily Statesman*. https://dailystatesman.com.gh/criminal-gold-syndicate-busted-over-2-7m-deal/

Duho, K. C. T., Abankwah, S. A., Mugo, G. K., Atampuri, M., Duho, V. S., & Adjei-Mensah, P. (2022). Impact of Covid-19 on Organised Crime in Ghana and Insights for a Post-Pandemic Context. *Dataking Policy Brief, 9*.

Duijn, P. A., Kashirin, V., & Sloot, P. M. (2014). The relative ineffectiveness of criminal network disruption. *Scientific Reports*, *4*(1), 4238. doi:10.1038/srep04238 PMID:24577374

Dukku, A., & Yunusa, A. (2022). Trafficking of Illicit Drugs in the West African Region: Factors, Implications and Solutions. *Gusau Journal of Sociology, 3*(2).

Dziwornu, M. G. (2021). Crime drop in Ghana? Some insights from crime patterns and trends. *Crime Prevention and Community Safety*, *23*(4), 433–449. doi:10.1057/s41300-021-00130-0

Ellis, S. (2016). *This present darkness: A history of Nigerian organized crime*. Oxford University Press.

Enact Observer. (n.d.). *Organised crime is infecting African and global supply chains*. Enact Observer. https://enactafrica.org/enact-observer/organised-crime-is-infecting-african-and-global-supply-chains on 16/01/2024

Ennin, D., & Mensah, R. O. (2019). Cybercrime in Ghana and the Reaction of the Law. *JL Pol'y & Globalization*, *84*, 36.

Finckenauer, J. O. (2005). Problems of definition: What is organized crime? *Trends in Organized Crime*, *8*(3), 63–83. doi:10.1007/s12117-005-1038-4

Ghana Police Service. (n.d.). *Anti-Human Trafficking Unit.* Ghana Police Service. https://www.police.gov.gh/anti-human-trafficking-unit---ahtu.html on 29/12/2023.

Ghana Police Service. (n.d.). *drug law enforcement unit – narcotics.* Ghana Police Service. https://police.gov.gh/en/index.php/drug-law-enforcement-unit-narcotics/#:~:text=The%20Narcotics%20Unit%20is%20a,of%20the%20Ghana%20Police%20Service

Ghanaian Times. (2021). Ghana loses $19.8m through fraudulent activities. *Ghanaian Times.* https://www.ghanaiantimes.com.gh/ghana-loses-19-8m-through-fraudulent-activities/

Ghanaian Times. (2023). Prosecute persons culpable of embezzling COVID-19 funds – SEND Ghana. *Ghanaian Times.* https://www.ghanaiantimes.com.gh/prosecute-persons-culpable-of-embezzling-covid-19-funds-send-ghana/

Ghanaweb. (2022). *Abuga Pele speaks about jail time and how he was denied opportunity to confront accusers.* Ghanaweb. https://www.ghanaweb.com/GhanaHomePage/NewsArchive/Abuga-Pele-speaks-about-jail-time-and-how-he-was-denied-opportunity-to-confront-accusers-1587737 on 05/01/2024

Ghanaweb. (2023). Police arrest 12 members of organised crime syndicate involved in carjacking, robbery and murder. *GhanaWeb.* https://www.ghanaweb.com/GhanaHomePage/NewsArchive/Police-arrest-12-members-of-organised-crime-syndicate-involved-in-carjacking-robbery-and-murder-1706498 on 07/01/2024

Global Organised Crime Index. (2023). *Ghana.* GOCI. https://ocindex.net/country/ghana on 28/12/2023

Graphic Online. (2018). NACOB sets wee and khat worth GH¢600,000 on fire. *Graphic.* https://www.graphic.com.gh/news/general-news/nacob-partners-destroy-seized-narcotics.html

Hodal, K. (2019). Illegal fishing by foreign trawlers costs Ghana $50m a year, researchers say. *The Guardian.* https://www.theguardian.com/environment/2019/jun/17/illegal-fishing-by-foreign-trawlers-costs-ghana-50-million-dollars-a-year-researchers-say on 18/01/2024

Hoggett, J., Redford, P., Toher, D., & White, P. (2019). Challenges for Police Leadership: Identity, Experience, Legitimacy, and Direct Entry. *Journal of Police and Criminal Psychology, 34*(2), 145–155. doi:10.1007/s11896-018-9264-2

Ibanga, D. A. (2017). *Patterns, trends, and issues of illicit wildlife hunting and trade: Analysis based on African environmental ethics.*

Jonathan, O. E., Olusola, A. J., Bernadin, T. C. A., & Inoussa, T. M. (2021). Impacts of crime on socio-economic development. *Mediterranean Journal of Social Sciences, 12*(5), 71. doi:10.36941/mjss-2021-0045

Kansanga, M. M., Dinko, D. H., Nyantakyi-Frimpong, H., Arku, G., & Luginaah, I. (2021). Scalar politics and black markets: The political ecology of illegal rosewood logging in Ghana. *Geoforum, 119*, 83–93. doi:10.1016/j.geoforum.2020.12.020

Kar, D., & Spanjers, J. (2017). Transnational crime and the developing world. *Global Financial Integrity*, 53-59.

Kennedy, M. (2016). F*ake U.S. Embassy In Ghana Operated For A Decade, State Department Says*. NPR. https://www.npr.org/sections/thetwo-way/2016/12/05/504426012/state-department-says-fake-u-s-embassy-in-ghana-operated-for-a-decade on 05/01/2024

Kennert, M., & Eligh, J. (2019). *A militarized political weapon: The Philippines' war on drugs*. GI-TOC.

Killingray, D. (1986). The maintenance of law and order in British colonial Africa. *African Affairs, 85*(340), 411–437. doi:10.1093/oxfordjournals.afraf.a097799

Kumah, R. K. (2022). *Determinants and Implications of Chinese Involvement in Informal Artisanal and Small-scale Gold Mining in Ghana: Perspectives from the Grassroots* [Doctoral dissertation, Queen's University (Canada)].

Livey, F. R. (2017). *International legal framework for combating transnational organised crime* [Doctoral dissertation, University of Glasgow].

Lucas, F. O. (2007). Criminal organizations and Judiciary Power. *Estudos Avançados, 21*, 107–117. doi:10.1590/S0103-40142007000300008

Merem, E. C., Twumasi, Y., Wesley, J., Isokpehi, P., Fageir, S., Crisler, M., & Nwagboso, E. (2018). Assessing the menace of illegal wildlife trade in the sub-Saharan African region. *Advancements in Life Sciences, 8*(1), 1–25. doi:10.5923/j.als.20180801.01

Ministry of Defence. (n.d.). *Narcotics Control Commission*. Ministry of Defense. https://www.mint.gov.gh/agencies/narcotic-control-board/ on 29/12/2023.

Ministry of Gender, Children, and Social Protection. (2022). *National Plan of Action for the Elimination of Human Trafficking in Ghana, 2017-2021*. Ministry of Gender, Children, and Social Protection. https://www.unicef.org/ghana/media/1851/file/National%20Plan%20of%20Action%20for%20the%20Elimination%20of%20Human%20Trafficking%20in%20Ghana.pdf

Miraglia, P., Ochoa, R., & Briscoe, I. (2012). *Transnational organised crime and fragile states.*

Mohammed, M. A. L. L. A. M. (2022). Can Corruption and Organized Crime Affect Economic Growth in the ECOWAS Region? *Journal of Monetary Economics, 17*(3), 411–436.

Obeng, A. S., & Yin, E. T. (2021). If I Die I Lose Everything: Understanding Poverty from the Perspective of Ankaful Residents in Ghana. *Asian Research Journal of Arts & Social Sciences, 15*(3), 32–44. doi:10.9734/arjass/2021/v15i330259

Ogunniyi, O. J., & Akpu, J. O. (2019). The Challenge of Drug Trafficking to Democratic Governance and Human Security in West Africa. *Africa Development. Afrique et Developpement, 44*(4), 29–50.

Okyere, S. (2017). 'Shock and Awe': A critique of the Ghana-centric child trafficking discourse. *Anti-Trafficking Review*, (9), 92–105. doi:10.14197/atr.20121797

Oliveira, A. P. (2023). *Organised crime is a human rights issue*. Global Initiative. https://globalinitiative.net/wp-content/uploads/2023/10/Ana-Paula-Oliveira-Four-reasons-why-organized-crime-is-a-human-rights-issue-GI-TOC-October-2023.pdf on 16/01/2024.

Overdevest, C., & Zeitlin, J. (2018). Experimentalism in transnational forest governance: Implementing European Union forest law enforcement, governance and trade (FLEGT) voluntary partnership agreements in Indonesia and Ghana. *Regulation & Governance, 12*(1), 64–87. doi:10.1111/rego.12180

Owusu, G., Oteng-Ababio, M., Owusu, A. Y., & Wrigley-Asante, C. (2016). Can poor neighbourhoods be correlated with crime? Evidence from urban Ghana. *Ghana Journal of Geography, 8*(1), 11–31.

Peprah, K. (2022). Drivers of Deforestation, Forest Degradation, and Management Responses in Ghana. In *Land Degradation Neutrality: Achieving SDG 15 by Forest Management* (pp. 61–79). Springer Nature Singapore. doi:10.1007/978-981-19-5478-8_4

Phale, M. O., & Kgosiemang, P. K. (2021). *Governance at a Glance: Botswana's APRM Experience*. Security Studies Collection.

Robertson, P. (2022). Philippines undercounts recent 'drug war' deaths. *Human Rights Watch*. https:// www.hrw.org/news/2022/11/17/philippines-undercounts-recent-drug-war-deaths on 17/01/2024

Sandor, A. (2016). *Assemblages of intervention: Politics, security, and drug trafficking in West Africa* [Doctoral dissertation, Université d'Ottawa/University of Ottawa].

Schultze-Kraft, M. (2014). *Getting real about an illicit 'external stressor': Transnational cocaine trafficking through West Africa* (IDS Evidence Report 72). Brighton: IDS. http://opendocs.ids.ac.uk/opendocs/handle/123456789/3966

Schultze-Kraft, M. (2016). *Organised crime, violence and development: Topic guide*. GSDRC, University of Birmingham.

Siegel, D. (2014). Women in transnational organized crime. *Trends in Organized Crime*, *17*(1), 52–65. doi:10.1007/s12117-013-9206-4

Siegel, L. J. (2001). Criminology: theories, patterns, and typologies (7th edition.) Wadsworth/Thomson Learning.

Singh, D. (2022). The Causes of Police Corruption and Working towards Prevention in Conflict-Stricken States. *Laws*, *11*(5), 69. doi:10.3390/laws11050069

Small Arms Survey. (2023). *Out of Control: The Trafficking of Improvised Explosive Device Components and Commercial Explosives in West Africa*. Small Arm Survey. https://www.smallarmssurvey.org/sites/default/files/resources/SAS-Report-24-IEDs-WEB.pdf

Sotande, E. O. (2016). *Transnational organised crime and illicit financial flows: Nigeria, West Africa and the global North* [Doctoral dissertation, University of Leeds].

Targba, A. (2023). Illegal Transnational Migration And Illicit Drug Trafficking In Nigeria. *Wukari International Studies Journal*, *7*(3), 236–249.

UN. (2023). *Our Common Agenda Policy Brief 9: A new agenda for peace*. UN. https://www.un.org/sites/un2.un.org/files/ our-common-agenda-policy-brief-new-agenda-for-peace-en.pdf on 17/01/2024.

UNODC. (2019). Global study on homicide: Executive summary, Vienna. UNODC.

US Attorney's Office. (2022). *Top Money Launderer For Ghana-Based Criminal Enterprise Sentenced To Nine Years.* USAO. https://www.justice.gov/usao-sdny/pr/top-money-launderer-ghana-based-criminal-enterprise-sentenced-nine-years on 07/01/2024

Wannenburg, G. (2005). Organised Crime in West Africa. *African Security Review*, *14*(4), 5–16. doi:10.1080/10246029.2005.9627583

Wayo, A. (2023). *The Role of Forensic Accounting in Combating Money Laundering in Ghana* [Doctoral dissertation, Northcentral University].

Williams, P. (2009). Illicit markets, weak states and violence: Iraq and Mexico. *Crime, Law, and Social Change*, *52*(3), 323–336. doi:10.1007/s10611-009-9194-0

Wright, A. (2013). *Organised crime*. Routledge. doi:10.4324/9781843926450

Yeebo, Y. (2017). The true story of the fake US embassy in Ghana. *The Guardian.* https://www.theguardian.com/world/2017/nov/28/the-true-story-of-the-fake-us-embassy-in-ghana on 05/01/2024

Yeh, S. S. (2022). *The End of Corruption and Impunity*. Rowman & Littlefield.

Yin, E. T. (2018). *Religion as an organizing principle in Ankaful maximum security prison, Ghana* [Doctoral dissertation, University of Cape Coast].

Yin, E. T. (2020). Religion, Rehabilitation, and Reintegration of Prison Inmates into Mainstream Society. Handbook of research on trends and issues in crime prevention, rehabilitation, and victim support, 398-414. IGI Global. doi:10.4018/978-1-7998-1286-9.ch023

Yin, E. T., Atupare, P. A., Kofie, N., Owusu, L. P., & Botchway, T. P. (2021). Rights and religious belief in maintaining prison social order. *UCC Faculty of Law Journal*, *1*(1), 1–16. doi:10.47963/ucclj.v1i1.217

Yin, E. T., Boateng, W., & Kofie, N. (2022). Family acceptance, economic situation, and faith community: The lived experiences of ex-convicts in Ghana. *Social Sciences & Humanities Open*, *5*(1), 100240. doi:10.1016/j.ssaho.2021.100240

Yin, E. T., & Kofie, N. (2021). The informal prison economy in Ghana: Patterns, exchanges, and institutional contradictions. *Cogent Social Sciences*, *7*(1), 2004673. doi:10.1080/23311886.2021.2004673

Yin, E. T., & Seiwoh, B. M. (2021). Costs and delays in accessing justice: A comparative analysis of Ghana and Sierra Leone. In Advancing Civil Justice Reform and Conflict Resolution in Africa and Asia: Comparative Analyses and Case Studies (pp. 112-139). IGI Global. doi:10.4018/978-1-7998-7898-8.ch007

APPENDIX: STATUTES

Anti-Money Laundering Act, 2008 (Act 749)
Criminal Offences Amendment Acts 2012 (Act 849)
Economic and Organized Crime Office Act 2010 (Act 804)
Ghana Human Trafficking Act 2005 (Act 694)
Narcotics Drugs (Control, Enforcement and Sanctions Law)/PNDC Law 236
Office of the Special Prosecutor Act 2017 (Act 959)

Chapter 6
Cyber Child Pornography:
A Socio-Legal Review

Baidyanath Mukherjee
https://orcid.org/0000-0002-1165-3432
AURO University, India

Arun Kumar Singh
Greater Noida College of Law, India

ABSTRACT

Child pornography on the internet is becoming a more noticeable concern in today's culture. Child pornographers have found an easy arena for spreading terrifying photographs of children being sexually assaulted with the development in home personal computer (PC) usage and more widely available access to the world wide web over the last decade. Detecting and prosecuting cyber child pornographers has also become a difficult task for police and attorneys throughout the world, with a high failure rate of putting culprits behind bars. Law enforcement agents' existing approaches for combating online child pornography might be regarded as archaic and ineffective. In this chapter, the authors will look at the key social and legal difficulties that people, legislators, and police officers face when it comes to online child pornography. This chapter will further focus on providing a solution and suggest innovative approaches to combat online child pornography.

DOI: 10.4018/979-8-3693-0327-6.ch006

INTRODUCTION

The absence of tangible borders on the Internet has heightened the societal apprehension surrounding child pornography, transcending geographical and legal boundaries. Understandably, discussions on this subject are frequently sidestepped in both social and academic spheres, given the distressing ordeals that young victims endure, often enduring prolonged suffering without intervention. A recent case reported by the Pimpri Chinchwad police exemplifies this issue, involving the filing of charges against seven internet users for uploading child pornography content online (Express News Service, 2022). Moreover, the state of Kerala has witnessed a sharp rise in the number of child pornography cases in the year 2022. According to the recently released report, in 2022, there were a total of 1,823 cases of children falling victim to cybercrimes, indicating a 32 per cent rise compared to the previous year's figure of 1,376. The cybercrimes against children encompassed various types, such as cyber pornography involving the hosting or publication of explicit materials featuring minors (1,171 cases), cyberstalking or bullying (158 cases), and other cybercrimes targeting children (416 cases)(Bose, 2023).

There is undeniable evidence that the Internet has led to an unprecedented surge in the development of child pornography, with one contributing factor being the significant reduction of entry barriers due to advancements in technology. The increased accessibility and user-friendliness of advanced editing software and cameras have simplified the creation and distribution of child pornography. In Indian Law, the term "Child Pornography" is explicitly defined under the Protection of Children from Sexual Offences Act. According to Section 2(da) of the Act, Child Pornography is characterized as a visual display depicting explicit sexual activity involving a child. (*The Protection of Children from Sexual Offences Act 2012*, 2012). It may be a video or a computer-generated picture that cannot be distinguished from a real child. It includes any image that depicts a youngster participating in such activities, whether generated, adapted, or modified. However, the internet has given child porn a clean slate, due to the ease of transmission from one paedophile to many other paedophiles and from one nation to many other nations. According to psychiatrists Kimberly Young and Alvin Cooper, two specialists who have examined online sexual behaviour, cybersex (whether it includes minors or not) is a kind of psychopathology and a manifestation of neurotic, obsessive behaviour. No doubt, it is a form of addiction. Cyber child pornography, in particular, is viewed as a sort of socio- and psychopathology, as an aspect of unhealthy power relations in which an adult exploits kids for his pleasures. Adults having unhealthy sexual desires for kids frequently initiate these acts of real-world abuse. The majority of cyber-supported sexual fantasy fulfilment with kids is found in ritualised rituals and fixations, typically of a sadistic kind (Uebel, 1999).

The constantly altering perspective of cyber technology has kept law enforcement authorities on edge, leaving them wrestling with laws riddled with gaps and plagued with inadequacy. The spread of obscene materials and ideas is one of cyberspace's character flaws. With the continued proliferation of literally hundreds of adult-oriented sexually explicit online sites, there has been concern and controversy over censorship and the legal concerns that accompany it. Governments and courts have always found it difficult to classify or differentiate illegal obscene or indecent items. The transmission of information deemed detrimental to children has traditionally been frowned upon by courts.

LITERATURE REVIEW

The scholarly exploration of cyber child pornography has been extensively addressed in various works, among which the study "Online Child Pornography: A Cultural Focus Literature Review" by María Inés Lovelle, Montserrat Yepes-Baldó, Marina Romeo, And Miguel Ángel Soria stands out(Lovelle et al., 2017). This work critically examines the socio-cultural and legal facets of online child pornography. Despite the global acknowledgement of child pornography as a criminal act, the review identifies a significant research gap—specifically, the limited attention given to cultural aspects within the scientific approach to this issue. The authors underscore the imperative to explore the cultural impact of cyber child pornography and stress the importance of incorporating the cultural dimension in the assessment of risk factors in aggressors. It is revealed that the scientific approach often focuses on a few cultural variables, such as country of birth or race, with the authors advocating for a broader consideration of cultural differences. They suggest that such differences can significantly influence the assessment of risk factors and that integrating the cultural dimension into law enforcement tasks could enhance predictions. This comprehensive review emphasizes the urgent need for further research into the cultural aspects of cyber child pornography, aiming to inform more effective socio-legal interventions and policies. Building on this foundation, the article "Role of Prohibitory Legislation in Preventing Online Sexual Abuse of Children: A Critical Socio-Legal" by Aswathy Prakash G (Prakash, 2018) provides a critical examination of the legal framework and public awareness surrounding online sexual abuse of children. While emphasizing the necessity for a robust legal framework and increased awareness to combat online sexual abuse, the paper identifies research gaps that merit further exploration. Specifically, it could delve deeper into the challenges faced in the implementation of prohibitory legislation and explore the evolving technological aspects of online threats to children. Additionally, the incorporation of case studies or real-life examples could lend a practical dimension to the socio-legal analysis, providing valuable insights for addressing the issue of cyber child pornography. Expanding the perspective to a regional context, the paper "Cybercrime in ASEAN: Anti-Child Pornography Legislation" by Robert Brian Smith offers a comprehensive analysis of anti-child pornography legislation in ASEAN countries(Smith, 2020). The paper emphasizes the importance of cooperation and harmonization of laws in combating cybercrime, particularly regarding the extraterritorial reach of legislation and the necessity for a coordinated response to address child pornography effectively. However, a notable research gap is identified as the paper does not delve into the implementation and enforcement of these laws. Additionally, it falls short in addressing the issue of cross-border cooperation and coordination in tackling cybercrime, crucial considerations in a region where countries possess different legal systems and procedures. In the systematic review titled "Child Sexual Abuse and the Internet" by Sana Ali, Hiba Abou Haykal, and Enaam Youssef Mohammed Youssef, a comprehensive overview of existing literature on online child sexual abuse is provided(Ali et al., 2023). While emphasizing the growing concern about this issue and the role of digital platforms in facilitating such abuse, the review reveals research gaps. It primarily focuses on the immediate impact on children's well-being, leaving unexplored the long-term effects on their mental health and social development. Moreover, a detailed analysis of the legal and policy frameworks governing online child sexual abuse is lacking, presenting an area for future research—potentially contributing valuable insights to your socio-legal review. Lastly, the article "Children at Risk: Legal and Societal Perceptions of the Potential Threat that the Possession of Child Pornography Poses to Society" by Suzanne Ost provides a comprehensive analysis of the legal and societal perceptions of child pornography(Ost, 2002). While examining reactions from the media, the public, law enforcement agencies, and politicians to the threat posed by child pornography, the article omits an exploration into the psychological and emotional harm experienced by child pornography victims. Additionally, a detailed analysis of the effectiveness of current legal and societal responses is absent. While questioning the legality of possessing child pornography, the article lacks a discussion on alternative approaches to addressing this issue. Overall, the existing literature provides a robust foundation for the research, and by examine diverse forms of cyber child abuse, comprehend the significance of cyber child pornography, juxtapose legislative frameworks in India and the USA, and propose innovative strategies to combat online child pornography, this article contributes significantly to the ongoing discourse on cyber child pornography from a socio-legal perspective.

OBJECTIVES FOR RESEARCH

- Conduct an analysis of various forms of cyber child abuse with a focus on understanding the implications of cyber child pornography;
- Compare the legislative frameworks pertaining to cyber child abuse in India and the USA;
- Propose innovative approaches to effectively combat the issue of online child pornography.

CYBER CHILD PORNOGRAPHY: A GLOBAL PROBLEM

The illicit activities of online child sexual abuse and exploitation encompass the use of information and communication technology to perpetrate sexual harm or exploit minors. The United Nations Economic and Social Commission for Asia and the Pacific (UN ESCAP) (1999) defines child sexual abuse as "contacts or interactions between a child and an older or more knowledgeable child or adult (stranger, sibling, or person in a position of authority such as a parent or caretaker) when the child is being used as an object for the older child's or adult's sexual needs. These contacts or interactions are carried out against the child using force, trickery, bribes, threats, or pressure." Child sexual exploitation involves child sexual abuse and/or other sexualized acts using children, which includes an exchange of some kind (e.g., affection, food, drugs, and shelter)(UNODC, 2015a). Those engaging in this offense exploit or seek to exploit "a position of vulnerability, differential power, or trust for sexual purposes" with the aim of gaining monetary or other advantages, such as sexual gratification(*Ending Online Child Sexual Exploitation and Abuse*, 2021).

Undoubtedly, the Internet has led to an unprecedented surge in the proliferation of child pornography, surpassing any previous historical instances. This surge is attributed, in part, to technological advancements that have significantly lowered the barriers to entry for producing and distributing child pornography. The increasing affordability and user-friendly nature of cameras and sophisticated multimedia editing software have streamlined the process of creating and disseminating child pornography. Defined by federal law in the United States as "a visual depiction of a minor engaged in sexually explicit conduct," child pornography has inflicted harm upon children for centuries. However, the Internet has revitalized child pornography due to its seamless transmission capabilities, allowing one paedophile to share with numerous others and facilitating the spread across different countries. A disturbing fact is that a minimum of 80% of individuals purchasing child pornography are actively involved in child molestation. Additionally, 36% of those exploiting children through the mail for child pornography purposes have been identified as actual child molesters. Child pornographers typically span in age from 10 to 65(Posey, 2005). When viewed as a socio- and psychopathology, cyber child pornography, in particular, emerges as an element within unhealthy power relations, wherein adults exploit minors for their own gratification. These instances of real-world abuse are often initiated by adults harbouring unhealthy sexual fantasies involving minors. In many cases, the fulfilment of these fantasies through cyberspace involves ritualized practices and fixations, primarily of a sadistic nature(Uebel, 1999). Moreover, experts emphasize that pornography is not only addictive but also progressively so. As individuals grow desensitized to the explicit content they encounter, they actively seek out more extreme and shocking material. Consequently, the alarming rise of vile and widespread child pornography on the Internet is hardly surprising, constituting at least one-third of online traffic. The disturbing content goes beyond explicit images of adults engaging in penetrative sex with two-month-old babies. For instance, the Wonderland Club, uncovered by the FBI and Scotland Yard in 2001, mandated prospective members to submit 10,000 original images of child pornography. This revelation offers a glimpse into the staggering volume of such images circulating globally(McCafferty, 2004).

International agreements, including the 1989 Convention on the Rights of the Child and the 2000 Optional Protocol to the Convention on the Rights of the Child on the sale of children, child prostitution, and child pornography, outline children's rights and specify the responsibility of states to shield children from sexual exploitation and abuse. Additionally, regional agreements, like the Council of Europe's 2007 Convention on the Protection of Children against Sexual Exploitation and Abuse (commonly known as the Lanzarote Convention), effective as of July 1, 2010, aim to prevent child sexual exploitation and abuse. These conventions work towards safeguarding victims, prosecuting perpetrators, and fostering national and international collaboration in identifying, investigating, prosecuting, and preventing such offenses(Rutai, 2020).

FORMS OF ONLINE CHILD ABUSE

While national, regional, and international laws strictly prohibit online child sexual exploitation and child sexual abuse, these forms of violence against children are delineated differently within these legal frameworks. Examples of criminal activities explicitly prohibited (to varying degrees) include online grooming, child sexual abuse material/child sexual exploitation material, and the live streaming of child sexual abuse. These are further discussed below:

Online Grooming

Child grooming, also known as the enticement or solicitation of children for sexual purposes, can be defined as the act whereby an adult "befriends" a child, often online (though offline grooming is also prevalent and should not be overlooked), with the intention of sexually abusing them(*What Is Child Grooming? Here Are the Six Steps a Predator Takes - Indiana Child Advocacy Centers and Chapter of NCA*, n.d.). Research and existing data indicate that grooming is predominantly carried out by males, while to a lesser extent, females also engage in soliciting children for sexual purposes and/or grooming them(Villacampa & Gómez, 2017).

In typical scenarios, the grooming process unfolds in stages, starting with the selection of a victim(Winters & Jeglic, 2017). Online, children engage with various social media platforms and communication apps, providing perpetrators with opportunities to access their accounts. Perpetrators select a victim based on factors such as the victim's "appeal/attractiveness" (in accordance with the perpetrators' desires), "ease of access" (determined by the privacy settings on the websites, platforms, and apps used by children), and/or "vulnerabilities" (for instance, if children share posts about isolation or feeling misunderstood)(Lanning, 2018; Ost & Mooney, 2013). Following the selection of a victim, the perpetrator initiates contact to establish a connection. Subsequently, the perpetrator endeavours to cultivate a friendship with the victim. Utilizing information gathered from online sources, the perpetrator deceives the victim by pretending to share common interests, hobbies, and similar family and social situations. This strategy aims to create a sense of connection, build rapport, and foster trust. The ultimate goal of the perpetrator is to progress the initial friendship into a deeper relationship(Aitken et al., 2018; O´Connell, 2003). Prior to engaging in sexual exploitation or abuse, the offender evaluates the risk of detection (such as inquiring whether the victim's parents or others monitor the child's accounts and/or digital devices), establishes the exclusivity of the relationship, emphasizes the necessity of secrecy, and isolates the child. It's important to note that there could be exceptions to these methods(Aitken et al., 2018). Studies have indicated that online grooming doesn't follow a linear process(de Santisteban et al., 2018); rather, it unfolds through a dynamic course influenced by the offender's motivation, capabilities, and the ability to manipulate and control the victim(Aitken et al., 2018). The ultimate objective of online grooming is to sexually exploit or abuse the victim. This can occur online, such as manipulating or coercing the victim into producing and sending sexually explicit images or videos to the perpetrator, or offline, for instance, by arranging a meeting with the victim in person for sexual abuse. In contrast to other international and regional instruments, such as the Optional Protocol to the Convention on the Rights of the Child on the Sale of Children, Child Prostitution, and Child Pornography of 2000, both the

Lanzarote Convention and Directive 2011/92/EU of the European Parliament and of the Council dated 13 December 2011, aimed at combating the Sexual Abuse and Sexual Exploitation of Children and Child Pornography, explicitly criminalize child grooming. Directive 2011/92/EU replaced Council Framework Decision 2004/68/JHA of 22 December 2003 on Combating the Sexual Exploitation of Children, including Child Pornography.

Article 23 of the Lanzarote Convention expressly forbids the "solicitation of children for sexual purposes" by criminalizing "the intentional proposal, through information and communication technologies, of an adult to meet a child...for the purpose of committing...[sexual abuse or producing child pornography]..., where this proposal has been followed by material acts leading to such a meeting." In parallel, Article 6 of Directive 2011/92/EU also prohibits the "solicitation of children for sexual purposes." Under Article 6(1) of the Directive, it is an offense to "propose, by means of information and communication technology, for an adult to meet a child who has not reached the age of sexual consent, for the purpose of committing...[sexual abuse and producing child pornography], where that proposal was followed by material acts leading to such a meeting" (such as traveling to an agreed-upon meeting place). Additionally, Article 6(2) of the Directive outlaws "an attempt, by means of information and communication technology, to commit...[child pornography offenses]...by an adult soliciting a child who has not reached the age of sexual consent to provide child pornography depicting that child."

Content Depicting the Sexual Abuse or Exploitation of Children

Child pornography is defined as the depiction, through any means, of a child involved in actual or simulated explicit sexual activities or the representation of a child's sexual parts for primarily sexual purposes, as stated in Article 2 of the UN Optional Protocol to the Convention on the Rights of the Child on the Sale of Children, Child Prostitution, and Child Pornography of 2000. This includes using a child to produce such depictions("International Centre For Missing & Exploited Children," 2017). Considering that the content portrays the sexual abuse of a child rather than consensual sexual activities, the terms "child sexual abuse material" or "child sexual exploitation material" are preferred. This choice aims to eliminate any connotations associated with the term "pornography"(Frangež et al., 2015). The term "child sexual abuse material" is employed for content depicting child sexual abuse, a subset of "child sexual exploitation material." Meanwhile, for "all other sexualized material featuring children," the term "child sexual exploitation material" is utilized(Interagency Working Group, 2017). Regional laws concerning the sexual exploitation of children have distinguished between child sexual abuse material and child sexual exploitation.

The term "child pornography" has been disapproved by international organizations, law enforcement agencies, academics, and child protection professionals. This rejection stems from its tendency to downplay the severe nature of violence against children, potentially placing blame on the child instead of the perpetrator, and the risk of implying consensual involvement. Despite this consensus, it's noteworthy that the term "child pornography" persists prominently in legal instruments from the past decade (e.g., the Convention on the Rights of the Child of 1989; the Optional Protocol to the Convention on the Rights of the Child on the Sale of Children, Child Prostitution and Child Pornography of 2000; the Council of Europe's Convention on Cybercrime of 2001; and the Lanzarote Convention of 2007, to name a few).

Material involving the exploitation and abuse of children is disseminated through various channels such as email, text messages, instant messaging, chat rooms, peer-to-peer file sharing networks (like eDonkey, BitTorrent, and Gigatribe), as well as on social media platforms. Additionally, both unencrypted and encrypted communication apps, such as Skype, Telegram, and WhatsApp, are used for the distribution of such content(Maras, 2016).

Material involving the sexual exploitation and abuse of children is exchanged on password-protected websites, bulletin boards, and forums. An illustrative example is the case of "Dreamboard," where individuals desiring membership had to submit an image depicting child sexual abuse material featuring a minor under twelve years old along with their application(U.S. Department of Justice, 2014). The person was given restricted access to the site's content if the photograph was approved as legitimate, and membership could only be kept up to date if the user kept adding images of child sexual assault. The user would have to create child sexual abuse content and upload it to the website, submit child sexual abuse stuff "that had never been seen before," and/or upload a sizable quantity of child sexual abuse materials if they desired more access to the content(U.S. Department of Justice, 2014). Members were advised to employ encryption to safeguard content access and elude detection by law enforcement agencies. While child sexual abuse material may exist on the surface web, Europol (2018) notes that the Darknet is increasingly utilized for the distribution of child sexual exploitation and abuse material, including more extreme forms of such content.

Streaming of Child Sexual Abuse

Live streaming of child sexual abuse entails the immediate broadcast of such incidents to viewers in distant locations. Although the live streaming of child sexual abuse often includes transmissions across international borders via the internet, it is crucial to highlight that certain countries have reported cases of domestic live streaming of child sexual abuse(Europol, 2018). The live streaming of child sexual abuse takes place in online chat rooms, social media platforms, and communication apps equipped with video chat features(Europol, 2018). Viewers engaging in the live streaming of child sexual abuse can adopt a passive role (i.e., pay to watch) or an active role by interacting with the child, the sexual abuser, and/or the facilitator of the child sexual abuse. In active participation, viewers may request specific physical acts (e.g., choking) and/or sexual acts to be performed on and/or by the child. This active involvement by the viewer is referred to as child sexual abuse to order and can occur either before or during the live streaming of child sexual abuse(UNODC, 2015b). A disgruntled Lostprophets singer, Ian Watkins, was convicted of child sexual assault, for inciting a mother to sexually abuse her kid over Skype sessions (The Queen vs. Ian Watkins and others, 2013). This case highlights that the live streaming of child sexual abuse is not solely driven by financial motives; rather, it can take place to fulfil romantic or sexual relationships, cater to the desires of sexual abusers and viewers, or unfold within the context of other abusive relationships (e.g., where the abuser may be following the directives of someone by whom they are also abused). Various financial methods, including digital currencies, cryptocurrencies, money transfers, online payment services, bank deposits, debit cards, and credit cards, have been utilized to pay for live streaming child sexual abuse(European Bank Authority, 2014).

The presence of economic disparities in nations, marked by elevated levels of poverty, unemployment, and job insecurity, has been recognized as a catalyst for the occurrence of live streaming child sexual abuse(Drejer et al., 2024). Live streaming child sexual abuse has been documented in areas like South East Asia, where the practice of coercing children to engage in sexual acts for financial support is not viewed as taboo or in violation of cultural and social norms within families (Drejer et al., 2024). In such instances, children are frequently coerced by facilitators, often a family or community member, to participate in sexual behaviour or become victims of sexual abuse while appearing in front of a webcam. In the Philippines, the facilitator rationalizes the sexual abuse of the child as a means of contributing to the family's financial needs, with the received money intended to support the entire family, including younger siblings (e.g., purchasing milk for a baby). Children rescued from these circumstances often bear a sense of guilt for not complying with the given instructions(Kumar, 2022).

SOCIAL DIFFICULTIES IN COMBATING ONLINE CHILD PORNOGRAPHY

Efforts to combat online child pornography face numerous social difficulties, including the anonymity of internet users, the global nature of the issue, and the challenge of enforcing laws across different legal jurisdictions (Schell et al., 2007). Additionally, the lack of cooperation and coordination among law enforcement agencies across countries poses a major hurdle in effectively combating online child pornography. Furthermore, the underground nature of the online child pornography industry makes it difficult to track and identify offenders, as they constantly employ sophisticated techniques to hide their activities and evade law enforcement. Moreover, the stigma surrounding victims of child pornography often leads to underreporting and reluctance to seek help or cooperate with authorities(Schell et al., 2007). Overall, these social difficulties create significant barriers in effectively combating online child pornography and require a multi-faceted approach involving international cooperation, technological advancements, and education and awareness campaigns to protect children and hold offenders accountable. In conclusion, social difficulties in combating online child pornography include factors such as the anonymity of internet users, the global nature of the issue, enforcement challenges across different legal jurisdictions, lack of cooperation among law enforcement agencies, underground nature of the industry, and stigma surrounding victims.

COMPARING ONLINE CHILD PORNOGRAPHY LAWS: USA VS. INDIA

The proliferation of child sexual abuse materials online has been facilitated by information and communication technology, particularly with the advent of end-to-end encryption and the dark web. Within the deep web, children are trafficked, solicited, and their images are exchanged, with varying ratings based on age and appearance. Online predators exploit the innocence and vulnerability of children, sometimes coercing them into creating explicit content, which is then sold for substantial sums globally. In India, the creation, production, and distribution of child pornographic materials constitute crimes under both the Information Technology Act, 2000 (amended in 2008), and the Indian Penal Code. Nevertheless, the menace persists due to the intricate nature of cyberspace legislation, which lacks sufficient deterrent power. The internet's freedom of anonymity allows individuals to register on social media platforms using any name or identity, facilitating the easy creation of false profiles by children misrepresenting their age and adults posing as minors. This freedom and anonymity enable adults to connect with minors online, transition the relationship offline, and engage in unlawful sexual activities. In an effort to address this issue, legislators and internet service providers have attempted to implement age verification processes to shield minors from inappropriate content or adult-oriented websites. However, these endeavours fall short of achieving the desired outcomes due to various factors. For instance, there is no universally applicable method of age verification that can be implemented across the jurisdiction of cyberspace. Additionally, there is a lack of consensus in defining "Child" across jurisdictions; while some consider anyone below 18 as a child, others adhere to age ranges between 16 and 20 years.

The Doe v. SexSearch.com(*Doe v. SexSearch*, 2007) case, heard in the United States District Court, exemplifies the challenge associated with insufficient age verification procedures on social networking sites, where users disclose their age during the registration process. SexSearch.com operates as an online adult dating service where members can connect for sexual encounters by creating profiles with specific information, including photos and videos. John Doe joined SexSearch.com and discovered Jane Roe's profile, which indicated her age as eighteen. After engaging in online conversations, they decided to meet at Jane Roe's home, where they had consensual sexual relations. However, it later emerged that Jane Roe was actually fourteen, and her registered age was false. Subsequently, John Doe faced charges of unlawful sexual conduct with a minor, carrying a potential fifteen-year prison sentence and potential lifelong registration as a sexual offender. Seeking legal recourse, Mr. Doe sued SexSearch.com, alleging that the platform failed to adequately screen minors during registration and falsely represented that all members were over 18. The court, however, dismissed his plea, citing that Mr. Doe was aware that SexSearch.com did not verify his age during registration. The court absolved SexSearch.com by pointing to a disclaimer in their terms and conditions, placing the responsibility on users to verify the information posted by others before contacting them through the platform. Additionally, the court noted that Mr. Doe could have taken steps to verify Jane Roe's age during their in-person meeting. As early as 2008, the United States took measures to protect children by initiating legal actions against major social networking sites involved in the distribution of sexually explicit or pornographic material on their platforms. These investigations led to settlements between MySpace, Facebook, and a coalition of U.S. State Attorneys General. In a settlement reached in January 2008 with forty-nine State Attorneys General, MySpace committed to implementing design and functionality changes on its site. Additionally, they agreed to develop tools specifically catering to parents, educators, and children. MySpace pledged cooperation with law enforcement to prevent and prosecute individuals misusing the internet, while also establishing new privacy protection standards. As part of their action plan, MySpace decided to hire a third party to compile a registry of email addresses provided by parents seeking to restrict their children's access to the website. They proposed banning anyone listed in the registry from creating a new profile or accessing their site. Furthermore, MySpace agreed to enhance the algorithm used to identify underage users.

During that same year, Facebook entered into a comparable settlement wherein it committed to incorporating over forty additional safeguards aimed at safeguarding young users from sexual predators and cyberbullies. As part of the agreement, Facebook also pledged to prohibit convicted sexual offenders from accessing the site and intended to restrict the online search capabilities of older users seeking subscribers under the age of eighteen. Furthermore, Facebook implemented a process to review users' profiles when they requested a change in their age, ensuring the legitimacy of such updates and preventing adults from posing as children(Metro News, 2019).

Furthermore, the United States has enacted the Children's Online Privacy Protection Act ("COPPA") in 2000, overseen by the Federal Trade Commission (FTC), to safeguard children under the age of 13. COPPA regulates websites directed at or frequently visited by children in this age group, prohibiting the collection of personal information online, such as full names, home addresses, email addresses, and hobbies. Under COPPA, interactions with children under thirteen and the collection, use, or retention of their data must adhere to specified guidelines. Verifiable consent from the child's parent is a prerequisite for operators before collecting, using, or disclosing personal information. Operators are also obligated to make reasonable efforts, considering available technology, to inform parents of their information practices, and parental consent must be obtained for these practices. The U.S. FTC has actively pursued legal action against websites primarily catering to children when they adopt questionable data collection practices.

The scenario in India differs from that in the United States. Recently, the issue of social media applications and children's privacy came under review by the Madurai bench of the Madras High Court in the case involving *S. Muthukumar v. The Telecom Regulatory Authorities of India and Others*. Following the acceptance of the petition, the Hon'ble High Court issued an interim order directing the central government to prohibit the TikTok app in India. The court expressed concerns about the app's potential danger to children, citing inappropriate content created by users that could expose children to sexual predators. Additionally, the court noted the live-streaming feature allowing users to send virtual "gifts" to creators, which could be purchased with real money. Subsequently, the central government instructed Google and Apple to remove TikTok from their App Stores. In response, TikTok appealed to the Supreme Court against the Madras High Court's interim order. The court appointed Mr. Arvind Datar as Amicus Curiae to assess the app's implications. Mr. Datar argued that banning the application is not a solution and emphasized the need to protect the rights of legitimate users. He referenced safeguards provided by the Information Technology Act, which protect intermediaries like TikTok from liability for content created by users. Mr. Datar contended that the Information Technology Act does not mandate intermediaries to screen all information hosted on their platforms. Ultimately, the Madras High Court lifted the ban, stating that India should consider enacting a comprehensive legislation, similar to COPPA (Children's Online Privacy Protection Act) of 2000, to safeguard children online.

Contemporary children may inadvertently encounter adult content, posing potential long-term consequences for their psychological and emotional well-being. The lack of parental control stands out as a significant factor contributing to children engaging in such activities. In today's world, a growing number of children are erecting barriers between themselves and their parents, exposing them to interactions with strangers and the risk of their photographs and other private details falling into the hands of predators and third parties.

Despite social media sites establishing minimum age requirements for their services, there is a notable absence of stringent enforcement of these rules. Age verification is lacking, allowing anyone to create a profile by falsifying their age. To mitigate these risks, parents and educators have the opportunity to educate children on safe online practices, teaching them how to recognize potential dangers and unhealthy online behaviors. Implementing secure internet connections at home and educational institutions, such as enabling VPN services, is crucial.

Cybercrime patterns against children in the online realm are relatively new, requiring specialized expertise and treatment for effective law enforcement.

COMBATING ONLINE EXPLOITATION AND ABUSE OF CHILDREN

To effectively combat child pornography, a comprehensive and innovative approach is needed. Conducting investigations by law enforcement is a key strategy in addressing online child sexual exploitation and abuse. National, regional, and international law enforcement agencies collaborate to investigate instances of online child sexual exploitation and abuse. An illustration of this cooperation is Operation Tantalio, where INTERPOL, Europol, and law enforcement agencies from 15 countries across Europe, Central America, and South America collaborated in investigating the distribution of child sexual abuse material through WhatsApp(Interpol, 2017). The presence of synchronized national laws, collaboration in criminal matters at the international level, including mutual legal assistance and extradition, as well as the existence of bilateral, regional, and multilateral conventions and agreements addressing child sexual exploitation and abuse, facilitates the coordinated efforts and cooperation among agencies in the international investigation of such cases. The effective enforcement of these laws, treaties, conventions, and agreements further strengthens the framework for international cooperation in combating child sexual exploitation. Covert law enforcement investigations have been carried out to uncover, probe, and bring to justice those involved in online child sexual exploitation and abuse. A notable example is the undercover operation involving the Kids the Light of Our Lives Internet chatroom, utilized as a medium for live-streaming child sexual abuse and the dissemination of material related to child sexual exploitation and abuse. Covert law enforcement operatives, affiliated with the Virtual Global Taskforce—a coalition of diverse law enforcement agencies worldwide with the overarching goal of establishing partnerships with non-member law enforcement agencies, non-government organizations, and the private sector to combat online child sexual exploitation and abuse—successfully penetrated the chatroom. These undercover officers gathered crucial evidence, leading to the successful prosecution of both the chatroom host and individuals utilizing the site.

Collaboration between government agencies and the private sector is crucial in combating online child sexual exploitation and abuse. This collaboration includes initiatives like restricting registered child sex offenders' access to platforms commonly used by children. An illustrative example is the 2012 Operation Game Over, where prominent companies such as Microsoft, Apple, Blizzard Entertainment, Electronic Arts, Disney Interactive Media Group, Warner Brothers, and Sony collectively removed over 3,500 accounts belonging to New York registered sex offenders from online video game platforms like Xbox Live and PlayStation(McCurley, 2012). Private entities, including Thorn, Facebook, Google, and others, have collaborated to establish an Industry Hash Sharing Platform, a cloud-based tool. The aim is to streamline the removal procedures for child sexual exploitation and abuse material from various online platforms.

Databases designed for investigative purposes, like INTERPOL's International Child Sexual Exploitation (ICSE) database, have been established to combat online child sexual exploitation and abuse. These databases play a crucial role in not only identifying child victims of sexual exploitation and abuse but also in pinpointing and investigating the perpetrators. An illustrative example is the identification of the leader of a network of sexual abusers in Japan. Authorities in Denmark and Australia uploaded videos featuring an unidentified child sexual abuse victim to ICSE, leading to the perpetrator's identification(Interpol, 2017). In the United States, the Child Victim Identification Program, operated by the National Centre for Missing and Exploited Children (NCMEC), functions as a central repository for child sexual abuse material. Similar to the ICSE database, the content within this database plays a crucial role in identifying both victims and perpetrators of child sexual exploitation and abuse. It aids in the investigation of individuals involved in child sexual abuse, including the abusers, consumers of child sexual abuse material, and those facilitating child sexual exploitation and abuse.

The vast expanse of the Internet, coupled with the multitude of online platforms, apps, and digital technologies available, provides perpetrators with the means to easily conceal their activities. Given the enormity of data and the abundance of online sites, traditional investigative methods for addressing child sexual exploitation and abuse fall short. Innovative technological solutions have the potential to expedite the identification of both perpetrators and victims while proactively removing materials related to child sexual exploitation and abuse. For instance, Terre des Hommes, an international children's rights organization, collaborated with partner institutions to develop "Sweetie," a virtual ten-year-old Filipina girl. This creation serves the purpose of engaging and communicating with online sexual predators, allowing for their public exposure and notifying relevant law enforcement agencies. Effectively addressing online child sexual exploitation and abuse demands a comprehensive strategy. This approach must encompass not only law enforcement tactics but also encompass laws, regulations, and policies. Additionally, it should involve the coordination of services provided to victims, cooperation among all institutions handling such cases, and educational programs along with awareness campaigns dedicated to combating these crimes and promoting Internet safety.

TECHNOLOGICAL APPROACH TO CURB CHILD PORNOGRAPHY

Child pornography on the internet has grown into a "big business." The internet propels evidence portraying sexual abuse of children into cyberspace, where it is shared, received, promoted, and sold by nearly anybody, memorialising the criminal even after the crime has occurred (The U.S. Department of Justice, 2010). Though child sexual abuse has occurred throughout history, it is seen as an aberrant subculture condemned to society's basement. The internet and other technologies transformed the child pornography industry from one that was secret to one that was freely available to everyone. Technology and the internet give cyber-pornographers of minors the tools they need to commit more crimes, go undetected, introduce new offenders, and enable "fresh exploitation of children." Child pornography started with the invention of the camera in the nineteenth century and has progressed ever since. Before the twenty-first century, child pornography was expensive and difficult to obtain, and the photos generated were for trading and personal collectors.

With the constant introduction of cutting-edge technology, there is a noticeable improvement in law enforcement everywhere, which usually leads to the reduction of crimes of all types and at all levels. At this time, technology-driven solutions have proven to be a boon for law enforcement agencies to bring solutions to child pornography.

Recently the Maharashtra Police's cyber wing has acquired technology named 'crawler' from Interpol to assist them in tracking down child pornography published online. The software employs a variety of processes, including nudity detection in photos and age recognition using face features, among other filters. It also has algorithms for searching for buzzwords related to child pornography, which can assist law enforcement authorities in tracking out communities that engage in these crimes. Based on these restrictions, the application 'crawler' searches the internet for photos, videos, and text. If they discover such media, it is added to the database, and police identify cases that may be classified as child pornography. At the beginning of this year, Interpol officials trained 12 Maharashtra cyber officers in the usage of this technology, following which they were given access to it. Last year, Interpol scheduled training for Kerala after numerous similar videos were uploaded from there.

In 2019, the National Centre for Missing and Exploited Children (NCMEC), a non-profit organisation located in the United States that seeks to prevent child exploitation, began exchanging information regarding child pornography in India with Indian agencies. These tips were obtained by the National Crime Records Bureau (NCRB), which sent them to the states where the child pornography event occurred. In the five months between September 2019 to January 2020, 25,000 incidents of child pornography were reported across the country (Thaver, 2020). Although Delhi tops the list of those suspected of uploading child pornography, Maharashtra, Gujarat, Uttar Pradesh, and West Bengal are the other top states, according to the statistics.

CONCLUSION AND SUGGESTION

A pressing necessity exists for a comprehensive and collaborative strategy to combat the abhorrent crime of cyber child pornography. Efforts should be directed towards both national and international levels to fortify laws, enhance law enforcement capabilities, and foster cross-border cooperation. The challenge in prosecuting cyber child pornographers globally stems from the absence of a proper definition for the crime and its broad jurisdiction. Recent global initiatives by trained professionals in identifying child pornographic content and the establishment of coalitions across wider geographical areas offer the potential for more effective collaboration among law enforcement agencies to curb this reprehensible crime. Addressing the issue demands a multifaceted approach, encompassing the delicate balance between individuals' right to free speech and the prevention of harm to minors. This involves educating potential targets, particularly women and children, and developing technological methods to identify online child pornographers. Advocacy for a multifaceted approach, involving technical, institutional, social, educational, and state-level initiatives, is essential. A code of behaviour for safeguarding children's online safety, emphasizing the responsibility of Internet Service Providers (ISPs) to detect and remove child sexual abuse material (CSAM), along with notifying law enforcement, is a key recommendation. Strengthening the National Commission for Protection of Child Rights (NCPCR) is vital, positioning it as a central entity in eradicating child pornography. Public education about the dangers and consequences of engaging in or consuming child pornography online, coupled with the provision of support and resources to victims and survivors, is critical. Addressing the socio-legal aspects of cyber child pornography is the key to creating a safer online environment for children, where their rights are safeguarded, and their well-being is prioritized. In conclusion, a comprehensive approach to the socio-legal aspects of cyber child pornography is imperative for fostering a secure online environment for children.

REFERENCES

Aitken, S., Gaskell, D., & Hodkinson, A. (2018). Online sexual grooming: Exploratory comparison of themes arising from male offenders' communications with male victims compared to female victims. *Deviant Behavior*, *39*(9), 1170–1190. doi:10.1080/01639625.2017.1410372

Ali, S., Haykal, H. A., & Youssef, E. Y. M. (2023). Child Sexual Abuse and the Internet—A Systematic Review. *Human Arenas*, *6*(2), 404–421. doi:10.1007/s42087-021-00228-9

Basuroy, T. (2022, March 15). *Total internet users in India*. Statista. https://www.statista.com/statistics/255146/number-of-internet-users-in-india/

Bose, M. (2023). Cybercrimes against children see 32% rise in a year, NCRB report shows. *Deccan Herald*. https://www.deccanherald.com/india/cybercrimes-against-children-see-32-rise-in-a-year-ncrb-report-shows-2799597

Brown, J. D. (2002, February). Mass media influences on sexuality. *Journal of Sex Research*, *39*(1), 42–45. doi:10.1080/00224490209552118 PMID:12476255

Correspondent, H. (2016, February 27). Block porn sites showing child pornography: SC | Latest News India. *Hindustan Times*. https://www.hindustantimes.com/india/tough-to-block-porn-sites-but-act-on-those-involving-children-sc/story-903nujBIFjtrrvSmqGPCbN.html

de Santisteban, P., del Hoyo, J., Alcázar-Córcoles, M. Á., & Gámez-Guadix, M. (2018). Progression, maintenance, and feedback of online child sexual grooming: A qualitative analysis of online predators. *Child Abuse & Neglect*, *80*, 203–215. doi:10.1016/j.chiabu.2018.03.026 PMID:29625326

Drejer, C., Riegler, M. A., Halvorsen, P., Johnson, M. S., & Baugerud, G. A. (2024). Livestreaming Technology and Online Child Sexual Exploitation and Abuse: A Scoping Review. *Trauma, Violence, \&. Trauma, Violence & Abuse*, *25*(1), 260–274. doi:10.1177/15248380221147564 PMID:36727734

Ending Online Child Sexual Exploitation and Abuse. (2021). UNICEF. www.unicef.org

European Bank Authority. (2014). *Annual Report*. EBA. doi:10.2853/34273

Europol. (2018). *Internet Organised Crime*. Europol. doi:10.2813/858843

Express News Service. (2022, May 6). Child pornography content: Pimpri Chinchwad police file cases against 7 internet users. *The Indian Express*. https://indianexpress.com/article/cities/pune/child-pornography-content-pimpri-chinchwad-police-file-cases-against-7-internet-users-7902290/

Frangež, D., Klancnik, A. T., Karer, M., Ludvigsen, B.-E., Kończyk, J., Perez, F. R., Veijalainen, M., & Lewin, M. (2015). The importance of terminology related to child sexual exploitation. *Revija za Kriminalistiko in Kriminologijo*, *66*, 291–299.

Hald, G. M., & Malamuth, N. M. (2014, April). Experimental Effects of Exposure to Pornography: The Moderating Effect of Personality and Mediating Effect of Sexual Arousal. *Archives of Sexual Behavior*, *44*(1), 99–109. doi:10.1007/s10508-014-0291-5 PMID:24729134

Interagency Working Group. (2017). Annual Report. In International Centre For Missing and Exploited Children. IWG.

International Centre For Missing & Exploited Children. (2017). In Bulletin of the Marx Memorial Library (Vol. 133, Issue 1). doi:10.3828/bbml.2001.133.4

Interpol. (2017). Annual Report 2017. In *INTERPOL* (*Vol. 5*). doi:10.7557/cage.6834

Kannan, S. (2020, April 11). Pornography gets a pandemic boost, India reports 95 per cent rise in viewing. *India Today*. https://www.indiatoday.in/news-analysis/story/pornography-gets-a-pandemic-boost-india-reports-95-per-cent-rise-in-viewing-1665940-2020-04-11

Kemp, S. (2022, February 15). *Digital 2022: India — DataReportal – Global Digital Insights*. DataReportal. https://datareportal.com/reports/digital-2022-india

Kumar, S. (2022). The Deep Web and Children Cyber Exploitation. In *Research Anthology on Child and Domestic Abuse and Its Prevention* (pp. 621–638). IGI Global. doi:10.4018/978-1-6684-5598-2.ch035

Lanning, K. (2018). The Evolution of Grooming: Concept and Term. *Journal of Interpersonal Violence*, *33*(1), 5–16. doi:10.1177/0886260517742046

Lovelle, M. I., Yepes-Baldó, M., Romeo, M., & Soria, M. Á. (2017). Online Child Pornography: A Cultural Focus Literature Review [Pornografía infantil online: una revisión literaria de enfoque cultural]. *Para La Estructura, 14*(2), 99.

MarasM.-H. (2016). *Cybercriminology.*

McCafferty, C. (2004). Only we can tackle porn. *Retrieved*, (March), 14.

McCurley, M. (2012). Operation: Game Over bans sex offenders from online games in New York. *Forbes*. https://www.engadget.com/2012-04-05-operation-game-over-bans-sex-offenders-from-online-games-in-new.html

Metro News. (2019). *Facebook cracks down on sex predators*. Metro News. https://metro.co.uk/2008/05/09/facebook-cracks-down-on-sex-predators-129843/

National Crime Records Bureau. (2021, September 9). *Untitled*. NCRB. https://ncrb.gov.in/sites/default/files/CII%202020%20Volume%201.pdf

O'Connell, R. (2003). *A TYPOLOGY OF CHILD CYBERSEXPLOITATION AND ONLINE GROOMING PRACTICES.* University of Central Lancashire. http://image.guardian.co.uk/sys-files/Society/documents/2003/07/17/Groomingreport.pdf

Ost, S. (2002). Children at Risk : Legal and Societal Perceptions of the Potential Threat That the Possession of Child Pornography Poses to Society. *Journal of Law and Society, 29*(3), 436–460. doi:10.1111/1467-6478.00227

Ost, S., & Mooney, J.-L. (2013). *Group localised grooming:what is it and what challenges does it pose for society and law?* Semantic Scholar. https://api.semanticscholar.org/CorpusID:73615323

Prakash, A. G. (2018). Role of Prohibitory Legislation in Preventing Online Sexual Abuse of Children: a Critical Socio-Legal Analysis. *Unitedworld Law Journal, 2*, 346–360. https://www.icmec.org/press/new-study-reveals-child-pornography-not-a-crime-in-most-countries/

Press Information Bureau, Government of India. (2020, January 25). *Press Information Bureau*. Press Information Bureau. https://pib.gov.in/PressReleseDetailm.aspx?PRID=1600505

Rotman, E. F. (2017). A Qualitative Study of What US Parents Say and Do When Their Young Children See Pornography. *Academic Pediatrics, 17*(8), 844–849. doi:10.1016/j.acap.2017.04.014 PMID:28450081

Rutai, Z. (2020). *The Lanzarote Committee: protecting children from sexual violence in Europe and beyond.*

Schell, B., Vargas Martin, M., Hung, P., & Rueda, L. (2007). Cyber child pornography: A review paper of the social and legal issues and remedies—and a proposed technological solution. *Aggression and Violent Behavior*, *12*(1), 45–63. doi:10.1016/j.avb.2006.03.003

Smith, R. B. (2020). CYBERCIME IN ASEAN: ANTI-CHILD PORNOGRAPHY LEGISLATION. *JOURNAL of INDONESIAN LEGAL STUDIES*, *5*(2), 277–292. doi:10.15294/jils.v5i2.37931

Thaver, M. (2020, December 15). Explained: How Maharashtra Police will use software to crack down on child porn. *The Indian Express*. https://indianexpress.com/article/explained/maharashtra-police-interpol-child-porn-software-7096513/

The Protection of Children from Sexual offences Act 2012. (2012). *The Gazette of India*.

The U.S. Department of Justice. (2010, August). *US Department of Justice*. Department of Justice. https://www.justice.gov/psc/docs/natstrategyreport.pdf

Uebel, M. (1999, January 1). *Toward a symptomatology of cyberporn*. YouTube. Retrieved July 14, 2022, from http://muse.jhu.edu/journals/theory_and_event/%20v003/3.4uebel.html

Uebel, M. (1999). Toward a Symptomatology of Cyberporn. *Theory & Event*, 3.

UNICEF. (n.d.). *Protecting children online*. UNICEF. https://www.unicef.org/protection/violence-against-children-online

UNODC. (2015a). *UNODC ANNUAL REPORT 2015*. UNDOC. www.unodc.org

UNODC. (2015b). *World Drug Report*. https://www.unodc.org/documents/wdr2015/World_Drug_Report_2015.pdf

U.S. Department of Justice. (2014). Dreamboard Member Sentenced to 45 Years in Prison for Participating in International Criminal Network Organized to Sexually Exploit Children. *Office of Public Affairs*. https://www.justice.gov/opa/pr/dreamboard-member-sentenced-45-years-prison-participating-international-criminal-network

Villacampa, C., & Gómez, M. J. (2017). Online child sexual grooming: Empirical findings on victimisation and perspectives on legal requirements. *International Review of Victimology*, *23*(2), 105–121. doi:10.1177/0269758016682585

What is child grooming? Here are the six steps a predator takes - Indiana Child Advocacy Centers and Chapter of NCA. (n.d.). Indiana Chapter of National Children's Alliance. https://incacs.org/what-is-child-grooming-here-are-the-six-steps-a-predator-takes/

Winters, G. M., & Jeglic, E. L. (2017). Stages of Sexual Grooming: Recognizing Potentially Predatory Behaviors of Child Molesters. *Deviant Behavior*, *38*(6), 724–733. doi:10.1080/01639625.2016.1197656

ENDNOTE

1 See also Cybercrime Module 2 and Trafficking in Persons Modules 12 and 14.

Chapter 7
Casual or Casualty?
Victimless Crime's Socio-Economic Impact in Indian Context

Himanshi Bhatia
Symbiosis Law School, Symbiosis International University, India

Prateek Sikchi
Symbiosis Law School, Nagpur, India & Symbiosis International University, Pune, India

ABSTRACT

The ultimate goal of society is to maintain social order. This can be attained by restricting the menace of crime. Within crime, there is a category of 'victimless crime' – which may sound oxymoronic. The victimless crimes cover those crimes where victims are not identifiable, or the illegal activity that occurs with the parties' consent. For decades there has been debate on whether victimless activity should be criminalized or not. The argument by the modernized world is in favor of decriminalization due to the lack of harm to others and freedom of the individual. This chapter hypothesizes that 'victimless crimes have victims – society as a whole, hence the term victimless is a façade. The chapter will attempt to establish the correlation between Mill's Harm Principle viz-a-viz modern victimless crimes. Thereafter, the chapter will discuss the various victimless crimes prevalent in India & their impact on the subcontinent. Lastly, the chapter will summarize the arguments with concluding remarks on the criminological aspect of victimless crimes.

DOI: 10.4018/979-8-3693-0327-6.ch007

INTRODUCTION: CRIMES WITH 'NO' VICTIM

One of the most debatable issues of the 21st century is that of '*crime & morality*' (Fuller, 1942). Due to evolving society with time & modern advancement, the rigidity of the moral norms has faded. The victimless crimes come under the *malum prohibitum* (evil acts that are prohibited) under the criminal code. Does the question arise on what basis few actions are not permitted? The answer to this lies in the 'morality' & 'other satellite crimes' associated with such crimes (Stewart, 1999) (Gross, 2012) (Silver & Silver, 2020).

Some of the victimless crimes prevailing in India are drug abuse, pornography, prostitution, gambling, etc. Even though such acts are usually consensual and rarely cause harm to any individual. The repercussions of such actions are quite persuasive on the social order. The satellite crimes or acts above stated victimless crimes harbors include human trafficking, rapes, theft, and even white-collar crimes. Notwithstanding the penalized crimes, these acts can even affect the GDP and Economy of the nation with the creation of the dependent nature of the offender on the resources of the state (National Research Council 2101 Constitution Ave Washington Dc 20418 & National Academies 500 Fifth Street Nw Washington Dc 20001, 1999) (Tankersley, 2021). The more the state's human resources indulge in the vicious cycle of gambling or drugs, the more the chances of the state progressing towards vulnerability due to non-efficient human resources.

This paper significantly deals with the societal impact of various victimless crimes. It deals with the latent costs incurred by the society, which penologically is not considered "victims" directly. The outbreak of the global pandemic has just increased the frequency of such crimes. Generally, harm in such crimes is borne by the offender himself; therefore, administration, due to lack of complainant, regards it as victimless. However, data & statistics of drug & gambling dependency (Kryszajtys et al., 2018) show the path of delinquency, which damages the societal order (victim herein).

The primary utilitarian concept inculcated in numerous criminal statutes across the globe is that of John Stuart Mill's *Harm Principle*. The paper will attempt to dissect the applicability of the harm principle on victimless crimes in today's world. Therefore, the issue of demand for the decriminalization of such crimes is to be pondered upon due to the absence of harm principle directly. Whether the Mill's Harm Principle justifies the criminality of victimless crimes? The criminological facet of the harm principle develops the responsibility of the offender towards the society only when the act affects others & the moment it concerns himself, he's not answerable (Ripstein, 2006).

Lastly, in the Indian scenario, illicit acts are already banned as per the special statutes, be it drugs, human trafficking for prostitution, pornography, or gambling.

While evaluating the crime cost to the society few parameters to be looked upon are victims cost, criminal's career cost, criminal justice system cost, and certain intangible costs. Although such costs are visible in any common crime, it is hidden under victimless crimes. This paper will take up victimless crimes for analyzing their cost on the Indian society as a whole.

MILL'S HARM PRINCIPLE APPLICABILITY

John Stuart Mill was among the famous English philosophers who propounded the utilitarian concept of the Harm Principle. His well-known work, "*On Liberty*", envisages the theory of co-relation between *offense* & *harm* on commission of any act. According to him, restricting liberty based on mere offense shall not be exercised by the state. The violations shall have the justification of harm on the other individual as a criterion of restricting the liberty of the offender (Macleod, 2016). He explains it as follows:

"That the only purpose for which power can be rightfully exercised over any member of a civilized community, against his will, is to prevent harm to others" (John Stuart Mill & Lindsay, 2016).

Though certain acts do not harm others yet, they're prohibited per se under the law. The reason behind these sanctions is an apprehension of harm to society. For instance, drunk driving or pollution regulations do not impose immediate or confirmed threats, but there is a possibility of it being harmful in the future course (Ripstein, 2006). Likewise, certain victimless crimes are considered aggravated offenses under the criminal code on the basis of harming effect attached to it.

This brings in the concept of '*Paternalism*' which refers to the curbing of the individual's sovereignty for the sake of protective (fatherly) intent (Thompson, 2013). Mill's harm principle is against this mechanism of authoritarian state control over the liberty of the individual irrespective of intent.

But within his critique on paternalism mill provided an exception wherein the state can regulate the individual's act. The mill's exception to paternalism is inadequacy that it can be used in the case of children or individuals with insufficient cognitive abilities (John Stuart Mill & Lindsay, 2016). His argument was based upon the rationale that such a class of people cannot take care of themselves; hence state can interfere with their actions with the help of paternalism (Oh, 2016).

In the context of victimless crimes, such a broad exception can cover even *drug-addicted individuals* who might lose control over their minds due to dependence on drugs. Similarly, the second exception of mill discusses the application of paternalism on the prohibition of the person selling him off as a slave to the market (Moore, 1991). Another crime that can be considered modern slavery is *'Prostitution,'* wherein women are regarded as property for sexual services to the male-dominated society. Prostitution is another prominent victimless crime that turns out to be the suitable analogy on mill's paternalism exception.

The modern liberals challenge the criminalization of victimless crimes on the basis of the mill's harm theory. Due to unidentifiable harm to any particular individual, they argue it as mere freedom of the offender (Dyzenhaus, 1992). Nevertheless, the apprehension of harm, responsibility towards the society & the paternalism exception imbibed the need for the criminalization of victimless crimes even in today's world. Mill's justifiability of harm principle was not absolute can be understood from his statement as follows

"As soon as any part of a person's conduct affects prejudicially the interests of others, society has jurisdiction over it, and the question whether the general welfare will or will not be promoted by interfering with it becomes open to discussion." (Macleod, 2016).

The traditional notion that acts shall be criminalized as an offense only when it fulfills the harm principle, i.e., causing harm to others without consent, holds no ground in victimless crimes. With the modernization of society, even crimes are evolving like online gambling, pornography, abortion, possession of contraband are just outcomes of modern times in one way or another. This calls for the evaluation of such crimes by considering all the social & economic hidden costs attached.

VICTIMLESS CRIMES IN INDIA

The ramifications of crime are usually borne by the innocent sufferer of that particular act. However, the concerning issue is what could be the price of this crime? What are its repercussions on the family & society of the victims? The primary evaluation of crime cost is still unknowable across the globe. The crime preventive mechanism demands such assessment on the impact of crime – socially, economically, psychologically, or upon the specific section of the state.

However, victimless crimes cause another dilemma that is for whom the cost is to be measured? If literally interpreted, it does not include any victim as such, and by the in-depth evaluation, we can count innumerable victims within the society. Therefore, deliberations reflect upon the question as consequences of crime affect whom & for what? Is it the offender himself or the community at large? For the manpower or economy of the state? The perception that some acts may be intolerable to one, maybe freedom, or beneficial to another is the facet of the criminological study (Secretariat, 1975).

While victimless crimes are usually denoted as moral wrongs for the immediate reason of being related to society. The Indian society is known for its diversity & different morals from that of the westernized world. The acceptance of homosexuality is yet to be achieved here. Before the decriminalization of homosexuality (*Navtej Singh Johar v. Union of India*, 2018), it was also under the purview of victimless crimes due to consensual acts of the parties involved.

Nevertheless, the above-stated progression does not dissolve the vulnerability of society. There are still certain so-called victimless offenses that need a study on their impact influence with regard to various other parameters. The next section of the paper will examine such few crimes, specifically in the Indian context & morality.

Drug Abuse

The consumption of drugs or psychoactive substances is not a new practice in India. Few substances like cannabis (bhang) have been socially accepted & widely used across the nation. Although usage of such psychoactive substances as cannabis & alcohol is prevalent in India for centuries yet the peril of drug abuse is not being discussed widely.

In the year 2018, half of the global population aged above 15 years were categorized as a consumer of alcohol (*Magnitude of Substance Use in India*, 2019). Similarly, approximately 3.9% of the world's population consumes cannabis aged between 16 to 64 years as per the estimates by the United Nations Office and Drugs and Crime (UNODC) – World Drug Report (2018). Whereas in India prevalence of alcohol usage is low but the dependency that is addiction level on alcohol is quite high (5.2% of the population) (Secretariat, 1975).

The above statistics depict the dependency rate of drug consumers concerning public health as a central issue. However, global & nations have yet not documented the impact of drug abuse on society within the sphere of criminal law. Some of the bottom-line factors which are due to drug abuse are as follows:

Economic Cost

Drug abuse is one of the major offenses which depreciates the state's exchequer multidimensionally. India's more than 1% of the GDP is lost to tobacco-related health expenditures & deaths alone (John et al., 2021). Tobacco is just one of the types of drug which is being widely used across the nation that immensely drains the economy. The study reveals that a total of 5.3% of the public & private health expenditures account for tobacco-related diseases in India annually (John et al.,

2021). The research concluded that on every INR 100 income from the excise taxes upon tobacco products, conversely INR 816 is imposed upon the society as the consumption burden (John et al., 2021).

Illicit Drug Trafficking is one of the major menaces to the Indian economy. The geographical location is one of the primary factors contributing to the Indian sub-continent as a breeding ground for illicit drug trade globally. India is surrounded by two main producing zones of opium production precisely that is *"Golden Crescent"* comprising Iran, Afghanistan & Pakistan & the *"Golden Triangle"* comprising Myanmar, Thailand & Laos (United Nations Office of Drugs and Crime, n.d.). These regions suffice the global demand for illicit heroin & drugs through their large production. The number of cases registered under the possession of drugs for trafficking was more than 25,000 during the year 2020 (*National Crime Records Bureau (NCRB), Indian Penal Code, Police Disposal of SLL Crime Cases (Crime Head-Wise)*, 2020).

Money laundering is quite a prevalent white-collar crime in India – illicit drug cultivation, manufacture & supply are a few channels through which it takes place. Such illicit drug money is usually used by the traffickers for terrorism financing & political influence (United Nations Office of Drugs and Crime, n.d.). This argument can be supported by the amount of drug items which was recovered from the anti-national elements was approximately 882 kg *(National Crime Records Bureau, Arms Taken Away from Police/CAPFs by Anti National Elements - 2020)* .As per the latest NCRB statistics, the sale & purchase of illicit drugs is also one of the motives behind the commission of cyber-crimes in India (*National Crime Records Bureau (NCRB), Cyber Crime Motives, 2020).*

Societal Cost

The rationale behind the drugs addiction is stated to be experimentation (curiosity) or peer pressure by the drug users. However, the momentary pleasure or experiment can cost huge to the society in the long run. Among the several hazards being associated with drug abuse, the most common is bodily disability along with the inability to perform even basic duties as a responsible citizen of the nation.

The complaint of memory loss, breathing issues, depression & poor sexual performance are just a few repercussions of drug consumption (United Nations Office of Drug and Crime UNODC, 2022). Criminal instincts & violence are the most visible consequences which that society encounters generally. When we discuss the issue of societal cost, the immediate victim in society is the family of the drug abuser.

The concept of *gender-based violence* can be traced in the drug abuse offense as well. There are numerous studies on the impact of drug abuse on the women of the family. It is considered a male dominant crime even now in some parts of the world including India. This impact can be economic, physical, or even mental harassment. Few satellite crimes associated with individual drug use are human trafficking, domestic violence & sexual exploitation of women (United Nations Office of Drug and Crime UNODC, 2022). The victimization of women by society due to lack of support further aggravates the situation.

Child delinquency is another consequence which the family of the drug addict suffers. Due to negligence of the child in the victimized family, there are high chances of child delinquency & even child labor as well. The homeless or street children are more prone to drugs addiction – the study depicts that these children have a history of family abuse & crime participation (International Narcotics Control Board, 2014, *Economic consequences of drug abuse)*. The number of juveniles in conflict with law cases reported under the Narcotics Drugs & Psychotropic Substances Act (The Narcotic Drugs and Psychotropic Substances Act, 1985) *hereinafter* NDPS Act was 264 across the country (International Narcotics Control Board, 2014,SLL Crimes - Juveniles in Conflict with Law - 2020). The crime statistics show that even the future of the country is trapped in the so-called victimless crime cycle.

Intoxicated Accidents are the outcome of driving motor vehicles while being high on any illicit substance. The influence of drugs on the body includes the imbalance of cognitive abilities, attention, coordination & other neurological functionalities (International Narcotics Control Board, 2014). The latest data of the Government empirical research shows 211,405 people died in road accidents due to alcohol or drugs consumption between the year 2008 to 2017 (Ministry of Road Transport and Highways Transport Research Wing, 2022). Drunk & driving is punishable under the Motor Vehicles Act, 1988 (s. 185) with minuscule punishment in comparison to the repercussion of the offense. The gaps are yet to be filled with intoxication association with the drug abuse presently by the Government of India.

Criminal Justice System Cost

The two major legislations covering drugs consumption & trafficking as a criminal offense are the Prevention of Illicit Traffic in Narcotic Drugs & Psychotropic Substances Act, 1988 & the NDPS Act, 1985. The consumption of any psychotropic substance or drug is punishable under Section 27 of the NDPS Act following the paternalistic approach of the government as discussed above.

However, with the criminalization of acts, it is obvious that state machinery will be called for to control the crime rate of that particular act. Under the Ministry of Home Affairs, the Narcotics Control Bureau (NCB) is the nodal agency which deals with drug-related crimes. Another ministry, Social Justice & Empowerment implements the policy for drug demand reduction, with NGOs' support.

Table 1. Police disposal of drugs related crime cases

Crime Head	Cases Pending Investigation from the previous year	Cases reported during the year	Cases reopened for investigation	Total cases for investigation
The NDPS Act, 1988	32230	59806	6	92042
a) Possession of drugs for personal consumption	18888	33246	0	52134
b) Possession of drugs for Trafficking	13342	26560	6	39908

Source: National Crime Record Bureau, *Crime in India* 2020 (Month)

The above-stated table predicts the burden of the cases under the different heads of drugs consumption & trafficking upon the police personnel in recent years

Table 2. Court disposal of drugs related crime cases

Crime Head	Cases Pending Trial from the previous year	Cases sent for trial during the year	Total Cases for trial	Cases abated by court
The NDPS Act, 1988	218111	54024	272135	33
a) Possession of drugs for personal consumption	119821	30014	149835	42
b) Possession of drugs for Trafficking	98290	24010	122300	36

Source: National Crime Record Bureau, *Crime in India* 2020 (Month)

Another component of the criminal justice system is courts, the above-stated table shows the huge load on the judicial system for the crime which does not even identify victims in the first place.

Correctional homes or de-addiction centers carry a huge cost under the aegis of the Central Government. For rehabilitation of drug offenders, the various de-addiction centers are established with many schemes like National Action Plan for Drug Demand Reduction Effective from April 01, 2020 (Ministry of social justice & empowerment), Prevention of Alcoholism & Substance (Drugs) Abuse and for Social Services Defense Effective from April 01, 2018, NashaMukt Bharat: Annual

Action Plan for 272 most affected districts, etc., These schemes & homes are just another cost which drains the state exchequer due to its impact on the society and future of the nation.

Pornography

The Digital Age's merits & demerits are some of the most controversial debates at present. Pornography or erotic entertainment is one of the products of the internet age. Pornography originates from the Greek word, which means *'writing about prostitutes'* depicting the life of prostitutes in the form of literature or art (Jenkins, 2019). However, the workable definition of pornography by Kuhn is 'pornography is a communication material provided for the purpose of sexually arousing or gratifying a user in isolation from others or in the company of others.'

Generally, consumption of pornographic material is not banned in many nations but recent trend depicts the negative consequences of excessive consumption of such nature. The emerging issue associated with it is that of public health & social norms. The boom of internet usage has directly increased the exposure to pornography. The convenient excess reveals that below the age of 18 estimated 60% of girls whereas 90% of boys have been exposed to such obscene materials (Vinnakota et al., 2021).

The alarming exposure to pornography has directly affected the crime rates in offenses related to sexual acts. The correlation between porn & sexual crimes is due to the content which is being served to the general public. According to a study, 94% of the porn scenes targets women, 88% include physical aggression and 48% contain verbal aggression as the mode of pleasure (Bridges et al., 2010).

The male-dominated acts & violence against women are some of the strands of crime against women in society. The gravity of the issue can be evaluated by the feminist controversial notion on pornography as *"pornography is the theory-rape is the practice"* (Morgan, 1980, pp. 134–140). Cyber pornography is regulated in India under various legislation like the Information Technology Act, 2000 (s. 67A, 67B) the Indian Penal Code (IPC, s. 292), and Indecent Representation of Women's act and the Young Person's (Harmful Publication) Act. However, India still lacks exclusive legislation which deals with pornography per se.

Crime Cost of Pornography

Pornography is not banned under the Indian legislation but it is the distribution, downloading & production which is punishable under the IT Act. The conundrum of porn ban was taken up in the case of *Kamlesh Vaswani* v. *Union of India W.P. 177/2013 (SC)*, wherein the petitioner pleaded that pornography influences the mind of sexual offenders with notions like that he can achieve sexual pleasures not just from sexual release but also the gratification of control & domination over women (generally depicted as a submissive partner).

The exploitation of Porn actors is one of the first results of the porn industry. Although, they're not considered as victims but the offenders under the criminal justice system. Numerous surveys have shown that usually these actors are pushed into pornography by fraud under the impression of modelling contracts (Aatreya, 2018). For the sake of continuous production, these actors are often harassed, tortured, blackmailed & even murdered in extreme cases due to demand pressure (Aatreya, 2018).

Revenge Porn is the recent trending crime in Indian society. Usually when relationships end the enraged partner avenges the loss by relying on cyber-crime of publicizing the intimate videos as porn content for the sake of revenge (Bansal & Agarwal, 2020). The vulnerability of such victims is not covered under any of the criminal legislation in India.

Porn-induced human trafficking is being recognized & documented in the recent NCRB data of India too. The latest statistics show that one of the purposes of human trafficking was child pornography in the year 2020 (*National Crime Records Bureau (NCRB), Victims Rescued -2020)*. Similarly, under the head of crime against women India recorded as many as 1655 cases relating to cyber pornography & obscenity in the previous year (*National Crime Records Bureau (NCRB), Cyber Crimes against Women -2020)*. Now, this can be the argument of how such crimes can be related to the viewer of porn. The high demand for pornographic materials by such viewers induces these crimes due to the flourishing porn industry in the sub-continent. India ranks third among the most porn-watching nations while fourth in terms of rape crime nations (Bridges et al., 2010).

The Productivity Cost of porn addicts is one of the intangible burdens on society. Just like drug addiction, porn addiction is a concern for the social environment. Generally, porn addiction affects the personal life of the viewer in terms of communication compatibility, sexual expectations, the biological clock of the body & many times the career of the person as well. These implications are not entertained or noticed by the family or society initially but subsequently, each of them pays the price of such consensual victimless crime ironically.

Gambling

Gambling or betting was considered a recreational activity in ancient times. It refers to consensus between two or more people for playing a game of chance involving stake which will become the possession of the winner. Thus, it happens to motivate gamblers for its economic benefits attached with it i.e., money or assets.

However, like other victimless crimes gambling has also a morality connotation. According to Manu, in the ancient Indian philosophy gambling was considered a self-destructing activity as it diminishes the wealth & honesty of the person. Gambling is usually taken up as a shortcut method of earning money with minimal skill & investment. Although, the consequences of such games are quite persuasive on the vulnerable section of society. The Hon'ble Supreme elucidates the harmful consequences of gambling in the landmark case of *State of Bombay v. RMD Chamarbaugwala* 1957 AIR 699 SC as follows:

"...which encourages a spirit of a reckless propensity for making easy gain by luck or chance, which leads to the loss of the hard-earned money of the undiscerning and improvident common man and thereby lowers his standard of living and drives him into a chronic state of indebtedness and eventually disrupts the peace and happiness of his humble home...."

The gambling & betting being the state subject (The Constitution of India, 1950) is usually regulated by the states considering the economy & revenues for the region. Likewise, the Government of Haryana passed a bill named the Public Gambling (Haryana Amendment) Bill of 2002, which aimed to create tourism opportunities in the state with the help of casino licensing & regulation. However, the amendment bill was reserved by the governor on a few grounds which also included "various criminal activities such as drug running, prostitution and extortion by organized crime syndicates".

The negative impact on the youth is also entertained by the legislators under the act of The Young Person's (Harmful Publications) Act, 1956 wherein penal consequences are attracted if any literature gambling or betting related is published under the 'harmful publication' category which may influence the young minds adversely. The number of juveniles in conflict with the law in the year 2020 due to gambling was 86 across the nation (*National Crime Records Bureau (NCRB), Juveniles in Conflict with Law -2020)*.

Similarly, any game of chance or contest which promotes gambling or betting activities comes under the *"unfair trade practices"* within the ambit of the Consumer Protection Act, 1986. Under the Information Technology (Intermediaries Guidelines) Rules, 2011 the 'intermediaries' or network service providers are held liable if they host any information which refers to or encourages gambling. However, the dilemma of economic boost in terms of revenue & morality plays a role in the above-stated regulation of gambling-related activities. The burden of such activities is what to be considered here on causal terms.

Impact On Family of Gamblers

Intimate Partner Violence (IPV) is one of the phenomena which is being taken up as one of the consequences of gambling. According to World Health Organization (2002), it refers to any act or behavior between the relationships that may cause harm in any form i.e., psychological, physical, or sexual. As per the studies, around one-third of people with a gambling addiction have reported the problem of IPV – 38% being the victims whereas 37% as the perpetrators of the IPV (Dowling, 2014). On the same grounds, 11% of IPV offenders have reported having gambling problems as well (Dowling, 2014).

Table 3. Gambler's phase in terms of conflict with the family

Denial Phase	***Occasional worries*** ***Keep concerns to self*** ***Make excuses for gambling***	***Consider gambling temporary*** ***Accepts increased gambling*** ***Questions unpaid bills***	***Unexplained financial crisis*** ***Accepts remorse of gambler***
Stress Phase	***Spouse spends less time with family*** ***Arguments*** ***Spouse feels rejected***	***Demands upon gambler*** ***Attempts to control gambling*** ***Provides bailouts***	***Avoids children, family*** ***Isolation Intense resentment***
Exhaustion Phase	***Thinking impaired*** ***Confusion*** ***Physical symptoms***	***Immobilization*** ***Rage***	***Doubts sanity*** ***Anxiety, Panic***
End Traits	**HELPLESSNESS HOPELESSNESS**	**MENTAL BREAKDOWN SUBSTANCE ABUSE**	**DIVORCE SUICIDAL THOUGHTS & ATTEMPTS**

Source: Australian Research centre

The above table depicts the phases of the gamblers considering its impact on their family & mental health. Though, India lacks substantive study on the internal private repercussions of gambling on the individual. The eventual results of the gambling addiction can show the legit victimization of the family & societal structure of the person involved in such "victimless activity" in long run. The end traits are what could be the most disastrous harm to any person.

'Loss Chasing' is another synonym for the gambling addiction wherein due to quick money temptation person plays for longer duration & traps under the vicious cycle of loss (Law Commission of India, 2018). Loss chasing often led to 'problem gambling' which is equivalent to the level of drug addiction. Such gamblers face withdrawal & cravings indicia when they're dispossessed of the gambling.

Crime burden due to gambling is registered under the Gambling Act. Accordingly, the crime rate in gambling head is as high as 11.5% for the year 2020 with a total share of 6.6% in the crime share (*National Crime Records Bureau (NCRB),* SLL Crimes (Crime Head-wise) - 2018-2020).

Economic Cost

The introduction of virtual currency in the Indian economy has also contributed to the rise of online gambling. Such gambling is usually out of the reach of law enforcement regulators. The studies in 2018 estimated that the online gambling market may rise to $1 billion by the year 2021(Law Commission of India, 2018).

Henceforth, the Reserve Bank of India (RBI) issued a circular on outlawing the usage of virtual currency in the year 2018 (Law Commission of India, 2018). Another prominent route for corruption in India is sports betting primarily cricket-related match-fixing or betting. Reports reveal that approximately INR 1,300 crore is invested in each international cricket match in one day format where the Indian team participates (Law Commission of India, 2018). Likewise, in the 2016 T-20 cricket world cup it is estimated that INR 30,000 crores were gambled via betting (George et al., 2020). Sports betting paves the way for illegal betting & black money in the Indian Economy.

Illegal betting is a threat to the economy due to fading out of profits from the taxation regime which consequently leads to black money marketing (Law Commission of India, 2018). The reason why gambling costs are heavy to the economy of the nation irrespective of connected revenue activities like casinos licensing revenue or tourism avenue.

'ZEMIOLOGY' IN VICTIMLESS CRIMES

The above discussion predicts the unknowability of the 'harm' to other actors in the commission of victimless crimes. The concept of harm in the criminal justice system is usually evaluated narrowly based on the penology attached to it. However, certain factors are being ignored by traditional criminology in the formation of the crime causal theory. Some of these include inequality, poverty, gender-based discrimination, geography, family history, unemployment, etc.

Therefore, the demand for a new discipline as the critique of traditional criminology comes into the picture that is ***'Zemiology'***. Zemiology originates from the Greek word *'zemia'* which means 'harm' and is mostly concerned with the 'social harm' study in relation to crimes. While the demand for justice is taken into consideration by the administration when there is substantial & noticeable harm or loss to the victims of crime. The complex & the present-day communities demand the recognition of the ***'social justice'*** within the ambit of the criminal justice system.

The various epistemology reveals that justice can be acquired easily against those crimes which are under the criminal law either substantially or procedurally, whereas the victims of social harm are at different pedestal due to non-recognition by the criminal justice system (Tombs, 2018). The harm caused due to victimless crimes like drugs or gambling is usually on society which does not directly find its position in the criminology or criminal justice system more or less.

The problem *of 'double victimization' i*s often associated with the crimes where the victims are under the jeopardy of the actions of the offenders along with the inabilities of the criminal justice system to ensure justice to such victims due to their ignorance of the magnitude of the harm (Tombs, 2018). For instance, the sexual violence due to access to 'pornography' does not come under the immediate crime & cause analogy due to notions of pornography being the victimless crime with no definite harm to another party.

Crime control is one of the tools which is usually relied upon by criminologists & the criminal justice system to curb the menace of crimes. The zemiological study also incorporates the idea of reduction of the crime itself & not as the critique of the criminal justice system or critical criminology (Copson, 2018). The reason behind the demand for social harm recognition is due to benign attitudes towards the crimes like prostitution, environmental pollution, suicide attempts, etc.

In such crimes, generally, the offender is given importance due to the act's impact on himself primarily & its counter effect on society secondarily. However, the behavioural science which criminology studies are the situations or psychology which contributes to the commission of the illegal activity is at the back foot. The concept that inequalities in society are not recognized as the 'harm' subsequently with no legal intervention to be sought upon can be the reference point for victimless crimes (Copson, 2018).

The vicious cycle of poverty & criminality is often related to each other in the majority of the cases in India. The fact that the motive behind gambling is usually the quick economic gains or the taking up the profession of prostitution due to economic compulsion is another societal deficiency. The victimless crimes though identify the offender as one who is at loss but the impact of inequality & social harm it might create within the community is yet to be researched.

Hence, if the question arises on why new concepts like zemiology shall be considered to control the victimless crimes? The simple answer lies with the ignorance of the social harm theory & the repercussions following it for the generations & the states. Critical criminology & zemiology, therefore, understands the contemporaneity of the offenses in the digital age with fast-moving economies.

CONCLUSION: FROM 'ANOMIE' TO 'RIGHTEOUSNESS'

The complex nature of victimless crimes as discussed in the paper brings us back to the question of what causes such crimes at first instance? Is it the society-induced criminality or psychology aspect of the individual? This led us to the famous ***"anomie theory"*** by Emile Durkheim. According to him, anomie refers to the normlessness in the society due to the lack of standards & purpose in the community (Encyclopedia Britannica, 2017). He gave this theory while studying another victimless crime i.e., *"suicide"*. The key reason for such a state was postulated him was the psychological impact on the society members due to the futile sensitivity backed with feelings of emptiness & despair. In such a scenario, often being righteousness is considered irrelevant, as what is desirable is still vague for such a society.

Through this paper, we have tried to discuss the effect of such "anomie" behavior on Indian society and how the term "victimless" is just ignoring the cost of such crimes in a larger context. Similarly, the question of the decriminalization of such crimes due to the absence of the mill's harm principle is being countered with the inter-linkage of mill's proviso with that of modern victimless crimes.

The State must act according to the paternalistic unit. The need for policy intervention by the State as highlighted by the authors is required to curb the menace of such crimes. While formulating such policy for victimless crimes, the costs of victimless crimes as discussed by the authors must be taken into consideration.

To recognize the crime causal & associated cost, we have discussed the study of 'zemiology' towards the end to analyze the social harm of such crimes. Therefore, along with the burden of such crimes, the legislators & scholars should also study the cause of such crimes vis-à-vis society from where self-harming offender germinates.

ACKNOWLEDGMENT

The authors would like to extend heartfelt appreciation to all the anonymous Peer reviewers and the Editor for their insightful comments. Particular thanks are due to Mr. Karun Sanjaya, Assistant Professor of Law, Symbiosis Law School, Nagpur, India for liasoning this publication opportunity and enlightening review on the manuscript. Acknowledgments are due to Prof. (Dr.) Kavita Singh, Professor of Law, the West Bengal National University of Juridical Sciences, Kolkata, India for developing a better understanding of the topic as course instructor for Criminology and also for facilitating the assessments as the current manuscript is the research output of the same.

REFERENCES

Aatreya, S. S. (2018). Obscenity and the Depiction of Women in Pornography: Revisiting the Kamlesh Vaswani Petition. *Nalsar Student Law Review, 13*(1). https://nslr.in/wp-content/uploads/2019/05/NSLR-Vol-13-Issue-1-No-1.pdf

Bansal, V., & Agarwal, I. (2020). Legality Of Pornographic Content Dissemination In India: A Critical Analysis. *Shimla Law Review, 3*, 43. https://www.hpnlu.ac.in/PDF/f0fb7022-a4e6-4ddd-8485-0f01543cabf5.pdf

Bridges, A. J., Wosnitzer, R., Scharrer, E., Sun, C., & Liberman, R. (2010). Aggression and sexual behavior in best-selling pornography videos: A content analysis update. *Violence Against Women, 16*(10), 1065–1085. doi:10.1177/1077801210382866 PMID:20980228

Copson, L. (2018). Beyond 'Criminology vs. Zemiology': Reconciling crime with social harm. In Zemiology: reconnecting crime and social harm (pp. 33–56). Palgrave Macmillan.

Dowling, N. (2014). *The Impact of Gambling Problems on Families*. Australian Gambling Research Centre. https://core.ac.uk/download/pdf/30673225.pdf

Dyzenhaus, D. (1992). John Stuart Mill and the Harm of Pornography. *Ethics, 102*(3), 534–551. doi:10.1086/293423

Encyclopedia Britannica. (2017). *Anomie | sociology*. Encyclopædia Britannica. https://www.britannica.com/topic/anomie

Fuller, R. C. (1942). Morals and the Criminal Law. *Journal of Criminal Law and Criminology (1931-1951), 32*(6), 624. doi:10.2307/1136815

George, S., Fenn, J., & Robonderdeep, K. (2020). An Overview of Gambling in India. *Global Journal of Medical, Pharmaceutical, and Biomedical Update, 15*(4), 4. doi:10.25259/GJMPBU_7_2020

Gross, H. (2012). Crime, Harm, and Moral Wrong. In *Crime and Punishment: A Concise Moral Critique*. Academic. doi:10.1093/acprof:oso/9780199644711.003.0007

International Narcotics Control Board. (2014). *Report of the International Narcotics Control Board for 2013*. United Nations. https://www.incb.org/documents/Publications/AnnualReports/AR2013/English/AR_2013_E.pdf

Jenkins, J. P. (2019). *Pornography | sociology*. Encyclopædia Britannica. https://www.britannica.com/topic/pornography

John, R. M., Sinha, P., Munish, V. G., & Tullu, F. T. (2021). Economic Costs of Diseases and Deaths Attributable to Tobacco Use in India, 2017-2018. *Nicotine & Tobacco Research: Official Journal of the Society for Research on Nicotine and Tobacco*, *23*(2), 294–301. doi:10.1093/ntr/ntaa154 PMID:32805055

Mill, J. & Lindsay, A. D. (2016). *On liberty and other essays*. Digireads.com Publishing.

Kryszajtys, D. T., Hahmann, T. E., Schuler, A., Hamilton-Wright, S., Ziegler, C. P., & Matheson, F. I. (2018). Problem Gambling and Delinquent Behaviours Among Adolescents: A Scoping Review. *Journal of Gambling Studies*, *34*(3), 893–914. doi:10.1007/s10899-018-9754-2 PMID:29470759

Law Commission of India. (2018). *Legal Framework: Gambling and Sports Betting Including In Cricket In India, Report No. 276* (p. 105). Government of India.

Macleod, C. (2016, August 25). *John Stuart Mill (Stanford Encyclopedia of Philosophy)*. Stanford.edu. https://plato.stanford.edu/entries/mill/

Magnitude of Substance Use in India (p. 34). (2019). Ministry of Social Justice and Empowerment, Government of India and NDDTC, AIIMS. https://socialjustice.gov.in/writereaddata/UploadFile/Survey%20Report.pdf

Ministry of Road Transport and Highways (Transport Research Wing). (2022). *Road Accidents in India 2022*. Government of India. https://morth.nic.in/sites/default/files/RA_2022_30_Oct.pdf

Moore, M. H. (1991). Drugs, the Criminal Law, and the Administration of Justice. *The Milbank Quarterly*, *69*(4), 529–560. doi:10.2307/3350227 PMID:1806801

Morgan, R. (1980). *Theory and Practice: Pornography and Rape, Take Back the Night: Women on Pornography*. William Morrow and Co.

National Crime Records Bureau (NCRB), Indian Penal Code, Police Disposal of SLL Crime Cases (Crime Head-wise). (2020). Ministry of Home Affairs.

National Research Council 2101 Constitution Ave Washington Dc 20418, & National Academies 500 Fifth Street Nw Washington Dc 20001. (1999). *Pathological Gambling: A Critical Review*. United States.

Navtej Singh Johar v. Union of India, (The Supreme Court of India, 2018). https://main.sci.gov.in/supremecourt/2016/14961/14961_2016_Judgement_06-Sep-2018.pdf

Oh, E. (2016). Mill on Paternalism. *Journal of Political Inquiry, 4.*

Ripstein, A. (2006). Beyond the Harm Principle. *Philosophy & Public Affairs, 34*(3), 215–245. doi:10.1111/j.1088-4963.2006.00066.x

Secretariat, U. N. (1975). *Economic and Social Consequences of Crime: New Challenges for Research and Planning*. OJP. https://www.ojp.gov/pdffiles1/Digitization/65619NCJRS.pdf

Silver, J. R., & Silver, E. (2020). The Nature and Role of Morality in Offending: A Moral Foundations Approach. *Journal of Research in Crime and Delinquency, 58*(3), 343–380. doi:10.1177/0022427820960201

Stewart, H. (1999). Legality and Morality in H.L.A. Hart's Theory of Criminal Law. *SMU Law Review, 52*(1). https://scholar.smu.edu/cgi/viewcontent.cgi?article=1693&context=smulr

Tankersley, J. (2021, November 25). Is pornography killing the economy? *Washington Post*. https://www.washingtonpost.com/news/wonk/wp/2013/09/06/is-pornography-killing-the-economy/

The Narcotic Drugs and Psychotropic Substances Act. (1985). LD. https://lddashboard.legislative.gov.in/actsofparliamentfromtheyear/narcotic-drugs-and-psychotropic-substances-act-1985

Thompson, L. J. (2013, December 23). *Paternalism | social science*. Encyclopedia Britannica. https://www.britannica.com/topic/paternalism

Tombs, S. (2018). For Pragmatism and Politics: Crime, Social Harm and Zemiology. In Zemiology: Reconnecting Crime and Social Harm (pp. 11–31). Palgrave Macmillan.

United Nations Office of Drug and Crime (UNODC). (2022). *World Drug Report 2022*. United Nations. https://www.unodc.org/unodc/en/data-and-analysis/world-drug-report-2022.html

United Nations Office of Drugs and Crime. (n.d.). Indian Ocean East. *Global Maritime Crime Programme*. UNDoC. https://www.unodc.org/unodc/en/piracy/indian-ocean-east.html

Vinnakota, D., Arafat, S. M. Y., & Kabir, R. (2021). Pornography and Sexual Violence Against Women in India: A Scoping Review. *Journal of Psychosexual Health*, *3*(3), 216–221. doi:10.1177/26318318211023935

Chapter 8
Exploring Reconciliation Prospects Amidst Identity and Governance Crisis in Manipur

Jyothis Mary
Hume Institute for Post-Graduate Studies, Lausanne, Switzerland

ABSTRACT

The conflicts in Manipur have a long socio-political history. The root causes behind these clashes are diverse and complex, including colonization, governance issues, drug trafficking, discrimination, geopolitics, and militarization. The ethnic groups and governments have failed to reconcile the differences peacefully. Through this chapter, the researcher is trying to provide an overview of the conflict and how this has affected the people of Manipur. The researcher will identify various dimensions of the conflict in Manipur and analyze how drug trafficking, land rights, and illegal migration are linked to ethnic violence between Kukis and Meiteis by highlighting the historical, cultural, and political aspects of the problem. Further, the existing policies and laws are analysed. Finally, the need for peace negotiations, the requirement for the disarmament of the communities, the need for investigation and trial of grave violations, and the necessity for establishing a truth and reconciliation commission will be discussed.

India is a country more diverse than many continents, yet united by its spirit, with its states embodying this very essence. The Northeast part of India, often referred to as the seven sisters of India, includes Arunachal Pradesh, Assam, Manipur, Meghalaya, Mizoram, Nagaland, and Tripura, is one of the most culturally diverse areas in the world. Historically, the Northeast region has been one of the world's prominent

DOI: 10.4018/979-8-3693-0327-6.ch008

migratory routes, making it a meeting ground for many races and communities (Kumar Das, 2007). Northeast India has a presence of more than 200 tribes with a rich heritage and distinct socio-cultural practices (National Council of Educational Research and Training, 2017). Manipur, also known as the 'land of jewels', is a multi-ethnic state with a population of 28, 55,794 (Census of India, 2011). With the presence of various ethnic groups, Manipur has evolved into a multi-ethnic, multi-cultural, multi-religious, and multi-linguistic society. Geographically, the state is divided into valley districts and hill districts. The valley is known as Imphal Valley and is surrounded by Naga Hill ranges and Lushai Hill ranges. Among population, 58.9% represents the population in the valley, and 41.1% indicates the population in the hills (Thaimei, 2021). The population of Manipur mainly consists of three ethnic groups: Meiteis, who dominate in the valleys; Kukis, and Nagas, who are inhibited on the surrounding hills. Among the Kukis and Nagas, there are 33 recognized tribal groups (Census of India, 2011). The population in Manipur is divided into four major categories: General, Other Backward Classes, Scheduled Caste, and Scheduled Tribes. The Meiteis belong to the non-tribal category and are mostly Hindus, and the Kukis and Nagas belong to the Scheduled Tribe category and are predominantly Christians.

Historically, Manipur was ruled by the Metei dynasty. The Meities and Nagas have been present in the valley and hills for centuries. The British conquered the Manipur kingdom in 1891(Khan, 2006). The Kukis were brought and settled by the Britishers surrounding the valley to protect the valley from attacks from the Naga tribes (Schoetz, 2023). As the Kukis had migrated during the 19th century, the Meiteis considered Kukis as outsiders or foreigners, although initially, the Kukis were not enemies but supporters of Meities. However, the Old Kukis are believed to have lived in the state traditionally, and only New Kukis migrated in the 19th century from the Laushai hills (Das, 2005). As the kings of Manipur and the British used the Kuki community against the Naga community to keep the Nagas under control, the conflict between these two communities arose (Kumar Sharma, 2016). The Nagas strongly resisted the efforts to control them or conquer the Naga-dominating parts of Manipur. The affiliation between Kukis and the British did not last long. During World War I, the Kukis refused to join the Labour Corps and declared war against the British, marking the beginning of the Anglo-Kuki War, 1917-1919 (Guite & Haokip, 2018). The war did not end in favour of the Kukis, as the British troops outnumbered them. In 1949, Manipur was integrated into the Indian Union as a 'C' state, then categorized as Union Territory in 1956, and later upgraded to statehood in 1971.

The ethnic tension between different groups in Manipur continued even after independence. The topography, socio-economic status, and historical factors such as ethnicity, tribal conflicts, migration, control over local resources, and extensive international borders contribute to a delicate situation in Manipur. Over the course of time, drug trafficking and narcotic trade have additionally played a role in accelerating the conflicts prevalent in Manipur.

Over the past few months, Manipur has witnessed an escalation in ethnic clashes between the Kuki and Meitei communities. Although the state repression by central and state governments is high in Manipur, the government is unable to control the ethnic violence successfully. The present violence is the result of decades-long conflict between tribals and non-tribals, mistrust among communities, governance issues, and uneven distribution of resources. Moreover, the conflict is an outcome of more serious issues such as illegal drug cultivation, illegal migration, identity crisis, land encroachments, and distress toward state actions. This chapter provides a comprehensive examination of all these issues and focuses on how illegal drug cultivation, drug trafficking, and migration are linked to the identity and governance crisis in Manipur. As the present conflict is majorly between the Meitei and Kuki communities, the chapter has limited its scope to the dispute between these two communities and delves into the historical and cultural aspects of the conflict. Further, the chapter explores and suggests peace-building mechanisms appropriate for the state to bring back harmony in Manipur.

THE HILLS-VALLEY DIVIDE

It is important to outline the hill-valley divide in Manipur to understand the existing conflict. All socio-economic, political, and cultural developments or non-developments in Manipur have to be seen through the prism of this divide (Hausing, 2009.). Before the arrival of the British, the hills were under the autonomous rule of Chiefs. During the colonial period, the hills and valley were differentiated and administered separately. The Britishers exercised direct rule in the valley and indirect rule partially in the hills, widening the gap between the hills and the valley. Moreover, the divide-and-rule policy of the British widened the cultural gap among the communities (Kumar Sharma, 2017). During the colonial period, the policies adopted excluded the hills as the hills were considered unproductive and economically unviable. Therefore, the gap in economic development between tribals and non-tribals increased.

This divide continued even after the British rule. Over the years, the inequality and gap between the hills and valley have grown, leading to continued ethnic conflicts. The valley region remained the center for all socio-political activities. The non-tribal people occupying the valley have more fertile land and are economically superior to the tribals in the hills. The valley people enjoyed more political power and marginalized the tribes in the hills. Due to the larger number of Meitei people residing in the valley, they have a higher number of representatives in the state assembly (only 19 seats are reserved for tribals out of 60 seats), giving them more power in decision-making. Since 1990, there have been only Meitei Chief Ministers for Manipur. The Meiteis are considered economically and politically powerful compared to the Kukis and Nagas, who live in deplorable conditions on the underdeveloped hills. The state governments in Manipur have always been alleged to have a bias in favour of Meiteis and use most of its funds are utilized towards the development of Imphal Valley while depriving the rightful developments in the hills.

The developments are different in valleys and hills. The Meiteis are in a more advanced and prosperous position compared to other ethnic communities in Manipur in terms of education, infrastructure, and employment. In contrast, the hill areas faced inadequacies in educational services, transportation, health care, hospitals, infrastructure, employment opportunities, and access to resources. The state resources concentrate on the valley, causing inequality toward the hill people. In this hills-valley divide, Kukis are more vulnerable compared to Nagas, who have already secured a homeland for themselves, Nagaland (Kipgen & Chowdhury, 2016).

This non-inclusive growth and the failure to address the legitimate aspirations of the hill people have led to political unrest, continued insurgency, ethnic violence, and demands for self-determination and autonomy movements in Manipur. For several decades, the Kuki homeland and Greater Nagaland movements demanded the right to self-determination and self-governance.

Demand for Kuki Homeland

Post-independence, the Northeast region witnessed the emergence of many ethnic-based insurgency groups, causing political unrest and ethnic violence. The formation of such groups is often driven by the concern of dominance by other ethnic or tribal groups along with the desire to protect their ethnic territoriality and natural resources, especially land. When the plea for self-determination and a separate homeland had been granted to many ethnic groups in North East India, such as Nagas (Nagaland), Mizo (Mizoram), Khasis, and Jaintias (Meghalaya), the same was denied for the Kukis.

Based on mythology, the Kuki-Chin groups believe they have a common origin, and they emerged from a cave called the 'Khul' or rock called 'Chhinlung' (Chungkhoseibaite,2016). Some believe Kukis are originally from the state settlement called 'Sinlung' (Das, 2005). Although the myths cannot be verified, many ethnic communities root their cultural history in such stories. A place called Zale'n-gam, 'the land of freedom', exists in the memories of Kuki Ancestors. Before the arrival of the British, the Kukis were one political sovereign; however, later, they were divided into three countries: India, Bangladesh, and Myanmar (Haokip, 2014).

The Kuki National Assembly in 1960 and the Kuki Zonal Chief Counsil in 1970 submitted a proposal for a separate Kuki state to the government of India. In the 1980s, Kuki armed groups and revolutionary organizations emerged to secure Kukiland by integrating all Kuki-inhibited areas within the Indian Union. The Kuki National Organisation, formed in 1980, started a strong national movement to form Zale'n-gam. There are around 15 armed groups under the Kuki National Organizations: Kuki National Army (kna), Kuki National Front-Military Council (knf-mc), Kuki National Front Zogam (knf), United Socialist Republican Army (usra), Zou Defence Volunteer (zdv), Zomi Revolutionary Front (zrf), United Kom-rem Revolutionary Army (ukra), Hmar National Army (hna), Kuki Liberation Army (kla), United Old Kuki Liberation Army (uokla), kla), Pakan Revolutionary Army (pka), Kuki Revolutionary Army (kra), Kuki National Front-Samuel (knf-s), Kuki Liberation Army (kla-p), and Kuki Liberation Army (kla-t) (Haokip, 2014). The demand of the Kuki National Organisation is for a separate statehood in India as well as in Myanmar. Initially, the organisation concentrated its operations in Myanmar; however, during the late 1990s, it shifted its focus to India. The Kuki State Demand Committee conducted several strikes and economic bandhs demanding Kukiland. To counter such strikes and insurgencies, the government of India imposed the Armed Forces (Special Powers) Act, 1958 in Manipur in 1980.

The Armed Forces (Special Powers) Act, 1958

The Act empowers the governor, state administrator, or central government to declare areas to be disturbed or dangerous, thereby using the armed forces. As per the Act, special powers are given to designated officers in the armed forces to fire upon or use force or even cause death when any person acts in contravention of the law in the disturbed area (Section 4). Furthermore, no prosecution or legal proceedings can be initiated against anyone acting according to this Act except with the prior permission of the central government (Section 6). This enormous power given under the Act to the armed forces led to large-scale violations of the human rights of the people of Manipur. The arbitrary use of special powers by the forces resulted in torture, extra-judicial execution, rape, and forced disappearances (Chawla, 2023).

The Suspension of Operations Agreement

In 2008, the Kuki National Organisation and the United People's Front signed the Suspension of Operations Agreement as an initiative to negotiate between the insurgent groups and the governments. The tripartite agreement aimed to initiate political dialogue between the insurgent groups, end hostilities, and settle the demands for a separate Kuki state. According to the agreement, the signatories should not undertake any activity threatening the integrity of the state. The agreement requires the insurgent groups to keep the weapons in locked storages, which security forces and insurgent groups will monitor.

LAND CONFLICTS IN MANIPUR

Unfortunately, land alone can be the cause of ethnic violence in Manipur., as it has an important role in shaping cultural and ethnic identity. The land is closely connected to the question of identity, politics, and power in Manipur. Land is considered the single most important physical possession for the scheduled tribes (Sitlhou, 2015). Moreover, indigenous people have a spiritual connection with lands.

The Meiteis hold only 10% of the land in Manipur, and the Kukis and Nagas hold 90% of the land (Madhusudhanan, 2023). Throughout the years, Manipur's economy remains predominantly agricultural. The people in Manipur mostly adhere to Jhum cultivation. The Kukis and Nagas practice shifting cultivation, while the Meteis practice terraced cultivation. The Kukis and Nagas mainly depend on land and forests for resources. They follow traditional farming practices and depend on farming for their survival.

The existence of both government legislation and customary laws in Manipur makes the land relations in Manipur complex. The tribals demand respect for culture and customs, thereby allowing for self-rule in the hills of Manipur. Kukis and Nagas have different traditional land ownership systems. Based on the traditional land system of Kukis, the whole land belongs to the Chief, the villagers might have permanent or temporary ownership over the land, and the land is distributed to the villagers for housing and cultivation (Sitlhou, 2015). The Chiefs have their own customary courts and traditional enforcement mechanisms to ensure the customary practices (Kipgen, 2017). The Naga tribe has a three-tier land system consisting of clan, village, and individual lands (Kumar Sharma, 2016). The Kukis and Nagas have an autonomous self-governing structure under traditional hereditary Chiefs (Kipgen, 2017). The tribal groups in Manipur have different forms of land ownership and management systems based on their customary practices.

During the colonial period, the Hill administration was brought under the British Government. However, the valley was under the princely administration. According to the Forest Act of 1878, the forests were categorized into three categories such as reserved, protected, and village forests. The governments gradually increased their control over the forest lands. With the introduction of the Indian Forest Act of 1927, the indigenous people in Manipur slowly lost their indigenous rights over the forest lands.

The Manipur Land Revenue and Land Reforms Act, 1960

Post-independence, land became a more complex issue in Manipur, and regulation became difficult as it had tribal and non-tribal populations. Implementing a uniform land law applicable to both hills and valley in Manipur would have endangered the rights of tribal people over the land. The Manipur Land Revenue and Land Reforms Act 1960 (hereinafter MLR&LR Act), one of Manipur's most important land laws, was adopted and applied throughout the valley and some parts of the hills. The MLR&LR Act empowers the state government to extend its application as a whole or any part to the hill area. Initially, the MLR&LR Act allowed the hills to practice customary ownership over the lands. As per the Act, all lands, forests, mines, and minerals are state property. Section 11, Chapter III of the Act specifies:

All lands, public roads, lanes and paths and bridges, ditches, dikes, and fences on or the same, the beds of the rivers, streams, nallahs, lakes and tanks and all canals and water courses, and all standing and flowing water and all rights in or over the same or appertaining thereto, which are not the property of any person and are hereby declared to be the property of any person are hereby declared to be the property of the Government.

Therefore, the state government has a legitimate power over lands and natural resources. For the MLR&LR Act to be applicable to a property, the state government must do a cadastral survey, and the land must be formally included in the land records. Previously, most of the lands in the hills were un-surveyed. However, over the years, large parts of hills were included under the Act. Through the extension of the Act to the hill areas, the government intends to remove the hill-valley divide geographically. Nevertheless, this has been widely opposed by the tribes occupying the hills.

The Act has a special provision (Section 158) for protecting the tribal areas, which prohibits the sale of tribal land to non-tribal people without the permission of the District Council or Deputy Commissioner. Therefore, the transfer of land by a person belonging to the scheduled tribe is not valid until it is transferred to another person of the scheduled tribe, with the consent in writing by the Deputy Commissioner, or the transfer is a mortgage to a cooperative society. Thus, the tribal people can purchase land in the valley, while the Meiteis cannot buy the land in the hills, which the Meiteis consider discriminatory. Furthermore, the Constitution of India, through Article 371 (C), protects the tribal areas in the hills by prohibiting non-tribal settlements and land acquisitions. The Manipur Hill Areas (Acquisition of Chief's Rights) Act, 1967, authorises the Manipur government to acquire the rights, titles, and interests of Chiefs over the hills. The Meities demand the extension of the MLR&LR Act to the hills, pointing to the scarcity of cultivable land in the valley and its abundance in the hills.

In 2015, three bills were passed in the Manipur State Assembly: (i) The Protection of Manipur People Bill, 2015 (ii) The Manipur Land Revenue and Land Reforms (Seventh Amendment) Bill, 2015 and (iii) The Manipur Shops and Establishments (Second Amendment) Bill, 2015, leading to protest from many tribal people. The tribals fear that the passing of these laws is an attempt by Meiteis to acquire land in the hills. The Minister of State in the Ministry of Home Affairs reported in the Rajya Sabha that nine people died in the protest against these bills.

Drug Trafficking and Illicit Drug Cultivation in Manipur

Manipur is alleged to have a historic drug problem. Ganga and Cannabis are widely used in Manipur for religious purposes. They also use raw Opium and Kanni during childbirth to reduce delivery pain. During the 1980s and 1990s, the State of Manipur witnessed an increase in drug addiction and the spread of HIV/Aids among drug users (Haiokip, 2020). With only .2% of India's total population, Manipur constitutes 8% of India's total HIV cases. 84% of the men got infected with HIV through needle sharing. Most of the drug users in Manipur are adolescents or young people, and nearly 10% of them are women (Priyokumar Singh, 2022)

The location of Manipur makes it a convenient route for the narcotics trade from the Golden Triangle. Heroin produced in the Golden Triangle enters Manipur through the India-Myanmar border, and the opium produced in Manipur is transported to Myanmar and smuggled back later as heroin. Smugglers use many well-identified and lesser-known routes to traffic drugs to Manipur. The drug money further leads to an increase in money laundering and corruption in Manipur. Nevertheless, recent concerns revolve around issues of poppy cultivation and transnational drug trafficking in Manipur. The government alleges that the drug mafia and illegal migrants orchestrate the ongoing violence.

Poppy Cultivation

Previously, Manipur was famous for high-quality Ganga production, but lately, the cultivation has shifted to poppy, which is more profitable (Naresh Singh & Kishorchannd Singh, 2023). There is a vast cultivation of poppy in the hills of Manipur. The hills of Manipur are ideal for the cultivation, propagation, and synthesis of opium poppy. Lately, the cultivation and manufacture of poppies have largely shifted from Myanmar to Manipur. The hill areas are widely used for poppy cultivation by clearing forest land. Apart from illegal cultivation and drug trafficking, poppy cultivation also causes environmental hazards in the hill areas, such as deforestation and soil erosion, and contributes to climate change. As per the India State of Forest Report (ISFR) 2019, the forest cover in Manipur has decreased by 499.10 sq. km compared to the ISFR 2017 (Forest Survey of India, 2019).

The primary reason for illegal poppy cultivation is rural poverty and unemployment coupled with difficulties farmers face with other crop cultivation due to a lack of infrastructure and lower prices. Additionally, cultivating poppy alongside other crops is easier. The farmers are hugely affected by the continued armed conflicts, insurgency problems, and ethnic conflicts, leading to insufficient income. Poppy cultivation and opium production provide off-season employment. Poppy cultivation is on a massive scale in several parts of Manipur, as it provides financial security to people and is the most profitable existing farming practice in Manipur. The substitute crops provided by the government, cardamom and lemongrass, do not generate profit to the extent that poppy cultivation does. Compared to other crops, poppies can be cultivated everywhere and have a high product value. In fact, it is difficult for any alternate crop to compete with opium in terms of price. Furthermore, due to the underdeveloped conditions, there are not many alternatives available to poor farmers besides poppy cultivation. Previously, the financial institutions were hesitant to give loans to the farmers from the hills due to a lack of collateral; however, now they receive loans faster as the creditor knows the people can pay back as they are involved in poppy cultivation (Singh, 2007). The income generated through poppy cultivation is mostly used by the farmers for educational expenses, health care, and housing.

War on Drugs Campaign by the State Government in Manipur

The present government launched a campaign called 'Nisha Thadokshi' and declared a 'war on drugs' in 2018 to combat drug trafficking, poppy cultivation, opium processing, and drug consumption. The campaign aims to destroy poppy cultivation in hilly areas, drug distribution, and narcotic trade. As part of the campaign, the government has introduced alternative crops such as cardamom and lemongrass to replace poppy cultivation. From 2017 to March 2023, 18,664.5 acres of poppy cultivation have been destroyed by law enforcement agencies ("First Information of Cognizable Crime Report Under Section 154 Criminal Procedure Code at Police Station," 2023). The Manipur police registered 620 cases under the Narcotics Drugs and Psychotropic Substances Act from 2022 to 2023, resulting in 724 arrests (PTI & PTI, 2023). Since 2017, 2518 people have been arrested for drug-related offenses. The government is also conducting drone-facilitated surveys, satellite mapping, and physical surveys to mark poppy cultivation and forest land. However, the Kukis allege the government's actions as selective targeting and aimed at stealing their ancestral lands. They also allege that the funding for poppy cultivation does not come from Myanmar but instead from Imphal Valley Meiteis (Bhattacharya, 2023).

MIGRATION CRISIS IN MANIPUR

The population of Manipur is inclusive of migrants and original people. Migration is a historical incident in Manipur and the heart of many conflicts. Many communities living in Manipur maintain social, cultural, and economic affinities with people across the border due to its historic cultural connections. The major migrant communities in Manipur are the Nepalis, the Bengolis, the Telis (Bhojpuris), and the Punjabis. However, the present problem regarding migration in Manipur is due to the influx of migrants from Myanmar. Manipur is also a national security concern area as it shares a long international border with Myanmar of 398 kilometers, most of which is unfenced. Among many other causes, the immigration of people from Myanmar is a major cause that accelerated the ethnic violence. Immigrants are migrating to Manipur for socio-political reasons rather than economic reasons. There has been an influx of migrants in the Northeast States after the Military Junta took over Myanmar. These refugees are mostly living in Kuki-inhabited villages. As India does not have a refugee law, these people are considered illegal migrants.

The Meiteis allege that there is sudden population growth in Manipur due to massive illegal migration from Myanmar. The illegal migration from Myanmar is seen as a threat to the demographic balance of Manipur by the Meiteis. Moreover, the Meiteis believe that migration is the primary cause of increased poppy cultivation and drug trade in Manipur. They fear the refugees will settle down in their lands and they will become minorities. The illegal migration from countries such as Myanmar, Bangladesh, and Nepal to Manipur created fear in Meiteis over employment opportunities, land encroachments, and resources. The Scheduled Tribe Demand Committee Manipur, while demanding the Scheduled Tribe category, emphasized that illegal immigrants from Myanmar threaten the Meitei community's culture, identity, and ancestral land.

Various origanisations representing Meiteis and Nagas in Manipur are demanding the implementation of the National Register of Citizens (hereinafter NRC) in the state as a response to the alleged population increase in illegal immigrants. In response to the demand for the NRC, the Chief Minister of Manipur announced in March 2023 a house-to-house survey to identify illegal migrants. The Cabinet Sub-Committee (CSC) on Identification of Illegal Immigrants in Manipur has identified 2187 illegal immigrants who have taken shelter in Manipur from Myanmar (Singh, 2023). The government started a drive to collect biometrics of illegal migrants, which is presumed to be put on the negative biometric list to prevent Myanmar nationals from acquiring Indian Citizenship. Apart from this, recently, the Manipur government started an eviction drive to clear illegal settlements from the forest areas. As part of this, many houses and churches were demolished. According to the data from the government, 291 encroachments were removed from forest land (Jain, 2023). Among these, 160 are Meitei evictions. The government states the eviction was not directed towards any specific community; on the contrary, the primary intention is to preserve forest land and deal with the climate crisis.

The Act Easy Policy in 2014 and the Free Movement Regime

When the British demarcated the India- Myanmar border, it divided people of the same culture, ethnicity, and family bonds into two different countries. India shares a land border of around 1643 Kilometers with Myanmar. As Myanmar is the only ASEAN country India shares a border with, it is India's land link to Southeast Asia. The government of India launched the Act Easy Policy in 2014 to promote dialogue, enhance cross-border cooperation, and foster economic stability in the Asia Pacific region. The major focus of the policy has been North East India and improving connectivity with North East India and ASEAN Nations. India also has a 'Neighbourhood First Policy', which intends to improve socio-economic development by focusing on bilateral engagements, trade, and connectivity with neighbouring countries. The economic development of the Northeast region is integral to the success of these two policies.

As part of the Act Easy Policy, India has a pact with Myanmar for the Free Movement Regime (herein after FMR), which allows tribes living on the borders of Northeast India to travel 16 kilometers on either side without a visa. Local nationals of both sides can stay in the other country for three days within 16 km on either side. The rationale behind the FMR was to allow ethnically connected people across the borders of India and Myanmar to move freely to strengthen their brotherhood and promote cultural assimilation. The regime also facilitates local trade and business as the people have been doing cross-border trade for a long time. However, one of the implications of this policy is that it promotes illegal migration and drug trafficking.

Only around 10% of the India-Myanmar border in Manipur is fenced. Complete fencing of the Indo-Myanmar border is not possible due to its difficult terrain. There are over 186 Border points. Border Points 32-130 pass through Manipur (Oinam, 2022). The areas in this region are underdeveloped and barely populated, fostering drug trafficking and illegal trade. The border region is isolated from the mainstream developments of both countries, and it lacks connectivity and infrastructure. Several insurgent groups have taken shelter in this region and engaged in illegal activities such as arms trading, drug smuggling, etc. Due to inaccessibility, lack of 24/7 surveillance, and lack of road communication, the region is exploited by criminals. Poor economic conditions and lack of employment opportunities force the people living near the border to carry and deliver drugs to mafias. The Manipur government considers the free regime movement hinders the state's efforts to hinder drug trafficking, and a large number of illegal migrants from Myanmar belonging to Kuki-Chin are crossing the border. Amidst the ethnic violence in Manipur, the State government requested the Central government to cancel the FMR and to complete border fencing to deal with the influx of migrants from Myanmar. The central government announced on 2nd January 2024 that it will end the FMR soon (Singh, 2024). Furthermore, the standing committee report on India's neighbouring policy has recommended monitoring the demographic changes caused by illegal migration on the borders.

DEMAND FOR SCHEDULED TRIBE STATUS BY MEITEIS

For a long time, the Meiteis have been demanding Scheduled Tribe status, which the Kukis and Nagas jointly oppose, as this might lead to further marginalisation of the tribal groups. The demand for Scheduled Tribe status first came in 1980. By obtaining reservation as a Scheduled Tribe, they could have quotas in public jobs and university courses. Most importantly, this would allow them to acquire property in the hill areas and provide them free access and full ownership of tribal lands. The Meitei community already enjoys job reservations under Scheduled Castes, Other Backward Classes, and Economically Backward Classes. The hill tribals fear that allowing Scheduled Tribe status to economically and educationally advanced Meiteis will allow them to purchase land in the hill areas and take away the state government jobs. Furthermore, the Scheduled Tribe status will allow the Meiteis to contest in elections from the present seats reserved for the Scheduled Tribes, i.e., for Kukis and Nagas, thereby facilitating the Meiteis to contest from all constituencies. In their defence for demanding the Scheduled Tribe status, Meteis argue that they were tribes before its merger with the Union of India, and they lost this status after the merger. Apart from this, they argue that the scheduled tribe status is required to protect their culture, language, ancestral property, and traditions (Deka, 2023).

In 2012, the Scheduled Tribes Demand Committee of Manipur Valley submitted a memorandum to the Governor and, later in 2013, met the Prime Minister of India, requesting the Scheduled Tribe status. In response, the central government asked the state government to submit a formal recommendation, to which the state government did not respond. Again, in 2022, the Meitei Tribe Union approached the Union Tribal Affairs Ministry, and the Ministry forwarded the letter to the Manipur State government, to which also they have not responded.

Later, the Meitei Tribe Union filed a writ petition at the Manipur High Court to consider providing tribal status to the Meitei community. On 19th April 2023, the High Court directed the state government to submit its recommendations for including the Meitei community in the Scheduled Tribe list. After the High Court's order, the Kuki organisations began to protest against the decision. The All-Tribal Students Union Manipur organised a peaceful 'tribal solidarity march' on 3 May 2023, which led to violent counter-protests, and ultimately, violence erupted between the tribal and non-tribal groups. However, the Supreme Court of India took a strong view against the Manipur High Court's order and stated it as factually incorrect.

The recent conflicts have deepened the hatred between the Kuki and Meitei groups, diminishing the scope for harmonization or political integration. There are several social media posts instigating the cleansing of tribals in the hills, reminding the Rwanda Genocide. Tragically, the clashes have resulted in loss of life, destruction of houses, religious and worship places being burned, rape and sexual assault, and displacement of people. More than 220 churches and 17 Hindu Temples have been destroyed (Jazeera, 2023). However, it was not until a shocking video went viral on social media, irrespective of the ban on the internet, showing Kuki women being paraded naked by Meitei men, that the issue gained widespread attention. Up until that point, the central government remained silent on the matter. The attackers threatened the victims to prevent them from reporting the incidents to the police or anyone else. Unfortunately, this was not an isolated incident in Manipur. It is important to acknowledge that women from both ethnic communities in Manipur face violence and become victims of this conflict. There has been a series of crimes committed against women since the beginning of the conflict. Women are being gang raped and brutally murdered by men. The Chief Minister himself has acknowledged that there are hundreds of such cases.

In the wake of the incident, numerous organizations, particularly women-led groups, have risen to protest against the central and state governments. People belonging to both communities are armed with various kinds of weapons. There is a complete breakdown of law and order and gross violations of human rights. The protest demonstrates the public's outrage and demand for accountability and justice. The Kuki community demands greater autonomy and a separate state administration from the existing State Government.

WAY FORWARD: PEACE BUILDING IN MANIPUR

The violence in Manipur is complex as it is linked to drug trafficking, governance issues, migration, and land conflicts. Indeed, there are no easy answers to the conflicts in Manipur. The state requires resolute action from the judiciary, legislative, and executive bodies to resolve the conflict in a meaningful and acceptable way, considering the aspirations of ethnic groups. As of now, the situation in Manipur is showing some signs of response and action. The police have taken some action by arresting a few suspects involved in the crimes against women. Additionally, the National Human Rights Commission has taken cognizance of the situation and issued a notice to the Manipur government demanding information about the steps taken to protect the people, especially women, in the aftermath of the incidents.

Comprehensive Reforms and Development

The state of Manipur requires a comprehensive, structural transformation in order to remove the gap between hills and valley by eradicating poverty, improving living conditions, increasing employment opportunities, and promoting equality. A transparent government and good governance must be instituted in Manipur. Sincere political efforts must be made to reduce the hill-valley divide, facilitating equal distribution of resources and funds. The development of hills must be the primary focus of governments to ensure equity and fairness. Furthermore, the Central government must focus on the state's overall development and equitable distribution of resources. The state administration must facilitate compensating the victims of the ongoing violence and reconstruction of villages and worship places damaged or destructed during the violence.

Various measures must be developed to address drug consumption, illicit use of crops, and organized crime associated with drug trafficking. To eradicate poppy cultivation in the hills, with the help of religious and ethnic associations, the farmers must be educated about the consequences and the fact that dependence on illicit cultivation is not sustainable for the long term. Rather than coercive methods like destroying the poppy cultivation, alternative methods by providing a better livelihood would be more effective. Farmers must be provided with alternative crops that can generate sufficient and stable legal income, better infrastructure to improve cultivation, and subsidies for agriculture. Ensuring social and community participation is imperative while developing policies for the community.

Initiatives and Observations by the Supreme Court of India

Concerning the atrocities committed by armed and police forces in Manipur, the Supreme Court in **Extra Judicial Execution Victim Families Association (EEVFAM) and Another. v. Union of India and Another held armed forces cannot claim blanket immunity from prosecution; thus, criminal proceedings can be initiated in case of excessive use of force causing the death of people. In 2016 and 2017, the Supreme Court directed the Central Bureau of Investigation to open investigations into the fake encounters by armed forces and police forces in Manipur.**

Based on the status report filed by the government of Manipur at the Supreme Court of India in Dinganglung Gangmei v. Mutum Churamani Meetei:

6,523 FIRs had been registered as on 25 July 2023. According to its status report, 150 deaths had taken place between 3 May 2023 and 9 June 2023, and 502 persons were reported to have been injured. The State reported that there were 5,101 cases of arson; 252 persons were arrested in connection with the FIRs, and 12,740 preventive arrests were made. The State informed the Court that 11 FIRs involved cases of violence against women and children, though this was subject to further verification. Seven arrests were reportedly made in connection with these 11 FIRs.

The Solicitor General of India stated at the court that the state of Manipur is taking appropriate measures to restore normalcy in the state. Fifty-two companies of Central Armed Forces and 103 Columns of Assam Rifles have been deployed to the state, peace meetings and flag marches are organised, relief camps are opened, food and medicine are provided, and helicopters and drones are used to monitor the situation.

In a petition filed by the Zomi Students Federation, it is submitted to the Supreme Court that several dead bodies are lying unidentified in mortuaries, and many people are missing. Some of the major cellular services are not working. There is a deficiency of drinking water, medicines, food, and shelter. The hill areas suffer a shortage of doctors.

The Supreme Court of India said violence against women in Manipur is of an unprecedented magnitude and cannot be excused. The Supreme Court announced that it would constitute a three-women committee with former judges of high courts to monitor the relief and rehabilitation work in Manipur. The Court also constituted a committee chaired by a retired judge with representatives from both communities to address the grievances and oversee the rehabilitation measures. The court has mandated the appointment of a special investigation team, enforcing the right to speedy trial, facilitating legal aid, the right to information, and providing medical aid and protection to victims and witnesses. Furthermore, the need for transformative and reparative justice for the victims of ethnic violence and dignity in disposing of the dead bodies were stated. Apart from this, the court suggested the appointment of a Commission of Inquiry to enquire into dereliction of duty by public servants.

In Manipur Tribal Forum Delhi v. The State of Manipur and Another, the Supreme Court directed the state government to pay interim relief of 10 Lakhs rupees to every tribal killed, reconstruct the buildings and churches destroyed during the violence, and provide security to tribals for safe return.

Initiatives by the Government of India to Combat Drug Trafficking

The Indian government has implemented various measures to address drug peddling and illicit supply of drugs in Manipur. In 2016, the government introduced the National Coordination Mechanism on Narcotics Control to enhance coordination among various ministries, departments, and law enforcement agencies dealing with narcotics at the central and state levels. The Anti-Narcotics Task Force in Manipur, headed by the Additional Director General of Police (Intelligence) and formed on 5 March 2022, is serving as a singular focal point for all narcotics-related issues. To curb drug smuggling along border areas, the Assam Rifles have been granted authority under the Narcotic Drugs and Psychotropic Substances (NDPS) Act, 1985, to seize drugs. A Special Task Force on Darknet and Crypto Currency has also been established to monitor suspicious transactions related to drugs conducted on the Darknet. Sub-Zonal Office of Narcotics Control Bureau (herein after NCB) in Imphal has been elevated to the Zonal level. The NCB collaborates with law enforcement agencies, sharing satellite imagery concerning illicit cultivation of Cannabis and Opium Poppy with Manipur Police, and actively participating in the destruction of such crops. Director General Level Talks and Field Level Officer meetings have been organized between the NCB, India, and the Central Committee for Drug Abuse Control, Myanmar, to address various drug-related issues with international implications. In alignment with the Ministry of Home Affairs directives, the NCB has identified two locations to install vehicle scanners at the international border and hinterland of Manipur to monitor and prevent the movement of drugs. Recognizing the transnational nature of the problem, the Government of India has entered into bilateral agreements with 27 countries, signed a Memoranda of Understanding with 16 countries, and established two Agreements on Security Cooperation (Ministry of Home Affairs, Government of India). These agreements aim to facilitate international cooperation in preventing the illicit trafficking of narcotic drugs and psychotropic substances.

Border Management

Considering the issues of illegal migration and trafficking of drugs and weapons, the Indo-Myanmar border management must be a priority for both central and state governments. However, as India and Myanmar share close cultural ties, cooperation for defence and security among the countries is key to continuing the friendly relationship. The bilateral mechanisms between the two countries must be strengthened. The government must put more effort into formulating better strategies for border management, such as integrated checkpoints and land points on finalized locations, by considering the historical and cultural aspects of the region. Improved security infrastructure, including establishing a smart fencing system and appointing forces to regulate and monitor entry and exit regularly, is essential to curb illegal migration from Myanmar. The government should prioritize promoting a sense of security and safety among the border population, establishing proposed Border Haats, as well as developing infrastructure and connectivity in the border region.

Peace Negotiations

There is an urgent need for peace talks with the two communities for a durable solution to the ongoing conflicts. The government of India has constituted a Peace Committee under the chairmanship of the governor of Manipur to facilitate peace talks and negotiations among the ethnic groups. The committee consists of the Chief Minister, a few Ministers of the State, Members of Parliament, Members of the Legislative Assembly, former civil servants, representatives of different ethnic groups, educationalists, artists, social workers, and litterateurs.

Peace talks with civil societies and insurgent groups have equal significance in restoring harmony within the state. The civil societies can contribute significantly through constant peace negotiation at the macro level, ensuring the coexistence between the ethnic communities. The civil societies can play a crucial role in doing the groundwork for mediating ceasefires and effectively promoting anti-drug campaigns.

Bringing the leaders from the Centre and neighbouring states at one level can make a difference in facilitating the dialogue between the ethnic groups. The neighbouring states, particularly Mizoram and Nagaland, can assist at the administrative level. The Kukis share ethnic ties with the Mizo people. Additionally, Mizoram's Chief Minister voiced for the protection of tribal minorities in Manipur. The people of Mizoram share a common history and culture with the people in Manipur; therefore, the state government of Mizoram can contribute positively towards the reconciliation and negotiation talks. Nagas can also be peacemakers in Manipur now.

Need for Transitional Justice Mechanisms

Manipur requires the creation of a new atmosphere, considering the nature of violence in the region. The situation demands the creation of extra-judicial mechanisms of justice. The underlying causes for the conflicts, such as poverty, marginalization, drug cultivation and trafficking, insecurity, and poor governance, should be addressed through a comprehensive process of transitional justice. Different actors, such as the government, armed forces, and insurgent groups, must take responsibility and contribute to the truth-seeking process. Many organizations, women's groups, and civil societies in Manipur demand the establishment of a truth commission. If not particularly for Manipur, the truth commission can be established collectively for the Northeast region. Creating a truth commission can be beneficial in performing investigations on ongoing and past conflicts, focusing on collective responsibilities, promoting reparations to victims, seeking information from victims of abuse, and, most importantly, ensuring transparency and accountability. The truth commission would enable the people in Manipur to share their stories, acknowledge past mistakes, and work towards healing.

Additionally, complete disarmament of all active insurgent groups in Manipur is imperative to bring back peace in the region, although executing this will be a challenge. Disarming and demobilizing the armed groups must be the priority of the governments. Political dialogue with the militant groups is critical to disarming the groups. The government must assure a dignified life in exchange for disarmament. Furthermore, amnesties and pardons can be introduced to deal with political offenses while ensuring actions against serious crimes and human rights violations. Special investigating teams and tribunals can be set up to determine gross human rights violations and reparations to victims. Restorative justice components, such as consulting the victims and affected communities, can be included while developing reparation programmes.

CONCLUSION

Manipur requires a future-oriented approach while appreciating and acknowledging the history and diversity of the ethnic groups. The government must simultaneously address multiple challenges such as land conflicts, illicit drug production, migration, fighting the insurgent groups, and development of the hill region. The situation demands quick and resolute action; however, bringing peace back to Manipur might take years of constant effort. The government must instill confidence in Kukis and Meiteis through equality and fairness. A comprehensive system focusing on truth, justice, reparations, and non-repetition must be adopted for peacebuilding in Manipur.

REFERENCES

A glimpse of the Indigenous tribes of Manipur (Part 1). (n.d.). MyGov blogs. https://blog.mygov.in/a-glimpse-of-the-indigenous-tribes-of-manipur-part-1/

Act East Policy. (n.d.). PIB. https://pib.gov.in/newsite/printrelease.aspx?relid=133837

Ani, & Ani. (2023, March 29). Massive rally held in Manipur to demand NRC in state. *The Print.* https://theprint.in/politics/massive-rally-held-in-manipur-to-demand-nrc-in-state/1480441/

Bhattacharya, S. (2023, June 14). How the Myanmar Crisis Threatens to Destabilize India's Manipur State. *The Diplomat*. https://thediplomat.com/2023/06/how-the-myanmar-crisis-threatens-to-destabilize-indias-manipur-state/

Chawla, N. (2023). Identity and violence in Manipur, India. *JSTOR Daily*. https://daily.jstor.org/identity-and-violence-in-manipur-india/

Chungkhoseibaite. (2016). Critical Study of Origin of Trans-National Tribes: The Kukis. *Journal Of International Academic Research for Multidisciplinary, 4*(8). https://www.jiarm.com/Sep2016/paper28752.pdf

Committee reports. (n.d.). PRS Legislative Research. https://prsindia.org/policy/report-summaries/india-s-neighbourhood-first-policy

Das, K. K. (2005). *Political and economic history of the Kukis of Manipur*. Shodhganga. https://shodhganga.inflibnet.ac.in/handle/10603/103911

Deka, K. (2023, May 6). Poppy cultivation, eviction drives, illegal influx, old scars—why Manipur is burning. *India Today*. https://www.indiatoday.in/india-today-insight/story/poppy-cultivation-eviction-drives-illegal-influx-old-scars-why-manipur-is-burning-2369831-2023-05-05

Dinganglung Gangmei Vs. Mutum Churamani Meetei & Ors. [Special Leave Petition (Civil) Diary No. 19206 of 2023]

EPW. (2014, October 31) Nationalism, ideology and consensual democracy *Economic and Political Weekly* https://www.epw.in/journal/2014/43-44/notes/nationalism-ideology-and-consensual-democracy.html

Extra Judicial Execution Victim Families Association (EEVFAM) and Another. v. Union of India and Another Writ Petition (Criminal) No.129 of 2012

First Information of Cognizable Crime Report under Section 154 Criminal Procedure Code at Police Station. (2023). Manipurpolice. https://www.manipurpolice.gov.in/wp-content/uploads/2023/10/FIR-NO.-60872023-IMPHAL-PS.pdf

Government of India constitutes Peace Committee in Manipur under the Chairpersonship of Governor, Manipur. (n.d.). PIB. https://pib.gov.in/PressReleasePage.aspx?PRID=1931248

Government of India. (2015, December 9). Ministry of Home Affairs. Rajya Sabha. Unstarred Question No. 1198. https://sansad.in/getFile/annex/237/Au1198.pdf?source=pqars

Guite, J., & Haokip, T. (2018). The Anglo-Kuki War, 1917–1919. *The Anglo-Kuki War, 1917–1919*. doi:10.4324/9780429431098

Haokip, T. (2020, November 30). *Anachronistic 'War on Drugs.'* https://papers.ssrn.com/sol3/papers.cfm?abstract_id=3739915

Hausing, K. K. S. (2009). *"Hills-valley divide as a site of conflict: Emerging dialogic space in Manipur," in Sanjib Baruah (ed.), Beyond counter-insurgency: Breaking the impasse in Northeast India (New Delhi: Oxford University Press, 2009), pp.263-89.* https://www.academia.edu/657205/_Hills_valley_divide_as_a_site_of_conflict_Emerging_dialogic_space_in_Manipur_in_Sanjib_Baruah_ed_Beyond_counter_insurgency_Breaking_the_impasse_in_Northeast_India_New_Delhi_Oxford_University_Press_2009_pp_263_89

Home | Government of India. (n.d.). https://censusindia.gov.in/census.website/

India-Myanmar - Bilateral Brief. (2020, May). MEA.

Jain, B. (2023, May 17). Manipur official: No tribal bias in evictions or in war on drugs. *The Times of India*. https://timesofindia.indiatimes.com/india/manipur-official-no-tribal-bias-in-evictions-or-in-war-on-drugs/articleshow/100291179.cms?from=mdr

Jazeera, A. (2023, August 9). Why ethnic violence in India's Manipur has been going on for three months. *Al Jazeera*. https://www.aljazeera.com/news/2023/8/9/why-ethnic-violence-in-indias-manipur-has-been-going-on-for-three-months

Kipgen, N. (2017). Land laws, ownership and tribal identity: the Manipur Experience. In Springer eBooks (pp. 111–126). doi:10.1007/978-981-10-5215-6_9

Kipgen, N., & Chowdhury, A. R. (2016). 'Contested state-craft' on the frontiers of the Indian nation: 'Hills Valley Divide' and the genealogy of Kuki ethnic nationalism in Manipur. *Studies in Ethnicity and Nationalism*, *16*(2), 283–303. doi:10.1111/sena.12184

Kumar Das, S. & East West Center Washington. (2007). Understanding Identity and Governance Crisis in Manipur. *Policy Studies*.

Kumar Sharma, S. & Vivekananda International Foundation. (2016). *Ethnic Conflict and Harmonization: A Study of Manipur*. Vif India. https://www.vifindia.org/

Lakshman, A. (2023, July 18). Manipur violence | After Kuki Inpi hardens stance, signs of fissures among groups demanding separation. *The Hindu*. https://www.thehindu.com/news/national/other-states/manipur-after-kuki-inpi-hardens-stance-signs-of-fissures-among-groups-demanding-separation/article67091479.ece

Madhusudhanan, K. (2023, June 9). Bridging the growing trust deficit in Manipur. *The Hindu*. https://www.thehindu.com/opinion/op-ed/bridging-the-growing-trust-deficit-in-manipur/article66947462.ece

Manipur Tribal Forum Delhi vs The State of Manipur and Another WP (C) No 540 of 2023

Mukherjee, K. (2017). Insurgency and peace building in the northeast Indian state of Manipur. *Democracy and Security*, *13*(3), 220–245. doi:10.1080/17419166.2017.1326308

MyGov.in | MyGov: A Platform for Citizen Engagement towards Good Governance in India. (n.d.). MyGov.in. https://www.mygov.in/

Singh, N., & Singh, K. (2023). The Poppy Menace in Manipur: Causes, Consequences and Responses. *European Chemical Bulletin*. doi: 10.48047/ecb/2023.12.si5a.073

National Council of Applied Economic Research. (2005). *Socio-Economic Impact of HIV and AIDS in Manipur*. UNDP. https://www.undp.org/sites/g/files/zskgke326/files/migration/in/socio_eco_impact_of_hiv_aids_in_manipur.pdf

EPW. (2014, October 31). Nationalism, ideology and consensual democracy. *Economic and Political Weekly*. https://www.epw.in/journal/2014/43-44/notes/nationalism-ideology-and-consensual-democracy.html

MyGov Blogs. (n.d.). "Nisha Thadoklasi", Manipur Govt declares war on drugs. *MyGov Blog*. https://blog.mygov.in/nisha-thadoklasi-manipur-govt-declares-war-on-drugs/

Oinam, A. (2022, November). *Revisiting Free Movement Regime (FMR): Challenges and Implications*. Claws. https://www.claws.in/static/IB-368_Revisiting-Free-Movement-Regime-FMR-Challenges-and-Implications.pdf

Priyokumar Meitei, S. (2010). Migration and Social Tensions in Manipur. *International Journal of Scientific Research*.

Priyokumar Singh, T. (2022). A Critical Analysis of Narco-Politics In Manipur. *International Journal of Multidisciplinary Educational Research*, *11*(1(5)).

PTI, & PTI. (2023, August 8). Drugs worth over Rs 1,610 crore seized by Assam Rifles in Manipur since July 2022. *Deccan Herald*. https://www.deccanherald.com/india/manipur/drugs-worth-over-rs-1610-crore-seized-by-assam-rifles-in-manipur-since-july-2022-2639227

Puia, R. (n.d.). *When boundaries matter: land, laws and territorial conflict in Manipur, Northeast India*. Academia. https://www.academia.edu/49356615/When_boundaries_matter_land_laws_and_territorial_conflict_in_Manipur_Northeast_India

RAJYA SABHA UNSTARRED QUESTION NO. 1198. (2015, September 9). MHA. https://www.mha.gov.in/MHA1/Par2017/pdfs/par2015-pdfs/rs-091215/1198.pdf

Schoetz, A. N. (2023, August 4). When did Kukis reach Manipur and how the past is shaping the state's present. *India Today*. https://www.indiatoday.in/history-of-it/story/manipur-violence-when-did-kukis-reach-manipur-and-how-past-is-shaping-states-present-2416215-2023-08-04

Singh, B. (2023, June 21). Over 2000 illegal immigrants took shelter in Manipur after military coup in Myanmar: CSC. *The Economic Times*. https://economictimes.indiatimes.com/news/india/over-2000-illegal-immigrants-took-shelter-in-manipur-after-military-coup-in-myanmar-csc/articleshow/101156422.cms

Singh, N., & Singh, K. (2023). The Poppy Menace in Manipur: Causes, Consequences and Responses. *European Chemical Bulletin*. doi:10.48047/ecb/2023.12.si5a.073

Singh, T. B. (2007). Poverty in Manipur. *Economic and Political Weekly*, *42*(3), 251–254. https://www.jstor.org/stable/4419165

Singh, V. (2024, January 2). *Free Movement Regime to end at Myanmar border*. The Hindu. https://www.thehindu.com/news/national/centre-set-to-scrap-free-movement-regime-with-myanmar-people-in-border-areas-will-require-visas/article67698536.ece

Sitlhou, H. (2015). Confronting the State: Land rights discourse in the Hills of Manipur. *Economic and Political Weekly*, *50*(30), 70–77. https://www.jstor.org/stable/24481977

Sumir Karmakar, D. H. N. S. Sumir Karmakar, & DHNS. (2023, July 29). Manipur starts collection of biometrics of "illegal migrants" from Myanmar amid massive rally by Meitei groups. *Deccan Herald*. https://www.deccanherald.com/india/manipur-starts-collection-of-biometrics-of-illegal-migrants-from-myanmar-amid-massive-rally-by-meitei-groups-1241977.html

The Wire. (n.d.). Supreme Court slams claim that Manipur fake encounter probe will "Demoralise" Army. *The Wire*. https://thewire.in/law/supreme-court-army-manipur-fake-encounter

Thaimei, S. (2021). Intercultural business communication and Culture Identity: A case study of Manipur. *Global Media Journal*, *13*(1).

The Hindu Bureau & The Hindu Bureau. (2023, August 9). Manipur violence case, live updates | SC constitutes committee of 3 former women judges to oversee humanitarian measures. *The Hindu*. https://www.thehindu.com/news/national/manipur-violence-row-supreme-court-kuki-meity-clash-live-updates/article67167206.ece

Webline Infosoft Pvt. Ltd., Dehradun. (n.d.). *Welcome to Forest Survey of India*. FSI. https://fsi.nic.in/isfr-volume-ii

The Wire. (n.d.). What's Behind the Manipur Violence and Why Stopping It Poses a Test for Modi. *The Wire*. https://thewire.in/security/manipur-violence-reasons-failure-and-solution-q-and-a

Why are farmers in Manipur cultivating poppy? (2019, November 23). Economic and Political Weekly. https://www.epw.in/engage/article/why-are-farmers-manipur-cultivating-poppy

Zomi Students Federation vs Union of India and Another WP (C) No 572 of 2023

Chapter 9
In the Name of the Holy Cow!
The Issue of Cow Vigilantism in Contemporary India

Bodhisattwa Som
REVA University, India

ABSTRACT

India's constitutional ethos establishes itself to be a secular country, believing in every citizen's right to follow their own religious beliefs. However, in the recent past, the evolution of Hindu nationalistic politics of hate, coupled with a monolithic and myopic viewpoint of construing the nation as a Hindu entity, has fanned the growth of fundamentalistic ideals of cow worship and cow protection. This has significantly led to the rise of non-state actors who employ any or all means possible of strong-arming minorities and the vulnerable sections of society in the name of cow protection. Thus, through this chapter, the author shall at the first instance argue the reasons for the rise of cow-vigilantism in India, situating it in a historical and socio-political context. The author's second argument would be to demonstrate how cow vigilantism has elevated to the status of organised crime in India. Finally, the author shall conclude with arguments suggesting ways to put an end to such heinous incidents of vigilantism and forge a way forward.

INTRODUCTION

India's Constitutional ethos establishes itself to be a secular country, believing in every citizen's right to follow their own religious beliefs. The Preamble of India's founding document, the Constitution establishes itself to be a secular nation. It also contains

DOI: 10.4018/979-8-3693-0327-6.ch009

the terms 'Liberty of thought belief, faith and worship.' It enumerates the Right to Freedom of Religion as a fundamental right. In fact, it is crucial to understand that the Indian ideal of secularism as reflected in the Constitution is different from its traditional Western conception. It strictly does not follow the separation of Church and State, but through a transformative process has acquired a distinct identity, not one of tolerating other religions (*sarva dharma sambhava),* but equal respect for all religions (Bhargava, 2007).

However, the ground reality may not reflect the value of a secular State that the founding fathers had envisioned for the country. This is a reality that they were well acquainted with, in the communally charged atmosphere during the horrors of an ongoing Partition, fuelled on vitriolic religious rioting (Rajeshwari, 2004) . The Constitutional Assembly charged with drafting the Constitution was indeed divided at that point of time between Hindu Nationalists, Hindu traditionalists and members advocating for secularism, with some even arguing for a *Hindu Rashtra* (a theocratic Hindu State) (Jafferlot, 2019). It is indeed quite an achievement that India's founding fathers successfully argued over and incorporated the 'composite culture' based secularism that is reflected in the Indian Constitution today. In fact, during the 1950's and 1970's this secular model worked well, relatively with leaders such as Nehru actively taking decisions to avoid a concoction of religion and politics (Jafferlot, 2019)[1]. With the rise of Hindu Nationalism since the 1980's and 1990's till the present day, the mixture of ethnoreligious conflict, historical revisionist modelled violence has only added extra *masala* to instigate and flare up the communally charged atmosphere within the country (Bose, 2018) .

However, India's tryst with destiny was short lived. India's past, as a nation remains both marred and married with communal violence, mainly between Hindus and Muslims, but also, to a lesser extent between Hindus and Sikhs and Hindus and Christians. (Rajeshwari, 2004 ; Jairath, 2005 ; Hasan, 1982). This has only increased after 2014, after the rise of the Hindu nationalist political party, the Bharatiya Janta Party (BJP), (Minority Rights Group International, 2017 ; Werleman, 2021 ; Ahuja, 2019). Communal violence in India shares an unholy nexus with electoral politics, with Hindu Nationalist parties appealing for *Hindu Ekta* (Hindu Unity) to accumulate support across caste lines (Varshney, 2002 ; Wilkinson, 2004) . Thus, studying the intricacies of communal violence in India in its entirety would be beyond the scope of the paper. Therefore, specifically, for the context of this chapter we shall focus on communal violence specifically rooted in cow vigilantism, since there has been a consistent increase in incidents of cow-vigilantism and lynching in almost all states of India (Jacob & Kamath, 2023) .

To perceive and understand the notion of cow vigilantism it becomes necessary to gain an understanding of the topic of vigilantism. To begin with, in any state, the enforcement of the law is the mandate of specific agencies owing their allegiance to the State. This is true since the genesis of the Police State in the 20th century and can be applied even to the modern welfare state. Generally, this authority is delegated by the State through exercising its administrative powers, to its crime prevention branch consisting of the police forces or other specialised agencies. The Weberian conception that the State, that should have the monopoly of violence, specifically in relation is widely accepted, and forms the basis of legitimacy to the State for the enforcement of criminal law (Anter, 2019) .

However, the very concept of vigilantism is an anti-thesis to this very ideal. Vigilantism consists of the same process for law enforcement performed by not the State or its agencies but by groups of citizens who are generally self-appointed. Naturally, they neither have the legal authority to enforce the criminal law nor the legitimacy of using violence against other citizens. In most cases they are guided by their own principles of what they conceptualise the law ought to be and not what the law is. This is mostly due to their lack of knowledge or ignorance regarding the laws of the State. The ideation of what they believe to be right or wrong forms the basis of them action. This can be grounded in *inter alia* bigotry, patriarchy, religious dogma as well as racial or sexual prejudice (Mareš & Bjørgo, 2019).

Cow vigilantism is thus an endemic problem in India, which also has vigilantism in other forms such as honour killings among inter-caste couples, moral policing and vigilantism against couples celebrating Valentines Day and vigilantism against inter-religious couples on the pretext of *love jihad* . To provide a working definition, it consists of the lynching of individuals belonging to religious or caste minorities by specific self-appointed protectors of the cow known as *gaurakshaks* (Cow Protectors). The basis for their violent actions has its foundational basis on the fact that the cow is considered sacred by the Hindus. Therefore, any transgressions or acts of violence against the cow is equated by the vigilantes to be an attack on Hindu religious beliefs, which spurs them into action. Their personal belief regarding their acts of vigilantism is that of protecting their and enforcing the law against cattle slaughter (Ahuja, 2019) . Post independent India has seen cow slaughter to be officially banned in some states in India by the State legislatures owing to Constitutional provisions (Patel, 2020) .

However, there remain pertinent questions surrounding involvement of any of the agencies of the State enforcing this law against cattle slaughter systematically. Rather, the involvement of cow vigilantes in enumerating and enforcing the law against cow slaughter is perhaps visually greater. The fact that these activities have systematically occurred in numerous states in India in a consistent manner raises its status to the level of organised crime. The societal impact and implications of this sort of organised crime practiced across state borders in India would be disproportionately affecting Muslims and Dalits and their intersectionality. The economic impact of such instances would be felt about them not receiving any income to sustain their families due to it being linked to their occupation, cattle trade.

Thus, through this paper I shall at the first instance argue the reasons for the rise of Cow-vigilantism in India situating it in a historical and socio-political context. My second argument would be to demonstrate parallels between Cow vigilantism and organised crime in India. Finally, I shall conclude this chapter by stating how Cow vigilantism must be considered a form of organised crime in the Indian context.

HISTORICAL AND SOCIO-POLITICAL CONTEXT OF COW VIGILANTISM

Understanding Hinduism and its Organisation

Hinduism, unlike other religions like Buddhism, Islam, or Christianity, is an amorphous religion (Damojipurapu, 2023). Compared to other religions in the world, it has no organisational hierarchical structure of beliefs that needs to be compulsorily adhered to. Generally, religions such as Buddhism, Christianity, Jainism, and Islam rely upon varied religious interpretations of a single Holy Book and derive strength and validity from an organised ecclesiastical organizational structure (Damojipurapu, 2023). Hinduism, on the other hand, is structurally bereft of any rigid canons, a singular sacred text or a single holy religious site or religious temple (Damojipurapu, 2023). Thus, Hinduism was not an organised religion but in fact focussed on the belief systems of the people. Pattanaik (2022), argues that in the Vedic Era Hinduism used to constitute *yajna* or exchange and it is only later in time that the idea of *devata* or *Bhagavan* (God) emerges. Before the advent of the Islamic rule or even the British Raj in India, there existed various religious sects within the Indian sub-continent with their own deities to worship, unique rituals and practices that were followed by the members within the same community (Thapar, 2014).

Hinduism was constitutive and cumulative of these various sects and did not structurally constitute a formalised, singular structure (Thapar, 2014). These sects each had a separate and unique origin with their beliefs systems also being distinct (Damojipurapu, 2023). Thapar (1989), succinctly terms it as a religion with no "a shared creed, catechism, theology, and ecclesiastical organization". It was only the *Varna Vyavastha* or the caste system that was the foundational ethos of Hinduism at that point in time (Claveyrolas, 2022). Even during the advent of Islamic rule within India during the fourteenth century, the writings of religious reformers Kabir, Chaitanya and even the works written in the Vijayanagar Empire indicate that the term *Hindu Dharma* was used in a cultural sense only (Pattanaik, 2022) . It was used a way of differentiating people who belonged to the *Hindu Dharma* or the native

Indian population from those who belonged to the *dharma* coming from the Turks, the *Turuka Dharma* (Pattanaik, 2022).

The term 'Hinduism' was only recently envisaged in the 19th Century by the famous religious reformer Raja Ram Mohan Roy (Pattanaik, 2022). Later, this term was used by colonisers, like the British, to denote the indigenous religion of India, as per their perception (Tharoor, 2018). According to Thapar (2014), the genesis of the nomenclature of the term 'Hindu' has geographical origins. It used to denote the inhabitants of the land beyond the Indus River. This is due to the fact the term 'Hindu' was the word for 'river' in the earlier Indo Aryan languages (Damojipurapu, 2023). As a proper noun it used to denote the river the Indus River (or the Sindh River), one of the biggest rivers on the north-western part of the Indian subcontinent (Damojipurapu, 2023). There exists a contradiction of opinions among scholars about existence and extent of the hostility of relationships among Hindus and Muslims in pre-colonial India (Talbot, 1995 ; Babur, 2000). The fact whether these differences were a result of British colonialism is also contested (Babur, 2000 ; Verghese, 2018). However, there can be no doubt that these differences vastly increased during the colonial rule, because of the divide and rule policy pursued by the British (Pandey G. 1992 ; Bennett, 1958).

Consider the simple fact of creation of colonial forms of knowledge in the foreign land of India whose cultures, practices, language, and legal system was at ends with post Enlightenment Britain. It was the British took it upon themselves the task of accumulating and codifying the the vast, scattered, and confusing law of the 'Hindoo' population, solely for fulfilling their self-interest (Cohn, 1996). During this period the emergence of a 'Hindu' identity was actualised with Hinduism being the religion of the native, indigenous population and Islam being a foreign conquering power (Jafferlot, 2007 ; Liu & Khan, 2015 ; Sylvie, 2010). Orientalists interested in the study of Sanskrit to formulate the law applicable in India to English for better colonial administration started classifying law into Hindu law and Muslim law (Cohn, 1996). They started taking the help of Brahminical priests and Muslim scholars during the process, in a sense conflating Hinduism with Brahminism (Cohn, 1996).

THE GENESIS OF HINDUISM AS AN ORGANISED RELIGION

At this point in time, numerous lost and forgotten religious works within Hinduism were translated by them to English. This led to the rediscovery and revival of several Hindu scriptures such as the Vedas and Upanishads, leading to a common class consciousness among some Hindus. The others were Hindu reformists were the nineteenth century religious reformists such as the Arya Samaj (Lipner, 2016 ; Zavos, 1999). They envisaged and advocated historical revivalist ideas of a great

Hindu civilisation[2] (who had been defeated by treacherous foreign invaders), whose former glory had to be restored (Jafferlot, 2007 ; Lipner, 2016 ; Zavos, 1999). Along with this, the importance of the text of the Vedas as the ultimate truth and the cultural racial superiority of the Hindus started to emerge (Zavos, 1999). This led to the emergence of a new kind of nationalism based on one's religious identity of being a Hindu, Hindu Nationalism.

There was a growth of early Hindu Nationalists groups in the early twentieth century like the Hindu Mahasabha, (which was started as Sarvadeshak Hindu Sabha) as an affront to the growing Muslim influence within the subcontinent (Bhagvan, 2008). This was primarily due to the policies of the British such as separate electorates brought about by the Morley Minto Reforms of 1919. These were primarily aimed at appeasing the Muslims and garnering their support, but consequently caused further communal divide. This created a sense of helplessness and inferiority complex among the Hindus, which led to the creation of the Hindu Mahasabha, an organisation representing Hindu assertiveness, unity, power, and solidarity (Jafferlot, 1998). The organisation was formed specifically in response to Muslim communal organisations such as the All India Muslim League formed in 1906 (Hansen, 1999). As a result of the stratification of the population and the divisive policies of the British, the gap between Hindus and Muslims became increasingly prominent and permanent in the form of communal antipathy and divisiveness (Damojipurapu, 2023 ; Jacob & Kamath, 2023 ; Pandey G., 1992). Hindu Nationalism as mentioned above started being recognised as a political doctrine by the 1920's its most prominent advocate being Vinayak Damodar Savarkar, who envisioned with great zeal, the idea of India becoming a *Hindu Rashtra* or Hindu State and came up with the concept of Hindutva (Bose, 2018). Hindutva was envisaged and incorporated by him as the modern, twentieth century politically Indian doctrine (Bose, 2018).

His conception of Indian national identity lay only in the followers of Hindu religion, whom he considered the original inhabitants of India. His definition of 'Hindu' included within its fold religions which branched off from Hinduism such as Jainism, Buddhism and Sikhism but excluded religions which were a result of foreign invasions and conquest such as Islam and Christianity (Savarkar, 1949 ; Mishra, 1999). Ironically, what is interesting is that Savarkar, the founder of Hindutva was against cow vigilantism. Personally, he was a proclaimed atheist and was sceptical of the religious fanaticism with which the orthodox Hindus worshipped the cow. He advocated for the protection of the cow under the values of gratitude, affection, compassion, and humanism due to its economic value (Bose, 2018). He stated that "attributing religious qualities to it fosters a superstitious mindset that destroys the nations' intellect and so it is a self-defeating one (Bose, 2018)." He encouraged the non-Hindus to dissolve the hatred they had towards the cow and instead work for its protecting it, purely for economic reasons not religious dogma (Bose, 2018). Thus, the very founder on whom Hindu fundamentalism and its conception of a theocratic Hindu State is based on, would not be a supporter of cow-vigilantism.

This ideology of Hindutva has been backed by the far-right ethno-religious paramilitary organisation, the *Rastriya Swayamsevak Sangh* (RSS). By the 1960's the Sangh family had increased its presence within the country. The turn of a few decades, to the 1980's and 1990's witnessed the mushrooming of other its branches, the Bhartiya Janata Party, political branch; the Bajrang Dal, the youth wing; and the Durga Vahini, the women's wing (Jacob & Kamath, 2023). These decades also saw the rise of right-wing fundamentalism throughout the territory of India and the worse communal clashes witnessed since the time of India.[3] (Mc.Guire, Reeves & Brasted, 1996).

As the Hindu Nationalist movement gathered force, the creation of such a Hindu theocratic state required the propagation of certain religious dogmas and principles which every Hindu had to adhere to. Since, the practice among Hindus was not standardised among the various sects, it became the project of the Hindu Nationalist movement to identify a uniform set of beliefs and practices, something that was ironically far removed from the very idea of Hinduism, but closer to the Abrahamic religions they antagonised and despised! The communal dividing lines drawn by the British eventually culminated in the partition of India along these religious lines itself [4], with the Congress party and Muslim League unable to resolve their differences (Pandey G., 2001).

DEMYSTIFYING THE HOLINESS OF THE COW IN RELATION TO HINDUISM

Of all the dogmas espoused by Hindu Nationalists, one of the dogmas that is important for this chapter is the religious sanctity of the cow to Hindu *dharma*. In the Hindu States envisioned by the Hindu Nationalists the cow had to be given a special religious, almost divine status and all Hindus had to agree to the mandate of not slaughtering it or consuming its meat. Historically, the cow was sacred in certain portions of the Indian subcontinent among certain upper castes historically but formed a part of the diet of people belonging to lower castes, well into the twentieth century (Simoons, 1979). Chigateri (2010), states that the ecological justification with respect to the sanctity ascribed to cows was a way of masking the 'prioritizing of dominant Hindu Caste identity' in injunctions given about cow protection.

Arguments in favour of the protection of the cow rooted in the Vedic scriptures, such as the Rigveda which were divine revelations (Agoramoorthy & Hsu, 2012 ; Khanna, 2017). This religious belief became dogmatic and entrenched among the followers of Hinduism, even though there existed contrary evidence in Hindu religious scriptures of this purported religious sanctity (Jha, 2009 ; Brown, 1964 ; Korom, 2000 ; Khanna, 2017). Jha, (2009), in fact, argues the fact that the Indo-Aryans who had migrated to the subcontinent considered beef to be a part of their diet and cites passages within the Rigveda which contain passages on its sacrificial value and allowing its consumption. He further provides historical evidence of scholars who had dispelled notions about the sanctity of the cow. Jha, (2009), does not focus on only the texts within the Rigveda but also other sources such as the later *Gryhasutras* and *Dharmasutras*, Buddhist scriptures, Jain Scriptures and laws made by the later Hindu lawmakers to buttress his argument dispelling the taboo around cow slaughter and eating beef. Thus, ancient Indian scriptures and religious texts of various religions permitted the sacrifice and consumption of the cow, so when did it all change?

The proscription around cow slaughter was perpetuated during the first millennium, (the beginning of the Middle Ages in India) when social structures increasingly started to become feudalised (Jha, 2009). Harris, (1977), states that at the time of 1000 B.C. there was a drastic increase in the population around the areas of the Gangetic plains along with deforestation, floods and droughts. Consequently, the size of farms grew smaller and thus the preservation of animals such as the cow, used for ploughing drastically increased (Harris, 1977). These economic centric reasons also are supported by other scholars as well (Simoons, 1979) . As a result due to the persistent economic crisis during those times, the cattle became the focal point of a religious ban on its slaughter and consumption, due to the simple fact that its death (by killing it) would sound a death knell to the farmer's livelihood (Harris, 1977 ; Simoons, 1979).

During this point in time, referred in the Puranic texts as *Kaliyuga*, social reconstruction and transformation thus took place as a result, leading to a ban on the slaughter of cows, for the reasons hypothesized above. (Jha, 2009 ; Brown, 1964) . However, the slaughter of the cow did not carry any uniform punishment, ranging from being treated as an untouchable to treating it as a minor sin (*upapātaka)* and not a major sin *(mahapātaka)* (Jha, 2009). It is during this period that we witness various medieval Brahminical literature prohibiting cow slaughter and elevating it to the status of religious dogma (Brown, 1964). The cloak of religion ascribed to the cow, especially the zebu breed[5] was insurance measure (Khanna, 2017 ; Joshi & Phillips, 1953) . It was to avert the disastrous socio-economic conditions due to natural disasters wreaking havoc in the Northern plains in India (Khanna, 2017).

We also find the role the cow played, as a political instrument. The Mughal emperors, prohibited cow slaughter in order respect the sentiments of the their Hindu subjects and more so to legitimise their rule; Maratha rulers such as Chhatrapati Shivaji (Jha, 2009 ; Brown, 1964 ; Khanna, 2017). We also find that the politicisation of the cow as being sacred to Hindus became a tool to spread communal divide and hatred between the Hindus and Muslims. The otherization of the Muslims began during this period as they were projected to be carnivorous, beef eaters who disrespected Hindu sentiments, which was not a true reflection of reality [6] (Brown, 1964 ; Jha, 2009) .

THE NEXUS OF HINDU FUNDAMENTALISM AND THE SACRED COW

Nonetheless the sacredness and holy sanctity of the cow became the focal point for uniting the Hindus. One of the finest examples where this was actualised was during the Sepoy Mutiny of 1848, often named the First War of Independence. This was a popular uprising by the masses against the British East India Company who were at the helm of affairs. The uprising started due to a very simple reason. The sepoys or Indian soldiers in the British army were issued a new military rifle, the Lee Enfield rifle. The cartridges of these rifles were greased with both pig[7] and cow fat and had to be torn open by one's mouth to load the bullet into the rifle. This naturally violated the religious sentiments of both Muslims and Hindus and ignited the spark of rebellion (Majumdar, 1957). To quell this rebellion, the East India Company was deprived of its powers and the British Crown assumed direct authority over India (Damojipurapu, 2023). This significant incident reflected the exhalated status of the cow among the Hindus, where an attack on the cow was an attack on the religion itself.

As mentioned earlier, there was a growing consciousness among Hindus in India in the late nineteenth century to organise themselves into a religion. Pushed on by the growing influence of Christian missionaries and the influx of Western sensibilities into nearly aspect of life, the Hindus felt a need to preserve their own traditions, which were Brahminical in nature (Damojipurapu, 2023). This included the preservation of cow. Jha (2009), aptly describes that "the cow became a tool of mass mobilisation", with the genesis of the organised cow protection movement through the Sikh Kuka or Namdhari sect in 1870.

This was further strengthened by Hindu reformist and revivalist movement such as the Arya Samaj, headed by Swami Dayanand Saraswati, who made developed the idea of sanctity and divinity of the cow. This made the animal a symbol of unity among the Hindus and became the match which would lite communal flares during the 1880's and 1890's between Hindus and Muslims. The hardened and unwavering stance of the Hindus with regard to cow slaughter was further solidified, evidenced by increasing litigation being pursued by them against Muslims for slaughtering cows during *Eid-al-Adha* or *Bakr'Id* (Jha, 2009 ; Damojipurapu, 2023). Furthermore, as the years rolled on by communal riots within Hindus and Muslims often occurred on the pretext of cow slaughter, in Azamgarh, Ayodhya, Shahabad etc (Jha, 2009) ; (Freitag, 1990 ; Pandey G., 1983). The seeds of communal divide had been sown by the British under the divide and rule policy had started to bear fruit.

COW PROTECTION/VIGILANTISM IN POST-INDEPENDENCE INDIA

By the middle of the 20th century, the protection of the cow had steeped into mainstream Hindu consciousness and became a cause for mobilisation even in secular political parties such as the Congress. The situation became so drastic from this period, that instead of Hinduism defining the cow-protection, cow-protection began to define Hinduism. The religious sanctity of the cow was broken from the shackles of personal religious beliefs and mass organisations to mainstream Indian politics, even by parties such as the Indian National Congress formed by the end of the 19th Century and active in the early 20th century the Indian National Congress had people with varying beliefs. Among them there were a large section of conservatives within the Congress who held the cow in high esteem religiously (Jafferlot, 2019). In fact, in 1940, a Special Committee formed by the Congress party had suggested the protection of cows (Garg, 2016). Many freedom fighters had provided assurances that the first goal of the Swadeshi Movement would be to bring about a prohibition on the slaughter on cows (Garg, 2016).

Therefore, it was not only the Hindu extremist parties that vouched for cow protection but also a large section of India's largest political party as well, among them senior national political figures such as Mahatma Gandhi (Department of Animal Husbandry and Dairying, n.d.). In fact, the protection of the cow through prohibiting cow slaughter was at a greater pedestal than India's independence for him. This stance is perhaps even more radical with respect to cow protection compared to Hindutva wadis (propagators and followers of Hindutva), for instance Savarkar! Cow protection was thus deeply embroiled within Indian politics and the ramifications of these chain of events have led to the chaos of cow vigilantism that has engulfed India.

Not only in politics, the Constitution of the newly independent India was also not spared when it came to cow protection! In the Constituent Assembly tasked with the task of drafting the constitution of India, neither of the early Draft Constitutions prepared by B.N.Rau or the Drafting Committee contained any provisions regarding cow slaughter. It was the conservative section of the Congress, mostly belonging to the upper castes who had brought forward the issue of cow protection before the Constituent Assembly, initially under the garb of economic reasons, but later regarding religious reasoning (Garg, 2016). This eventually paved the way for cow protection to find its way into the Constitution, specifically Article 48 in Part IV, Directive Principles of State Policy, albeit based on economic reasons.[8] Part IV of the Indian Constitution contains broad directives to implement law and policy in the future, to be achieved by the State. They are non-justiciable in nature, compared to the justiciable Fundamental Rights present in Part III of the Constitution.

Nearly two decades after having achieved independence the cow remained the central focus of politics in India. The year 1966 saw the mass scale mobilisation and violence in the national capital as numerous communal organisations joined hands to protest in front of the Parliament to enact specific laws banning cow slaughter (Damojipurapu, 2023).The protection given to the cow through anti cow slaughter laws became common place in the post independent Indian republic by the enactment of the national law, the Prevention to Cruelty to Animals Act, 1960. This empowered the police with search and seizure powers to ensure that animals are not treated with cruelty. Furthermore, cow slaughter provisions got the status of being a serious offence because in most of the laws it was a cognizable, non-bailable offence with the burden of proof being on the accused. It also saw several states enact legislation prohibiting cattle slaughter (Patel, 2020).

In addition to cow protection laws the state has also tried to impose some measures through the executive calling for a ban on cow slaughter. In late May 2017, India's Environment Ministry implemented new rule with respect to the Regulation of Livestock Markets under the Prevention of Cruelty to Animals Act. These rules mandate all buyers and settlers at animal markets countrywide to sign an undertaking affirming that any cattle traded will be used solely for agricultural purposes (Minority Rights Group International; Centre for Study of Society and Secularism, 2017). This move been questioned by critics to be a manifestation of a clandestine national ban. This has been done by effectively making it illegal for cattle to be sold for slaughter. Others have raised concerns surrounding the legality of such measures, enumerating the lack of jurisdiction the central government has over animal markets (The Scroll, 2017).

Even the judicial arm of the State, the Supreme Court of India in many cases before it has upheld the prevention of cow slaughter laws in many states, first addressed by the Supreme Court in the *Hanif Quareshi* case (Mohammad Hanif Quareshi v. State of Bihar, 1958). In response to a petition filed by Muslim butchers arguing that cattle slaughter laws infringed their fundamental rights under Articles 14, 19(1)(g) and 25, it was held that both the right to equality under Article 14 and the freedom to practice religion were not violated. Regarding their right to practice their trade or profession, the court characterised the absolute ban sans any criterion for testing the usefulness of cattle to be an 'excessive restriction', but by contrast still upheld in its *ratio decidendi*, the total ban on the slaughter of *"cows of all ages, and calves of cows."* In another judgement, the Supreme Court, unequivocally yet controversially upheld the total ban of all types of cattle, not limited to cattle. The reasoning given by the court was clothed in the economic benefits of cattle, not only in terms of their manure being useful, but also it being used as a source of biofuel (State of Gujarat v. Mirzapur Moti Kureshi Kassab Jamat, 2006).

The most significant development about cow protection has been the rise of Hindu nationalism after the resounding victory of the right-wing Hindu nationalist party, the Bharatiya Janta Party since 2014 and their re-election in 2019. One of the ways to implement the Hindutva agenda has been through the working of vigilante groups such as the Bajrang Dal (Jafferlot, 2021). These groups have now been active in protection of the Cow from the people who according to them, butcher them or transport them from butchering, and are ready to use violence to stop them with no fear of the apparatus of the State being used against them (A.Gowen, 2018). It is not only the Bajrang Dal who can be characterised as the sole outfit tasked with cow protection we find that other specific outfits for it such as the Gau Raksha Dal (Cow Protection Organisation) as well. This organisation is spread across numerous states such as Uttar Pradesh, Rajasthan, Himachal Pradesh, Gujarat, Madhya Pradesh, Maharashtra, Goa, Delhi, and Haryana. These groups primarily have the backing of the state to carry on their activities and have thus in a rising number of cases unleashed unrelenting violence against Muslims and Dalits whom they suspect have caused harm to cows. If such groups continue to have a free run, without the intervention of the State through its organs it would lead to a violation of a many fundamental rights of individuals and would be a fraud on the Constitutional mandate of the right to equality, life, religion, and the right to practice any trade or profession under Articles 14, 21, 25 and 19(1)(g).

This section thus showed the rise of Hinduism as a collective organised religion with its fundamental tenets being linked by religious extremists to cow protection. It placed in a socio-legal, political context. The entire process did not happen over a few years but was a product of decades worth of collective religious activism, stretching from pre-independence times. This chapter thus is a reflection how historically the idea of the cow being sacred to Hindus based on religious scriptures was crystallised into the minds of the ordinary Hindu. It also brings forward to light the fact how this animal and its religious virtue was politicised and milked by pre-independence leaders of Hindu nationalistic political parties and how even after independence it continued to remain a political tool dispensable at the hand of the majority to oppress the minority.

The next part of the chapter would be a discussion how cow vigilantism could be looked as an organised crime. The *modus operandi* of cow protection groups would be analysed and compared to the general understanding of how organised crime works to make the evaluation.

COW VIGILANTISM AS ORGANISED CRIME

Understanding Organised Crime

According to the United Nations, organised crime is comparatively different from other forms of crimes which occur generally. The central point of distinction is with regard to its planned, organisational nature as opposed to unplanned, sporadic, separate acts of violence carried out by separate individuals (United Nations Office on Drugs and Crime, 2018) In fact a working definition given by the organisation highlights the fact its continued existence is maintained "through the corruption of public officials and the use of intimidation, threats or force to protect its operations." (United Nations Office on Drugs and Crime, 2018). Legally, the definition of organised crime can also be found in Article 2 of the United Nations Convention against Transnational Crime which states the term 'Organised Criminal Group' to " *mean a structured group of three or more persons, existing for a period of time and acting in concert with the aim of committing one or more serious crimes or offences established in accordance with this Convention, to obtain, directly or indirectly, a financial or other material benefit*" (United Nations Office on Drugs and Crime, 2000).

Vigilantism as Organised Crime

Johnston (1996), has tried to categorise vigilantism as a form of organised crime and have identified some basic characteristics of vigilantism which include – (i) planning and premeditation by the vigilantes; (ii) voluntary participation; (iii) it being a form of 'autonomous citizenship' and, as such social movement; (iv) utilisation or intimidation to the use of force; (v) the reason for its inception being tied an established order being under threat from the transgression, the potential transgression, or the imputed institutionalized norms; (vi) its main objective being to control crime or other social infraction assurances (or 'guarantees') of security both to participants and to others. Moreover, his characterisation becomes extremely vital because he establishes the criminological basis for understanding the phenomena of vigilantism. Thus, if we focus on the definitions of organised crime as given by the United Nations and the six identifiers of vigilantism as a concept, we find that there are some similarities namely their common organisational structure; their formation to commit crimes, particular violent crimes; the role of the State governments in allowing these groups to prosper due to their similar ideological similarities and pure vote bank politics of majority appeasement.

Characterising Cow Vigilantism as Organised Crime

Provided these definitions and then understanding of vigilantism as an organised crime, I shall try to characterise whether the functioning of cow vigilante groups satisfies these definitions. It becomes poignant to understand the *modus operandi* of cow protection organisations. Post 2014, there has been a consistent increase in incidents of cow-vigilantism in almost all states of India, particularly states where the cow has been politicised to a greater extent, such as Uttar Pradesh, Haryana, Gujarat, Karnataka etc. (BBC News, 2023 ; (Human Rights Watch, 2019 ; Maskara, 2021).

According to one study, 97% of such attacks have happened post 2014 with 24 out of 28 people killed in the attacks being Muslim (Abraham & Rao, 2017). Another worrying trend has been the number of cow vigilantism cases that have been covered by the media, with four cow-related hate crimes being reported from 2010-2014, distinguishable from 71 cases between 2015 and 2018 (Jafri, 2023). The perpetrators of these crimes, calling themselves *Gaurakshaks* or cow protectors are mostly Brahmins, as stated by the chairman of one such vigilante organisation, Bharatiya Gau Raksha Dal, on being asked about the composition of some 6000 vigilantes in his organisation (BGRD) (Masoodi, 2016). Within this community of cow-protectors, layers of patriarchy are embedded, visible with the presence of very few female *Gaurakshaks*, although the trend seems to be shifting with the advent of elite, tech savvy, new age women gau-rakshaks in places like NCR and Gujarat (Kissu, 2023 ; Dave, 2016). The present community of *gaurakshaks* is growing with not only the blue coloured workers or unemployed men, but lawyers, auditors, self-employed persons also being incorporated into this mould, of their free will (Ganapatye, 2023). Such people have diversified the caste pool of *gaurakshaks* with castes such as the Jat, Gujjar, Yadav, Bania, Agrawal, Thakur and Rajput being included (Ganapatye, 2023).

Instances of cow vigilantism, through the years 2016 to 2020, have resulted in over 50 deaths from instances of lynching or mob violence (Maskara, 2021). Incidental to this there has also been a monumental increase of cases involving political violence related to cows, increasing to 40% in 2017 as compared to 2016, and further doubling in 2018 (Maskara, 2021). The year 2020 saw a decrease in instances of political violence related to cows, presumably due to the lockdown imposed by the government due to the Coronavirus pandemic, but even then, 16 politically violent events were reported, resulting in nine fatalities (Maskara, 2021).

Most of victims would involve a cattle trader or traders, mostly Muslims or Dalits who would be carrying cattle in their vehicles for either selling or transporting them (Maskara, 2021). Dalits also became vulnerable targets to these attacks due to their caste enforced occupational connection to disposing off the carcasses of the cows (Maskara, 2021). Cow vigilante groups in India do not operate in isolation but in concert in various regions in the cow belt States they belong to. Scholars have pointed towards the fact that they operate on social media through WhatsApp groups, YouTube communities and even Meta, Instagram, and X groups to identify their targets and publicize them in order to demonstrate to their political patronage their loyalty towards protecting core Hindu beliefs and punishing all those who break the law, through whatever means possible (Zafri, 2023 ; Ward, 2020). They would be stopped by cow vigilantes who would conduct a search in the vehicle. They would then automatically suspect and accuse the cattle traders of transporting the cattle for the purpose of slaughtering them. If they find any cattle, the persons in the vehicle would be dragged out and beaten to death or grievously injured with rods, sticks or even bare hands and feet (Human Rights Watch, 2019 ; Minority Rights Group International, 2017). In some cases, the victims would be left on the road dead or on the verge of death or even lynched. In other cases, the victims of these atrocities would be burnt to death or hung from a tree (BBC News, 2023 ; Citizens for Justice and Peace, 2023). The most harrowing part of these instances is the role of social media after these instances happen where such vigilantes record such incidents and post them within their circles on various social media platforms which have thousands of members or subscribes, with some vigilantes attaining a level of celebrity status (Zafri, 2023 ; Jafferlot, 2021 ; Ward, 2020).

These instances of vigilantism with the involvement of the cow are not isolated instances. They have a greater propensity of happening in the cow-belt states where vigilantes do not have the fear of being prosecuted by the State. In fact, the police and authorities work hand in hand with them and in many cases their actions are cheered on, and their leaders are cheered or felicitated by the police along with the crowds who come out to support them (Zafri, 2023) . For many young vigilantes they do not have any innate sense of fear, but there exists an innate state of self-confidence even after being arrested by the authorities and jailed as they know that when they would be released, they would be cheered on and garlanded (Jafferlot, 2021). This emboldens the cow vigilantes in to thinking that whatever transgressions they are pursuing is to uphold the law, mainly the law relating to cow slaughter. The silence or inaction by the State in these instances is a kind of tacit approval for their activities, with even the official statistics of people lynched to death through the actions of cow vigilantes not being in the hands of officials (Human Rights Watch, 2019).

Therefore, a study of all these instances highlights the fact that how cow vigilantism can also be considered a form of organised crime carried out by right wing fundamentalist Hindu groups against minorities like Muslims and Dalits in India. This form of vigilantism exhibits characteristics of organised crime due to the following reasons – firstly, the existence of a common organisational structure of the right-wing Hindu groups engaged in cow vigilantism with most of them being young unemployed men or men working in the informal sector. These groups also have their organisational structure also within the social media realm with common Facebook, YouTube, X and WhatsApp groups through which they share news of instances of cattle transportation, spurring them into action. They also make sure that they do make videos of instances of making videos on those violating cow protection laws having beaten them up or injured them, naming, and shaming them or forcing them to chant religious slogans contrary to their religious beliefs (Farooq, 2022 ; Ward, 2020). Secondly, in almost all instance of cow vigilantism violence is seen as the norm of punishing those individuals who transgress Hindu religious dogma about sacredness of the cow. In almost all instances the victims are never given the chance of defending themselves. Thirdly, the response of the State governments particularly in the cow belt states, where cow protection is more religiously followed and where vigilantes are more active, in tackling such a grievous issue has been lesser than lukewarm (Human Rights Watch, 2019).

There is also a financial or economic aspect to these instances of cow-vigilantism that is generally undermined. An economic incentive to continue cow protection-based violence would be to further ideals of Hindu majoritarianism within the country. Since, such form of cow vigilantism affects Muslims the most (who control multi-billion-dollar beef trade) in India, it seeks to strangulate and oppress their economic power (Akram, Nasar, Safdar, & Sher, 2021). Also, the cows captured to be ‘protected’ by the cow vigilantes would have also have to be sheltered and monitored health wise (Akram, Nasar, Safdar, & Sher, 2021). This serves the economic interests of political parties and politicians who want to profit from it by securing favourable business contracts (Akram, Nasar, Safdar, & Sher, 2021). In fact, the Indian government has spent over $41 million for cow sheds, the state of Gujarat had proposed a budget of Rs. 500 crore for cow protection and the Uttar Pradesh government has spent a whopping Rs. 1681.61 crores for the protection of more than 9,15,125 cows (Akram, Nasar, Safdar, & Sher, 2021 ; Express News Service, 2022 ; The Hindu Bureau, 2023). Instances of bribery and extortion, with the threat of cow vigilantism or blocking vehicles carrying cows is also common in places such as Punjab where cow vigilantes and the police work hand in hand (Akram, Nasar, Safdar, & Sher, 2021 ; Goyal, 2016). So while cow-vigilantism is tied to religious fundamentalist notions of unleashing violence on minorities it is also tied to being a source of income or business for others.

Therefore, it is demonstrated that the *modus operandi* and the corresponding features how cow vigilantism is carried out is an act of vigilantism, due to their overwhelming overlapping characteristics. It also has similar corresponding features to organised crime syndicates, perhaps not technically with the way it has generally been understood, but contextually in the Indian context with similar ways of organisational structure and way of functioning. There are also economic incentives which seek to benefit the State and cow vigilantes in upholding the status quo.

CONCLUSION AND SUGGESTIONS

This chapter has studied the phenomena of cow vigilantism, which is a problem a secular country like India continues to grapple with. It poses as an affront to the ideals of secularism, liberty of thought, fraternity and unity enshrined in the Preamble of the Constitution and manifested in the fundamental rights to religion, equality, freedom of expression and the right to life and personal liberty. The origins of the phenomena bare its roots the colonial policy of dividing the Muslim and Hindu population and effectively ruling them, which invertedly gave rise to the monstrosities of Hindu nationalism within India and Islamic fundamentalism in Pakistan. The rise of Hindu nationalism over the years in India in a clandestine fashion was not moribund but slowly taking roots within society. This communal vitriol has gained traction over the past few years and has affected the minorities within our society in every harmful way possible. The chapter has highlighted how the importance given to the cow within the Hindu religion eventually led to the formation of laws against laws against cow slaughter. Cow vigilantes chanced upon this opportunity to unleash a violence of the law previously only given to the Executive within the state. Such is the ferocity and particularness of operations of these groups throughout India over the years, it can effectively be classified as a form of organised crime.

The monopoly of violence given to the State has slowly eroded to mob violence being carried out by these groups while the State tacitly watches on and has a laid-back approach in tackling these issues, with justice not seeing the light of day. To tackle this menace in society, there is an urgent need to legislate a Union law prohibiting lynching, with specific provisions dealing with cases of cow vigilantism. Further, there must also be an enactment of legislation criminalising acts in which there are explicit cases of communal violence. It must also be noted that the mere enactment of the legislation is not enough if the Executive, through institutions like the police forces, does not act upon it. The oft cited repeated argument of having a specific Union law ensuring witness protection would also help in the implementation of both these laws. The existing laws on cattle protection can also be relooked and modified through the establishment of an expert committee consisting of farmers, legal experts, agriculturalists and members of the civil society (Human Rights Watch, 2019).

The Executive branch of the State must take the responsibility of ensuring that minorities are not beaten up, lynched, harassed, or killed in the name of protection of religion. Accountability should not be a word thrown in the air, but rather actually realised when perpetrators of such acts of cow vigilantism roam free with impunity. Investigation into matters involving such incidents must be prompt, impartial and not politically influenced with proper oversight mechanisms within the police department. Ensuring the implementation of such measures targeted against acts of cow vigilantism would demonstrably prove that there is no betrayal of the faith of millions of Indians on the State but also prove the fact that we defraud the Constitutional values our forefathers envisioned the Indian State to be built upon.

REFERENCES

Agoramoorthy, G., & Hsu, M. J. (2012). The significance of cows in Indian society between sacredness and economy. *Anthropological Notebooks*, *18*(3), 5–12.

Ahuja, J. (2019). Protecting Holy Cows: Hindu Vigilantism against Muslims in India. In T. Bjørgo & M. Mareš (Eds.), *Vigilantism against Migrants and Minorities* (pp. 55–69). Routledge. doi:10.4324/9780429485619-4

Anter, A. (2019). The Modern State and its Monopoly on Violence. In E. Hanke, L. Scaff, & S. Whimster, The Oxford Handbook of Hans Weber (pp. 226-236). New York, United Stateas: Oxford University Press.

Babur, Z. (2000). Religious Nationalism, Violence and the Hindutva Movement in India. *Dialectical Anthropology*, *25*(1), 61–76. doi:10.1023/A:1007197222204

BBC News. (2023, May 8). *Deaths raise fresh fears over cow vigilantism in India*. BBC News. https://www.bbc.com/news/world-asia-india-65229522

Bennett, F. M. (1958, February). Muslim and Hindu: The Sensitive Areas. *The Atlantic*. https://www.theatlantic.com/magazine/archive/1958/02/muslim-and-hindu/305462/

Bhagvan, M. (2008). Princely States and the Hindu Imaginery: Exploring the Cartography of Hindu Nationalism in Colonial India. *The Journal of Asian Studies*, *67*(3), 881–915.

Bhargava, R. (2007). The Distinctiveness of Indian Secularism. In *M.N.Srinivas, The Future of Secularism* (pp. 20–54). Oxford University Press.

Bose, S. (2018). *Secular States, Religious Politics India, Turkey, and the Future of Secularism*. Cambridge University Press. doi:10.1017/9781108559461

Brown, W. N. (1964, February). *The Sanctity of the cow in Hinduism*. Retrieved from The Economic Weekly: https://www.epw.in/system/files/pdf/1964_16/5-6-7/the_sanctity_of_the_cow_in_hinduism.pdf

Chigateri, S. (2010). Negotiating the 'sacred' cow: Cow slaughter and the Regulation of Difference in India. In M. Mookherjee, Democracy, Religious Pluralism and the Liberal Dilemma of Accomodation (pp. 137-159). Springer.

Citizens for Justice and Peace. (2023, March 28). *Cow vigilantism incidents continue to go unchecked in northern India*. CJP. https://cjp.org.in/cow-vigilantism-incidents-continue-to-go-unchecked-in-northern-india/

Claveyrolas, M. (2022). Hinduism and Caste System. In S. Joddka & J. Naudet (Eds.), *The Oxford Handbook of Caste* (pp. 236–246). Oxford University Press.

Cohn, B. S. (1996). *Colonialism and its forms of Knowledge: The British in India* (S. B. Ortner, N. B. Dirks, & G. Eley, Eds.). Princeton University Press.

Damojipurapu, M. (2023). Patterns and Risks in Contemporary Religion Based Hate Speech in India. In M. Bergsmo, & K. Manocha, Religion, Hateful Expression and Violence (pp. 209-274). Brussels, Belgium: Torkel Opsahl Academic EPublisher.

Department of Animal Husbandry and Dairying. (n.d.). *ANNEX II (6) Views of Mahatma Gandhi on Cow protection*. Department of Animal Husbandry and Dairying, Ministry of Fisheries, Animal Husbandry and Dairying, Government of India. https://dahd.nic.in/hi/related-links/annex-ii-6-views-mahatma-gandhi-cow-protection#:~:text=Cow%20protection%20to%20me%20is,identity%20with%20all%20that%20lives

Farooq, G. (2022). Old Conflicts in New Media Assemblages: India's Cow Vigilantism and YouTube. *Asiascape: Digital Asia*, *9*(1-2), 47–70. doi:10.1163/22142312-bja10027

Freitag, S. B. (1990). *Collective Action and Community: Public Arena and the Emergence of Communalism in North India*. Oxford University Press.

Garg, L. (2016, October 15). *Examining the Constituent Assembly Debates on Cow Protection*. The Wire. https://thewire.in/law/unveiling-indias-long-history-of-hypocrisy-on-cow-slaughter-laws

Gowen, A. (2018, September 3). 'We Don't Have Any Fear': India's Angry Young Men and Its Lynch Mob Crisis. *Washington Post*. https://www. washingtonpost. com /world /asia pacific /we -dont -have -. . . - a0aa -11e8 -a3dd -2a1991f075d5 story. html? utm term =. 6a0084f604cd

Guire, Mc. J., Reeves, P., & Brasted, H. (1996). Politics of Violence: From Ayodhya to Behrampada. New Delhi: Sage.

Hansen, T. B. (1999). *The Saffron Wave: Democracy and Hindu Nationalism in Modern India*. Princeton University Press. doi:10.1515/9781400823055

Harris, M. (1977). *Cannibals and Kings: The Origins of Cultures*. Vintage Books, a division of Random House, Inc.

Hasan, Z. K. (1982, February). Communalism and Communal Violence in India. *Social Scientist (New Delhi)*, *10*(2), 25–39. doi:10.2307/3516974

Human Rights Watch. (2019, February 18). *Violent Cow Protection in India Vigilante Groups Attack Minorities*. Human Rights Watch. https://www.hrw.org/report/2019/02/19/violent-cow-protection-india/vigilante-groups-attack-minorities

Jacob, C., & Kamath, M. (2023, March 9). 'Kill Two Million of Them': Institutionalised Hate Speech, Impunity and 21st Century Atrocities in India. *Global Responsibility to Protect*, *15*(2-3), 209–245. doi:10.1163/1875984X-20230002

Jafferlot, C. (1998). *The Hindu Nationalist Movement in India*. New York: Columbia University Press.

Jafferlot, C. (2007). Hindu Nationalism: A Reader. Oxforsdshire: Princeton University Press. doi:10.1515/9781400828036

Jafferlot, C. (2019, April 4). *The Fate of Secularism in India*. Carnegie Endowment for International Peace. https://carnegieendowment.org/2019/04/04/fate-of-secularism-in-india-pub-78689

Jafferlot, C. (2021). *Modi's India Hindu Nationalism and the Rise of an Ethnic Democracy*. Princeton University Press.

Jairath, V. K. (2005, September-December). Studying Communal Rights in India: Some Methodological Issues. *Sociological Bulletin*, *54*(3), 443–462. doi:10.1177/0038022920050309

Jha, D. (2009). *The Myth of the Holy Cow*. Navayana Publishing.

Johnston, L. (1996). What is Vigilantism. *British Journal of Criminology*, *36*(2), 220–236. doi:10.1093/oxfordjournals.bjc.a014083

Joshi, N. R., & Phillips, R. W. (1953). *Zebu Cattle of India and Pakistan: A FAO Study*. Food and Agriculture Organization of the United Nations.

Khanna, V. (2017). The Holy Cow: Unravelling the Mystery of its Holiness. *Millenial Asia*, 217-233.

Korom, F. J. (2000). Holy Cow! The Apotheosis of Zebu, or Why the Cow Is Sacred in Hinduism. *Asian Folklore Studies*, *59*(2), 181–203. doi:10.2307/1178915

Lipner, J. (2016). Hindu Fundamentalism. In J. Dunn (Ed.), *Fundamentalisms: Threats and ideologies in the modern world* (pp. 93–116). I.B. Tauris and Co. Ltd.

Liu, J. H., & Khan, S. S. (2015). Nation building through historical narratives in pre-independence India: Gandhi, Nehru, Savarkar, and Golwalkar as entrepreneurs of identity. In M. Hanne, W. Crano, & J. Mio (Eds.), *Warring with words: Narrative and Metaphor in Politics* (pp. 211–237). Psychology Press.

Majumdar, R. (1957). *The Sepoy Mutiny and The Revolt of 1857*. Calcutta Oriental Press Private Limited.

Mareš, M., & Bjørgo, T. (2019). *Vigilantism against Migrants and Minorities: Concepts of Goals and Current Research*. Routledge.

Maskara, S. (2021, May 3). *Cow Protection Legislation and Vigilante Violence in India*. ACLED Bringing Clarity to Crisis. https://acleddata.com/2021/05/03/cow-protection-legislation-and-vigilante-violence-in-india/

Minority Rights Group International, & the Centre for Study of Society and Secularism. (2017, June). *A Narrowing Space: Violence and Discrimination against India's Religious Minorities*. Centre for Study of Society and Secularism and Minority Rights Group International. https://minorityrights.org/wp-content/uploads/2017/06/MRG_Rep_India_Jun17-2.pdf

Mishra, A. (1999). Savarkar and the Discourse on Islam in Pre-Independent India. *Journal of Asian History*, *33*(2), 142–184.

Mohammad Hanif Quareshi v. State of Bihar (Supreme Court of India 1958).

Pandey, G. (1983). Rallying around the Cow. In R. Guha (Ed.), *Subaltern Studies* (Vol. 2, pp. 60–129). Oxford University Press.

Pandey, G. (1992). *The Construction of Communalism in Colonial North India*. Oxford University Press.

Pandey, G. (2001). *Remembering Partition: Violence, Nationalism, and History in India*. Cambridge University Press. doi:10.1017/CBO9780511613173

Patel, A. (2020, December 30). *The Dark Chronology Of India's Cow-Slaughter Laws*. Article 14. https://article-14.com/post/the-dark-chronology-of-india-s-cow-slaughter-laws

Pattanaik, D. (2022, February 15). *Who created the term Hinduism? And why did the British feel the need to defend Hinduism?* Scroll. https://scroll.in/article/1017342/who-created-the-term-hinduism-and-why-did-the-british-feel-the-need-to-defend-hinduism

Rajeshwari, B. (2004, March). *Communal Riots in India A Chronology (1947-2003).* Retrieved from Institute of Peace and Conflict Studies: http://www.nagarikmancha.org/images/1242-Documents-Communal_Riots_in_India.pdf

Savarkar, V. D. (1949). *Hindu Rashtra Darshan.*

Simoons, F. J., Batra, S. M., Chakravarti, A. K., Diener, P., Ferro-Luzzi, G. E., Harris, M., Heston, A., Hoffpauir, R., Lodrick, D. O., Malik, S. L., Mey, W. E., Mishra, S. N., Palmieri, R. P., Pimentel, D., Robkin, E. E., Schwabe, C. W., Schwartzberg, J. E., Suryanarayana, M., & Wagner, P. L. (1979, September). Questions in the Sacred Cow Controversy. *Current Anthropology*, *20*(3), 467–493. doi:10.1086/202319

State of Gujarat v. Mirzapur Moti Kureshi Kassab Jamat (Supreme Court of India 2006).

Sylvie, G. (2010). *The construction of history and nationalism in India: Textbooks, controversies and politics.* Routledge.

Talbot, C. (1995). Inscribing the Other, Inscribing the Self: Hindu-Muslim Identities in Pre- Colonial India. *Comparative Studies in Society and History*, *37*(4), 692–722. doi:10.1017/S0010417500019927

Thapar, R. (1989). Imagined Religious Communities? Ancient History and the Modern Search for a Hindu Identity. *Modern Asian Studies*, *23*(2), 209–231. doi:10.1017/S0026749X00001049

Thapar, R. (2014). *The Past as Present:Forging Contemporary Identities through History.* Aleph Book Company.

Tharoor, S. (2018). *Why I am a Hindu.* Aleph Book Company.

The Scroll. (2017, May 29). *Reading the law: government seems to be on thin ice as it bans trade on cattle for slaughter.* Scroll. https://scroll.in/article/838954/reading-the-law-government-is-on-thin-ice-as-it-imposes-de-facto-cattle-slaughter-ban#:~:text=The%20Rules%20have%20come%20in,for%20slaughter%20from%20animal%20fairs

United Nations Office on Drugs and Crime. (2000, Novemeber 15). *United Nations Convention against Transnational Organized Crime and the Protocols Thereto.* United Nations Office on Drugs and Crime. https://www.unodc.org/documents/treaties/UNTOC/Publications/TOC%20Convention/TOCebook-e.pdf

United Nations Office on Drugs and Crime. (2018, April). *Defining Organised Crime.* United nations Office on Drugs and Crime: https://www.unodc.org/e4j/zh/organized-crime/module-1/key-issues/defining-organized-crime.html

Varshney, A. (2002). *Ethnic Conflict and Civic Life: Hindus and Muslims in India*. Yale University Press.

Verghese, A. (2018, 5 June). *Did Hindu-Muslim conflicts in India really start with British rule?* Scroll. https://scroll.in/article/880832/did-hindu-muslim-conflicts-in-india-really-start-with-british-rule

Ward, M. (2020). Walls and Cows: Social Media, Vigilante Vantage, and Political Discourse. *Political Discourse. Social Media + Society*, *6*(2). doi:10.1177/2056305120928513

Werleman, C. (2021). Rising Violence against Muslims in India Under Modi and BJP Rule. *Insight Turkey*, *23*(2), 39–50. doi:10.25253/99.2021232.3

Wilkinson, S. I. (2004). *Votes and Violence: Electoral Competition and Ethnic Riots in India*. Cambridge University Press. doi:10.1017/CBO9780511510458

Zafri, A. (2023, February 2023). *India's 'cow protectors' are getting away with murder*. Codastory. https://www.codastory.com/disinformation/india-cow-vigilantes/

Zavos, J. (1999, April). The Arya Samaj and the antecedents of Hindu nationalism. *International Journal of Hindu Studies*, *3*(1), 58–63. doi:10.1007/s11407-999-0008-x

ENDNOTES

1 For instance, introducing Section 123 in the Representation of People's Act, 1951, which disallows politicians from campaigning on religious reasons.

2 They were against the supremacy of the Vedas; the rigidity of the caste system and sought to unify all Hindus under the ambit of Hinduism.

3 These include the Bombay Riots which engulfed the city of Mumbai from (December 1992-January 1993); the Demolition of the Babri Masjid in 1992-1993 and the Gujarat Riots in the year 2000.

4 Pakistan, an Islamic, theocratic state was created and separated itself from India, which incorporated itself into a secular state.

5 Zebu breed of cattle, native to India which has the ability to thrive in the harsh Indian tropical conditions, as stated in a study conducted by the United Nations Food and Agricultural Organisation.

6 Consider the case of the Shin people, Muslims belonging to Dardistan (present day Pakistan) in the late Nineteenth Century who consider the existence of the cow to be a cardinal sin, similar to how other Muslims view pigs. The cow is treated with such abhorrence and hostility that they distance themselves from

cows; avoid any way of direct contact; refuse to consume cow's milk or utilize cow dung and reject beef as food.

7 Considered to be unclean by Muslims, while cows were had a sacred status in the minds of most Hindus in the 19th Century.

8 Article 48 of the Constitution of India, Organization of Agriculture and Animal Husbandry - The State shall endeavour to organise agriculture and animal husbandry on modern and scientific lines and shall, in particular, take steps for preserving and improving the breeds, and prohibiting the slaughter, of cows and calves and other milch and draught cattle.

Chapter 10
The Influence of Organized Crime on Electricity Theft and Power Infrastructure Vandalism in South Africa

Phathutshedzo Madumi
University of Stellenbosch, South Africa

ABSTRACT

This chapter examines the underlying reasons, repercussions, and issues related to organized crime's influence on electricity theft and power infrastructure damage in South Africa in depth. It goes to the incentives that drive organized crime groups as well as the flaws in the power distribution structure that allow such illegal activity. Furthermore, the chapter investigates the socioeconomic effects of these crimes on customers, businesses, and communities, putting light on the broad scope of these illegal acts. As crucial strategies, the chapter advocates stronger security measures, legislative reforms, community engagement, international cooperation, and public-private partnerships. South Africa can alleviate the impact of the ongoing electricity crisis, restore stability to the energy sector, and protect key infrastructure by taking a comprehensive approach. This chapter aims to give useful insights for policymakers, researchers, and practitioners working to prevent organized crime's effect on the nation's energy sector.

DOI: 10.4018/979-8-3693-0327-6.ch010

INTRODUCTION

At this moment in South Africa, narratives and visuals related to organized crime, particularly in the electricity sector, are almost inescapable. Although the media consistently highlights the gravity of contemporary criminal threats, policymakers and law enforcement often fall short in implementing appropriate responses to address these challenges effectively. Indeed, as organized crime continues to be a growing concern for policy in South Africa, the government's ability to effectively tackle these syndicate groups seems to be increasingly inadequate. Indeed, South Africa has been grappling with a persistent electricity crisis, which has posed significant challenges for the nation. The frequent occurrence of blackouts and load shedding has adversely affected businesses, households, and the overall economy. A major factor contributing to this crisis is the state-owned energy provider, Eskom, which is facing immense distress. Echoing similar sentiments, Theron (2018) contends that Eskom, alongside fellow state-owned entities like Transnet, Telkom, and municipalities, grapples with challenges tied to infrastructure theft. The persisting issue revolves around the substantial value of pilfered materials, implying organized criminal involvement propelled by syndicates within the context of copper theft.

According to Sidebottom, Ashby, and Johnson (2014), metal prices are an example of a macroeconomic environmental element that influences criminals' decision-making in terms of crime opportunity. Assuming all other conditions remain constant, a rise in metal prices is expected to increase the appeal of metal theft, resulting in an increase in the frequency of such criminal operations. Electricity theft and power infrastructure vandalism have emerged as significant challenges in South Africa. The rampant electricity theft exacerbates the issue of unplanned power outages, further complicating the already dire situation for Eskom. These problems not only lead to revenue losses for the energy provider but also put additional strain on an already struggling electricity grid, making it even more challenging to maintain a stable and reliable power supply for the country. Addressing these issues is crucial to mitigate the impact of the ongoing electricity crisis and restore stability to the energy sector.

It is vital to recognize that organized crime, along with its root causes, repercussions, and attempts to curb it, presents a complex and multifaceted reality. Clearly, understanding and addressing organized crime requires a comprehensive and nuanced approach. The intricate nature of organized crime involves various factors contributing to its existence, far-reaching consequences for individuals and society, and complex efforts to combat and prevent it. Policymakers, law enforcement agencies, and communities need to collaborate and implement effective strategies to tackle this multifaceted challenge effectively.

Organized crimes such as electricity theft and power infrastructure vandalism have a negative impact on the economy, leading to reduced productivity and investment.

Unsurprisingly, the extent to which organized crime has contributed to this critical situation is a matter of debate. Some argue that the crises are a result of electricity theft, infrastructure vandalism, mismanagement, and a lack of political will, while others point to broader economic and social factors as the root causes. This chapter aims to explore and analyze the significant influence of organized crime in the rampant issue of electricity theft and power infrastructure vandalism in South Africa. It provides a comprehensive examination of the underlying causes, consequences, and challenges associated with this phenomenon. The chapter will delve into the intricate relationship between organized crime groups, the energy sector, and the broader societal implications. The objectives of this chapter are to:

1. Examine the various techniques employed by organized crime groups to steal electricity.
2. Analyse the socio-economic consequences of electricity theft and power infrastructure vandalism on consumers, businesses, and communities.
3. Explore potential solutions to address organized crime on electricity theft and power infrastructure vandalism.

In addition, this chapter will utilize qualitative literature assessment drawing largely from key secondary sources of existing studies on the topic. It will also analyze relevant data from government and industry sources. In conclusion, this chapter provides a comprehensive outline for examining the influence of organized crime on electricity theft and power infrastructure vandalism in South Africa. By analyzing the causes, consequences, challenges, and countermeasures, this chapter aims to contribute to the understanding of this issue and provide valuable insights for policymakers, researchers, and practitioners involved in combating organized crime's impact on the energy sector.

DEFINITIONS AND CHARACTERISTICS OF ORGANIZED CRIME

Organized crime has multiple definitions and characteristics. Goga (2014) defines "organized crime" as encompassing unlawful actions perpetrated by a criminal organization or syndicate, collaborating with the aim of achieving a shared objective, typically centred around financial gains. According to Roelofse (2009), organized crime can be understood as a business entity with inherent features such as planning, hierarchy, division of labour, intelligence, market research, organizational culture, discipline, and contracting. This business-like operation is primarily motivated by profit and power, without being bound by legal and moral constraints. In addition,

Albanese (2015) suggests that the definition of organized crime is derived from a consensus among writers over the past several years and can be stated as follows:

Organized crime is a continuing criminal enterprise that rationally works to profit from illicit activities that are often in great public demand. Its continuing existence is maintained through the use of force, threats, monopoly control, and/or the corruption of public officials. (Albanese, 2015, p. 4)

In addition, Albanese (2015) put forward that organized crime is characterized by its closed and selective membership, driven by ideological or political motives behind its actions, necessitating specialized skills for planning and executing specific activities and functioning under a strict code of secrecy. Similarly, Richards (1999) outlines the characteristics of organized crime groups or criminal organizations, as employed by the Criminal Intelligence Directorate of the Royal Canadian Mounted Police. In the same way, Roth (2010) identifies corruption, violence, continuity, structure, discipline, absence of ideology, engagement in multiple enterprises, adherence to rules and regulations, codes of conduct, and sophistication as the key features on his list.

Liddick (2009) employs the term "attributes" in lieu of elements and outlines the frequently cited characteristics associated with organized crime. These attributes encompass hierarchy, the pursuit of rational profit through criminal actions, the application of force or threats, the corruption of public officials, addressing public service demands, establishing monopoly control over illicit markets, maintaining restricted membership, lacking ideological motives, specializing in work tasks, adhering to codes of secrecy, and engaging in extensive planning. Equivalently, the characteristics comprise an accumulation of profits, long-term existence, a structured approach to advance the group's criminal activities, resorting to violence to achieve objectives, and the capacity to corrupt government officials, police officials, and/or corporate figures (Carter, 1997).

Organized crime syndicates engage in a wide range of activities. Clinard and Meier (2011, p. 162) identify seven major actions. Illegal gaming, racketeering, illegal drug distribution, usury or loan sharking, illicit prostitution, reselling stolen or hijacked commodities, and managing legitimate enterprises are examples. Others who followed and expanded on his theories produced the scholarly notion that some organized crime groups function rationally and economically. Similar to their respectable counterparts, businessmen who work for profit maximization with Allum and Sands (2004); Broude and others Teichman (2009); D'Andria (2011); Sellin (1963); Vaknin (2000).Power; profit; premeditated crime; structured organizational scheme; self-preservation; success; access to goods through crime; continued activity; secrecy of operation; control; corruption; complex detection;

efforts to obtain immunity; intimidation and the use of force; non-impulsiveness, according to Dobovek (2012, p. 43).

Organized criminal groups are distinguished by their organized structure (especially in the realm of criminal business), and their major purpose is the generation of money through unlawful operations. They retain their position in society through threats, violence, bribery of state officials, and extortion, and have a major effect on individuals, small communities, regions, or entire states (FBI, 2014). The more their ability to cause harm, the bigger the threat they pose to society (von Lampe, 2016).

BRIEF OVERVIEW OF ORGANIZED CRIME IN THE SOUTH AFRICAN CONTEXT

Various alterations and developments have distinguished the nature of the transition of organized crime in South Africa. As the country's political, social, and economic landscapes have changed throughout time, organized crime has adapted and evolved in response. The transition from well-known and structured criminal organizations widespread during apartheid to more flexible and dispersed criminal networks in the post-apartheid era is an important feature of the change. This transformation has enabled criminal organizations to capitalize on new opportunities, broaden their operations, and expand their influence in many areas of society.

For decades, police officers have been confronted with the problem of organized crime, white-collar crime, and corruption on a daily basis. The South African state has encountered a variety of obstacles since the end of apartheid. One of these has been the growing threat of organized crime, which has had a significant impact on public perception. The story has been one of organized crime, which is becoming more sophisticated and lethal, as opposed to a declining and under-equipped state (Goga, 2014). When a state fails to provide jobs, goods, or other services, or does so at exorbitant prices, organized crime steps in (Allum and Siebert, 2003; Clinard and Meier, 2011) by providing counterfeit designer clothes, medicine, tools, or any other counterfeit product known to man.

During the transition, organized crime groups have exploited vulnerabilities inside state institutions and engaged in corrupt behaviors. This has enabled criminal enterprises to penetrate multiple levels of government, law enforcement agencies, and other vital institutions, impeding effective law enforcement and perpetuating their illicit activities. Furthermore, socioeconomic problems such as poverty, unemployment, and inequality continue to contribute to the country's rise and continuation of organized crime. These elements foster an environment in which criminal organizations can attract new members and gain support from disillusioned people looking for alternate methods of survival.

Organized crime is frequently linked to the political, economic, and financial structures in which it functions. According to Singh (2022), corruption protects criminals from the reach of the criminal justice system by involving law enforcement authorities. Furthermore, criminals might use corrupt methods to influence political decisions and penetrate state institutions and lawful enterprises.

The links between criminals and the South African government initially surfaced between 2009 and 2018, while Jacob Zuma was president. The Zondo Commission, a four-year investigation into Zuma's administration that concluded this year, uncovered ties between the government and alleged wrongdoers, with the three Gupta brothers, originally from India, who managed to become part of Zuma's inner circle being the most notable individuals. The Gupta family has constantly denied any involvement in illegal activities since shifting to the United Arab Emirates in 2018. Likewise, Jacob Zuma, who is currently on trial for corruption, has maintained his innocence (Pilling, 2023).

Former Eskom CEO Andre Marinus de Ruyter attributes the power outages in part to the extended neglect of coal-fired power plants by the African National Congress, which have reached an average age of 42 years. He also points to sabotage as a contributing factor. De Ruyter asserts that criminal organizations are involved in stealing critical infrastructure components like pylons, bolts, copper, and aluminum wires, with the intention of melting them down and reselling them. These criminal groups also engage in coal theft. Additionally, they exacerbate the situation by issuing contracts to repair the damage they've caused, further increasing their revenues (Pilling, 2023).

In addition, De Ruyter emphasizes that complaints of inexplicable issues continue while the country suffers from rolling blackouts (Moodley, 2022). One of the most profitable strategies used by criminal groups, he claims, is the theft of coal in transit to Eskom power stations, which is subsequently resold abroad. Stolen trucks are rerouted to former landfill regions known as blending sites, where high-quality coal is exchanged for garbage or debris. Water and metal waste are used to fill the gap, allowing thieves to benefit from the scam (Pilling, 2023). According to an intelligence report, the implicated criminal organizations operating within Eskom include the Presidential Cartel, the Mesh-Kings Cartel, the Legendaries Cartel, and the Chief Cartel, as reported by Bloom (2023).

In some instances, fraudulent activities occur within the coal procurement process. For example, consider the scenario involving Power Station A, Mine A, and Trucking Company A. Power Station A is responsible for procuring a specific grade and quantity of coal from Mine A. This coal is then transported directly from the mine by Trucking Company A and is sealed during the transportation process. However, there is a potential for collaboration or illicit payments between Mine A and/or Trucking Company A and a member of a cartel (van Diemen,2023).

In these cases, the truck responsible for transporting the high-grade coal intended for Power Station A may take deceptive actions. It might disable its GPS tracker upon entering a location commonly referred to as a "black site." At this point, the genuine load of high-quality coal is substituted with lower-quality coal. Another truck, referred to as Truck B, then acquires the superior coal at a reduced price, while Power Station A ends up receiving the subpar coal product (van Diemen,2023).

Overall, the shift of South African organized crime is a dynamic and complicated process driven by historical events, socioeconomic situations, technical breakthroughs, and globalization. Addressing this issue necessitates a broad approach that involves efficient law enforcement, addressing core causes, improving international cooperation, and strengthening anti-corruption organizations.

CAUSES AND DYNAMICS OF ELECTRICITY THEFT

South Africa's critical infrastructure is in jeopardy because of years of chronic mismanagement and widespread thievery. Considerable amounts of copper cable and other vital metal components are removed from the country's railways, power grid, and communication network daily, resulting in a considerable decrease in capacity and operating efficiency. Electricity theft can be defined as the unauthorized use of electricity from a utility provider, typically without a legal contract or a valid obligation to manipulate the measurement of its consumption (Smith, 2003).

Power theft has serious consequences for both the victims and the perpetrators. The consequences of power theft are particularly serious since illegally obtained electricity has an impact on Eskom's financial returns. According to Eskom (2016:3), "electricity theft and the subsequent energy losses experienced by Eskom and municipalities contribute to the escalation of electricity tariffs." Tariff rises have consequences not only for individuals involved in electricity theft but also for the entire community. As a result, prices for basic necessities such as food and other necessary commodities rise. Furthermore, households with illicit connections use electricity more than those who buy it. This produces a negative loop that is a direct result of electricity theft.

Different economic variables influence an individual's decision to engage in criminal conduct (Becker,1968). The perceived likelihood of being captured and convicted, the severity of the related consequences, and the availability of legal options for earning a living are among these considerations. On the other side, a society's socioeconomic position might influence power theft within it. According to a study by Depura, Wang, Devabhaktuni, and Gudi (2010), customers' economic problems have a significant impact on electricity theft. In other words, persons who are unable to pay for power may resort to stealing it through unlawful connections.

As a result, one could claim that Eskom associates illicit connections with economic issues, whereas meter tampering is associated with variables such as greed and opportunism.

Figure 1. Illegal electricity connections
(IOL, 2022)

Illegal electrical hookups are frequent in South African towns, cities, and rural areas. Figure 1 depicts the prevalence of illegal electrical connections. While energy theft is commonly associated with low-income persons, recent disclosures show that businesses and agricultural enterprises are also involved in this illegal practice. Electricity theft has serious implications, including overloading the electrical grid, which leads to power outages. These interruptions, in turn, have far-reaching consequences, including lost production and traffic congestion.

According to Herzog (2005), it is reasonable to conclude that economic hardship might lead to a stressful scenario characterized by scarcity, which may increase the chance of individuals resorting to criminal actions to meet their personal or family requirements. This could help explain why businesses are typically prime targets for criminal activity, especially during economic downturns, because they provide easy access to resources sought after by criminals (Bressler, 2009). According to Bressler (2009), crimes against enterprises are classified into two types: those committed by personnel within the corporation and those committed by third parties.

Copper theft is a national problem in South Africa, committed by both individuals and organized groups motivated by the potential of quick financial rewards and a wide range of vulnerable targets. In their quest for rich returns, these criminals target electrical substations, cellular towers, landline telephone lines, trains, water wells, construction sites, and empty dwellings. Copper theft from these sources disrupts the regular operation of electricity, communication, transportation, water distribution, heating, as well as security and emergency services, ultimately jeopardizing both public safety and national security (FBI, 2014).

It is also clear that the widespread use of copper has led to a surge in its price, rendering it an attractive incentive for criminals. Even though licensed scrap merchants are required not to purchase copper from questionable sources, the strong financial incentives often cause them to ignore the origin of the copper. As a result of this issue, analysts argued for increased regulation in the used goods market, which resulted in the passage of a new law targeted at attaining this goal. Additionally, as Tokerlson pointed out in 2010, the visibility, accessibility, lack of adequate protection, and the relatively straightforward process of stealing and selling copper make it a top choice for criminal enterprises. Construction sites, vacant homes, railways, and key infrastructure are excellent targets for opportunistic and well-organized thieves prepared to go to any length to obtain valuable metals.

POWER INFRASTRUCTURE VANDALISM AND ORGANIZED CRIME

Vandalism is conceptually framed by Ward's (1973) classical definition, which describes it as the purposeful infliction of property damage through certain behaviors. This contrasts with the damage caused by deterioration, erosion, and other natural processes. Wilson (1988) uses the same conceptual framework, describing vandalism as the result of deliberate or careless activities intended for the built environment. According to Ikejemba and Schuur (2018), the government's inefficiency and failure to create jobs, provide social security, and meet other basic necessities can breed discontent among the public, eventually leading to infrastructure vandalism. Arguably, the underlying causes of vandalism are deeply established in society's socio-structural foundations, particularly the material circumstances of the people, the state, and the larger economy. Ikejemba and Schuur (2018) further contended that chronic government inequities within a society would lead residents to turn to infrastructure damage and robbery as a way of economic survival.

There is widespread concern about organized crime infiltrating South African government institutions, primarily through corrupt methods. Economically, organized crime has the ability to create enormous economic upheaval and damage. Without question, South Africa is experiencing huge disruptions in service delivery, with serious consequences for the economy and the daily lives of its residents. The annual expense of combating criminal devastation is in the billions of South African rands. If quick action is not taken, the damage done to the very structure of the South African state may become irreparable. According to Shaw (1998), organized crime has grown significantly since the start of South Africa's democratic transition in 1990. It should be highlighted that criminal actions involving cable theft and damage occur throughout South Africa's major cities, rather than in specific geographic areas. This common occurrence is attributed to the several challenges associated with urban expansion, including increased unemployment, acute poverty, squalor, rising inequality, and perceived social deprivation.

According to Bressler (2009), vandalism is one of the types of criminal acts committed against enterprises by persons who are not involved with the organization. Wilful or malicious damage to property, such as equipment or buildings (Scott, La Vigne, & Palmer, 2007). In South Africa, the main metals targeted by vandals are copper and aluminium (Yorke-Smith, 2010). Furthermore, these criminals have also taken aim at diesel and petrol pipelines, along with water infrastructure. Concurrently, corruption has hampered the effectiveness of critical utilities. Vandalism frequently leads to a power outage. In many cases, customers are uninformed of the underlying cause of the power loss and merely lodge concerns about the outage itself. As a result, the electrical utility personnel must conduct an investigation to establish the true reason for the outage.

The theft of important components and materials, particularly copper, a highly sought-after worldwide commodity required for railway, electrical, and communication networks, has been the most noticeable and far-reaching effect of this issue. It is also commonly employed in the construction of water infrastructure. According to S&P Global (2021), the global price of copper more than doubled between April 2020 and June 2021. This has resulted in an unparalleled spike in copper theft across South Africa's networks, resulting in the loss of hundreds of kilometers of copper cable. Because of security issues, theft has become easier. South Africa's massive infrastructure networks provide a substantial problem. For example, Eskom CEO André de Ruyter stated that the 390,000 kilometers of distribution and transmission lines make stationing guards at every pylon physically impractical. However, there have been cases where security procedures have been botched, allowing burglars to take advantage of the situation (Writer 2021).

To get copper, thieves often work at night, armed with trucks, pulleys, industrial cutting tools, and tractors. These criminals are divided into two categories: organized crime syndicates, which are responsible for large-scale stealing, and subsistence thieves, who steal smaller amounts, frequently a few meters at a time. It should be noted that these persons may be hired by syndicates to steal copper wires and pipes. As reported by Shabalala (2021) the stolen metal is then sold to local scrap merchants, who process it into ingots and granules that do not require scrap export permits and are nearly identical to lawfully processed copper. Stolen copper is mostly shipped through South African ports to China, the world's largest copper consumer. Exporters occasionally utilize codes linked to commodities such as shoes or textiles to avoid discovery. It is suspected that stolen copper from Zimbabwe is being shipped through South Africa (Shabalala, 2021).

During the COVID-19 lockdown, over 80% of railway stations were vandalized, primarily due to a lack of security measures. Metrorail Gauteng was reported to have lost more than R76 million owing to train station theft and vandalism in September 2021(Makwea, 2021). Criminal assaults on the South African railway network have witnessed a surge in recent years, primarily focusing on the theft of copper used in overhead power cables. According to Greyling (2023), Transnet reported a 177% increase in copper cable theft over the previous five years in October 2021, with an alarming 1,000 kilometers of cable taken between January and October 2021. A note published in December 2021 by Transnet revealed that a staggering 33.5 kilometers of overhead copper cable were stolen in just the first week of that month (Transnet, 2021). Figure 2 depicts the magnitude of Transnet's losses as a result of cable theft from 2016 to 2023.

Figure 2. Total cost of Transnet cable theft
(Greyling, 2023)

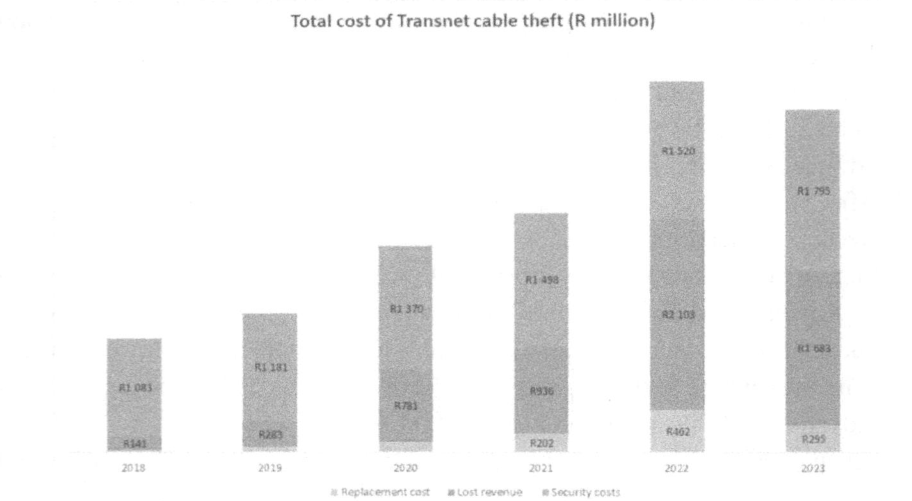

Equally, it is believed that individuals affiliated with the taxi sector in the Western Cape have deliberately destroyed railway infrastructure in order to force commuters to choose more expensive taxi services as part of organized criminal operations. In April 2022, a taxi driver was sentenced to 20 years in prison for setting fire to a train in 2020, costing PRASA R3.5 million. He admitted that when there were more taxis on the road, his revenues increased (Mthethwa, 2022). As aforementioned,

Copper theft against electricity infrastructure is carried out by both low-level individual thieves and organized syndicates, some of whom are well-armed. For example, in March 2022, ten criminals armed with AK-47s stole 135 meters of cable from a Johannesburg substation. In other cases, deception is used, with burglars disguising themselves as municipal personnel while secretly cutting underground wire (Slabbert, 2022).

Illegal connections and meter manipulation exacerbate the electricity grid's problems. While this type of criminal behavior is not necessarily organized, it can lead to transformer explosions, resulting in extensive power outages in impacted areas. Eskom claimed in August 2020 that it had expended its resources on removing illegal connections and rebuilding exploded transformers, each of which cost between R80,000 and R100,000 (Ntuli, 2020). It's critical to understand that lengthy power outages can aggravate and perhaps instigate aggressive conduct among those who are involved in illicit connections and meter tampering. For example, in June 2020, two Eskom employees were kidnapped and forced to restore an illegal electrical supply, indicating the potential for escalation in such scenarios (News24, 2020).

At times, illegal connections pose considerable hazards in critical conditions, including the possibility of death via electrocution and the destruction of electrical infrastructure. Furthermore, there are economic consequences for utility consumers who are not participating in illegal activity, such as power outages that result in financial losses (Lewis 2015).

CONSEQUENCES AND IMPACT ON SOUTH AFRICAN SOCIETY

The impact of organized crime is often debated in democratic regimes such as South Africa (Allum and Seibert, 2003). There is no doubt that copper cable theft is on the rise in South Africa, harming vital companies such as Eskom, Telkom, and Transnet, which are critical in the fields of energy, telecommunications, and railroads. Copper theft is a public safety concern. It can impact housing, public lighting, and traffic lights, causing a hazard to the community. It can also injure or kill those stealing it and can harm both members of the public and utility workers. As copper is used to transport high and extra-high voltages, exposed wires can cause serious injury to death. Although it's prohibited for scrap yards to exchange 'cash' money for copper – some still do, which makes it easier for criminals to make quick cash. Unfortunately, a lot of copper thefts occur by repeat offenders who are looking for quick financial gains.

There are two types of repercussions to power outages: direct and indirect. The sudden stoppage of activities or services that rely on electricity is referred to as a direct effect. For example, direct effects include food deterioration, data loss, and the inability of life-support systems in hospitals and homes to function correctly. Indirect effects, on the other hand, occur as a result of disrupted activities or services. Indirect effects include property damage from occurrences like arson and looting, as well as increased feelings of insecurity. These consequences are further classified based on whether they can be stated in monetary terms, in which case they are referred to as economic impacts. The interruption of leisure or work activity has a social consequence. Organizational, procedural, administrative, and other changes made in response to blackout conditions fall under the category of operational impacts.

Von Ketelhodt and Wöcke (2008) observed that Small and Medium Enterprises (SMEs) were considered especially significant for the country's ongoing developmental phase. As a result, the effects of the energy crisis are far-reaching for these businesses, with many of them facing lower trade or productivity because of the burden of overhead expenses while unable to conduct business. Most SMEs rely largely on a constant electrical supply, and power disruptions pose significant issues. It may be argued that a disproportionately large fraction of these enterprises also believed they had suffered losses in their operations as a result of the lack of a consistent electrical supply.

The power outage resulted in a considerable decrease in household income for people working in occupations that require electricity. Employees who rely on specialized power equipment, for example, typically face more significant cutbacks in their regular working hours. On the other hand, a successful act of vandalism against an electricity infrastructure results in a power outage for all customers connected to that transformer. In some situations, this vandalism may also cause a transient failure that affects other parts of the electrical network.

Furthermore, with the emergence of international markets and technological advancements, organized crime in South Africa has become increasingly multinational. illegal networks now use worldwide connections to participate in activities such as drug trafficking, human smuggling, cybercrime, and money laundering, making it more difficult to combat these illegal operations within national borders. Hence, Reichl, Schmidthaler, & Schneider (2013) maintains that knowing the need to sustain a continuous supply of electricity is critical. This understanding is critical in finding a balance between the benefits of improving electrical dependability and making infrastructure improvements.

CHALLENGES AND COUNTERMEASURES

This chapter attempts to investigate the complex relationship between organized crime and its impact on energy theft and power infrastructure destruction in South Africa. The country has been dealing with an ongoing electricity crisis, typified by regular blackouts and load shedding, with the state-owned energy supplier, Eskom, in serious trouble. The main reasons for this issue include a variety of factors such as electricity theft, power infrastructure vandalism, financial mismanagement, unsustainable debt levels, outdated infrastructure, and insufficient investment. These variables have combined to produce a complex and difficult situation, making it difficult to find a quick and long-term solution to the electricity crisis. Electricity theft and power infrastructure vandalism have emerged as major factors in this crisis, resulting in revenue losses for energy providers and increased strain on the grid.

One big difficulty with copper cable theft is the possibility of profiting from it by police enforcement and private security organizations, which is a troubling prospect for those investigating organized crime. This issue is akin to racketeering principles in that private security firms have a vested interest in the problem continuing rather than being resolved completely. Despite the lack of tangible evidence of their performance, some of these companies have received significant contracts to prevent copper theft and protect state assets. To acquire a better understanding of this, compare the loss figures of Transnet and Telkom, which rely on outsourced private security groups, with Eskom, which has just switched to an in-house security approach to solve the issue.

In South Africa, organized crime in the energy sector is like a disease that is tough to treat. Instead, it has metastasized and spread throughout the organization's entire structure. This negative influence can be discovered in a variety of ways, from encountering resistance in installing controls and conducting investigations to encountering challenges in initiating disciplinary actions. The South African Police Service (SAPS) has even formed a multidisciplinary squad to disrupt and combat criminal syndicates operating at Eskom power plants. However, as more evidence is unearthed, it becomes clear that the amount of corruption and malfeasance is significantly worse than can be seen.

Whether in a city, town, suburb, or rural area, the following scenario has become all too common and frustrating in South Africa today: widespread and uncontrolled infrastructure destruction. Transmission lines have been tampered with, and railway lines, energy-supplying substations, and transformers have all been regular targets for criminal gangs. As foot troops, these organizations usually recruit young and destitute drug users.

It is apparent that electricity is vital to the South African economy, and its disruption has the potential to severely impact the nation's economic stability. It is also important to recognize that addressing South Africa's power challenges necessitates a multifaceted approach. Consequently, this chapter presents the following recommendations:

1. Enhanced Security Measures: Implement robust security measures at critical infrastructure sites, including power substations, railway stations, and construction sites. This should involve the use of technology such as surveillance cameras, alarms, and security personnel to deter and detect vandalism and theft.
2. Legislative Reforms: Strengthen legislation related to metal theft and vandalism, including stricter penalties for offenders. Enforce the existing laws effectively, and consider introducing new regulations to address emerging threats in the field of organized crime.
3. Community Engagement: Promote community awareness and involvement in the prevention of electricity theft and power infrastructure vandalism. Encourage citizens to report suspicious activities and engage in community watch programs to protect critical infrastructure.
4. International Cooperation: Collaborate with international law enforcement agencies to track and combat transnational organized crime networks involved in metal theft and infrastructure vandalism. Sharing information and intelligence can help identify and dismantle criminal operations.
5. Diversification of Energy Sources: Explore and implement a diverse mix of energy sources, including renewables (solar, wind, hydro), natural gas, and nuclear power, to reduce reliance on a single energy type and enhance energy security.
6. Public-Private Partnerships: Foster partnerships between government agencies, private sector companies, and non-governmental organizations to tackle organized crime's impact on the energy sector. Collaborative efforts can lead to more effective prevention and mitigation strategies.
7. Improved Governance and Transparency: Enhance transparency and accountability within the energy sector to combat corruption and mismanagement, ensuring that resources are allocated efficiently and effectively.

Addressing organized crime's influence on energy theft and power infrastructure vandalism in South Africa requires a comprehensive and collaborative approach that takes into account the core reasons, legal frameworks, and security measures. Combating these illegal behaviours must also consider the larger socioeconomic background, as well as the necessity for job opportunities and alternatives for people at risk of engaging in criminal behaviour. Moreover, implementing the aforementioned recommendation can serve as the foundation for a comprehensive strategy to address South Africa's power difficulties while also ensuring a stable and reliable energy supply for the country's economic growth and development. Finally, tackling this issue is critical for restoring stability to South Africa's energy sector and safeguarding citizens' safety and well-being.

CONCLUSION

The impact of organized crime on energy theft and vandalism in South Africa is a multidimensional and complicated subject with far-reaching implications. This chapter has examined many facets of the problem, ranging from the evolution of organized crime in South Africa to the reasons and drives behind these illegal operations. It has also investigated the methods used by organized crime groups to steal energy, flaws in the power distribution system that allows theft, and socioeconomic factors that contribute to the prevalence of electricity theft. In South Africa, organized crime has evolved from classic, hierarchical criminal organizations to more flexible and multinational criminal networks, making it difficult to combat their activities within national borders. Corruption inside state institutions has facilitated their influence and operations even further.

Electricity theft and power infrastructure vandalism affect a wide range of stakeholders, ranging from utility companies such as Eskom to consumers and the general public. Beyond financial losses, the consequences of these criminal acts have an influence on public safety and service delivery. Copper theft has become a serious worry due to the high value of copper and the ease with which it can be stolen and sold. Economic incentives for copper theft have increased criminal activity targeting infrastructure such as railroads, power substations, and communication networks. Combating organized crime in this setting has been complicated by the presence of both organized syndicates and individual thieves, often with varying degrees of experience. The situation has been worsened by regulatory barriers, corruption, and insufficient security practices.

REFERENCES

Albanese, J. S. (2015). *Organized crime: From the mob to transnational organized crime*. Routledge.

Allum, F., & Sands, J. (2004). Explaining organized crime in Europe: Are economists always right? *Crime, Law, and Social Change*, *41*(2), 133–160. doi:10.1023/B:CRIS.0000016223.49968.17

Allum, F., & Siebert, R. (2003). Organized crime: A threat to democracy? In F. Allum & R. Siebert (Eds.), *Organized Crime and the Challenge to Democracy* (pp. 1–22). Routledge., Retrieved from http://www.tandfebooks.com/isbn/9780203426418

Becker, G. (1968). Crime and Punishment: An Economic Approach. *Journal of political economy, 76*(2), 169-217.

Bloom, K. (2023). Introducing the four crime cartels that have brought Eskom and South Africa to their knees. *Daily Maverick.* https://www.dailymaverick.co.za/article/2023-02-27-introducing-the-four-crime-cartels-that-have-brought-eskom-and-south-africa-to-their-knees/

Bressler, M. (2009). The Impact of Crime on Business: A Model for Prevention, Detection & Remedy. *Journal of Management and Marketing Research*, 1–13.

Broude, T., & Teichman, D. (2009). Outsourcing and insourcing crime: The political economy of globalized criminal activity. *Vanderbilt Law Review*, *62*(3), 795–848.

Carter, D. L. (1997). *International Organised Crime: Emerging Trends in Entrepreneurial Crime*. Sage Publications.

Clinard, M. B., & Meier, R. F. (2011). *Sociology of Deviant Behavior* (14th ed.). Wadsworth Cengage Learning.

D'Andria, D. (2011). Investment strategies of criminal organisations. *Policy Studies*, *32*(1), 1–19. doi:10.1080/01442872.2010.520558

Depuru, S. S. S. R., Wang, L., Devabhaktuni, V., & Gudi, N. (2010). Measures and setbacks for controlling electricity theft. *Proc. IEEE North American Power Symposium*, Arlington, TX. 10.1109/NAPS.2010.5619966

Dobovšek, B. (2012). *Korupcija v tranziciji*. Ljubljana, Slovenia: Fakulteta za varnostne vede.

Federal Bureau of Investigation (FBI). (2014). *Reports and publications*. FBI. https://www.fbi.gov/stats-services/publications

Goga, K. (2014). *Responses to organized crime in a democratic South Africa*. Institute for Security Studies.

Greyling, D. (2023). Transnet cable theft disaster. *Daily Investor.* https://dailyinvestor.com/south-africa/33912/transnet-cable-theft-disaster/

Herzog, S. (2005). The Relationship between Economic Hardship and Crime: The case of Israel and the Palestinians. *Sociological Perspectives*, *48*(2), 189–211. doi:10.1525/sop.2005.48.2.189

Ikejemba, E., & Schuur, P. (2018). Analyzing the impact of theft and vandalism in relation to the sustainability of renewable energy projects in Sub-Saharan Africa. *Sustainability (Basel)*, *10*(3), 814. doi:10.3390/su10030814

IOL. (2022). *Illegal electricity connections and a spike in vandalism of electricity infrastructure in recent months across the city and the province is costing millions of rand*. IOL. https://www.iol.co.za/capeargus/news/vandalism-of-electricity-infrastructure-and-illegal-connections-costing-millions-of-rand-352c2318-03a3-4d53-8360-51cff7296a90

Lewis, F. B. (2015). Costly 'throw-ups': Electricity theft and power disruptions. *The Electricity Journal*, *28*(7), 118–135. doi:10.1016/j.tej.2015.07.009

Liddick, D. R. (2009). *An empirical, theoretical and historical overview of organised crime*. Edwin Mellen Press.

Moodley, P. (2022). *Sabotage at power stations widespread*. Eskom CEO. https://www.sabcnews.com/sabcnews/sabotage-at-power-stations-widespread-eskom-ceo/

Mthethwa, C. (2022). Cape Town taxi employee who burnt train so he could 'get paid more' sentenced to 20 years. *News24*. https://www.news24.com/news24/southafrica/news/cape-town-taxi-employee-who-burnt-train-so-he-could-get-paid-more-sentenced-to-20-years-20220423

News24. (2020). Eskom workers 'held hostage', forced to restore illegal electricity connections. *News24*. https://www.news24.com/news24/southafrica/news/eskom-workers-held-hostage-forced-to-restore-illegal-electricity-connections-20200629

Ntuli, N. (2020). Eskom gives up on thieves. *News24*. https://www.news24.com/witness/news/eskom-gives-up-on-thieves-20200811

Pilling, D. (2023). *Scandal at South Africa's Eskom: the CEO and the cyanide-laced coffee*. AFR. https://www.afr.com/world/africa/scandal-at-south-africa-s-eskom-the-ceo-and-the-cyanide-laced-coffee-20230303

Reichl, J., Schmidthaler, M., & Schneider, F. (2013). Power Outage Cost Evaluation: Reasoning, Methods and an Application. *Journal of Scientific Research and Reports*, *2*(1), 249–276. doi:10.9734/JSRR/2013/3167

Richards, J. R. (1999). *Transnational criminal organizations, cybercrime and money laundering: A handbook for law enforcement officers, auditors, and financial investigators*. CRC Press.

Roelofse, C. J. (2009). *Organised Crime in South Africa. Urbanization, Policing and Security: Global Perspectives*. CRC Press.

Roth, M.P. (2010). *Organised Crime*. Upper Saddle River: prentice Hall.

Scott, M. J., La Vigne, N. G., & Palmer, T. (2007). *Preventing Vandalism.* The Urban Institute Justice Policy Center.

Sellin, T. (1963). Organized crime: A business enterprise. *The Annals of the American Academy of Political and Social Science, 347*(1), 12–19. doi:10.1177/000271626334700103

Shabalala, Z. (2021). *How the illicit copper trade is sapping South Africa.* Reuters. https://www.reuters.com/world/africa/exclusive-how-illicit-copper-trade-is-sapping-south-africa-2021-10-15/

Shaw, M. (1998). Organised crime in post-apartheid South Africa: Safety and governance programme (Occasional paper no 28). Institute for security studies.

Sidebottom, A., Ashby, M., & Johnson, S. D. (2014). Copper cable theft: Revisiting the price-theft hypothesis. *Journal of Research in Crime and Delinquency, 51*(5), 684–700. doi:10.1177/0022427814521216

Singh, D. (2022). The Causes of Police Corruption and Working towards Prevention in Conflict-Stricken States. *Laws, 11*(5), 69. doi:10.3390/laws11050069

Slabbert, A. (2022). Cable thieves now armed with AK-47s. *News24.* https://www.news24.com/citypress/news/cable-thieves-now-armed-withak-47s-20220410

Smith, T. B. (2003). Electricity theft- comparative analysis. *Energy Policy, 32*(18), 2067–2076. doi:10.1016/S0301-4215(03)00182-4

Theron, A. (2018). *Copper theft remains a concern.* ESI Africa. https://www.esi-africa.com/southern-africa/copper-theftremains-a-serious-concern-eskom/

Torkelson, E. (2010). *Who profits from Copper Theft?* ISS. http://www.iss.co.za/iss_today.php?ID=1059

Transnet. (2021). *The impact of cable theft and vandalism of Transnet property.* Twitter. https://twitter.com/ReliableTFR/status/1458393093754036224

Vaknin, S. (2000). The criminality of transition. In M. Pagon (Ed.), Policing in Central and Eastern Europe: Ethics, Integrity and Human Rights (pp. 61–70). Ljubljana, Slovenia: Fakulteta za policijsko-varnostne vede [College of Police and SecurityStudies].

van Diemen, D. (2023). Filthy seam of sabotage – how thieving cartels are plunging South Africa into darkness. *Daily Mavrick.* https://www.dailymaverick.co.za/article/2023-03-04-eskom-sabotage-cartels-power-cuts/

Von Ketelhodt, A., & Wöcke, A. (2008). The impact of electricity crises on the consumption behaviour of small and medium enterprises. *Journal of Energy in Southern Africa, 19(*1), 4-12. doi:10.17159/2413-3051/2008/v19i1a3321

von Lampe, K. (2016). *Organized Crime: Analyzing illegal activities, criminal structures, and extra-legal governance*. Sage. doi:10.4135/9781506305110

Ward, C. (1973). *Vandalism*. The Architecturel Press.

Wilson, P. (1988). Preventing Vandalism and Graffiti. *Journal of Security Administration*, *11*(2), 28–35.

Writer, S. (2021). Evidence of Eskom being destroyed from the inside: report. *Business Tech*. https://businesstech.co.za/news/energy/539754/evidence-of-eskom-being-destroyed-from-the-inside-report/

Yorke-Smith, L. (2010). *Solving Copper Theft*. Hi-Tech Security Solutions. http://www.securitysa.com/article.aspx?pklarticleid=5905

Chapter 11
Outside and Out of Mind:
Organized Criminal Enterprises and the Fleecing of Flora and Fauna

Joshua Todd Shadwick
Southeast Missouri State University, USA

ABSTRACT

Organized crime is a noted facilitator of drugs, weapons, and human trafficking. Overlooked, however, is the involvement of these criminal enterprises regarding flora (i.e., plants) and fauna (i.e., animals) crimes. For example, the trafficking of wildlife and wildlife parts globally. The need to better understand the impact these criminal units is espoused by multiple stakeholders. Subsequently, this chapter will discuss the impact organized crime has on wildlife and the environment through an international lens.

INTRODUCTION

Organized crime has received a great deal of attention regarding drug and human trafficking (Jones et al., 2022). These offenses can, at times, obscure the fact that these criminal enterprises also traffic in flora (i.e., plants) and fauna (i.e., animals) (Felbab-Brown, 2017). Subsequently, crimes against wildlife and the environment go largely underenforced and underexplored (Felbab-Brown, 2017; Wolf, 2011). The obscurity of these offenses further incentivizes the draw to these criminal acts, given the lucrative ability to turn a profit with little oversight. For example, scholars have noted the value associated with the trafficking of wildlife across different species (Moreto & Pires, 2018; Nurse, 2015; Pires et al., 2023). Thus, non-profits,

DOI: 10.4018/979-8-3693-0327-6.ch011

practitioners, and academics espouse the impact organized criminal units have on wildlife and the environment (Corwin, 2009; Crow e et al., 2013; Gore et al., 2023; Jacobs et al., 2014; Keskin et al., 2022; Stadler et al., 2023).

In short, institutions and individuals charged with protecting wildlife and the environment have taken notice of crimes against wildlife and the environment. The ability to inform and educate interested parties is crucial to addressing offenses against animals and the environment (Kahler et al., 2023; Moreto & Pires, 2018; Nurse, 2015). For this chapter, wildlife crime will encapsulate a multitude of different offenses ranging from poaching to the trafficking of wildlife and their parts. Moreover, environmental harm will capture actions ranging from illegal dumping toxic materials into the environment to clandestine logging operations (Burns & Lynch, 2004; Nores, 2010, 2019; Wolf, 2011). These flora- and fauna-related harms involve actions that occur on the outskirts of legal and ethical standards and outside common-place policing strategies (Felbab-Brown, 2017). Subsequently, organized crime leverages these events' obscurity and maximizes potential gains while negatively impacting the environment and wildlife.

Understanding the criminal networks and wildlife crime nexus is established through multiple information sources beyond typical academic outlets (Felbab-Brown, 2017; Moreto & Pires, 2018; Nuwer, 2018). For example, investigative journalists such as Nuwer (2018) highlight the complex structures of these enterprises, from the individuals securing wildlife or wildlife parts for transport to the individuals orchestrating the transfer of these animals or items to other parts of the world. An element consistent within the literature is that organized traffickers move prominent species (i.e., rhinos) along with lesser-known species (i.e., pangolin). Therefore, individuals and institutions interested in dismantling these networks must be cognizant of all animals.

Other outlets, such as work by wildlife enforcement practitioners, provide unique insight into wildlife and environmental crimes. Work by Nores (2010, 2019) underlines the complex issues these organized groups present to the environment and public safety. More specifically, the impact clandestine grow operations present regarding violence used by criminal groups and the environmental impact associated with illegal dumping. The latter point is magnified when the chemicals used in the illegal grow operations saturate the topsoil and radiate into water sources (Burns & Lynch, 2004; Nores, 2010, 2019). The underlying supposition to these cases is that multiple areas can be impacted initially and in the long term. Moreover, these events occur within urban centers and rural communities (Nores, 2010, 2019).

Therefore, this chapter aims to unpack what is known about the impact these groups have both domestically and internationally regarding wildlife and environmental crime. Moreover, contextual backcloths such as urban and rural landscapes will be included so motivated parties understand that the issue is not limited to a particular locale. This discussion will include current reporting and documentation strategies used to combat these offenses. Intervention strategies will be examined to see what tactics and tools are currently deployed to help disable and dismantle these criminal enterprises.

This chapter will primarily discuss and examine the impact of organized crime on wildlife and the environment through an international lens. This international lens illustrates that networks are not isolated to a particular country's borders (Keskin et al., 2022; Nuwer, 2018; Pires et al., 2023). Instead, networks stretch beyond a singular continent or country (Pires et al., 2023). For example, Nuwver (2018) and others (Moreto & Pires, 2018; Pires et al., 2023) have identified how key individuals may be located on a different continent than the individuals engaged in collecting and harvesting animals. An example of this issue in motion is the trafficking and poaching of African wildlife, where individuals collect animals for the illegal pet trade, Traditional Chinese Medicine (TCM), or for consumption (Corwin, 2009; Moreto & Pires, 2018; Nuwver, 2018). Therefore, to understand these networks, individuals and institutions need to disentangle and understand why a particular animal or plant is being pursued. Put simply, context forges clarity.

ORGANIZED CRIME RELATED TO WILDLIFE AND ENVIRONMENTAL CRIMES

The theorized involvement of organized crime syndicates with wildlife and environmental crimes has been a documented phenomenon (Felbab-Brown, 2017; Nuwer, 2011, 2018; Wolf, 2011; Wyatt, 2009). This occurrence is understandable given the lucrative nature of these crimes to other international crimes, such as drug, weapon, or human trafficking. For illustration purposes, INTERPOL (2022) argues that environmental crimes are the third largest crime category globally. The high profits and reduced enforcement capabilities result in a low-risk venture for organized crime syndicates (Moreto & Pires, 2018).

The ability to use established connections and smuggling routes further bolsters the likelihood of organized criminal group engagement (Moreto & Pires, 2018; Nuwer, 2018). Moreover, wildlife trafficking can encompass both live animals (i.e., parrots, pangolins, turtles) and animal parts (i.e., rhino horns, shark fins, tiger claws) (Nuwer, 2018; Moreto & Pires, 2018; Wasser et al., 2018; Wyatt, 2009). Trafficking is not, however, limited to only animals and animal parts. When examining trafficked plants, the Saguaro cactus and other cactus varieties have been used for financial gain. For example, Operation Atacama, conducted in Italy, documented the collection of 1,000 cactuses valued at $1.2 million on the black market (IUCN, 2020; Nuwer,

2021). This operation illustrates a point: fins, feathers, and fruits can all serve as potential vessels for exploitation.

Conversely, the concern over the involvement of transnational organized crime has, been met with reservation (Felbab-Brown, 2017; Moreto & Pires, 2018). This guarded acceptance is due to the limited evidence surrounding this topic (Felbab-Brown, 2017; Moreto & Pires, 2018; Pires et al., 2023). For example, there is no central or global database on wildlife transactions (Felbab-Brown, 2017; Nurse, 2015). The patchwork of databases illustrates the difficulty in quantifying these crimes and the movement of plants, animals, and animal parts, both domestically and internationally. This limitation is understandable, given the variation in reporting strategies between countries and across continents (Moreto & Pires, 2018). Subsequently, scholars have advocated for a data directory to help stitch together these various data sources to enhance investigations moving forward (Gore et al., 2023).

More specifically, Gore and colleagues (2023) underscore the importance of leveraging multiple resources to construct a more holistic lens involving flora- and fauna-related trafficking incidents. The ability to overlay multiple animals (i.e., rhino, pangolin), plants (i.e., ginseng, cacti), and protected area-related data together assist with constructing context and understanding, both initially and long-term. In turn, granular insights can be triangulated using repeated measures (Gore et al., 2023). The ability to link different data sources, such as enforcement or consumer-oriented data, provides a platform to decipher unique attributes associated with a particular plant or animal.

As such, scholars have argued that the involvement of transnational organized crime groups should be taken from a trade- or consumptive- specific lens (Moreto & Lemieux, 2015; Moreto & Pires, 2018). The ability to critically examine the trafficking of a specific animal (Wyatt, 2009) or the removal of a particular plant (Marteache & Pires, 2020; Wyatt, 2014) assists interested parties understand specific context. For example, Pires and colleagues (2016) found little support for organized crime involvement in the parrot pet trade within Bolivia and Peru. However, scholarship has noted the involvement of organized crime with elephant ivory (Titeca, 2019; Wasser et al., 2018), rhino horns (Haas & Ferreira, 2016; Hübschle, 2014; Nuwer, 2018), falcon trade (Wyatt, 2009), and the illegal timber trade (Wyatt, 2014). Therefore, motivated parties should understand the reasons (e.g., TCM, pet trade) why a particular animal or plant is being trafficked and how organized groups can potentially integrate themselves into the trafficking equation.

The underlying supposition is that combatting wildlife and environmental crimes requires asymmetrical thinking. Subsequently, scholars have further argued that research and investigations into organized crime and wildlife crime should not focus solely on males being the offenders (Hübschle, 2014). Work by both Nuwer (2018) and Hübschle (2014) highlights the critical role women play within organized crime syndicates and the rhino horn trafficking from Africa into Asia, ranging from the initial harvesting of an animal to the end consumer. Research illustrates that males and females commit these complex crimes (Felbab-Brown, 2017; Nuwer, 2018).

Moreover, research by Wyatt (2009) and others (Felbab-Brown, 2017; Moreto & Pires, 2018) illustrate that organized crime is not limited to only Africa. Instead, it extends into other countries, and the operational structure associated with these crimes, such as fur and raptor sales, varies depending on the commodity. For example, Wyatt's (2009) work noted the complex structure used in the illegal fur trade within Russia; conversely, a simple chain network structure was utilized for the raptor trade. Scholarship also notes that the nationalities of these criminal groups also tend to vary depending on the exact crime type, where Chinese-based groups were involved with rhino horns (Nuwer, 2018) and Arab-based groups were involved with the falcon trade (Wyatt, 2009).

Moreover, scholarship has also documented the involvement of organized crime in relation to environmental crimes. An example is the deforestation practices within the Brazilian Amazon (Hobbs, 2023). Although no specific region was specified for the group involved. It can be surmised that the criminal group most likely originates from that region given its remote location. The incentive to engage in these environmental crimes represent the relative low detection and punishment risks (Hobbs, 2023). Institutions and individuals charged with wildlife and environmental protection should consider the different flora (e.g., sandalwood, redwood, rosewood, cacti) and fauna (e.g., bears, tigers, pangolins) present within a particular area (Hobbs, 2023; Marteache & Pires, 2020; Moreto & Pires, 2018; Nuwer, 2018). By being aware of what is found within a region, country, or state, allows various stakeholders to better understand what to look for regarding potential exploitation pathways.

Environmental harm is another environmental issue associated with organized crime (Nores, 2010, 2019; Wolf, 2011). More specifically, pollution-based harms for a particular country or region. These issues may include the illegal disposal of hazardous waste or price fixing for waste disposal services (Wolf, 2011). For example, prior scholarship has documented an organized crime group in Italy illegally dumping hazardous waste (Massari & Monzini, 2004). Government-based corruption is likely to be included with these crimes (Wolf, 2011). Therefore, stakeholders need to consider the potential for government-based corruption that helps facilitate wildlife and environmental crimes (Moreto & Pires, 2018; Nuwer, 2018). Likewise, institutions and individuals charged with investigating these crimes need to consider what is being removed or added that negatively impacts flora and fauna.

Thus, clarity is captured through context-specific understanding (e.g., what precisely is being trafficked). Or what pollution-related actions are occurring that result in environmental harm. In other words, broad generalizations regarding the involvement and influence of transnational organized groups should be used cautiously

(Moreto & Pires, 2018). Interested parties should not readily assume that a criminal syndicate is behind every wildlife and environmental crime. Instead, institutions and individuals should dissect these crimes so that they can be understood on a granular level to help facilitate the detection of organized criminal groups. Moreover, a crime dissection should include information to integrate potential intervention strategies at the crime-specific level. We now turn toward a more in-depth discussion on intervention strategies.

INTERVENTION STRATEGIES

Interventions, like tools in a toolbox, vary according to the wildlife or environmental problem. However, deploying an effective strategy hinge on the context of the crime to which it is being applied specifically (Goldstein, 1990; Moreto & Pires, 2018). This point will be discussed in further detail later; suffice it to say that details matter. Regardless of the intervention strategy, a key element that needs to be an underlining feature is the initial and continued support of the community (Felbab-Brown, 2017). Individuals and institutions must be aware of the community context where intervention strategies are being integrated. For example, issues associated with poverty and using wildlife as a food source (i.e., bushmeat) within Africa are well-documented (Brown, 2017; Moreto & Pires, 2018; Nuwer, 2018). Therefore, to help facilitate community support for practices meant to minimize poaching for bushmeat purposes, institutions need to address the reasons behind the problem (Felbab-Brown, 2017). In other words, facilitating programs associated with ecotourism and alternative livelihood practices can serve as foundational elements for positive community advancement (Felbab-Brown, 2017). The underlying supposition is that positive change for wildlife occurs through the enrichment of communities and citizens.

Intervention strategies focused on enriching communities and the environment can be represented through Community-based natural resource management (CBNRM). CBNRM programs address three potential outcomes: environmental conservation, community empowerment, and social equality (Felbab-Brown, 2017). These elements can be interpreted as conservation, human rights, and poverty reduction (Felbab-Brown, 2017). An example of a CBNRM program in motion is Zimbabwe's CAMPFIRE program (Communal Areas Management Program for Indigenous Resources) (Felbab-Brown, 2017). This program focused on empowering locals by providing monetary funds from safari hunting to stay at the local level instead of at the national level. The funds, in turn, are used to help establish wells and other critical infrastructure items while facilitating initial and sustained sound ecological practices (Tchakatumba et al., 2019). In essence, the ability to facilitate citizen and community empowerment supports the willingness of community members to manage resources and report offenses (Felbab-Brown, 2017; Leavitt et al., 2020). In turn, community empowerment coupled with active reporting practices provide the bedrock for other intervention strategies.

Establishing active community participation and reporting facilitates a more robust image of wildlife and environmental crimes. This refined understanding assists with ways to curb these offenses. When considering potential intervention techniques, instruments such as "The 25 Techniques of Situational Crime Prevention" can be valuable tools for facilitating interventions (Cornish & Clark, 2003; Fauna & Flora International, 2021). The pillars, *increasing effort, increasing risk, reducing provocation, reducing rewards, and removing excuses,* help to facilitate potential intervention points. For example, focusing on *increasing effort* can make it harder for organized groups to remove a target species (Fauna & Flora International, 2021). Likewise, institutions could focus on *reducing rewards* by increasing the identification of plants and animals (Fauna & Flora International, 2021; Moreto & Pires, 2018). Another technique is to overlap situational crime techniques (Cornish & Clark, 2003; Viollanz et al., 2021) with what is CRAVED (concealable, removable, available, valuable, enjoyable, and disposable) (Moreto & Pires, 2018). The underlying supposition is that these techniques reduce opportunities, and CRAVED helps illustrate which flora or fauna will be targeted within a particular area.

To further minimize opportunities, understanding the overlap of people, places, and times relative to different chain events (i.e., preparation, pre-activity, illegal activity, and post-activity) forms a platform for integrating intervention strategies (Felbab-Brown, 2017; Fauna & Flora International, 2021). Dissecting a criminal event allows an investigator to examine the context leading up to, during, and after the commission of a crime to help identify potential areas to integrate intervention strategies (Fauna & Flora International, 2021). In other words, the investigator breaks the criminal event into several smaller steps so critical points are not overlooked. In Nuwer's (2018) work, the process of capturing, retaining, and transporting wildlife for various reasons (i.e., TCM, pet trade) illustrates the different chain events. The relative importance associated with the poachers, handlers, and final consumers specific to these different events or transition periods illustrates the complexities associated with combating wildlife and environmental crimes. Thus, the ability of investigators to dissect a crime into smaller parts can aid in identifying a key element in addressing the crime initially and in understanding how criminal practices evolve.

Regardless, intervention practices must be integrated into actionable work plans. Coupled with this practice is the constant evaluation and sharing of lessons learned from an intervention practice (Fauna & Flora International, 2021). Moreover, intervention strategies must be crime-specific (Moreto & Pires, 2018). This contextual factor means interested parties should understand the driving forces specific to different animal and plant species. For example, the Asian and African Pangolins have been targeted for their use in TCM and as a social status symbol.

In contrast, the Saguaro cactus has been poached due to its symbol of the American desert (Moreto & Pires, 2018). Although not consumptive, the process of removing the cactus from its natural habitat to a relegated spot as landscape art can be viewed as a disruption to the environment. The ability to disentangle different wildlife and environmental crimes from one another provides institutions with a greater understanding of motives and actionable steps. With these intervention techniques in mind, we now turn toward a discussion on recommendations.

RECOMMENDATIONS

Recommendations for addressing organized crime surrounding wildlife and environmental crime are multipronged. First, continued efforts to support public awareness and appreciation must be garnered and fostered for animals and their habitats. Moreover, empowering local communities and facilitating sustained infrastructure support is another element that needs to occur. Zimbabwe's CAMPFIRE represents the potential of this conservation model, as it addresses some of the underlying problems associated with wildlife crime (Felbab-Brown, 2017). Stakeholders should also continue to explore ego-tourism outlets to facilitate revenue and public awareness. The ability to bring revenue and attention to prominent and non-prominent species through non-consummative means bolsters the inherent value that should be given to animals and their habitats (Moreto & Pires, 2018). Furthermore, interested parties should not isolate public awareness to one country or continent. The reason is that wildlife and environmental exploitation has been documented globally and across prominent (e.g., gorillas, tigers) and lesser publicized (e.g., eels, parrots) animals (Felbab-Brown, 2017; Moreto & Pires, 2018; Nuwers, 2018).

The second component to address is to help consolidate wildlife crime data into one dataset. To help illustrate this point, within the United States, there is NIBRS (National Incident-Based Reporting System) where crimes (e.g., violent, property, drug) are collected from thousands of law enforcement agencies across the nation (FBI, 2012). In turn, data is collected on the crime count and specific information involving a particular incident (e.g., crime location, weapon use). Currently, however, no national-based dataset exists that captures the various environment- and wildlife-related crimes across all 50 states. Therefore, the ability to consolidate these crime types into one dataset would help illustrate the breadth and depth of these crimes within the United States. The creation of this national-level wildlife and environmental crime dataset could be used as a model for international data collection efforts. Statutory reporting of wildlife and environmental crimes would allow the extent of the problem to be established both nationally and internationally (Nurse, 2015). The ability of practitioners and researchers to better understand issues would be enhanced since much can be gathered from aggregating crime data (Gore et al., 2023; Nurse, 2015). A better understanding associated with the scale of the offenses would help allocate resources devoted to addressing these crimes.

The third component is to increase scholarship and training specific to wildlife and environmental crimes. Scholars have argued that this area of scholarship has been largely overlooked within the academic community (Felbab-Brown, 2017; Moreto & Pires, 2018; Nurse, 2015; Wolf, 2011). Part and parcel of this problem is the lack of quantitative-based studies associated with these crimes (Lynch & Pires, 2019). In turn, treating this research area as a niche subject matter undermines the important need to expand it beyond conjecture within the ivory towers of academia. Subsequently, we should examine wildlife and environmental crimes with the same intensity as other criminal offenses. Integrating established criminological tools, such as situational crime prevention, would facilitate a more refined understanding specific to wildlife and environmental crimes (Moreto & Pires, 2018).

Couched within refining criminological tools (i.e., CRAVED) is the need to understand the influence online practices have on the commission of these crimes. More specifically, the ability to take the knowledge associated with the physical environment and overlay it with the digital landscape is one area that needs attention. Programs such as the wildlife trafficking cybercrime program represent the inherent need to understand online and physical factors associated with committing these offenses (U.S. Fish & Wildlife Service, n.d.). Understandably, the "marketplace" for illicit animal parts and animals has shifted to a digital interface. Subsequently, CITES (n.d.) denotes that wildlife cybercrime occurs when it is enabled or facilitated using communication technology interfaces such as the dark web or social network platforms. Bridging the gap in what is known about the environment, both physical and digital, is needed for both research and practice.

When taken collectively, these recommendations illustrate the need to leverage resources continually. Researchers and investigators should consider that offenders and offenses are not static (Felbab-Brown, 2017). Instead, the practices used by those engaging in the trafficking of flora and fauna are likely to change over time (Moreto & Pires, 2018). Moreover, item and animal desirability will likely ebb and flow with social and cultural changes. Understanding the human dynamics associated with the consumptive use of wildlife, both legal and illegal, will further aid in bridging resources.

CONCLUSION

This chapter aims to empower individuals' and institutions' responses to wildlife and environmental crimes. Moreover, a discussion on the extent organized criminal groups were involved with these offenses. These groups, at times, are involved in flora- and fauna-related crimes (Hobbs, 2023; Hübschle, 2014; Nuwer, 2018; Titeca, 2019). Practitioners and academics, however, should not readily assume that crime syndicates are behind every offense (Felbab-Brown, 2017). Instead, academics and practitioners must focus on the importance of building and fostering social ties with external stakeholders. Active engagement with the communities and enhanced reporting practices both domestically and internationally represent platforms needed regardless of the extent to which organized groups are involved.

In addition, wildlife and environmental law enforcement agency leaders should consider the importance of senior law enforcement officials' institutional knowledge and community relationships. Retaining that information and maintaining community ties across law enforcement officials is crucial to addressing these complex crimes (Felbab-Brown, 2017; Moreto & Pires, 2018). Turnover among experienced officers and onboarding of new, less-experienced officers are events that will occur within these agencies. By being proactive, agencies can minimize the loss of information across officers and ensure community ties are maintained over time.

The value associated with community ties and empowerment must be considered in the fight against wildlife and environmental crimes. It can be surmised that effective intervention strategies against organized groups are likely will likely cause these criminal enterprises to displace to another area or animal to exploit (Felbab-Brown, 2017). Information sharing and continued interactions with community organizations aid in understanding the movement of crime domestically and internationally.

Coupled with community ties are the improved data collection efforts for wildlife and environmental crimes. The ability to link information and events across states and nations can facilitate an enhanced understanding of these events for practitioners and academics. Furthermore, disentangling unique attributes such as the method of take (e.g., trap, firearm), location, and time associated with these events aids in providing clarity and context. Therefore, the call for refined practices is now; do not let it go unanswered.

REFERENCES

Felbab-Brown (2017). The extinction market: Wildlife trafficking and how to counter it. Oxford University Press.

Burns, R. G., & Lynch, M. J. (2004). *Environmental crime: A sourcebook*. LFB Scholarly Pub LLC.

CITES. (n.d.). *Combating Wildlife Cybercrime*. CITES. https://cites.org/eng/prog/imp/

combating_wildlife_cybercrime_draft#:~:text=Wildlife%20crime%20linked%20to%20the%20Internet%20is%20defined%20in%20the,the%20dark%20web%2C%20online%20marketplaces.

Cornish, D. B., & Clarke, R. V. (2003). Opportunities, precipitators and criminal decisions: A reply to Wortley's critique of situational crime prevention. *Crime Prevention Studies*, *16*, 41–96.

Corwin, J. (2009). *100 Heartbeats: The race to save Earth's most endangered species*. Rodale Inc.

Crow, M. S., Shelley, T. O. C., & Stretesky, P. B. (2013). Camouflage-collar crime: An examination of wildlife crime and characteristics of offenders in Florida. *Deviant Behavior*, *34*(8), 635–652. doi:10.1080/01639625.2012.759049

Fauna & Flora International (2021). *Using situational crime prevention to address illegal wildlife trade: A toolkit*. Flora & Fauna International.

F.B.I. (2012). *About the NIBRS*. U.S. Department of Justice-Federal Burearu of Investigation. https://ucr.fbi.gov/nibrs/2012/resources/about-the-nibrs

Felbab-Brown, V. (2017). *The Extinction Market: Wildlife trafficking and how to counter it*. Oxford University Press.

Goldstein, H. (1990). *Excellence in problem-oriented policing*. In New York NY: Police Executive Research Forum.

Gore, M. L., Hilend, R., Prell, J. O., Griffin, E., Macdonald, J. R., Keskin, B. B., Ferber, A., & Dilkina, B. (2023). A data directory to facilitate investigations on worldwide wildlife trafficking. *Big Earth Data*, *7*(2), 1–11. doi:10.1080/20964471.2023.2193281

Haas, T. C., & Ferreira, S. M. (2016). Combating rhino horn trafficking: The need to disrupt criminal networks. *PLoS One*, *11*(11), e0167040. doi:10.1371/journal.pone.0167040 PMID:27870917

Hobbs, S. (2023). From chains to chainsaws: Modern slavery and deforestation in the Brazilian Amazon. *Nature and Space,* 1-28.

Hübschle, A. (2014). Of bogus hunters, queenpins and mules: The varied roles of women in transnational organized crime in Southern Africa. *Trends in Organized Crime*, *17*(1-2), 31–51. doi:10.1007/s12117-013-9202-8

INTERPOL. (2022). *Stepping up the global fight against wildlife crime through a united response*. INTERPOL. https://www.interpol.int/en/News-and-Events/News/2022/Stepping-up-the-global-fight-against-wildlife-crime-through-a-united-response

IUCN. (2020). *"Operation Atacama", the recovery of trafficked threatened cacti*. International Union for Conservation of Nature. https://www.iucn.org/news/species-survival-commission/202012/operacion-atacama-recovery-trafficked-threatened-cacti

Jacobs, M. H., Vaske, J. J., & Sijtsma, M. T. (2014). Predictive potential of wildlife value orientations for acceptability of management interventions. *Journal for Nature Conservation*, *22*(4), 377–383. doi:10.1016/j.jnc.2014.03.005

Jones, N. P., Chindea, I. A., Argomedo, D. W., & Sullivan, J. P. (2022). A Social Network Analysis of Mexico's Dark Network Alliance Structure. *Journal of Strategic Security*, *15*(4), 76–105. doi:10.5038/1944-0472.15.4.2046

Kahler, J. S., Reynald, D. M., & Gore, M. L. (2023). "I let it go:" Quantifying residential guardianship intentions when witnessing wildlife poaching. *Biological Conservation*, *277*, 109829. doi:10.1016/j.biocon.2022.109829

Keskin, B. B., Griffin, E. C., Prell, J. O., Dilkina, B., Ferber, A., MacDonald, J., & Gore, M. L. (2022). Quantitative investigation of wildlife trafficking supply chains: A review. *Omega*, 102780.

Leavitt, K., Wodahl, E. J., & Schweitzer, K. (2020). Citizen willingness to report wildlife crime. *Deviant Behavior*. doi:10.1080/01639625.2020.1738643

Lynch, M. J., & Pires, S. F. (Eds.). (2019). *Quantitative studies in green and conservation criminology: The measurement of environmental harm and crime*. Routledge. doi:10.4324/9780429453946

Marteache, N., & Pires, S. F. (2020). Choice structuring properties of natural resource theft: An examination of redwood burl poaching. *Deviant Behavior*, *41*(3), 311–328. doi:10.1080/01639625.2019.1565518

Massari, M., & Monzini, P. (2004). Dirty business in Italy: Case study of illegal trafficking in hazardous waste. *Global Crime*, *6*(3), 285–304. doi:10.1080/17440570500273416

Moreto, W. D., & Lemieux, A. M. (2015). From CRAVED to CAPTURED: Introducing a product-based framework to examine illegal wildlife markets. *European Journal on Criminal Policy and Research, 21*(3), 303–320. doi:10.1007/s10610-014-9268-0

Moreto, W. D., & Pires, S. F. (2018). *Wildlife crime: An environmental criminology and crime science perspective*. Carolina Academic Press.

Nores, J. (2010). *War in the woods: Combating the marijuana cartels on America's public lands*. Lyons Press.

Nores, J. (2019). *Hidden War: How special operations game wardens are reclaiming America's wildland from the drug cartels*. Gun Digest Books.

Nurse, A. (2015). *Policing wildlife: Perspectives on the enforcement of wildlife legislation*. Springer Publishing. doi:10.1057/9781137400017

Nuwer, R. L. (2018). *Poached: Inside the dark world of wildlife trafficking*. Scribe Publications.

Nuwer, R. L. (2021). Global cactus traffickers are cleaning out the deserts. *The New York Times*. https://www.nytimes.com/2021/05/20/science/cactus-trafficking-chile.html#:~:text="Just%20about%20every%20plant%20you,can%20take%20a%20serious%20toll.

Pires, S. F., Schneider, J. L., & Herrera, M. (2016). Organized crime or crime that is organized? The parrot trade in the neotropics. *Trends in Organized Crime, 19*(1), 4–20. doi:10.1007/s12117-015-9259-7

Pires, S. F., Thomson, R. W., Petrossian, G. A., & Sosnowski, M. C. (2023). A Social Network Analysis of Large-Scale Wildlife Seizures Made at US Ports of Entry. *Deviant Behavior, 44*(8), 1–14. doi:10.1080/01639625.2023.2169211

Stadler, W. A., Jonson, C. L., & Gialopsos, B. M. (2023). Are we loving our national parks to death? A call for research on crime and law enforcement in the US national park system. *Criminal Justice Review, 48*(1), 85–105. doi:10.1177/07340168211015726

Tchakatumba, P. K., Gandiwa, E., Mwakiwa, E., Clegg, B., & Nyasha, S. (2019). Does the CAMPFIRE programme ensure economic benefits from wildlife to households in Zimbabwe? *Ecosystems and People (Abingdon, England), 15*(1), 119–135. doi:10.1080/26395916.2019.1599070

Titeca, K. (2019). Illegal ivory trade as transnational organized crime? An empirical study into ivory traders in Uganda. *British Journal of Criminology, 59*(1), 24–44. doi:10.1093/bjc/azy009

U.S. Fish & Wildlife Service. (n.d.). *Office of Law Enforcement Training and Development Unit*. U.S. Fish & Wildlife Service. https://www.fws.gov/program/office-law-enforcement-training-and-development-unit/what-we-do

Viollaz, J., Long, B., Trung, C. T., Kempinski, J., Rawson, B. M., Quang, H. X., Hiền, N. N., Liên, N. T. B., Dũng, C. T., Huyền, H. T., McWhirter, R., Dung, N. T. T., & Gore, M. L. (2021). Using crime script analysis to understand wildlife poaching in Vietnam. *Ambio*, *50*(7), 1378–1393. doi:10.1007/s13280-020-01498-3 PMID:33738731

Wasser, S. K., Torkelson, A., Winters, M., Horeaux, Y., Tucker, S., Otiende, M. Y., Sitam, F. A. T., Buckleton, J., & Weir, B. S. (2018). Combating transnational organized crime by linking multiple large ivory seizures to the same dealer. *Science Advances*, *4*(9), 1–10. doi:10.1126/sciadv.aat0625 PMID:30255141

Wolf, B. (2011). 'Green-Collar Crime': Environmental Crime and Justice in the Sociological Perspective. *Sociology Compass*, *5*(7), 499–511. doi:10.1111/j.1751-9020.2011.00381.x

Wyatt, T. (2009). Exploring the organization of Russia Far East's illegal wildlife trade: Two case studies of the illegal fur and illegal falcon trades. *Global Crime*, *10*(1-2), 144–154. doi:10.1080/17440570902783947

Wyatt, T. (2014). The Russian Far East's illegal timber trade: An organized crime? *Crime, Law, and Social Change*, *61*(1), 15–35. doi:10.1007/s10611-013-9461-y

Chapter 12
Empowering Community Actors:
Training Taxi and Private Hire Vehicle Drivers as Allies in Combating Organized Crime

Mohammed Abdel-Haq
University of Bolton, UK & Hume Institute for Postgraduate Studies, Lausanne, Switzerland

Alicia Danielsson
University of Bolton, UK & Hume Institute for Postgraduate Studies, Lausanne, Switzerland

ABSTRACT

This chapter explores the integral role of taxi and Private Hire Vehicle (PHV) services in combating organized crime, with a specific focus on child sexual exploitation as highlighted by cases like Operation Stovewood. The research scrutinizes the socio-economic impacts of organized crime on individuals and communities, emphasizing the need for a collaborative approach to address these issues. It particularly examines the involvement of the taxi and PHV industry in these crimes and advocates for effective public-private collaboration in tackling organized crime.

DOI: 10.4018/979-8-3693-0327-6.ch012

Organized crime, including activities like human trafficking and extortion, undermines societal stability, fostering violence and eroding public trust in institutions. The chapter presents a disturbing dimension of this crime: the exploitation of certain taxi/PHV drivers in child sexual exploitation scandals, as seen in investigations across cities like Rotherham. This revelation has led to a critical inquiry into taxi and PHV licensing, aiming to address regulatory gaps and ensure the safeguarding of vulnerable individuals.

The research adopts a comprehensive methodology, analyzing Operation Stovewood as a case study and reviewing academic and government reports on the effectiveness of policies and legal frameworks governing taxi and PHV licensing. It also explores the ethical and legal responsibilities of regulating taxi and PHV services, balancing safety measures with privacy rights.

Key to this discourse is the necessity of public-private collaboration in combating organized crime. The strategic positioning of taxi and PHV drivers as local surveillance agents offers a unique opportunity in this fight. The chapter proposes comprehensive training, legal structures, and ethical guidelines to empower drivers in this role, supplemented by technological advancements like CCTV in taxis and PHVs.

INTRODUCTION

Following a series of alarming revelations of large-scale child sexual exploitation rings in Northern England, a spotlight has been cast on the role of taxi and Private Hire Vehicle (PHV) services in such crimes, prompting a critical inquiry by the Task and Finish Group into taxi and PHV licensing. This research delves into the socio-economic impacts of organized crime on individuals and communities, underscoring the imperative for a collaborative approach to combat these deep-rooted issues. It particularly scrutinizes the involvement of the taxi and PHV trade in these crimes, reflecting on the broader need for effective public-private collaboration in tackling organized crime (Task and Finish Group on Taxi and Private Hire Vehicle Licensing, 2018).

Organized crime, which encompasses illicit activities such as drug trafficking, human trafficking, and extortion, poses a severe threat to societal stability. It expands deep into the fabric of communities, fostering violence and corruption, thereby undermining public trust in institutions and impeding economic development. The direct impact of these criminal enterprises is evident in the heightened violence and insecurity experienced by individuals, while the indirect effects manifest in the erosion of institutional credibility and economic harm.

A disturbing aspect of organized crime that has come to the fore is the involvement of certain taxi/PHV drivers in child sexual exploitation scandals, as uncovered in investigations across cities like Rotherham. These revelations have not only exposed the opportunistic exploitation of the night-time economy by some within the taxi and PHV industry, but also highlighted significant regulatory and monitoring gaps in taxi and PHV licensing. In response, the Task and Finish Group's inquiry aims to address these gaps by advocating for stricter regulations and practices in taxi and PHV licensing, thus ensuring better safeguarding of vulnerable individuals (Task and Finish Group on Taxi and Private Hire Vehicle Licensing, 2018).

The fight against organized crime, especially in the context of protecting children and vulnerable communities, necessitates a unified response that bridges public authorities, law enforcement, and the private sector. This collaborative approach is particularly vital in sectors like taxi and PHV services, where systemic vulnerabilities have been exploited. Empowering community actors such as taxi and PHV drivers through training and equipping them to recognize and report signs of exploitation and other criminal activities emerges as a crucial strategy in this context.

The methodology of this research is comprehensive, incorporating an analysis of Operation Stovewood as a case study, combined with in-depth reviews of academic and government reports. This is complemented by a detailed examination of the existing policies and legal frameworks governing taxi and PHV licensing, assessing their effectiveness in ensuring public safety.

A significant consideration in this discourse is the ethical and legal responsibilities that surround the regulation of taxi and PHV services. This includes addressing the vicarious accountability of local authorities in ensuring proper regulation and the protection of taxi and PHV drivers who, in good faith, report criminal activities. Furthermore, the research navigates the delicate balance between implementing safety measures like CCTV in taxis and PHVs and respecting the privacy rights of individuals.

The Impact of Organised Crime on Individuals and Society and the Call for Collaboration

Organised crime, a pervasive and insidious force, poses a significant threat to societal and economic stability. Its wide-reaching influence permeates various facets of daily life, presenting formidable challenges that necessitate innovative, collaborative responses from both the public and private sectors (Levi & Maguire, 2004; Watson, Sousa-Santos & Howes, 2021; Waardenburg, Groenleer & De Jong, 2020). This examination seeks to illuminate the multifaceted effects of organised crime and emphasizes the critical need for a collective approach to address these issues.

The socio-economic impact of organised crime on communities is profound and multi-dimensional. Activities such as drug trafficking, human trafficking, money laundering, and extortion, conducted by criminal enterprises, contribute to the erosion of societal fabric. This erosion manifests in the perpetuation of violence, fostering of corruption, and a consequential undermining of trust in public institutions. The resultant social destabilisation detrimentally affects individual quality of life and impedes economic development (Di Maggio & Lo Verde, 2023; Jakubiec & Kuliński, 2023; Martinez Cristaldo, 2023).

One of the most immediate and visible repercussions of organised crime is the perpetuation of violence. Criminal enterprises engage in territorial disputes, power struggles, and vendettas, often resulting in violence spilling into the public sphere. This violence poses a direct threat to individuals' lives and instills fear and insecurity among the broader population, effectively making citizens prisoners within their own neighbourhoods (El Ghamari & Gabriela Bartoszewicz, 2020; Üngör, 2020; Rader, 2023).

In parallel, organised crime's impact extends to the corruption and weakening of institutions. The credibility and effectiveness of public institutions, including law enforcement, judiciary, and government agencies, are compromised by this infiltration, leading to a loss of public trust and confidence. As citizens perceive these institutions as compromised, their likelihood of cooperating with authorities, reporting crimes, or engaging in community-building efforts diminishes significantly (Baradel, 2020; Braithwaite, 2022; Strečanský, 2023; Hirsch Ballin, 2022).

Economically, the impact of organised crime is equally profound. Illicit activities generate substantial illicit revenue, distorting economic systems and diverting capital from legitimate businesses and investments (Otusanya & Adeyeye, 2022; Singh, 2023; Zabyelina & Thachuk, (Eds.). 2022; Obaga, 2021). This distortion hinders economic growth and development, stifling entrepreneurship and legitimate economic activity, particularly in areas heavily infiltrated by organised crime. Entrepreneurs and business owners in such areas often find themselves subjected to extortion, racketeering, or forced to pay "protection money" to criminal syndicates (Piemontese, 2023; Vaia & Bisogno, 2020; Sollecito, 2023).

The social fabric of communities experiences significant disintegration as organised crime spreads its influence. Families, torn apart by addiction, violence, or involvement in criminal activities, endure immense emotional and psychological strain. Children raised in such environments face a heightened risk of replicating criminal behaviour patterns or becoming victims themselves (Coomber, Donnermeyer, McElrath & Scott, 2014; McLean, 2019; Thornberry (Ed.), 2018; Wright, Tibbetts & Daigle, 2014).

Organised crime's exploitation of vulnerable individuals represents one of its most harrowing consequences. Human trafficking, a grave manifestation of this exploitation, involves the recruitment, transportation, and exploitation of individuals for purposes such as forced labor, sexual exploitation, or organ trafficking (Aronowitz & Veldhuizen, 2021; Shelley, 2013; Caparini, 2014; Meneses Falcón, Urío Rodríguez & Uroz Olivares, 2019). Vulnerable populations, including migrants, refugees, and marginalized communities, are disproportionately affected. The exploitation of children within these networks is particularly distressing, subjecting them to forced labor, sexual abuse, and recruitment into criminal activities (Gallagher, 2015; Edwards, 2007; Yousaf, 2018; Nagle, 2013).

The involvement of organised crime in the drug trade amplifies its social toll. Drug cartels and criminal networks profit from the sale of illegal narcotics, entrapping individuals in cycles of addiction and despair (Reuter, 2014; McCarthy-Jones, Doyle & Turner, 2020; Mallory, 2011; Raineri & Strazzari, 2023). Vulnerable communities, characterised by poverty and limited access to education and healthcare, are disproportionately affected. Organised crime preys on the desperation of individuals in these communities, offering drugs as an escape from harsh realities, ensnaring them in a vicious cycle of addiction (Berry, 2020; Davies, Powling & Symmonds, 2024; Windle, Moyle & Coomber, 2020; Deuchar, McLeanand & Holligan, 2021; Lefevre, Hickle & Larkin, 2020).

The global impact of organised crime, unfettered by geographical borders, affects regions and countries worldwide. The interconnectedness of modern economies and communication systems has facilitated the expansion of criminal networks, enabling them to exploit vulnerabilities on a global scale (Clark, Fraser & Hamilton-Smith, 2021; Danielsson, 2023; Palermo, 2020). This globalization presents challenges for international cooperation and necessitates coordinated efforts among nations to combat it effectively (Bright & Whelan, 2020; Danielsson, 2023; Hignett, 2021; Bouchard, 2020; Coutinho, Diviák, Bright & Koskinen, 2020).

The socio-economic toll of organised crime is extensive and multifaceted, encompassing violence, corruption, economic distortion, social disintegration, and global ramifications. Addressing this complex challenge requires collaboration between public and private actors, with community actors, such as taxi and PHV drivers, playing a crucial role in addressing these issues at the local level.

In the introduction to this critical examination, it is imperative to acknowledge that over the past two decades, a series of major scandals involving large-scale, organized, group-based child sexual exploitation rings, predominantly in the north of England, have emerged into public consciousness. These revelations have not only triggered extensive investigations but also attracted significant media attention, thereby shifting the public understanding and recognition of the nature of child sexual exploitation. Before 2010, the comprehension of such exploitation was limited to a handful of significant cases. However, the last decade has witnessed a paradigm shift, marked by an increase in law enforcement activity and a growing awareness of the complexities surrounding child sexual abuse. High-profile investigations in Telford, Rochdale, Rotherham, Oxford, Bristol, Newcastle, North Wales, and other regions have illuminated the distressing reality of sexual exploitation of children by groups, propelling this grievous issue from the shadows into the spotlight. Yet, it is crucial to acknowledge that much work remains to be done to fully comprehend this form of offending, particularly in light of significant underreporting (Task and Finish Group on Taxi and Private Hire Vehicle Licensing, 2018; Home Office, 2020, Department for Transport, 2019).

A notable aspect of these cases is the involvement of individuals associated with the night-time economy, particularly taxi and PHV drivers, as well as employees of restaurants and takeaways. Reports, including the seminal Jay Report in Rotherham, have underscored the role of taxis and PHVs in these exploitation rings. These cases reveal the often-opportunistic nature of the offending, where children present in night-time environments are more vulnerable and lack protection. Offenders, through their employment, have access to potential victims, exploiting these opportunities to perpetrate abuse. This pattern of abuse is not dissimilar to that observed in other environments, such as custodial institutions, where frequent access to potential victims is also a factor (Home Office, 2020).

The evidence points to a significant role of public spaces in group-based child sexual exploitation (CSE) offenses, highlighting the necessity of creating safer public spaces as a pivotal aspect of prevention strategies. This necessitates a collaborative approach involving local agencies, including law enforcement, local businesses in the night-time economy, and safeguarding partners. Many areas have already made strides in fostering partnership working and information-sharing, especially with businesses such as hotels, taxi and PHV firms, and licensed premises. These efforts are crucial to raise awareness and enhance understanding of exploitation indicators. Furthermore, the utilization of the full range of disruption powers, including licensing and regulatory levers held by local authorities, is essential. This approach not only ensures the safety of public transport but also demonstrates the potential of underutilized reporting methods in combatting such heinous crimes. The spotlight on the accountability of public authorities in these instances underscores the urgent need to safeguard vulnerable populations and prevent future atrocities.

In developing this comprehensive analysis on the role of taxi and PHV drivers in combating organized crime, particularly focusing on child sexual exploitation and modern slavery, our methodology embraces a nuanced and integrative approach. At the core of this study is an extensive literature review that delves into academic journals, government reports, and existing literature on organized crime. This review is critical in offering a broad understanding of the roles and responsibilities of taxi and PHV drivers within this context, while also examining the legal frameworks and ethical considerations that underpin the industry.

A key component of our methodology is the analysis of the Operation Stovewood, as the foundational case study of this research. By closely examining this real-world example, the study gains insights into the practical application of theoretical concepts, understanding the dynamics of multi-agency collaboration, and the impact of community participation in combating complex criminal activities. This case study serves as a crucial source of information, providing a detailed look at the challenges faced, strategies employed, and the outcomes achieved in the fight against organized crime.

In framing the methodology for this research, it is essential to clarify the selection of Operation Stovewood as the central case study, especially in the context of numerous high-profile incidents of child sexual exploitation (CSE) that have surfaced across various cities in the UK. While acknowledging the significance of other major incidents in cities like Telford, Rochdale, Oxford, and Bristol, the choice of Operation Stovewood is a deliberate one, based on several factors that align closely with the aims of this chapter and the overall research.

Operation Stovewood (National Crime Agency, 2015; National Crime Agency, 2023), initiated in 2014 and spearheaded by the National Crime Agency, stands as the largest investigation into non-familial CSE in the UK, focusing on allegations of abuse in Rotherham between 1997 and 2013. This operation's extensive scope – both in terms of time span and the breadth of incidents examined – makes it an unparalleled case study for understanding the complexities and dynamics of organized CSE. This choice aligns with the research's aim to delve into the systemic, societal, and law enforcement responses to such exploitation.

Several key aspects justify the selection of Operation Stovewood for this study:

Scale and Impact: With around 200 officers involved, Operation Stovewood is unprecedented in scale, having recorded numerous crimes, arrests, and survivor identifications. Its comprehensive nature provides a broad spectrum of data and insights into the functioning of organized CSE rings.

Depth of Investigation: The operation's thorough and independent nature of investigation, stemming from Professor Alexis Jay's independent review, offers a detailed and unbiased exploration of the systemic management of CSE. This depth is crucial for an in-depth understanding of both the successes and failures in handling such exploitation.

Ongoing Nature: The continuing nature of Operation Stovewood's investigation, with the expectation to extend into 2027, offers a dynamic perspective into both historical and evolving patterns of CSE within organized crime. This allows for a real-time analysis of changing strategies, tactics of offenders, and evolving law enforcement responses.

Public and Media Attention: The extensive media coverage and public interest in Operation Stovewood underscore its societal relevance and impact. The operation has significantly contributed to raising public awareness and understanding of group-based CSE, thus informing the broader discourse surrounding these crimes.

Policy and Practice Implications: Insights from Operation Stovewood can inform broader policy-making and practices in child protection and law enforcement. The lessons learned from this operation are pivotal in shaping future strategies to combat similar crimes effectively.

In addition to these methods, the study also incorporates an in-depth policy and legal analysis. This involves scrutinizing the existing policies, laws, and regulations that govern taxi and PHV drivers, assessing their effectiveness in ensuring passenger safety and in equipping drivers to actively participate in crime prevention.

Although not employed as the primary methodlogy, the study integrates elements of autoethnographical methods from one of the authors, adding a personal and experiential dimension to the research. This inclusion enriches the analysis by offering an intimate perspective that complements the more objective data collected. It provides a unique lens through which the subject matter is viewed, adding depth and personal relevance to the findings (Cilliers & Viljoen, 2021).

Adhering to strict ethical guidelines throughout the study, especially considering the sensitive nature of the topics under discussion, is paramount (Bos, 2020; De Sousa & De Sousa, 2023).

By weaving together these diverse methodological strands, our study aims to offer a comprehensive and insightful exploration of the role of taxi and PHV drivers in the broader context of organized crime. The integration of literature review, case study analysis, policy examination, and autoethnographical insights creates a rich tapestry of understanding, aimed at providing evidence-based recommendations and enhancing the effectiveness of taxi and PHV drivers in this critical societal role.

THE IMPERATIVE FOR PUBLIC-PRIVATE COLLABORATION

The necessity of a concerted public-private collaboration in the realm of combating organised crime cannot be overstated. The intricate and adaptive nature of organised crime requires a unified approach, wherein public authorities and private entities synergize their efforts to tackle this formidable adversary (Bueger & Edmunds, 2020; Villani, 2020; Rizzuti, 2022; Davies, Malik, Jokinen & Haapasaari, 2023; Spapens, Abraham, van Dijk & Hofstra, 2021). In this discourse, we delve into the rationale behind the imperative for such collaboration, underscoring the indispensability of amalgamating the strengths of both sectors in this crucial endeavor.

Organised crime is a complex, multi-dimensional phenomenon that transcends national borders and legal jurisdictions (Danielsson, 2023). Criminal networks, characterized by their sophistication and adaptability, employ advanced technology, financial acumen, and intricate knowledge of legal systems to circumvent detection and prosecution. Addressing these multifarious challenges necessitates a diverse amalgamation of resources and skills (Danielsson, 2023).

The public sector, embodied by law enforcement agencies and other governmental bodies, holds the legal authority and investigative prowess essential for the pursuit of organised crime. These agencies are equipped with the requisite infrastructure and resources to conduct complex investigations, effectuate arrests, and bring criminal elements to justice (Goldstein, Sances & You, 2020; Seepma, de Blok & Van Donk, 2021; Sitompul & Hasibuan, 2021; Velasco, 2022).

Concurrently, the private sector contributes a unique repository of expertise and resources. Private entities often possess access to critical intelligence, financial records, and expansive business networks, all of which can be instrumental in identifying and dismantling illicit activities (Sage-Passant, 2023; Pimentel, 2022; Świątkowska, 2020; Ehe, 2020). Moreover, these entities are well-positioned to implement preventive measures within their respective industries and supply chains, thereby bolstering efforts to thwart organised crime (Fazely, 2020; Monk, 2021; Thommandru & Maratovich, 2024).

The combat against organised crime mandates the mobilisation of vast information and resources. Through collaborative efforts, public and private actors can pool their knowledge, data, and capabilities, thus forging a more comprehensive and effective response mechanism (Skidmore, 2022; Pournara, 2020; Bright & Whelan, 2020; Morgan, Brown, Voce & Cubitt, 2020; Pastor, Mignet, Mattes, Gurzawska, Nitsch & Wright, 2021).

Information sharing stands as a potent tool in this battle. Private actors can proffer insights into suspicious financial transactions, vulnerabilities in supply chains, or emerging criminal trends to law enforcement agencies. Conversely, public authorities can equip private entities with intelligence regarding known criminal networks and their activities (Maxwell & Artingstall, 2017; Olley, 2019; Comolli (Ed.), 2018; Akhgar & Yates (Eds.), 2011).

Resource allocation benefits significantly from such collaboration. Public-private partnerships enable the leveraging of funding, technology, and personnel from both sectors, facilitating a more efficacious approach to tackling organised crime. This collaborative model proves particularly beneficial in addressing potential resource shortfalls in either the public or private sector (Uhl, Kučera, Hayrapetyan, Gartner, Leuven & Stockreiter, 2020; Hardouin, 2009: den Boer, 2021).

Organised crime frequently operates across national frontiers, presenting an array of legal and jurisdictional challenges. Collaborative efforts are paramount in navigating these complexities. Public-private collaboration can enhance legal cooperation, ensuring the pursuit and apprehension of criminals irrespective of their geographic location (Zabyelina & Thachuk (Eds.), 2022; Cara, 2012; Finklea, 2011; Christensen, Rayment-McHugh, Prenzler, Chiu & Webster, 2021).

Cross-border investigations necessitate coordination among law enforcement agencies from various countries. Private entities can play a critical role by sharing information and aiding in such coordinated efforts (Danielsson, 2023).

Preventing organised crime is as vital as responding to it. Public-private collaboration can significantly enhance prevention and preparedness measures. Private industries are capable of establishing guidelines, best practices, and standards to mitigate the risk of criminal infiltration. This includes the implementation of robust compliance programs, thorough due diligence on business partners, and heightened employee awareness (Bunt & Schoot, 2003; Seivold, 2023; Zabyelina & Thachuk (Eds.), 2022; Doig & Sproat, 2020; Sauve, Woodley, Jones & Akhtari, 2023).

Collaboration can also lead to the development of early warning systems that detect and respond to emergent threats. By monitoring trends and sharing intelligence, public and private actors can maintain a proactive stance against criminal activities (Basheer & Alkhatib, 2021; Kayode-Ajala, 2023; Tyagi, 2021).

Overall, the imperative for public-private collaboration in combating organised crime is clearly evident. The complexity of the challenge, coupled with the necessity to mobilize information and resources and overcome legal and jurisdictional hurdles, underscores the need for a collaborative approach. By harnessing the strengths of both the public and private sectors, such efforts have the potential to forge a more resilient and effective response to organised crime, contributing significantly to safer and more secure communities (Bright & Whelan, 2020); Tagziria & de Lugo, 2023; Ishikawa & Kryvoi (Eds.), 2023).

This collaboration must also adhere to fundamental human rights principles and international obligations, ensuring that the response to organised crime is not only effective but also just and ethical (Watson, Sousa-Santos & Howes, 2021; Darcy, 2022; Guercke, 2021; Harré, 2022). The complexity of organised crime often intersects with severe human rights violations, with criminal enterprises engaging in activities that infringe upon the rights and dignity of individuals, especially the most vulnerable, such as victims of human trafficking and forced labor (Currie & Douglas, 2021; Kataria & Gautam, 2022; Jones, 2020; Degani & De Stefani, 2020; Rubio Grundell, 2022) .

Under the international human rights framework, states have obligations to protect individuals within their jurisdiction from human rights abuses. This includes safeguarding the right to life, liberty, and security of persons and preventing torture, slavery, and human trafficking (Karenga, 2022; Moeckli, Shah, Sivakumaran & Harris (Eds.), 2022; Pisillo Mazzeschi & Pisillo Mazzeschi, 2021; Karenga, 2022). The social contract theory, a cornerstone of political philosophy, further underscores the relationship between states and citizens (Sasan, 2021; Besley, 2020; Boucher & Kelly, 2003). In this context, citizens relinquish certain freedoms to the state in exchange for protection and the rule of law. The rule of law ensures that state power is exercised within defined legal boundaries and in accordance with human rights principles (Lautenbach, 2013; Beatty, 1994).

States bear the primary responsibility for upholding the social contract, ensuring the safety, security, and rights of their citizens. This extends to the prevention and prosecution of organised crime, particularly when it involves human rights abuses. States are required not only to refrain from violating rights but also to take proactive measures to protect individuals. When organised crime threatens human rights, states must enact and enforce laws, allocate resources, and collaborate with other actors to prevent and address these violations (Rothstein, 2021; Ratner, 2001; Abramson, 2003; Verdier & Stephan, 2021; Rabkin & Lerner, 2022).

Accountability mechanisms are crucial in safeguarding human rights and combating organised crime. State organs and bodies, including local authorities and other public entities, play critical roles in this regard. When human rights violations are preventable or should have been known to the state, it underscores the state's failure to uphold its obligations (Guercke, 2021; Campesi, 2020; Murphy, 2020; Heerdt, 2021). Such violations may result from inadequate law enforcement, insufficient victim support, or gaps in legal frameworks. Vulnerable individuals, such as victims of trafficking or exploitation, require heightened protection (Richie-Zavaleta, Baranik, Mersch, Ataiants & Rhodes, 2021; Green, 2021). States should prioritize the implementation of policies and practices that prevent their victimization and provide robust support services.

Public-private collaboration can extend to accountability measures. Independent oversight bodies, civil society organizations, and international entities can play roles in holding state organs accountable for human rights violations and abuse related to organised crime (Hughes, 2020; Missoni & Alesani, 2023; Murphy & De Vrieze, 2020; Arun, Ashraf, Jayasinghe & Soobaroyen, 2023).

In summary, public-private collaboration in combating organised crime should be framed within the context of states' positive human rights duties and obligations under international law. Upholding the social contract, the rule of law, and accountability mechanisms are essential to protect vulnerable populations from exploitation. Collaboration should emphasize not only the prevention and prosecution of organised crime but also the safeguarding of fundamental human rights, ultimately contributing to a more just and secure society.

The State's Ethical Obligations in Protecting Citizens from Organised Crime

The social contract theory and the role of the state in this context are central to understanding the ethical obligations towards citizens. This theory implies that the state has ethical obligations towards its citizens, including the duty to safeguard their security and rights (Weale, 2020; Seabright, Stieglitz & Van der Straeten, 2021; Rothstein, 2021). When organised crime threatens the well-being and rights of individuals, the state is ethically bound to take active measures to counteract this threat.

Positive human rights duties, as established in international human rights instruments, obligate states not only to refrain from infringing on rights but also to proactively protect and fulfill them (Donnelly & Whelan, 2020; Smith, 2022; Ramcharan, 2021). In the context of organised crime, these duties carry profound ethical imperatives. Vulnerable populations, including victims of human trafficking and exploitation, underscore the ethical importance of positive human rights duties (Simović & Šikman, 2020; Currie & Douglas, 2021; O'Neill, 2023). States have a moral obligation to prioritize the protection of those who are most susceptible to harm and abuse. The ethical challenge lies in balancing the state's duty to combat organised crime with its duty to respect the rights and dignity of all individuals, including suspects and perpetrators. Ethical governance demands that measures taken to combat crime do not result in disproportionate harm or violations of individual rights (Lazarus, 2012; Sorochinsky, 2009; Prescott & Levenson, 2010; Ozymy & Jarrell, 2020; Gallen & Mhuirthile (Eds.), 2021).

The rule of law is a foundational concept that ensures that state power is exercised within the confines of established legal frameworks and principles (Napolitano, 2020; Waldron, 2021; Pavel, 2021). It carries ethical implications related to the just and equitable treatment of individuals. Upholding the rule of law is an ethical imperative because it guarantees fairness, due process, and the protection of individual rights in the face of criminal accusations. It also prevents the arbitrary use of state power and safeguards against abuses in the name of security (Smokov, Horoshko, Korniienko & Medvedenko, 2022; Carrera, Mitsilegas & Stefan, 2021; Lillo Lobos, 2022).

Accountability mechanisms are essential ethical safeguards to ensure that state organs and public entities fulfill their responsibilities (Breuer & Leininger, 2021; Van Niekerk & Sebakamotse, 2020; Janenova & Knox, 2020; Elhaw & Rabee, 2024; Schönsteiner, 2022). When human rights violations occur in the context of organised crime, accountability mechanisms serve as ethical checks and balances, holding those responsible accountable for their actions or inactions (Neyroud, 2022; Prenzler, 2021; Oriolo, 2023).

It follows that the imperative for public-private collaboration in combating organised crime is deeply rooted in philosophical and ethical considerations. The social contract theory underscores the state's ethical obligation to protect its citizens, while positive human rights duties emphasize the moral imperative of safeguarding vulnerable populations. The rule of law and accountability mechanisms serve as ethical safeguards to ensure that state actions align with principles of justice and respect for human rights. By embracing these philosophical and conceptual foundations, public and private actors can work collaboratively with a shared ethical commitment to combating organised crime while upholding human rights and the principles of justice.

Central to our discussion is the role of community actors, with a specific focus on taxi and PHV drivers. Beyond their primary function as transportation providers, taxi and PHV drivers are uniquely positioned to become valuable allies in the fight against organised crime. Their frequent interactions with diverse members of society grant them insights into local communities that can aid in identifying and preventing criminal activities.

As we look deeper into the issue, we will explore how these community actors, particularly minicab drivers, can be trained and empowered to actively participate in crime prevention. By harnessing their knowledge and skills, we aim to enhance their ability to serve as vigilant guardians of community safety.

CASE STUDY: AN EXAMINATION OF OPERATION STOVEWOOD

Operation Stovewood stands as an instructive case study in the field of law enforcement, particularly in addressing the complexities of child sexual exploitation (CSE). Initiated by the National Crime Agency (NCA) in response to the grave CSE crisis in Rotherham, as delineated in the Jay Report, this operation was characterized by its expansive scope, encompassing non-familial CSE incidents in Rotherham between 1997 and 2013 (Jay, 2014). The operation's methodical approach, challenges encountered, and the collaborative framework employed offer valuable insights into the dynamics of multidisciplinary investigations and the crucial role of community-based intelligence in combatting CSE.

The foundation of Operation Stovewood was its multi-agency approach. This collaborative framework brought together diverse entities such as the South Yorkshire Police, Rotherham Metropolitan Borough Council, health agencies, and child protection services. The melding of these agencies was vital to address the multifaceted nature of CSE, necessitating not only law enforcement's involvement but also the engagement of social services, healthcare providers, and community support mechanisms (Hamer, 2022; Avalos, 2020; Maslen & Paine, 2019; Peach, Allen, Brown, Sanghera, Sharif, Lees & Senior, 2015; Slope, 2022).

Strategic coordination was pivotal to the operation's success. Orchestrated by the NCA, the operation aimed to ensure a cohesive approach among the involved agencies, avoiding duplication of efforts against offenders and facilitating a synergistic working relationship. This coordination was key in streamlining the investigation, optimizing resource allocation, and reducing victim fatigue, a potential consequence of repetitive interviews or inquiries by different entities (National Crime Agency, 2015; Hamer, 2022).

A central aspect of this collaborative investigation was the effective sharing of information. Operation Stovewood underlined the need for a framework enabling the timely and secure exchange of data and intelligence among involved stakeholders. This was instrumental in identifying patterns of abuse, linking disparate cases, and comprehending the broader exploitation network (Alison, Alison, Shortland & Surmon-Bohr, 2020; Williams, 2023).

Community engagement in intelligence gathering was underscored as a significant element of the operation. The willingness of the community to come forward with information was essential for the success of the operation. Building trust with the community, particularly among minority groups where cultural or social barriers might impede reporting, was a focused endeavor of the operation (National Crime Agency, 2015; Hamer, 2022).

The operation adopted a victim-centric approach, enhancing the effectiveness of community-based intelligence. By ensuring that the welfare of victims was prioritized and that appropriate support was provided, the operation gained crucial insights from victims' testimonies, essential for understanding the nature and extent of the exploitation.

Proactive outreach initiatives were identified as crucial in gathering community-based intelligence. Operation Stovewood demonstrated the importance of awareness campaigns and educational programs to inform the public about the indicators of CSE and to encourage reporting. Building confidence in the investigation process among victims, partners, and the public involved regular updates on the progress of the investigation, maintaining transparency in operations, and reassurance that all reports and information would be taken seriously and acted upon (Rotherham Metropolitan Borough Council, 2018).

A noteworthy aspect of Operation Stovewood was the identification of taxi and PHV drivers as one of the groups involved in the exploitation network. This involvement was part of a broader pattern of exploitation uncovered by the operation, which highlighted the systemic nature of the abuse and the various means by which perpetrators were able to access and exploit vulnerable children and young people (Home Office, 2020).

The involvement of taxi and PHV drivers in facilitating exploitation, such as providing access and transportation to vulnerable children and teenagers, became a focal point of investigation and response. In some instances, taxi and PHV drivers developed a trust relationship with their young passengers, which was then exploited either by the drivers themselves becoming direct perpetrators of abuse or aiding others in the exploitation network. Regulatory measures, including enhanced background checks and specific training on child protection, were implemented in response to the findings of the investigation (Home Office 2020; Task and Finish Group on Taxi and Private Hire Vehicle Licensing, 2018).

As such, Operation Stovewood provides pivotal insights into the dynamics of collaborative investigations and community-based intelligence in addressing CSE. The multi-agency approach, strategic coordination, effective information sharing, community engagement, and the focus on a victim-centric approach are critical elements that contributed to the operation's effectiveness. These insights not only aided the current investigation but also set a precedent for future operations dealing with complex and sensitive issues.

Government Actions since the revelations of Operation Stovewood

The findings and revelations from operation Stovewood highlighted an urgent need for reform. In the following, some of the steps that followed are discussed, in particular in light of the need to address necessary improvements to the regulation of Taxi's and PHV. The key emphasis in this section is placed on the Task and Finish Group's recommendations on taxi and PHV licensing.

The Statutory Taxi and Private Hire Vehicle Standards underwent significant updates in 2017 and 2022, primarily in response to concerns about the safety of passengers, particularly children and vulnerable adults, and the involvement of taxi and private hire vehicle (PHV) services in crimes. These updates reflect the high-risk nature of the industry, with reports of sexual assaults and abuse by drivers being alarming (Department for Transport, 2022).

Under the Policing and Crime Act 2017, the Secretary of State for Transport was granted the authority to issue statutory guidance to protect passengers, specifically children and vulnerable individuals, during taxi and PHV services. This guidance covers those under 18 and aligns with the Care Act 2014's definition of "vulnerable individual." While the focus is on safeguarding specific groups, these standards benefit all passengers, and the Department for Transport (DfT) expects uniform implementation unless compelling local reasons exist (Department for Transport, 2022; Task and Finish Group on Taxi and Private Hire Vehicle Licensing, 2018).

Despite devolution, the statutory taxi and private hire vehicle standards continue to apply in Wales. Licensing authorities have a statutory duty to prioritize safeguarding and promoting children's welfare, including implementing whistleblowing procedures, safe recruitment practices, and clear policies for addressing allegations against individuals working with children (Department for Transport, 2022).

These updates reflect substantial industry changes and lessons learned since 2010, offering comprehensive guidance on assessing the suitability of individuals and operators for licensing, safeguarding children and vulnerable adults, complying with the Immigration Act 2016, and Common Law Police Disclosure. In conclusion, these regulatory updates demonstrate the UK government's commitment to enhancing passenger safety and preventing abuse and exploitation in the taxi and PHV industry, providing a robust framework for effective regulation by local authorities and licensing bodies (Department for Transport, 2022; Task and Finish Group on Taxi and Private Hire Vehicle Licensing, 2018).

The taxi and private hire vehicle (PHV) industry in England, while offering essential transportation services, has faced growing concerns about safety and regulation. In response to these pressing issues, the Task and Finish Group, assembled under the leadership of the then Minister of State for Transport, the Rt Hon John Hayes CBE MP, embarked on a comprehensive investigation. This group, convened in 2017, aimed to address these concerns and make recommendations to protect passengers, particularly vulnerable individuals, and rebuild trust in the industry (Task and Finish Group on Taxi and Private Hire Vehicle Licensing, 2018).

The Crucial Priority: Safety

Throughout its investigations, the Task and Finish Group had placed a resounding emphasis on the critical importance of safety in the taxi and Private Hire Vehicle (PHV) industry. This focus arose from an understanding that passenger trust was rooted in the assurance of safety and security, as much as convenience, in their chosen mode of transportation. The enclosed environment of taxis and PHVs brought to the fore the vulnerabilities faced by both passengers and drivers, necessitating a thorough examination of safety measures (Task and Finish Group on Taxi and Private Hire Vehicle Licensing, 2018).

A particularly alarming aspect uncovered during the group's investigations was the occurrence of child sexual exploitation and other forms of abuse by a minority of licensed taxi and PHV drivers. These reprehensible acts highlighted the urgent need to implement robust preventive measures to protect vulnerable passengers, especially children. While it was acknowledged that the majority of drivers abided by the law, the actions of a few had the potential to significantly erode public confidence and tarnish the industry's reputation. The disturbing insights from the Casey and Jay reports served as a sobering reminder of the consequences of inaction, stressing the imperative to act swiftly in instituting reforms to prevent further victimization (Task and Finish Group on Taxi and Private Hire Vehicle Licensing, 2018; Rotherham Metropolitan Borough Council. 2018; Home Office, 2020).

In response to these pressing concerns, the Task and Finish Group proposed a set of comprehensive recommendations aimed at overhauling the safety standards in the taxi and PHV sector. Foremost among these was the establishment of national safety standards, to be implemented as Statutory Guidance for local licensing authorities. This move aimed to create a uniform and rigorous framework across the industry, ensuring thorough checks and balances to protect passengers (Task and Finish Group on Taxi and Private Hire Vehicle Licensing, 2018; Parliamentlive.tv, 2019).

To further bolster passenger safety and maintain accountability, the group advocated for the mandatory installation of CCTV, both visual and audio, in all licensed vehicles. This measure was to be complemented by strict adherence to data protection protocols. Recognizing the potential financial strain this could place on small businesses, the group encouraged government and local authorities to find ways to mitigate these costs (Task and Finish Group on Taxi and Private Hire Vehicle Licensing, 2018; Rotherham Metropolitan Borough Council, 2018; Home Office, 2020).

Advancements in technology had opened up new avenues for enhancing safety, leading the group to propose the integration of GPS tracking in the minimum standards for CCTV systems in taxis and PHVs. This addition was expected to significantly boost public safety measures (Task and Finish Group on Taxi and Private Hire Vehicle Licensing, 2018; Home Office, 2020).

Another key recommendation involved the clear identification of licensed vehicles to avoid public confusion and distinguish them from unlicensed counterparts. This measure was intended to enhance the visibility and recognition of licensed taxis and PHVs (Task and Finish Group on Taxi and Private Hire Vehicle Licensing, 2018; Home Office, 2020).

The group underscored the importance of comprehensive background checks for drivers, including enhanced Disclosure and Barring Service (DBS) checks. Regular updates and record-keeping through the DBS update service were crucial to maintain current and accurate information (Task and Finish Group on Taxi and Private Hire Vehicle Licensing, 2018; Home Office, 2020).

In line with improving accountability and information sharing, the group suggested the creation of a register for drivers who had had their licenses refused or revoked. They also proposed establishing a national database encompassing all licensed taxi and PHV drivers, vehicles, and operators (Task and Finish Group on Taxi and Private Hire Vehicle Licensing, 2018; Home Office, 2020).

Finally, the group recognized the critical role of driver training and engagement in identifying and reporting signs of abuse and exploitation, particularly in cases of child sexual abuse. Equipping drivers with the necessary skills and knowledge was deemed essential for enhancing the overall safety of passengers (Task and Finish Group on Taxi and Private Hire Vehicle Licensing, 2018; Home Office, 2020).

Through these recommendations, the Task and Finish Group aimed to bring about a transformative change in the taxi and PHV industry, ensuring a safer and more secure environment for both passengers and drivers.

The recommendations presented by the Task and Finish Group represent a comprehensive, proactive approach to combating abuse and exploitation within the taxi and PHV industry. These measures prioritize passenger safety, promote transparency and accountability, and aim to restore public trust in the sector. As these recommendations are implemented and enforced, the industry can move towards a future where passengers can have confidence in the safety and integrity of their chosen mode of transportation.

The evidence session with the Chair of the Task and Finish Group on Taxi and Private Hire Vehicle Licensing (TFG) in the UK Parliament was a critical examination of the challenges facing the taxi and private hire industry. The central focus of this one-off session was to explore ways to prevent abuse, exploitation, and enhance the security and wellbeing of the public utilizing these services. The evidence provided during the session underscored the urgent need for comprehensive reforms to ensure public safety and restore trust in the industry (Parliamentlive.tv, 2019).

The session began with a stark assertion by Professor Abdel-Haq, the Chair of TFG, who emphasized the immediate risk to public safety posed by the current state of the industry. He noted that when individuals enter a taxi or private hire vehicle, they do so with the expectation of safety, and this expectation is not currently being met. The evidence presented pointed to a pressing need for prompt action to address the shortcomings in the sector (Parliamentlive.tv, 2019).

One of the key issues discussed was the abuse and exploitation of passengers, particularly vulnerable individuals. Professor Abdel-Haq highlighted cases of sexual abuse and exploitation within the industry and called for urgent measures to prevent such incidents. The evidence strongly indicated that without legislative reforms and increased oversight, passengers would continue to be at risk (Parliamentlive.tv, 2019).

Enhancing the security and wellbeing of the public was a major focus of the evidence session. One of the key proposals discussed was the introduction of CCTV cameras in taxis and PHVs. Professor Abdel-Haq argued that these vehicles should be considered public spaces rather than private ones, given their role in providing transportation services to the public. The introduction of CCTV cameras was seen as a vital step in deterring criminal behavior, protecting both passengers and drivers, and improving overall public safety (Parliamentlive.tv, 2019).

Another critical aspect of enhancing security and wellbeing was the issue of cross-border hiring. The evidence session raised concerns about drivers obtaining licenses in one area and working in another, potentially bypassing safety regulations. The need for coordination between local authorities and standardized enforcement mechanisms to ensure compliance with safety standards was emphasized as a means to address this challenge effectively (Parliamentlive.tv, 2019).

Furthermore, the evidence session highlighted the importance of robust training for drivers, especially concerning issues such as safeguarding passengers and assisting individuals with disabilities. The proposal that training in specific areas should be part of minimum standards for licensing was widely supported as a way to ensure that drivers are well-equipped to provide safe and inclusive services (Parliamentlive.tv, 2019).

While the evidence session shed light on the urgent need for reform in the taxi and PHV industry to enhance public safety and prevent abuse, there was disappointment regarding the government's response. The government's use of terms such as "best endeavours" and "when time allows" raised concerns about the lack of urgency in addressing these critical issues. Professor Abdel-Haq stressed the importance of clear timeframes and decisive action to prevent further abuse.

THE ROLE OF TAXI AND PRIVATE HIRE VEHICLE DRIVERS IN COMBATING ORGANIZED CRIME

This analytical discourse delves into the nuanced and multifaceted role of taxi and PHV drivers in the context of organized crime, particularly in combating modern slavery and sexual exploitation, as highlighted by cases like Operation Stovewood. It critically evaluates the strategic position of taxi and PHV drivers within community fabrics, their legal and moral obligations, and the intricate ethical dilemmas they encounter in the battle against organized criminal activities.

Taxi and Private Hire Vehicle Drivers as Local Surveillance Agents, Strategic Positioning and Observational Advantage

The role of taxi and Private Hire Vehicle (PHV) drivers in the domain of organized crime prevention, especially in the contexts of modern slavery and sexual exploitation, demands a thorough and nuanced examination. This critical analysis delves into the multifaceted aspects of taxi and PHV drivers' roles as local sentinels, exploring the depths of their potential contributions, challenges they face, and the broader implications of their involvement in combating these heinous crimes.

Taxi and PHV drivers, due to the nature of their profession, are strategically positioned within the urban tapestry, moving across various sociocultural and economic segments of the city. This unique positioning provides them with a distinct observational advantage. They have access to both the public and private spheres of urban life, witnessing a range of interactions and behaviors that remain unseen to most (Eisapareh, Nazari, Kaveh, Cousins & Mokarami, 2023; Home Office 2020).

Their vantage point is not merely physical but also social. Taxi and PHV drivers engage with a cross-section of society, from the marginalized to the affluent, gaining insights into diverse human behaviors and social dynamics. This unique social interface positions them to notice anomalies in passenger behavior or interactions that could hint at underlying criminal activities (Eisapareh, Nazari, Kaveh, Cousins & Mokarami, 2023; Mweene, 2022; Xing, 2022; Home Office, 2020).

The indicators of organized crime, particularly human trafficking and sexual exploitation, are often subtle and easily overlooked. Taxi and PHV drivers, through their routine interactions, may observe signs such as passengers showing signs of fear or distress, individuals who appear to be controlled or directed by another, or unusual patterns of travel, such as frequent trips to known areas of illicit activity. The ability to recognize these signs is crucial and can be enhanced through specific training programs focusing on identifying and understanding the nuances of such criminal activities (Home Office 2020; Campos & Sánchez, 2021).

Despite their strategic position, taxi and PHV drivers face significant challenges in effectively contributing to crime prevention. The transient nature of their interactions with passengers often limits their ability to make detailed observations. Furthermore, the need to balance attentiveness to potential criminal indicators with respect for passenger privacy and norms of professional conduct presents a complex ethical challenge.

There is also the challenge of the urban environment itself – a space where anonymity and transience can mask illicit activities. The ever-changing urban landscape, with its flux of people and activities, can make it difficult for taxi and PHV drivers to discern patterns or behaviors indicative of organized crime (Gambetta & Hamill, 2005; Broad & Gadd, 2022; Cooper, Aarhaug & Scott, 2023; Burton, McGregor & Laycock, 2020; Home Office 2020).

For taxi and PHV drivers to effectively function as local sentinels, comprehensive training is imperative. Such training should encompass not only the identification of potential indicators of trafficking and exploitation but also effective communication with law enforcement, understanding of legal obligations, and methods for reporting suspicious activities without compromising personal safety or passenger trust (Task and Finish Group on Taxi and Private Hire Vehicle Licensing, 2018).

Capacity building in this context also involves creating awareness among taxi and PHV drivers about the broader societal impact of organized crime and their potential role in mitigating these activities. Empowering them with knowledge and skills goes beyond the practical aspects of crime reporting to fostering a sense of civic responsibility and community engagement (Task and Finish Group on Taxi and Private Hire Vehicle Licensing, 2018, Home Office, 2020; Local Government Association, 2015; Home Office, 2016; Hertfordhire Modern Slavery Partnership, 2022).

The legal structure governing taxi and PHV drivers is pivotal in leveraging their role in combating organized crime. Most jurisdictions enforce background checks and licensing for taxi and PHV drivers, which is a preliminary filter ensuring a level of professionalism and trustworthiness. These legal structures often encompass directives specific to organized crime. For instance, taxi and PHV drivers may be legally bound to report unlawful activities they observe, with a particular emphasis on signs of human trafficking or exploitation. Some regions have taken proactive measures by mandating specialized training for taxi and PHV drivers, empowering them with the skills to identify and respond effectively to trafficking indicators (Hertfordhire Modern Slavery Partnership, 2022; Hampshire Safeguarding Children Partnership, 2020; Oxfordshire Safeguarding Adults Board, 2023; Dartford Borough Council, 2020).

Furthermore, the legal duties of taxi and PHV drivers extend to cooperation with law enforcement, often providing crucial insights or evidence for criminal cases. However, it is essential that legal protections are in place to shield taxi and PHV drivers from possible retaliations, such as threats or harm from criminal networks.

Ethical Dilemmas and the Path to Resolving Them

In the realm of countering organized crime, the role of taxi and PHV drivers transcends the mere provision of transport services, embedding them deeply within the ethical fabric of community welfare and justice. This position, while pivotal, is replete with intricate ethical complexities that necessitate careful navigation and strategic resolution.

Taxi and PHV drivers, in their capacity as frontline observers, are often privy to situations that may indicate the presence of victims of crimes such as human trafficking or sexual exploitation. Herein lies an ethical responsibility to remain vigilant and proactive, a duty that extends beyond the confines of legal obligations. However, the path to fulfilling this responsibility is strewn with challenges. The primary dilemma faced by taxi and PHV drivers is the delicate balance between respecting passenger privacy and protecting potential victims. This task demands discernment, as the line between intrusive probing into personal affairs and remaining alert to signs of criminal activity is often blurred and fraught with the risk of misinterpretation.

Compounding this dilemma is the possibility of misjudgment, where limited information can lead to unfounded accusations with serious implications. The ethical breach and legal repercussions of such scenarios place an additional burden on the decision-making process of taxi and PHV drivers. Furthermore, the act of engaging with or reporting individuals linked to organized crime introduces a significant personal risk, encompassing threats to their physical safety.

To effectively address these ethical challenges, a structured decision-making framework is indispensable. Such a framework encompasses several key elements. Firstly, it includes comprehensive guidelines that aid taxi and PHV drivers in identifying legitimate signs of criminal activities, relying on objective criteria rather than personal biases or stereotypes. Alongside this, established protocols for reporting suspicious activities are crucial. These protocols should ensure that drivers can make reports in a manner that is both safe and responsible (College of Policing, 2023; UNODC, 2020; Institute of Licencing, 2018; Licensing Committee, 2019).

Moreover, the framework should prioritize regular training sessions, not only focusing on the recognition of crime indicators but also emphasizing ethical judgment, respect for passenger rights, and the avoidance of profiling. This training should be accompanied by accessible support services, including counseling and legal advice, to assist taxi and PHV drivers in managing the emotional and ethical weight of their role (Home Office, 2020; Task and Finish Group on Taxi and Private Hire Vehicle Licensing, 2018).

Lastly, and perhaps most critically, the framework must provide legal and institutional support for taxi and PHV drivers who, in good faith, report crimes. This support is crucial in safeguarding them from the legal consequences of unintentional false accusations and in ensuring their protection from potential retaliatory actions. The establishment of strong whistleblower protections is crucial in fostering a culture of reporting and accountability. Taxi and PHV drivers, as frontline observers of city life, often witness activities that may be linked to organized crime. However, the fear of repercussions - both from criminal elements and legal complexities - can deter them from reporting these observations (Home Office, 2020; Task and Finish Group on Taxi and Private Hire Vehicle Licensing, 2018).

Effective whistleblower protection mechanisms must provide anonymity, legal safeguards, and assurances against retaliation. These protections would encourage taxi and PHV drivers to report suspicious activities without fear of personal or professional harm. It is also vital to create awareness among drivers about these protections and the importance of their role in crime prevention (South Cambridgeshire District Council, 2022; Department for Transport, 2019).

In essence, the role of taxi and PHV drivers in the fight against organized crime demands an approach that intertwines clear guidelines, ethical training, robust support systems, and legal protections. By equipping taxi and PHV drivers with the necessary tools for informed and ethically sound decision-making, and by ensuring they are supported in this challenging role, their contribution to community safety and justice can be significantly enhanced, upholding the highest standards of ethical practice.

Vicarious Accountability and the Reciprocal Liability of Local Authorities

The intricate concept of vicarious accountability, particularly in the context of taxi drivers' involvement in countering organized crime, introduces a nuanced layer of complexity that demands a comprehensive and critical exploration. In this realm, taxi drivers often function as de facto agents of local authorities, their interactions with the public placing them in a unique position where their actions or inactions, especially in matters of public safety and crime, can inadvertently cast a reflection on the authorities themselves (Dumba, 2017; Andreangeli, 2020; Barrett, 2010; Department for Transport, 2022). This perception imbues local authorities with a profound sense of vicarious responsibility, compelling them to ensure that taxi drivers are not only adequately trained and informed but also sufficiently equipped and protected to contribute effectively to crime prevention.

This burden of vicarious responsibility extends beyond mere training and encompasses a broader duty of care that local authorities owe to both the public and the taxi drivers (Deakin, 2018; Strauss, 1980; Sharma, 2023; Strugała, 2021; Amaxopoulou, Durovic & Lech, 2021). This duty involves more than implementing comprehensive training programs; it includes equipping taxi drivers with essential tools and resources such as emergency communication systems and access to law enforcement support, enhancing their capacity to act as community sentinels.

The legal framework governing the vicarious liability of local authorities in relation to the actions of taxi drivers is often complex and necessitates clarity. Local authorities potentially bear liability for actions taken by taxi drivers, especially when such actions arise directly from their professional responsibilities. This legal standpoint underscores the need for clear guidelines and policies that outline the expected extent of actions and responsibilities of taxi drivers in their role against organized crime.

Addressing this reciprocal dynamic between taxi drivers and local authorities requires the establishment of robust collaborative frameworks. Such partnerships should aim to forge a cohesive approach encompassing training, resource allocation, and adherence to legal standards. Collaboration can also extend to intelligence sharing, aiding taxi drivers in more effectively identifying and reporting criminal activities.

A critical aspect of this relationship is balancing the autonomy of taxi drivers with appropriate oversight by local authorities. While it is essential for drivers to maintain independence in their operations, there must be mechanisms in place to ensure that their actions align with broader public safety objectives and legal standards. This balance is delicate and requires ongoing dialogue and adaptation to the ever-changing urban and criminal landscapes.

Ensuring that taxi drivers are protected and supported in their role is an essential component of vicarious accountability. Protection includes safeguarding them against potential retaliation from criminal elements and providing legal and psychological support if they face consequences as a result of their reporting activities. These support systems are crucial not only for the well-being of the drivers but also for maintaining their trust and willingness to engage in crime prevention initiatives.

In conclusion, the concept of vicarious accountability and reciprocal liability in the context of taxi drivers and local authorities is a complex issue that demands a multifaceted approach (Eisenberg, 1987; Overall, 2016; Bailey-Harris & Harris, 2002). It necessitates comprehensive strategies that encompass training, legal clarity, collaborative frameworks, balanced oversight, and robust support systems. Effectively addressing these aspects is vital to leverage the unique position of taxi drivers in combating organized crime, while ensuring their safety and aligning their efforts with the broader goals of public safety.

Advancing Taxi and Private Hire Vehicle Drivers' Roles through Technological Integration and Accountability

The integration of technology such as Closed-Circuit Television (CCTV) in taxis and PHVs represents a significant advancement in evidence collection and driver safety. CCTV systems serve multiple functions: they act as a deterrent to potential criminal activities within the taxi or PHV, provide crucial evidence in the event of a crime, and enhance the overall safety of both drivers and passengers. The visual and audio recordings can be pivotal in investigations, offering irrefutable evidence of interactions and transactions that occur within the vehicle.

However, the implementation of such technology must be critically analyzed. Privacy concerns are paramount, as constant surveillance raises questions about the right to privacy for both drivers and passengers. There is a need for a balanced approach that respects individual privacy while ensuring public safety. Clear guidelines and regulations on the usage, storage, and access to this footage are essential to address these concerns.

Moreover, the effectiveness of CCTV in taxis and PHVs extends beyond mere surveillance. It can act as a psychological barrier to crime, where the presence of a camera may deter potential offenders, including those who might exploit or coerce passengers into criminal activities. It also offers a sense of security to drivers, who often work alone and are vulnerable to assault or other criminal acts (Home Office, 2020; Task and Finish Group on Taxi and Private Hire Vehicle Licensing, 2018).

CONCLUSION: A CASE FOR EMPOWERING COMMUNITY ACTORS: TRAINING TAXI AND PRIVATE HIRE VEHICLE DRIVERS AS ALLIES IN COMBATING ORGANIZED CRIME

Organized crime, with its multifaceted and pervasive influence, poses a significant threat to societal stability and individual well-being. Its far-reaching impact necessitates a collaborative approach involving both public and private sectors, including community actors like taxi and PHV drivers. This comprehensive analysis has illuminated the diverse socio-economic impacts of organized crime and the critical role of public-private collaboration in combating it, particularly in the context of child sexual exploitation (CSE) and modern slavery.

The profound socio-economic toll of organized crime on communities is characterized by violence, corruption, economic distortion, and social disintegration. It calls for an urgent and collective response that transcends traditional law enforcement methods. The strategic positioning of taxi and PHV drivers as local surveillance agents presents a unique opportunity in this fight. Their everyday interactions and mobility across various societal segments provide them with an observational advantage crucial in identifying potential criminal activities, including those related to human trafficking and sexual exploitation.

However, leveraging the role of taxi and PHV drivers in crime prevention is not without challenges. It requires a nuanced approach that balances ethical considerations, respect for passenger privacy, and the need for vigilance against criminal activities. Comprehensive training, legal structures, and ethical guidelines are essential to empower taxi and PHV drivers to act responsibly and effectively in this capacity. The introduction of technology, such as CCTV in taxis and PHVs, further enhances their ability to contribute to public safety, though it raises important questions about privacy and data protection.

The collaborative framework employed in operations like Stovewood, which addressed CSE in Rotherham, underscores the importance of multi-agency cooperation in tackling organized crime. Such collaborations enhance information sharing, resource allocation, and provide a cohesive approach to complex investigations. They also highlight the necessity of involving community actors in intelligence gathering and crime prevention strategies.

The Task and Finish Group's recommendations on taxi and PHV licensing reflect a significant step toward improving passenger safety and rebuilding trust in the industry. These recommendations include national safety standards, mandatory installation of CCTV, enhanced background checks, and comprehensive training for drivers. Implementing these measures will be pivotal in preventing abuse and exploitation within the industry.

Moreover, the concept of vicarious accountability places an ethical and legal responsibility on local authorities to ensure that taxi and PHV drivers are adequately trained, equipped, and supported in their role as community guardians against organized crime. This reciprocal liability underscores the need for local authorities to collaborate closely with taxi and PHV drivers, providing them with the necessary tools and resources to fulfill their role effectively and safely.

In the final concluding remarks of this study, it is crucial to emphasize the specific role that PHV drivers played in the Rotherham Child Sex Abuse Scandal, as extensively investigated by Operation Stovewood, and in other similar cases across England over the past two decades. The findings indicate that, in these instances, PHV drivers were predominantly involved either as perpetrators or as facilitators of the abuse and exploitation. This involvement ranged from direct participation in criminal activities to providing logistical support that enabled the perpetration of these heinous acts.

However, this chapter has posited a critical argument from both legal and pragmatic perspectives, suggesting that the very circumstances which allowed taxi drivers to be effectively involved in such exploitation can be transformed into a key instrument for effective prevention in the future. It highlights an important dichotomy: while a minority of drivers were implicated in these crimes, the majority are decent, law-abiding citizens who play a crucial role in their communities.

This study advocates for the potential of taxi and PHV drivers as a vital, yet underutilized, resource in the fight against organized crime, particularly child sexual exploitation. Taxi and PHV drivers' extensive access to and interaction with local communities position them uniquely to observe and report suspicious activities. However, leveraging this potential requires a two-pronged approach: comprehensive training and robust support mechanisms.

Training programs designed specifically for taxi and PHV drivers should focus not only on identifying signs of exploitation and abuse but also on legal responsibilities and ethical considerations in reporting such incidents. This training must be accompanied by support mechanisms that protect the drivers from potential repercussions of reporting and encourage them to come forward without fear of retaliation or legal consequences.

Moreover, this approach calls for a collaborative effort between law enforcement, local authorities, and the taxi and PHV industry. By fostering a culture of awareness and vigilance, and by equipping taxi and PHV drivers with the necessary tools and knowledge, these stakeholders can transform taxi and PHV drivers into proactive agents in the detection and prevention of organized crime.

As such, while the involvement of taxi and PHV drivers in the Rotherham scandal and similar cases across England has shed light on a grim reality, it also uncovers an opportunity for positive change. By capitalizing on the extensive community reach and the day-to-day interactions of taxi and PHV drivers, and by empowering them through training and support, there is a significant opportunity to enhance community safety and combat organized crime more effectively. The majority of law-abiding taxi and PHV drivers can be transformed into a formidable frontline defense against child sexual exploitation, exemplifying how a profession, once entangled in a narrative of crime, can pivot towards becoming a critical ally in safeguarding society.

Overall, this chapter has argued that an integration of taxi and PHV drivers as allies in combating organized crime represents a significant advancement in community-based crime prevention strategies. By harnessing their strategic position, observational skills, and local knowledge, taxi and PHV drivers can play a crucial role in identifying and reporting criminal activities. However, this integration must be supported by comprehensive training, ethical guidelines, legal protections, and technological advancements to ensure effectiveness, respect for privacy, and the safety of both drivers and passengers. As this approach gains traction, it holds the potential to contribute significantly to safer and more secure communities, demonstrating the power of collaborative efforts in the ongoing battle against organized crime.

REFERENCES

Abramson, K. (2003). Beyond consent, toward safeguarding human rights: Implementing the United Nations Trafficking Protocol. *Harv. Int'l LJ*, *44*, 473.

Akhgar, B., & Yates, S. (Eds.). (2011). *Intelligence Management: Knowledge Driven Frameworks for Combating Terrorism and Organized Crime*. Springer Science & Business Media.

Alison, L. J., Alison, E., Shortland, N., & Surmon-Bohr, F. (2020). *ORBIT: The science of rapport-based interviewing for law enforcement, security, and military*. Oxford University Press.

Amaxopoulou, M., Durovic, M., & Lech, F. (2021). Regulation of Uber in the UK. Global Perspectives on Legal Challenges Posed by Ridesharing Companies: A Case Study of Uber, 101-135.

Andreangeli, A. (2020). Taxi services, platforms and Article 101 TFEU: Changing the shape of the transport intermediation services industry? *Mkt. & Competition L. Rev.*, *4*, 41.

Aronowitz, A. A., & Veldhuizen, M. E. (2021). The human trafficking–organized crime nexus. In *Routledge handbook of transnational organized crime* (pp. 232–252). Routledge.

Arun, T., Ashraf, J., Jayasinghe, K., & Soobaroyen, T. (2023). Accounting, accountability and governance in emerging economies: a development perspective. In Handbook of Accounting, Accountability and Governance (pp. 215-236). Edward Elgar Publishing.

Avalos, L. (2020). Reversing the Decriminalization of Sexual Violence. *Nev. LJ*, *21*, 1.

Bailey-Harris, R., & Harris, M. (2002). Local authorities and child protection-the mosaic of accountability. *Child and Family Law Quarterly*, *14*, 117.

Baradel, M. (2020). *The puzzle of yakuza's longevity: The endurance of the yakuza and its implications for theories of organised criminality* (Doctoral dissertation, Birkbeck, University of London).

Barrett, S. D. (2010). The sustained impacts of taxi deregulation. *Economic Affairs*, *30*(1), 61–65.

Basheer, R., & Alkhatib, B. (2021). Threats from the dark: A review over dark web investigation research for cyber threat intelligence. *Journal of Computer Networks and Communications*, *2021*, 1–21.

Beatty, D. (1994). Human rights and the rules of law. In *Human Rights and Judicial Review: A Comparative Perspective* (pp. 1–56). Brill Nijhoff.

Berry, M. (2020). *Organised crime in Red City: An ethnographic study of drugs, vice and violence* (Doctoral dissertation, Cardiff University).

Besley, T. (2020). State capacity, reciprocity, and the social contract. *Econometrica*, *88*(4), 1307–1335.

Bos, J. (2020). *Research ethics for students in the social sciences*. Springer Nature.

Bouchard, M. (2020). Collaboration and boundaries in organized crime: A network perspective. *Crime and Justice*, *49*(1), 425–469.

Boucher, D., & Kelly, P. (2003). *The social contract from Hobbes to Rawls*. Routledge.

Braithwaite, J. (2022). *Macrocriminology and freedom*. ANU Press.

Breuer, A., & Leininger, J. (2021). Horizontal accountability for SDG implementation: A comparative cross-national analysis of emerging national accountability regimes. *Sustainability*, *13*(13), 7002.

Bright, D., & Whelan, C. (2020). *Organised crime and law enforcement: A network perspective*. Routledge.

Broad, R., & Gadd, D. (2022). *Demystifying modern slavery*. Taylor & Francis.

Bueger, C., & Edmunds, T. (2020). Blue crime: Conceptualising transnational organised crime at sea. *Marine Policy*, *119*, 104067.

Bunt, H. V. D., & Schoot, C. V. D. (2003). Prevention of Organised Crime. A situational approach.

Burton, S., McGregor, M., & Laycock, G. (2020). MINICAB DRIVERS IN LONDON. Problem-Oriented Policing: Successful Case Studies.

Campesi, G. (2020). Police accountability and human rights at the Italian borders. *Fundamental Rights Challenges in Border Controls and Expulsion of Irregular Immigrants in the European Union: Complaint Mechanisms and Access to Justice*, 125-147.

Campos, J. R., & Sánchez, C. G. (2021). Irregular Migration And Human Trafficking For The Purpose Of Sexual Exploitation: An Analysis Of Public Policy Instruments For Combating It In Chiapas, Mexico. *Young Migrants Crossing Multiple Borders to the North*, *36*, 75.

Caparini, M. (2014). Human trafficking and organized crime. Trafficking in Human Beings: Learning from Asian and European Experiences (Singapore: Konrad Adenauer Stiftung, East Asian Institute, European Policy Centre, EU Centre in Singapore, 2014).

Cara, A. (2012). Investigating and combating organized crime in EU.

Carrera, S., Mitsilegas, V., & Stefan, M. (2021). Criminal justice, fundamental rights and the rule of law in the digital age. Report of a CEPS and QMUL Task Force.

Christensen, L. S., Rayment-McHugh, S., Prenzler, T., Chiu, Y. N., & Webster, J. (2021). The theory and evidence behind law enforcement strategies that combat child sexual abuse material. *International Journal of Police Science & Management*, *23*(4), 392–405.

Cilliers, L., & Viljoen, K. (2021). A framework of ethical issues to consider when conducting internet-based research. *South African Journal of Information Management*, *23*(1), 1–9.

Clark, A., Fraser, A., & Hamilton-Smith, N. (2021). Networked territorialism: The routes and roots of organised crime. *Trends in Organized Crime*, *24*, 246–262.

College of Policing. (2023). Investigation introduction. https://www.college.police.uk/app/investigation/investigation-introduction

Comolli, V. (Ed.). (2018). *Organized crime and illicit trade: How to respond to this strategic challenge in old and new domains*. Springer.

Coomber, R., Donnermeyer, J. F., McElrath, K., & Scott, J. (2014). Key concepts in crime and society. *Sage (Atlanta, Ga.)*.

Cooper, J. M., Aarhaug, J., & Scott, J. (2023). *Taxi, Limousine, and Transport Network Company Regulation: Recurring Challenges*. Taylor & Francis.

Coutinho, J. A., Diviák, T., Bright, D., & Koskinen, J. (2020). Multilevel determinants of collaboration between organised criminal groups. *Social Networks*, *63*, 56–69.

Currie, R. J., & Douglas, S. (2021). Human rights and transnational organized crime. In *Routledge handbook of transnational organized crime* (pp. 388–408). Routledge.

Currie, R. J., & Douglas, S. (2021). Human rights and transnational organized crime. In *Routledge handbook of transnational organized crime* (pp. 388–408). Routledge.

Danielsson, A. (2023). Tackling Digital Entrepreneurship Within the Illicit Economy: The Evolving Fight Against Serious and Organized Crime Within a Digitally Facilitated Sex Industry. In Digital Entrepreneurship and Co-Creating Value Through Digital Encounters (pp. 118-144). IGI Global.

Darcy, S. (2022). International Law and Collaboration: A Tentative Embrace. *Collaboration in Authoritarian and Armed Conflict Settings*, *248*, 244–267.

Dartford Borough Council. (2020). Modern Anti-Slavery and Human Trafficking Statement 2020-21.

Davies, J., Malik, H. M., Jokinen, A., & Haapasaari, S. (2023). Private and public co-operation in preventing and addressing corporate crime: The case of labour trafficking in the Finnish construction industry. *Crime, Law, and Social Change*, 1–19.

Davies, L., Powling, L., & Symmonds, J. (2024). Assessing and Managing the Risk of Organised Crime, Human Trafficking and Modern Slavery. In *Managing Clinical Risk* (pp. 341–378). Routledge.

De Sousa, A., & De Sousa (2023) R. Ethics in Child Sexual Abuse Research, Global Bioethics Enquiry; 11(2)

Deakin, S. (2018). Organisational torts: Vicarious liability versus non-delegable duty. *The Cambridge Law Journal*, *77*(1), 15–18.

Degani, P., & De Stefani, P. (2020). Addressing Migrant Women's Intersecting Vulnerabilities. Refugee Protection, Anti-trafficking and Anti-violence Referral Patterns in Italy. *Peace Human Rights Governance, 4*(Peace Human Rights Governance 4/1), 113-152.

den Boer, E. V. (2021). Countering Criminal Facilitation Through Public–Private Cooperation in The Netherlands. *International Security Management: New Solutions to Complexity*, 463-476.

Department for Transport. (2019). Taxi and Private Hire Vehicle Licensing: Protecting Users.

Department for Transport. (2022). Taxi and Private Hire Vehicle Licensing Best Practice Guidance for Licensing Authorities in England

Department for Transport. (2022, November 25). Statutory taxi and private hire vehicle standards. GOV.UK. https://www.gov.uk/government/publications/statutory-taxi-and-private-hire-vehicle-standards/statutory-taxi-and-private-hire-vehicle-standards

Deuchar, R., McLeanand, R., & Holligan, C. (2021). Framing and Re-Framing the Experiences of Youth in Disadvantaged Scottish Communities. In Gangs, Drugs and Youth Adversity (pp. 129-146). Bristol University Press.

Di Maggio, U., & Lo Verde, F. M. (2023). Organized Crime as Global Social Problem. In *The Palgrave Handbook of Global Social Problems* (pp. 1–24). Springer International Publishing.

Doig, A., & Sproat, P. A. (2020). Local responses to a national initiative on organised crime and local government procurement fraud. *Journal of Financial Crime*, *27*(1), 78–91.

Donnelly, J., & Whelan, D. J. (2020). *International human rights*. Routledge.

Dumba, S. (2017). Informal public transport driver behaviour and regulatory policy linkage: An expose. *Journal of Transport and Supply Chain Management*, *11*(1), 1–16.

Edwards, A. (2007). Traffic in human beings: At the intersection of criminal justice, human rights, asylum/migration and labor. *Denv. J. Int'l L. & Pol'y*, *36*, 9.

Ehe, R. (2020). The role of Open Source Intelligence in the Fight against Transnational Organized Crime-A European Perspective.

Eisapareh, K., Nazari, M., Kaveh, M. H., Cousins, R., & Mokarami, H. (2023). Effects of an educational intervention program based on the PRECEDE–PROCEED model for anger management and driving performance of urban taxi drivers: A comparison of traditional and online methods. *Safety Science*, *157*, 105933.

Eisenberg, M. R. (1987). The Vicarious Liability of Governmental Entities: Judicial and Legislative Attempts to Reduce Accountability for Tortious Acts. *Ann. Surv. Am.*, *L*, 637.

El Ghamari, M., & Gabriela Bartoszewicz, M. (2020). (Un) sustainable development of minors in Libyan refugee camps in the context of conflict-induced migration. *Sustainability*, *12*(11), 4537.

Elhaw, A. E. M., & Rabee, I. (2024). From Slavery to Modern Slavery, Trafficking in Human Beings (Challenges and Solutions) At the Regional and International Level. *Migration Letters : An International Journal of Migration Studies*, *21*(S1), 271–300.

Fazely, A. (2020). *Identity crimes in the UK: An examination of the strategies employed by front-line practitioners in the public and private sector to detect, prevent and mitigate against this crime* (Doctoral dissertation, Middlesex University).

Finklea, K. M. (2011, July). The interplay of borders, turf, cyberspace, and jurisdiction: Issues confronting US law enforcement. Congressional Research Service, Library of Congress.

Gallagher, A. T. (2015). Exploitation in migration: Unacceptable but inevitable. *Journal of International Affairs*, *68*(2), 55.

Gallen, J., & Mhuirthile, T. N. (Eds.). (2021). *Law, Responsibility and Vulnerability: State Accountability and Responsiveness*. Routledge.

Gambetta, D., & Hamill, H. (2005). *Streetwise: How taxi drivers establish customer's trustworthiness*. Russell Sage Foundation.

Goldstein, R., Sances, M. W., & You, H. Y. (2020). Exploitative revenues, law enforcement, and the quality of government service. *Urban Affairs Review*, *56*(1), 5–31.

Green, J. (2021). Closing the accountability gap in corporate supply chains for violations of the Trafficking Victims Protection Act. *Business and Human Rights Journal*, *6*(3), 449–489.

Guercke, L. (2021). State Responsibility for a Failure to Prevent Violations of the Right to Life by Organised Criminal Groups: Disappearances in Mexico. *Human Rights Law Review*, *21*(2), 329–357.

Hamer, R. (2022). Travelling though trauma: voices in partnership, 2020-2022-service evaluation.

Hampshire Safeguarding Children Partnership. (2020). HIPS Child Exploitation Strategy.

Hardouin, P. (2009). Banks governance and public-private partnership in preventing and confronting organized crime, corruption and terrorism financing. *Journal of Financial Crime*, *16*(3), 199–209.

Harré, T. (2022). Human traffickers' fair trial rights and transnational criminal law. *Anti-trafficking review*, (18), 159-173.

Heerdt, D. (2021). *Blurred lines of responsibility and accountability: Human rights abuses at mega-sporting events*. Intersentia.

Hertfordhire Modern Slavery Partnership. (2022, October 28). Training and resources. Hertfordshire Modern Slavery Partnership. https://www.stopexploitationherts.org.uk/index.php/training-and-resources/.

Hignett, K. (2021). Transnational organized crime and the global village. In *Routledge handbook of transnational organized crime* (pp. 305–317). Routledge.

Hirsch Ballin, E. (2022). Trust Beyond Borders: Selected Papers on the Significance of Human Rights and the Rule of Law.

Home Office. (March 2016). Modern Crime Prevention Strategy.

Hughes, D. (2020). Differentiating the Corporation: Accountability and International Humanitarian Law. *Mich. J. Int'l L.*, *42*, 47.

Institute of Licencing. (2018). Guidance on determining the suitability of applicants and licensees in the hackney and private hire trades.

Ishikawa, T., & Kryvoi, Y. (Eds.). (2023). *Public and Private Governance of Cybersecurity: Challenges and Potential*. Cambridge University Press.

Islam, F. (2023). Human Trafficking Law Enforcement Over the Victims and Offenders: The Perspective of Anti-Trafficking Stakeholders. *Victims & Offenders*, 1–29.

Jakubiec, W., & Kuliński, M. (2023). The phenomenon of economic crime: Threats and contemporary trends. *Scientific Journal of Bielsko-Biala School of Finance and Law*, *27*(3), 55–58.

Janenova, S., & Knox, C. (2020). Combatting corruption in Kazakhstan: A role for ethics commissioners? *Public Administration and Development*, *40*(3), 186–195.

Jay, A. Independent Inquiry into Child Sexual Exploitation in Rotherham 1997–2013 (Rotherham

Jones, J. (2020). Is It Time to Open a Conversation About a New United Nations Treaty to Fight Human Trafficking That Focuses on Victim Protection and Human Rights? The Palgrave International Handbook of Human Trafficking, 1803-1818.

Karenga, P. V. S. (2022). International Human Rights Laws and Trafficking in Persons. In *A West African Model to Address Human Trafficking* (pp. 199–210). Springer International Publishing.

Karenga, P. V. S. (2022). States' Obligations Under International Human Rights Law. In *A West African Model to Address Human Trafficking* (pp. 227–249). Springer International Publishing.

Kataria, G., & Gautam, M. (2022). Exploring Complex Dynamics Of Narcoterrorism And Its Impact On Human Rights In Indian Context. *Journal of Pharmaceutical Negative Results*, 4729–4740.

Kayode-Ajala, O. (2023). Applications of Cyber Threat Intelligence (CTI) in financial institutions and challenges in its adoption. *Applied Research in Artificial Intelligence and Cloud Computing*, *6*(8), 1–21.

Lautenbach, G. (2013). *The concept of the rule of law and the European Court of Human Rights*. OUP Oxford.

Lazarus, L. (2012). Positive obligations and criminal justice: Duties to protect or coerce?.

Lefevre, M., Hickle, K., & Larkin, R. (2020). Child Criminal Exploitation in the South East of England: family experiences and professional responses.

Levi, M., & Maguire, M. (2004). Reducing and preventing organised crime: An evidence-based critique. *Crime, Law, and Social Change*, *41*, 397–469.

Licensing Committee. (2019). Taxi & Private Hire Licensing – New Statutory Guidance from the Department of Transport.

Lillo Lobos, R. (2022). The Right to Access to Justice as a Key to Understand the Right to a Fair Trial in Civil Matters. In *Understanding Due Process in Non-Criminal Matters: How to Harmonize Procedural Guarantees with the Right to Access to Justice* (pp. 251–281). Springer International Publishing.

Local Government Association. (2015). Tackling serious and organised crime a local response.

Mallory, S. (2011). *Understanding organized crime*. Jones & Bartlett Publishers.

Martinez Cristaldo, C. E. (2023). The impact of institutional weakness on the presence of organised crime: A case study on Paraguay and organised crime in the Triple Frontier.

Maslen, H., & Paine, C. (2019). When should the police investigate cases of non-recent child sexual abuse? *Criminal Justice Ethics*, *38*(2), 65–102.

Maxwell, N. J., & Artingstall, D. (2017). *The role of financial information-sharing partnerships in the disruption of crime*. Royal United Services Institute for Defence and Security Studies.

McCarthy-Jones, A., Doyle, C., & Turner, M. (2020). From hierarchies to networks: The organizational evolution of the international drug trade. *International Journal of Law, Crime and Justice*, *63*, 100436.

McLean, R. (2019). *Gangs, drugs and (dis) organised crime*. Bristol University Press.

Meneses Falcón, M. D. C., Urío Rodríguez, S. J., & Uroz Olivares, J. (2019). Financing of trafficking in human beings in Spain.

Metropolitan Borough Council. Rotherham 2014)

Missoni, E., & Alesani, D. (2023). *Management of International Institutions and NGOs: Insights for Global Leaders*. Taylor & Francis.

Moeckli, D., Shah, S., Sivakumaran, S., & Harris, D. (Eds.). (2022). *International human rights law*. Oxford University Press.

Monk, M. (2021). Emergent trends in the Chinese counterfeit pharmaceutical supply chain and opportunities for public-private reform.

Morgan, A., Brown, R., Voce, I., & Cubitt, T. (2020). Organised and transnational crime. *Australian Policing: Critical Issues in 21st Century Police Practice*, 315.

Murphy, J., & De Vrieze, F. (2020). *Parliaments and independent oversight institutions. Global and countryspecific analysis of parliaments' relationships with Supreme Audit*. Anti-Corruption and Human Rights Institutions.

Murphy, S. D. (2020). Codifying the Obligations of States Relating to the Prevention of Atrocities. *Case W. Res. J. Int'l L.*, *52*, 27.

Mweene, O. (2022). Construction of interpersonal helping behaviours exhibited among pirate taxi drivers in the city of Lusaka: an embedded mixed methods design (Doctoral dissertation, The University of Zambia).

Nagle, L. E. (2013). How Conflict and Displacement Fuel Human Trafficking and Abuse of Vulnerable Groups. The Case of Colombia and Opportunities for Real Action and Innovative Solutions. *Groningen Journal of International Law, 1*(2).

Napolitano, G. (2020). The Rule of Law. The Oxford Handbook of Comparative Administrative Law, 421.

National Crime Agency. (2015). Memorandum of Understanding Concerning Operation Stovewoos.

Neyroud, P. (2022). Policing "Landscapes" for the Rule of Law and Public Protection: The State of Evidence on Organisational Policies, Structures, and Human Resources. *Cambridge Journal of Evidence-Based Policing*, *6*(3-4), 140–161.

Ngo, N. (2021). Child sexual abuse violence against human dignity of children. *International Journal of Research*, *10*(15), 97–108.

Obaga, A. (2021). *Illicit Financial Flows: a Legal Analysis of Tax Avoidance by Financial Institutions in Kenya* (Doctoral dissertation, University of Nairobi).

Olley, N. (2019). 207 Transnational policing and organised crime. *The Development of Transnational Policing: Past, Present and Future*, 207-238.

O'Neill, M. (2023). *The Transnational Crime of Human Trafficking: A Human Security Approach*. Taylor & Francis.

Oriolo, A. (2023). The rule of law, transnational crimes, and the human rights-based approach in the European Union: The Court of Justice as Ultimate Guardian of the 'Good' Laws. In *Solidarity and Rule of Law: The New Dimension of EU Security* (pp. 201–226). Springer International Publishing.

Otusanya, O. J., & Adeyeye, G. B. (2022). The dark side of tax havens in money laundering, capital flight and corruption in developing countries: Some evidence from Nigeria. *Journal of Financial Crime*, *29*(1), 62–100.

Overall, L. (2016). Abuse in Foster Care and Potential Liability for Local Authorities: Can liability be imposed through vicarious liability or a non-delegable duty?.

Oxfordshire Safeguarding Adults Board. (2023, August 3). Other training. https://www.osab.co.uk/learning-zone/osab-core-adult-safeguarding-courses/traiing-hosted-by-osab/other-training/

Ozymy, J., & Jarrell, M. L. (2020). Of Sex Crimes and Fencelines: How Recognition of Environmental Justice Communities as Crime Victims Under State and Federal Law Can Help Secure Environmental Justice. *Pace Environmental Law Review*, *38*, 109.

Palermo, G. (2020). Transnational Organized Crime: The Branching of Mafias Into the Global Era. In Handbook of Research on Trends and Issues in Crime Prevention, Rehabilitation, and Victim Support (pp. 124-143). Igi Global.

Parliamentlive.tv. (2019, March 27). Transport Committee Wednesday 27 March 2019. episode, London.

Pastor, R., Mignet, F., Mattes, T., Gurzawska, A., Nitsch, H., & Wright, D. (2021). COPKIT: Technology and Knowledge for Early Warning/Early Action-Led Policing in Fighting Organised Crime and Terrorism. In *Technology Development for Security Practitioners* (pp. 121–133). Springer International Publishing.

Pavel, C. E. (2021). The international rule of law. In *Legitimacy Beyond the State* (pp. 52–71). Routledge.

Peach, D., Allen, D., Brown, P., Sanghera, K., Sharif, R., Lees, J., & Senior, J. (2015). Needs analysis report following the sexual exploitation of children in Rotherham.

Piemontese, L. (2023). Uncovering illegal and underground economies: The case of mafia extortion racketeering. *Journal of Public Economics*, *227*, 104997.

Pimentel, S. (2022). *Non-Traditional Collectors: Case Studies and Implications for the Private Sector* (Doctoral dissertation, San Diego State University).

Pisillo Mazzeschi, R., & Pisillo Mazzeschi, R. (2021). Protection of Liberty and Security of the Person. *International Human Rights Law: Theory and Practice*, 329-341.

Pournara, M. (2020). *Strategic police decision-making in tackling organised crime* (Doctoral dissertation, Cardiff University).

Prenzler, T. (2021). *Ethics and accountability in criminal justice: Towards a universal standard*. Australian Academic Press.

Prescott, D. S., & Levenson, J. S. (2010). Sex offender treatment is not punishment. *Journal of Sexual Aggression*, *16*(3), 275–285.

Rabkin, J. A., & Lerner, C. S. (2022). Criminal justice is local: Why states disregard universal jurisdiction for human rights abuses. *Vand. J. Transnat'l L.*, *55*, 375.

Rader, M. M. G. (2023). *Organized Crime: A Test of Durkheim's Theory of Punishment and Society* (Doctoral dissertation, University of South Alabama).

Raineri, L., & Strazzari, F. (2023). The data that we do (not) have: Studying drug trafficking and organised crime in Africa. *Trends in Organized Crime*, •••, 1–21.

Ramcharan, B. G. (2021). *The concept and present status of the international protection of human rights: forty years after the universal declaration* (Vol. 13). BRILL.

Ratner, S. R. (2001). Corporations and human rights: a theory of legal responsibility. *yale LJ, 111*, 443.

Reuter, P. (2014). Drug markets and organized crime. The Oxford handbook of organized crime, 359-381.

Richie-Zavaleta, A. C., Baranik, S., Mersch, S., Ataiants, J., & Rhodes, S. M. (2021). From victimization to restoration: Multi-disciplinary collaborative approaches to care and support victims and survivors of human trafficking. *Journal of Human Trafficking*, *7*(3), 291–307.

Rizzuti, A. (2022). Organised food crime: An analysis of the involvements of organised crime groups in the food sector in England and Italy. *Crime, Law, and Social Change*, *78*(5), 463–482.

Rotherham Metropolitan Borough Council. (2018) Commissioners' Timeline of key headlines / progress to the Ministry of Housing, Communities and Local Government February 2015 – February 2018 (3 Years)

Rothstein, B. (2021). *Controlling corruption: The social contract approach*. Oxford University Press.

Rothstein, B. (2021). *Controlling corruption: The social contract approach*. Oxford University Press.

Rubio Grundell, L. (2022). The Intersection of Security and Neo-abolitionism in the EU's Anti-trafficking Policies. In *Security Meets Gender Equality in the EU: The Politics of Trafficking in Women for Sexual Exploitation* (pp. 119–163). Springer International Publishing.

Sage-Passant, L. (2023) *The security intelligence services of the private sector* (Doctoral dissertation, Loughborough University).

Sasan, J. M. V. (2021). The Social Contract Theories of Thomas Hobbes and John Locke: Comparative Analysis.

Sauve, B., Woodley, J., Jones, N. J., & Akhtari, S. (2023). Methods of preventing corruption: a review and analysis of select approaches.

Schönsteiner, J. (2022). Inter-American Elements for a Systemic Approach to State-Owned Enterprises' Human Rights Obligations. *Business and Human Rights Journal*, *7*(3), 397–417.

Seabright, P., Stieglitz, J., & Van der Straeten, K. (2021). Evaluating social contract theory in the light of evolutionary social science. *Evolutionary Human Sciences*, *3*, e20.

Seepma, A. P., de Blok, C., & Van Donk, D. P. (2021). Designing digital public service supply chains: Four country-based cases in criminal justice. *Supply Chain Management*, *26*(3), 418–446.

Seivold, G. (2023). What We've Learned: Lessons from the World's Leading Security Companies on Partnerships and Privatization. In *Handbook on Public and Private Security* (pp. 321–346). Springer International Publishing.

Sharma, N. (2023). EXAMINING THE LEGAL 'RELATIONSHIP' BETWEEN THE TAXI OWNER AND THE TAXI DRIVER IN FIJI: A CASE FOR REFORM. DRP Thesis.

Shelley, L. (2013). Human trafficking as a form of transnational crime. In *Human trafficking* (pp. 116–137). Willan.

Simović, M., & Šikman, M. (2020), HUMAN RIGHTS AND ORGANISED CRIME-LIMITATION OF HUMAN RIGHTS V. PREVENTION OF ORGANISED CRIME. In *International Scientific Conference "Towards a Better Future: Human rights, Organized crime and Digital society"* (p. 129).

Singh, P. (2023). Money Laundering and Abuse of the Financial System. *Issue 2 Indian JL & Legal Rsch.*, *5*, 1.

Sitompul, A., & Hasibuan, P. (2021). The Morality of Law Enforcement Agencies (Police, Prosecutor's Office, KPK) in Money Laundering With the Origin of the Corruption. *European Science Review*, (9-10), 55–63.

Skidmore, M. (2022). *Empirical Research to Contextualise Serious and Organised Crimes and Develop Perspectives on Effective Crime Control in the UK* (Doctoral dissertation, University of Portsmouth).

Slope, R. (2022). *Care in the Iron Cage: A Weberian Analysis of Failings in Care.* Taylor & Francis.

Smith, R. K. (2022). *International human rights law.* Oxford University Press.

Smokov, S. M., Horoshko, V. V., Korniienko, M. V., & Medvedenko, S. V. (2022). Rule of Law as a Principle of Criminal Procedure (on materials of the European Court of Human Rights). *Pakistan Journal of Criminology, 14*(3).

Sollecito, A. (2023). *Honor behind Human Trafficking Absenteeism in Italian Mafias." A comparative study among Italian.* Nigerian and Albanian Mafias.

Sorochinsky, M. (2009). Prosecuting Torturers, Protecting Child Molesters: Toward a Power Balance Model of Criminal Process for International Human Rights Law. *Mich. J. Int'l L., 31*, 157.

South Cambridgeshire District Council. (2022). South Cambridgeshire District Council Modern Slavery Statement 2022-23.

Spapens, A., Abraham, M., van Dijk, B., & Hofstra, D. (2021). 25 years of tackling large-scale drug crime in the Netherlands. *CIROC Newsletter*, (3), 2–3.

Strauss, D. P. (1980). Vicarious Municipal Liability: Creating a Consistent Remedial Policy for Local Government Violations of Civil Rights. *Cal. WL Rev., 16*, 58.

Strečanský, B. (2023). Dancing on a Thin Ice: Civil Society in Slovakia. *Contested Civic Spaces: A European Perspective, 22*, 193.

Strugała, R. (2021). The sharing economy as the contemporary challenge for the law of torts. In *Digital Technologies and the Law of Obligations* (pp. 45–53). Routledge.

Świątkowska, J. (2020). Tackling cybercrime to unleash developing countries' digital potential. *Pathways for Prosperity Commission Background Paper Series, 33*, 2020–01.

Tagziria, L., & de Lugo, L. B. R. B. (2023) West Africa Organised Crime Resilience Framework.

Task and Finish Group on Taxi and Private Hire Vehicle Licensing. (2018). Taxi and Private Hire Vehicle Licensing Steps towards a safer and more robust system.

Thommandru, A., & Maratovich, F. F. (2024). Leveraging new emerging technologies to enhance the anticorruption arsenal: Assimilating India's experiential insights into Uzbekistan's criminoverse. *Multidisciplinary Reviews, 7*(3), 2024058–2024058.

Thornberry, T. P. (Ed.). (2018). *Developmental theories of crime and delinquency.* Routledge.

Tyagi, A. (2021). *Early warning identity threat and mitigation system* (Doctoral dissertation).

Uhl, A., Kučera, J., Hayrapetyan, L., Gartner, M., Leuven, K. U., & Stockreiter, S. (2020). Private Sector Engagement in the Prevention of Organized Crime.

Üngör, U. Ü. (2020). *Paramilitarism: Mass violence in the shadow of the state.* Oxford University Press.

UNODC. (2020, April). Organized crime module 6 key issues: Ethical perspective - moral failure in decision-making. Organized Crime Module 6 Key Issues: Ethical Perspective - Moral Failure in Decision-Making. https://www.unodc.org/e4j/en/organized-crime/module-6/key-issues/ethical-perspective.html

Vaia, G., & Bisogno, M. (2020). Fighting organised crime and mafia-type firms: the role of public administrations. *Fighting organised crime and mafia-type firms*, 1-130.

Van Niekerk, T., & Sebakamotse, J. K. T. (2020). A few critical observations of current oversight and accountability challenges of financial management of municipalities in the Free State province: An ethical dilemma. Journal for Christian Scholarship= Tydskrif vir Christelike Wetenskap, 56(3-4), 269-293.

Velasco, C. (2022, May). Cybercrime and Artificial Intelligence. An overview of the work of international organizations on criminal justice and the international applicable instruments. In *ERA Forum* (Vol. 23, No. 1, pp. 109-126). Berlin/ Heidelberg: Springer Berlin Heidelberg.

Verdier, P. H., & Stephan, P. B. (2021). International Human Rights and Multinational Corporations: An FCPA Approach. *BUL Rev.*, *101*, 1359.

Villani, S. (2020). Fight Against Organized Crime and Resilience to Climate Change: A Relationship of Mutual Causality. The Palgrave Handbook of Climate Resilient Societies, 1-28.

Waardenburg, M., Groenleer, M., & De Jong, J. (2020). Designing environments for experimentation, learning and innovation in public policy and governance. *Policy and Politics*, *48*(1), 67–87.

Waldron, J. (2021). The rule of law and the role of courts. *Global Constitutionalism*, *10*(1), 91–105.

Watson, D., Sousa-Santos, J. L., & Howes, L. (2021). Transnational and organised crime in Pacific Island countries and territories: Police capacity to respond to the emerging security threat.

Watson, D., Sousa-Santos, J. L., & Howes, L. (2021). Transnational and organised crime in Pacific Island countries and territories: Police capacity to respond to the emerging security threat.

Weale, A. (2020). MODERN SOCIAL CONTRACT THEORY C. Oxford University Press.

Williams, B. (2023). *Policing Mental Health, Vulnerability and Risk*. Critical Publishing.

Windle, J., Moyle, L., & Coomber, R. (2020). 'Vulnerable'kids going country: Children and young People's involvement in county lines drug dealing. *Youth Justice*, *20*(1-2), 64–78.

Wright, J. P., Tibbetts, S. G., & Daigle, L. E. (2014). *Criminals in the making: Criminality across the life course*. Sage Publications.

Xing, J. L. (2022). Driving as communities: Chinese taxi drivers' technology, job, and mobility choices under the pressure of e-hailing. *Mobilities*, *17*(5), 676–694.

Yousaf, F. N. (2018). Forced migration, human trafficking, and human security. *Current Sociology*, *66*(2), 209–225.

Zabyelina, Y., & Thachuk, K. L. (Eds.). (2022). *The Private Sector and Organized Crime: Criminal Entrepreneurship, Illicit Profits, and Private Sector Security Governance*. Taylor & Francis.

KEY TERMS AND DEFINITIONS

Child Sexual Exploitation: - Child Sexual Exploitation (CSE) is a form of abuse of a sexual nature aimed at people under 18 years of age.

Taxi and PHV Services: - Refers to transportation services provided to the public, including traditional taxis licensed to pick up passengers without prior booking and Private Hire Vehicles (PHVs) that must be pre-booked.

Public-Private Collaboration: - A cooperative arrangement between public entities (governments) and private sectors.

Socio-Economic Impact: - The effect of an activity on the economic conditions and social well-being of a community.

Regulatory Gaps: - Situations where existing regulations do not adequately cover or address specific issues, leading to areas where activities are not properly controlled or monitored.

Community Surveillance: - Monitoring activities conducted by community members or organizations to ensure safety, security, and compliance with norms or regulations within a community.

Legal and Ethical Responsibilities: - Obligations that individuals or organizations must adhere to, as defined by law and ethical standards, to ensure fairness, justice, and respect for rights.

Compilation of References

A glimpse of the Indigenous tribes of Manipur (Part 1). (n.d.). MyGov blogs. https://blog.mygov.in/a-glimpse-of-the-indigenous-tribes-of-manipur-part-1/

Aatreya, S. S. (2018). Obscenity and the Depiction of Women in Pornography: Revisiting the Kamlesh Vaswani Petition. *Nalsar Student Law Review, 13*(1). https://nslr.in/wp-content/uploads/2019/05/NSLR-Vol-13-Issue-1-No-1.pdf

Abdulai, A. G. (2009). Political will in combating corruption in developing and transition economies: A comparative study of Singapore, Hong Kong and Ghana. *Journal of Financial Crime*, *16*(4), 387–417. doi:10.1108/13590790910993753

Abramson, K. (2003). Beyond consent, toward safeguarding human rights: Implementing the United Nations Trafficking Protocol. *Harv. Int'l LJ*, *44*, 473.

Ackermann, J. B. (2003). *Money laundering*. Open Science. https://openscience.ge/bitstream/1/497/1/samagistro%20gurguchiani.pdf

Act East Policy. (n.d.). PIB. https://pib.gov.in/newsite/printrelease.aspx?relid=133837

Adam, I., & Adongo, C. A. (2016). Do backpackers suffer crime? An empirical investigation of crime perpetrated against backpackers in Ghana. *Journal of Hospitality and Tourism Management*, *27*, 60–67. doi:10.1016/j.jhtm.2016.03.003

ADF. (2023). *Illegal Fish Dumping by Chinese Trawlers Rising in Ghana*. ADF. https://adf-magazine.com/2023/03/illegal-fish-dumping-by-chinese-trawlers-rising-in-ghana/#:~:text=Chinese%20trawlers%20have%20committed%20acts,in%20the%20past%20two%20decades

Adler, F., Mueller, G. O. W., & Laufer, W. S. (2013). Criminology, (8th Edition). New York.

African Union. (2002). Draft Action Plan to Combat Trafficking in Human Beings Especially Women and Children. *AF-EU/MIN.CONF (II)/3.*

Africanews. (2023). Ghana Auditor General reveals violations in use of Covid 19 funds. *Africa News*. https://www.africanews.com/2023/01/23/ghana-auditor-general-reveals-violations-in-use-of-covid-19-funds//

Agariga, F., Abugre, S., & Appiah, M. (2021). Spatio-temporal changes in land use and forest cover in the Asutifi North District of Ahafo Region of Ghana,(1986–2020). *Environmental Challenges*, *5*, 100209. doi:10.1016/j.envc.2021.100209

Agboli, J. M. (2023). Implications of legalisation of cannabis cultivation in Ghana: A critical review. *Drugs, Habits and Social Policy*. doi:10.1108/DHS-06-2023-0023

Agoramoorthy, G., & Hsu, M. J. (2012). The significance of cows in Indian society between sacredness and economy. *Anthropological Notebooks*, *18*(3), 5–12.

Agyapong, D., Asiamah, M., & Addo-Danquah, M. (2016). Organised Crime, Foreing Direct Investment and Economic Growth in Ghana. *British Journal of Economics. Management & Trade*, *15*(4), 1–12.

Ahuja, J. (2019). Protecting Holy Cows: Hindu Vigilantism against Muslims in India. In T. Bjørgo & M. Mareš (Eds.), *Vigilantism against Migrants and Minorities* (pp. 55–69). Routledge. doi:10.4324/9780429485619-4

Aitken, S., Gaskell, D., & Hodkinson, A. (2018). Online sexual grooming: Exploratory comparison of themes arising from male offenders' communications with male victims compared to female victims. *Deviant Behavior*, *39*(9), 1170–1190. doi:10.1080/01639625.2017.1410372

Akelola, S. (2012). *Fraud in the banking industry: A case study of Kenya*. Nottingham Trent University.

Akhgar, B., & Yates, S. (Eds.). (2011). *Intelligence Management: Knowledge Driven Frameworks for Combating Terrorism and Organized Crime*. Springer Science & Business Media.

Albanese, J. S. (2015). *Organized crime: From the mob to transnational organized crime*. Routledge.

Albanese, J. S. (2021). Organized crime as financial crime: The nature of organized crime as reflected in prosecutions and research. *Victims & Offenders*, *16*(3), 431–443. doi:10.1080/15564886.2020.1823543

Albanese, J. S. (2023). Development and Surges of Organized Crime: An Application of Enterprise Theory. In *Organized Crime in the 21st Century: Motivations, Opportunities, and Constraints* (pp. 11–24). Springer International Publishing. doi:10.1007/978-3-031-21576-6_2

Alexander, K. (2000). The Legalization of the International Anti-money Laundering Regime: The Role of the Financial Action Task Force. *Centre for Business Research. C- 8.*

Ali, S., Haykal, H. A., & Youssef, E. Y. M. (2023). Child Sexual Abuse and the Internet—A Systematic Review. *Human Arenas*, *6*(2), 404–421. doi:10.1007/s42087-021-00228-9

Alison, L. J., Alison, E., Shortland, N., & Surmon-Bohr, F. (2020). *ORBIT: The science of rapport-based interviewing for law enforcement, security, and military*. Oxford University Press.

Allum, F., & Sands, J. (2004). Explaining organized crime in Europe: Are economists always right? *Crime, Law, and Social Change*, *41*(2), 133–160. doi:10.1023/B:CRIS.0000016223.49968.17

Allum, F., & Siebert, R. (2003). Organized crime: A threat to democracy? In F. Allum & R. Siebert (Eds.), *Organized Crime and the Challenge to Democracy* (pp. 1–22). Routledge., Retrieved from http://www.tandfebooks.com/isbn/9780203426418

Amaxopoulou, M., Durovic, M., & Lech, F. (2021). Regulation of Uber in the UK. Global Perspectives on Legal Challenges Posed by Ridesharing Companies: A Case Study of Uber, 101-135.

Amoah, R. (2020). *Public Perceptions of Human Rights Abuses of the Ghana Police Service in the Jomoro Municipality* [Doctoral dissertation, University of Cape Coast].

Amponsah, S., Isshaq, Z., & Agyapong, D. (2019). Determinants of tax stamp evasion in rural districts in Ghana: A case of Twifu Atti-Morkwa and Hemang lower Denkyira districts. *International Journal of Law and Management*, *61*(1), 73–90. doi:10.1108/IJLMA-08-2017-0190

Andell, P., James, D., & Maitra, D. (2023). County lines and the transformation of middle drug markets within a local organised crime context. In *Understanding Drug Dealing and Illicit Drug Markets* (pp. 245–264). Routledge.

Andreangeli, A. (2020). Taxi services, platforms and Article 101 TFEU: Changing the shape of the transport intermediation services industry? *Mkt. & Competition L. Rev.*, *4*, 41.

Anheier, H. K., Lang, M., & Toepler, S. (2019). Civil society in times of change: Shrinking, changing and expanding spaces and the need for new regulatory approaches. *Economics*, *13*(1), 20190008. doi:10.5018/economics-ejournal.ja.2019-8

Ani, & Ani. (2023, March 29). Massive rally held in Manipur to demand NRC in state. *The Print*. https://theprint.in/politics/massive-rally-held-in-manipur-to-demand-nrc-in-state/1480441/

Aning, K. (2007). Are there emerging West African criminal networks? The case of Ghana. *Global Crime*, *8*(3), 193–212. doi:10.1080/17440570701507729

Anter, A. (2019). The Modern State and its Monopoly on Violence. In E. Hanke, L. Scaff, & S. Whimster, The Oxford Handbook of Hans Weber (pp. 226-236). New York, United Stateas: Oxford University Press.

Anti-money laundering unit. (2004). *An overview of the UN conventions and the international standards concerning anti-money laundering legislation*. NGLP. http://www.nplg.gov.ge/dlibrary/collect/0002/000828/Dis.Shashiashvili%20G.pdf

Appiahene-Gyamfi, J. (2021). Policing in Ghana. *Global Perspectives in Policing and Law Enforcement, 1*.

Appiahene-Gyamfi, J. (2003). Urban crime trends and patterns in Ghana: The case of Accra. *Journal of Criminal Justice*, *31*(1), 13–23. doi:10.1016/S0047-2352(02)00196-4

Aranega, A. D. T. (2023). *The Crime-Geopolitics Nexus and Transnational Environmental Crimes in the Amazon Forest* (Doctoral dissertation, PUC-Rio).

Aronowitz, A. A., & Veldhuizen, M. E. (2021). The human trafficking–organized crime nexus. In *Routledge handbook of transnational organized crime* (pp. 232–252). Routledge.

Arskova, J., & Allum, F. (2014). Introduction: Women and transnational organized crime. *Trends in Organized Crime*, *17*(1-2), 1–15. doi:10.1007/s12117-014-9223-y

Arun, T., Ashraf, J., Jayasinghe, K., & Soobaroyen, T. (2023). Accounting, accountability and governance in emerging economies: a development perspective. In Handbook of Accounting, Accountability and Governance (pp. 215-236). Edward Elgar Publishing.

Asanidze, S. (2012). *Criminological characterization of legalization of illegal income (money laundering)*. Grigol Robakidze University. http://www.nplg.gov.ge/dlibrary/collect/0002/000576/Asanidze%20S%2B.pdf

Atampugre, G., Mensah, E., Boateng, E., Mabhaudhi, T., & Cofie, O. O. (2022). *Situational analysis of a social-ecological landscape in the Ahafo Ano Southwest District of Ghana*. Research Gate.

Atta-Asamoah, A. (2014). *Transnational security challenges and statehood in Africa: A case study of drug trafficking in Ghana*. Research Gate.

AU. (2014). *Comprehensive Assessment of Drug Trafficking and Organised Crime in West and Central Africa*. AU. https://au.int/sites/default/files/documents/30220-doc-organized_crime_in_west_and_central_africa_-_july_2014_-_abridged_summary_english.pdf

Avalos, L. (2020). Reversing the Decriminalization of Sexual Violence. *Nev. LJ*, *21*, 1.

Ayres, T. (2020). *The War on Drugs and its invisible collateral damage* (A. Brisman & N. South, Eds.).

Azure, J. F. (2009). *The customs excise and preventive service and cross border crimes management: a case study of the eastern frontier of Ghana* [Doctoral dissertation, Kwame Nkrumah University of Science and Technology].

Babur, Z. (2000). Religious Nationalism, Violence and the Hindutva Movement in India. *Dialectical Anthropology*, *25*(1), 61–76. doi:10.1023/A:1007197222204

Badet, G., Damiba, L., Engueléguélé, S. B., Gaima, E., Iwuamadi, C. K., Ndiaye, S., & Williams, S. (2016). *Effectiveness of anti-corruption agencies in West Africa*. Open Society Foundations.

Bailey-Harris, R., & Harris, M. (2002). Local authorities and child protection-the mosaic of accountability. *Child and Family Law Quarterly*, *14*, 117.

Bansal, V., & Agarwal, I. (2020). Legality Of Pornographic Content Dissemination In India: A Critical Analysis. *Shimla Law Review*, *3*, 43. https://www.hpnlu.ac.in/PDF/f0fb7022-a4e6-4ddd-8485-0f01543cabf5.pdf

Baradel, M. (2020). *The puzzle of yakuza's longevity: The endurance of the yakuza and its implications for theories of organised criminality* (Doctoral dissertation, Birkbeck, University of London).

Barrett, S. D. (2010). The sustained impacts of taxi deregulation. *Economic Affairs*, *30*(1), 61–65.

Basheer, R., & Alkhatib, B. (2021). Threats from the dark: A review over dark web investigation research for cyber threat intelligence. *Journal of Computer Networks and Communications*, *2021*, 1–21.

Basuroy, T. (2022, March 15). *Total internet users in India*. Statista. https://www.statista.com/statistics/255146/number-of-internet-users-in-india/

BBC News. (2023, May 8). *Deaths raise fresh fears over cow vigilantism in India*. BBC News. https://www.bbc.com/news/world-asia-india-65229522

Beatty, D. (1994). Human rights and the rules of law. In *Human Rights and Judicial Review: A Comparative Perspective* (pp. 1–56). Brill Nijhoff.

Becker, G. (1968). Crime and Punishment: An Economic Approach. *Journal of political economy*, *76*(2), 169-217.

Bello, P. O., & Olutola, A. A. (2020). The conundrum of human trafficking in Africa. *Modern slavery and human trafficking*, 15-27.

Bennett, F. M. (1958, February). Muslim and Hindu: The Sensitive Areas. *The Atlantic*. https://www.theatlantic.com/magazine/archive/1958/02/muslim-and-hindu/305462/

Beristain, M. J. O. (2021). Impact of globalization and use of violence within Italian and Mexican criminal groups. *Sapienza Universitá di Roma. Working Paper*, (4).

Berry, M. (2020). *Organised crime in Red City: An ethnographic study of drugs, vice and violence* (Doctoral dissertation, Cardiff University).

Besley, T. (2020). State capacity, reciprocity, and the social contract. *Econometrica*, *88*(4), 1307–1335.

Bhagvan, M. (2008). Princely States and the Hindu Imaginery: Exploring the Cartography of Hindu Nationalism in Colonial India. *The Journal of Asian Studies*, *67*(3), 881–915.

Bhargava, R. (2007). The Distinctiveness of Indian Secularism. In *M.N.Srinivas, The Future of Secularism* (pp. 20–54). Oxford University Press.

Bhattacharya, S. (2023, June 14). How the Myanmar Crisis Threatens to Destabilize India's Manipur State. *The Diplomat*. https://thediplomat.com/2023/06/how-the-myanmar-crisis-threatens-to-destabilize-indias-manipur-state/

Bloom, K. (2023). Introducing the four crime cartels that have brought Eskom and South Africa to their knees. *Daily Maverick*. https://www.dailymaverick.co.za/article/2023-02-27-introducing-the-four-crime-cartels-that-have-brought-eskom-and-south-africa-to-their-knees/

Boakye, J. (2020). Enforcement of logging regulations in Ghana: Perspectives of frontline regulatory officers. *Forest Policy and Economics*, *115*, 102138. doi:10.1016/j.forpol.2020.102138

Bøås, M., & Strazzari, F. (2020). Governance, Fragility and Insurgency in the Sahel: A hybrid political order in the making. *The International Spectator*, *55*(4), 1–17.

Bonsu, P. (2011). *The effect of the distribution of illicit drugs on a transit country-a case study of Ghana* [Master's thesis, Institutt for statsvitenskap].

Bose, M. (2023). Cybercrimes against children see 32% rise in a year, NCRB report shows. *Deccan Herald*. https://www.deccanherald.com/india/cybercrimes-against-children-see-32-rise-in-a-year-ncrb-report-shows-2799597

Bose, S. (2018). *Secular States, Religious Politics India, Turkey, and the Future of Secularism*. Cambridge University Press. doi:10.1017/9781108559461

Bos, J. (2020). *Research ethics for students in the social sciences*. Springer Nature.

Bouchard, M. (2020). Collaboration and boundaries in organized crime: A network perspective. *Crime and Justice*, *49*(1), 425–469.

Boucher, D., & Kelly, P. (2003). *The social contract from Hobbes to Rawls*. Routledge.

Braithwaite, J. (2022). *Macrocriminology and freedom*. ANU Press.

Bressler, M. (2009). The Impact of Crime on Business: A Model for Prevention, Detection & Remedy. *Journal of Management and Marketing Research*, 1–13.

Breuer, A., & Leininger, J. (2021). Horizontal accountability for SDG implementation: A comparative cross-national analysis of emerging national accountability regimes. *Sustainability*, *13*(13), 7002.

Bridges, A. J., Wosnitzer, R., Scharrer, E., Sun, C., & Liberman, R. (2010). Aggression and sexual behavior in best-selling pornography videos: A content analysis update. *Violence Against Women*, *16*(10), 1065–1085. doi:10.1177/1077801210382866 PMID:20980228

Bright, D., & Whelan, C. (2020). *Organised crime and law enforcement: A network perspective*. Routledge.

Briskey, M. (2023). Organized Crime and Penury in Pakistan: The Hybrid Exploitation of the Poor and Powerless. In The Routledge Handbook of Poverty in the Global South (pp. 284-301). Routledge India.

Broadhurst, R. (2017). Cybercrime: Thieves, Swindlers, Bandits, and Privateers in Cyberspace. In The Oxford Handbook of Cyber Security. Oxford Press.

Broad, R., & Gadd, D. (2022). *Demystifying modern slavery*. Taylor & Francis.

Broude, T., & Teichman, D. (2009). Outsourcing and insourcing crime: The political economy of globalized criminal activity. *Vanderbilt Law Review*, *62*(3), 795–848.

Brown, W. N. (1964, February). *The Sanctity of the cow in Hinduism.* Retrieved from The Economic Weekly: https://www.epw.in/system/files/pdf/1964_16/5-6-7/the_sanctity_of_the_cow_in_hinduism.pdf

Brown, D. E. (2013). *The challenge of drug trafficking to democratic governance and human security in West Africa* (Vol. 8). Army War College Press.

Brown, J. D. (2002, February). Mass media influences on sexuality. *Journal of Sex Research, 39*(1), 42–45. doi:10.1080/00224490209552118 PMID:12476255

Bueger, C., & Edmunds, T. (2020). Blue crime: Conceptualising transnational organised crime at sea. *Marine Policy, 119*, 104067.

Bunt, H. V. D., & Schoot, C. V. D. (2003). Prevention of Organised Crime. A situational approach.

Burns, R. G., & Lynch, M. J. (2004). *Environmental crime: A sourcebook.* LFB Scholarly Pub LLC.

Burton, S., McGregor, M., & Laycock, G. (2020). MINICAB DRIVERS IN LONDON. Problem-Oriented Policing: Successful Case Studies.

Calderoni, F., Comunale, T., Campedelli, G. M., Marchesi, M., Manzi, D., & Frualdo, N. (2022). Organized crime groups: A systematic review of individual-level risk factors related to recruitment. *Campbell Systematic Reviews, 18*(1), e1218. doi:10.1002/cl2.1218 PMID:36913220

Campesi, G. (2020). Police accountability and human rights at the Italian borders. *Fundamental Rights Challenges in Border Controls and Expulsion of Irregular Immigrants in the European Union: Complaint Mechanisms and Access to Justice*, 125-147.

Campos, J. R., & Sánchez, C. G. (2021). Irregular Migration And Human Trafficking For The Purpose Of Sexual Exploitation: An Analysis Of Public Policy Instruments For Combating It In Chiapas, Mexico. *Young Migrants Crossing Multiple Borders to the North, 36*, 75.

Caparini, M. (2014). Human trafficking and organized crime. Trafficking in Human Beings: Learning from Asian and European Experiences (Singapore: Konrad Adenauer Stiftung, East Asian Institute, European Policy Centre, EU Centre in Singapore, 2014).

Cara, A. (2012). Investigating and combating organized crime in EU.

Carrera, S., Mitsilegas, V., & Stefan, M. (2021). Criminal justice, fundamental rights and the rule of law in the digital age. Report of a CEPS and QMUL Task Force.

Carter, D. L. (1997). *International Organised Crime: Emerging Trends in Entrepreneurial Crime.* Sage Publications.

Casas-Zamora, K. (Ed.). (2013). *Dangerous liaisons: Organized crime and political finance in Latin America and beyond.* Brookings Institution Press.

Catino, M. (2020). Italian organized crime since 1950. *Crime and Justice, 49*(1), 69–140. doi:10.1086/707319

Chawla, N. (2023). Identity and violence in Manipur, India. *JSTOR Daily*. https://daily.jstor.org/identity-and-violence-in-manipur-india/

Chernikova, L. (2012). *The role of the banking sector in the fight against money laundering: domestic and foreign experience - National interests: priorities and security*. Aspect Press.

Chigateri, S. (2010). Negotiating the 'sacred' cow: Cow slaughter and the Regulation of Difference in India. In M. Mookherjee, Democracy, Religious Pluralism and the Liberal Dilemma of Accomodation (pp. 137-159). Springer.

Chouvy, P. A. (2019). Cannabis cultivation in the world: Heritages, trends and challenges. *EchoGéo*, (48), 48. doi:10.4000/echogeo.17591

Christensen, L. S., Rayment-McHugh, S., Prenzler, T., Chiu, Y. N., & Webster, J. (2021). The theory and evidence behind law enforcement strategies that combat child sexual abuse material. *International Journal of Police Science & Management*, *23*(4), 392–405.

Chungkhoseibaite. (2016). Critical Study of Origin of Trans-National Tribes: The Kukis. *Journal Of International Academic Research for Multidisciplinary*, *4*(8). https://www.jiarm.com/Sep2016/paper28752.pdf

Cilliers, L., & Viljoen, K. (2021). A framework of ethical issues to consider when conducting internet-based research. *South African Journal of Information Management*, *23*(1), 1–9.

CITES. (n.d.). *Combating Wildlife Cybercrime*. CITES. https://cites.org/eng/prog/imp/

Citizens for Justice and Peace. (2023, March 28). *Cow vigilantism incidents continue to go unchecked in northern India*. CJP. https://cjp.org.in/cow-vigilantism-incidents-continue-to-go-unchecked-in-northern-india/

Clark, A., Fraser, A., & Hamilton-Smith, N. (2021). Networked territorialism: The routes and roots of organised crime. *Trends in Organized Crime*, *24*, 246–262.

Claveyrolas, M. (2022). Hinduism and Caste System. In S. Joddka & J. Naudet (Eds.), *The Oxford Handbook of Caste* (pp. 236–246). Oxford University Press.

Clinard, M. B., & Meier, R. F. (2011). *Sociology of Deviant Behavior* (14th ed.). Wadsworth Cengage Learning.

Cohn, B. S. (1996). *Colonialism and its forms of Knowledge: The British in India* (S. B. Ortner, N. B. Dirks, & G. Eley, Eds.). Princeton University Press.

College of Policing. (2023). Investigation introduction. https://www.college.police.uk/app/investigation/investigation-introduction

Çomak, H., Şeker, B. Ş., Civelek, Y., & Bozkuş, Ç. A. (Eds.). (2022). *Cyber Environment and International Politics* (Vol. 12). Transnational Press London.

combating_wildlife_cybercrime_draft#:~:text=Wildlife%20crime%20linked%20to%20the%20Internet%20is%20defined%20in%20the,the%20dark%20web%2C%20online%20marketplaces.

Committee reports. (n.d.). PRS Legislative Research. https://prsindia.org/policy/report-summaries/india-s-neighbourhood-first-policy

Comolli, V. (2021). Organized crime during and after the pandemic. In *Global Security in Times of Covid-19: Brave New World?* (pp. 245–271). Springer International Publishing.

Comolli, V. (Ed.). (2018). *Organized crime and illicit trade: How to respond to this strategic challenge in old and new domains*. Springer.

Coomber, R., Donnermeyer, J. F., McElrath, K., & Scott, J. (2014). Key concepts in crime and society. *Sage (Atlanta, Ga.)*.

Cooper, J. M., Aarhaug, J., & Scott, J. (2023). *Taxi, Limousine, and Transport Network Company Regulation: Recurring Challenges*. Taylor & Francis.

Copson, L. (2018). Beyond 'Criminology vs. Zemiology': Reconciling crime with social harm. In Zemiology: reconnecting crime and social harm (pp. 33–56). Palgrave Macmillan.

Cornish, D. B., & Clarke, R. V. (2003). Opportunities, precipitators and criminal decisions: A reply to Wortley's critique of situational crime prevention. *Crime Prevention Studies*, *16*, 41–96.

Correspondent, H. (2016, February 27). Block porn sites showing child pornography: SC | Latest News India. *Hindustan Times*. https://www.hindustantimes.com/india/tough-to-block-porn-sites-but-act-on-those-involving-children-sc/story-903nujBIFjtrrvSmqGPCbN.html

Corwin, J. (2009). *100 Heartbeats: The race to save Earth's most endangered species*. Rodale Inc.

Coutinho, J. A., Diviák, T., Bright, D., & Koskinen, J. (2020). Multilevel determinants of collaboration between organised criminal groups. *Social Networks*, *63*, 56–69.

Crow, M. S., Shelley, T. O. C., & Stretesky, P. B. (2013). Camouflage-collar crime: An examination of wildlife crime and characteristics of offenders in Florida. *Deviant Behavior*, *34*(8), 635–652. doi:10.1080/01639625.2012.759049

Currie, R. J., & Douglas, S. (2021). Human rights and transnational organized crime. In *Routledge handbook of transnational organized crime* (pp. 388–408). Routledge.

D'Andria, D. (2011). Investment strategies of criminal organisations. *Policy Studies*, *32*(1), 1–19. doi:10.1080/01442872.2010.520558

Daily Statesman. (2023). Criminal gold syndicate busted over $2.7m deal. *Daily Statesman*. https://dailystatesman.com.gh/criminal-gold-syndicate-busted-over-2-7m-deal/

Damojipurapu, M. (2023). Patterns and Risks in Contemporary Religion Based Hate Speech in India. In M. Bergsmo, & K. Manocha, Religion, Hateful Expression and Violence (pp. 209-274). Brussels, Belgium: Torkel Opsahl Academic EPublisher.

Danielsson, A. (2023). Tackling Digital Entrepreneurship Within the Illicit Economy: The Evolving Fight Against Serious and Organized Crime Within a Digitally Facilitated Sex Industry. In Digital Entrepreneurship and Co-Creating Value Through Digital Encounters (pp. 118-144). IGI Global.

Danielsson, A. (2023). Tackling Digital Entrepreneurship Within the Illicit Economy: The Evolving Fight Against Serious and Organized Crime Within a Digitally Facilitated Sex Industry. In Digital Entrepreneurship and Co-Creating Value Through Digital Encounters (pp. 118-144). IGI Global.

Darcy, S. (2022). International Law and Collaboration: A Tentative Embrace. *Collaboration in Authoritarian and Armed Conflict Settings*, *248*, 244–267.

Dartford Borough Council. (2020). Modern Anti-Slavery and Human Trafficking Statement 2020-21.

Das, K. K. (2005). *Political and economic history of the Kukis of Manipur*. Shodhganga. https://shodhganga.inflibnet.ac.in/handle/10603/103911

Davies, J., Malik, H. M., Jokinen, A., & Haapasaari, S. (2023). Private and public co-operation in preventing and addressing corporate crime: The case of labour trafficking in the Finnish construction industry. *Crime, Law, and Social Change*, •••, 1–19.

Davies, L., Powling, L., & Symmonds, J. (2024). Assessing and Managing the Risk of Organised Crime, Human Trafficking and Modern Slavery. In *Managing Clinical Risk* (pp. 341–378). Routledge.

de Santisteban, P., del Hoyo, J., Alcázar-Córcoles, M. Á., & Gámez-Guadix, M. (2018). Progression, maintenance, and feedback of online child sexual grooming: A qualitative analysis of online predators. *Child Abuse & Neglect*, *80*, 203–215. doi:10.1016/j.chiabu.2018.03.026 PMID:29625326

De Schutter, A., & Duquet, N. (2023). The nexus between drug markets and gun violence in the European Union.

De Sousa, A., & De Sousa (2023) R. Ethics in Child Sexual Abuse Research, Global Bioethics Enquiry; 11(2)

Deakin, S. (2018). Organisational torts: Vicarious liability versus non-delegable duty. *The Cambridge Law Journal*, *77*(1), 15–18.

Degani, P., & De Stefani, P. (2020). Addressing Migrant Women's Intersecting Vulnerabilities. Refugee Protection, Anti-trafficking and Anti-violence Referral Patterns in Italy. *Peace Human Rights Governance, 4*(Peace Human Rights Governance 4/1), 113-152.

Deka, K. (2023, May 6). Poppy cultivation, eviction drives, illegal influx, old scars—why Manipur is burning. *India Today*. https://www.indiatoday.in/india-today-insight/story/poppy-cultivation-eviction-drives-illegal-influx-old-scars-why-manipur-is-burning-2369831-2023-05-05

den Boer, E. V. (2021). Countering Criminal Facilitation Through Public–Private Cooperation in The Netherlands. *International Security Management: New Solutions to Complexity*, 463-476.

Department for Transport. (2019). Taxi and Private Hire Vehicle Licensing: Protecting Users.

Department for Transport. (2022). Taxi and Private Hire Vehicle Licensing Best Practice Guidance for Licensing Authorities in England

Department for Transport. (2022, November 25). Statutory taxi and private hire vehicle standards. GOV.UK. https://www.gov.uk/government/publications/statutory-taxi-and-private-hire-vehicle-standards/statutory-taxi-and-private-hire-vehicle-standards

Department of Animal Husbandry and Dairying. (n.d.). *ANNEX II (6) Views of Mahatma Gandhi on Cow protection.* Department of Animal Husbandry and Dairying, Ministry of Fisheries, Animal Husbandry and Dairying, Government of India. https://dahd.nic.in/hi/related-links/annex-ii-6-views-mahatma-gandhi-cow-protection#:~:text=Cow%20protection%20to%20me%20is,identity%20with%20all%20that%20lives

Depuru, S. S. S. R., Wang, L., Devabhaktuni, V., & Gudi, N. (2010). Measures and setbacks for controlling electricity theft. *Proc. IEEE North American Power Symposium*, Arlington, TX. 10.1109/NAPS.2010.5619966

Deuchar, R., McLeanand, R., & Holligan, C. (2021). Framing and Re-Framing the Experiences of Youth in Disadvantaged Scottish Communities. In Gangs, Drugs and Youth Adversity (pp. 129-146). Bristol University Press.

Di Maggio, U., & Lo Verde, F. M. (2023). Organized Crime as Global Social Problem. In *The Palgrave Handbook of Global Social Problems* (pp. 1–24). Springer International Publishing.

Di Nicola, A. (2022). Towards digital organized crime and digital sociology of organized crime. *Trends in Organized Crime*, •••, 1–20.

Dinganglung Gangmei Vs. Mutum Churamani Meetei & Ors. [Special Leave Petition (Civil) Diary No. 19206 of 2023]

Dobovšek, B. (2012). *Korupcija v tranziciji.* Ljubljana, Slovenia: Fakulteta za varnostne vede.

Doig, A., & Sproat, P. A. (2020). Local responses to a national initiative on organised crime and local government procurement fraud. *Journal of Financial Crime*, *27*(1), 78–91.

Donnelly, J., & Whelan, D. J. (2020). *International human rights*. Routledge.

Dowling, N. (2014). *The Impact of Gambling Problems on Families.* Australian Gambling Research Centre. https://core.ac.uk/download/pdf/30673225.pdf

Drejer, C., Riegler, M. A., Halvorsen, P., Johnson, M. S., & Baugerud, G. A. (2024). Livestreaming Technology and Online Child Sexual Exploitation and Abuse: A Scoping Review. *Trauma, Violence, \&. Trauma, Violence & Abuse*, *25*(1), 260–274. doi:10.1177/15248380221147564 PMID:36727734

Duho, K. C. T., Abankwah, S. A., Mugo, G. K., Atampuri, M., Duho, V. S., & Adjei-Mensah, P. (2022). Impact of Covid-19 on Organised Crime in Ghana and Insights for a Post-Pandemic Context. *Dataking Policy Brief, 9.*

Duijn, P. A., Kashirin, V., & Sloot, P. M. (2014). The relative ineffectiveness of criminal network disruption. *Scientific Reports*, *4*(1), 4238. doi:10.1038/srep04238 PMID:24577374

Dukku, A., & Yunusa, A. (2022). Trafficking of Illicit Drugs in the West African Region: Factors, Implications and Solutions. *Gusau Journal of Sociology, 3*(2).

Dumba, S. (2017). Informal public transport driver behaviour and regulatory policy linkage: An expose. *Journal of Transport and Supply Chain Management*, *11*(1), 1–16.

Dyzenhaus, D. (1992). John Stuart Mill and the Harm of Pornography. *Ethics*, *102*(3), 534–551. doi:10.1086/293423

Dziwornu, M. G. (2021). Crime drop in Ghana? Some insights from crime patterns and trends. *Crime Prevention and Community Safety*, *23*(4), 433–449. doi:10.1057/s41300-021-00130-0

Edwards, A. (2007). Traffic in human beings: At the intersection of criminal justice, human rights, asylum/migration and labor. *Denv. J. Int'l L. & Pol'y*, *36*, 9.

Ehe, R. (2020). The role of Open Source Intelligence in the Fight against Transnational Organized Crime-A European Perspective.

Eisapareh, K., Nazari, M., Kaveh, M. H., Cousins, R., & Mokarami, H. (2023). Effects of an educational intervention program based on the PRECEDE–PROCEED model for anger management and driving performance of urban taxi drivers: A comparison of traditional and online methods. *Safety Science*, *157*, 105933.

Eisenberg, M. R. (1987). The Vicarious Liability of Governmental Entities: Judicial and Legislative Attempts to Reduce Accountability for Tortious Acts. *Ann. Surv. Am.*, *L*, 637.

El Ghamari, M., & Gabriela Bartoszewicz, M. (2020). (Un) sustainable development of minors in Libyan refugee camps in the context of conflict-induced migration. *Sustainability*, *12*(11), 4537.

Elhaw, A. E. M., & Rabee, I. (2024). From Slavery to Modern Slavery, Trafficking in Human Beings (Challenges and Solutions) At the Regional and International Level. *Migration Letters : An International Journal of Migration Studies*, *21*(S1), 271–300.

Elliott, L. (2022). Transnational environmental crime and development. In *The Routledge Handbook of Global Development* (pp. 233–244). Routledge.

Ellis, S. (2016). *This present darkness: A history of Nigerian organized crime*. Oxford University Press.

Enact Observer. (n.d.). *Organised crime is infecting African and global supply chains*. Enact Observer. https://enactafrica.org/enact-observer/organised-crime-is-infecting-african-and-global-supply-chains on 16/01/2024

Encyclopedia Britannica. (2017). *Anomie | sociology*. Encyclopædia Britannica. https://www.britannica.com/topic/anomie

Ending Online Child Sexual Exploitation and Abuse. (2021). UNICEF. www.unicef.org

England, A. (2022). Financial crimes watchdog puts UAE on 'grey list. *The Financial Times*.

Ennin, D., & Mensah, R. O. (2019). Cybercrime in Ghana and the Reaction of the Law. *JL Pol'y & Globalization*, *84*, 36.

EPW. (2014, October 31) Nationalism, ideology and consensual democracy *Economic and Political Weekly* https://www.epw.in/journal/2014/43-44/notes/nationalism-ideology-and-consensual-democracy.html

EPW. (2014, October 31). Nationalism, ideology and consensual democracy. *Economic and Political Weekly.* https://www.epw.in/journal/2014/43-44/notes/nationalism-ideology-and-consensual-democracy.html

European Bank Authority. (2014). *Annual Report*. EBA. doi:10.2853/34273

European Commission, Communication from the Commission to the European Parliament, the Council, the EESC and the Committee of the Regions on the EU Strategy to tackle Organised Crime 2021-2025, COM(2021) 170 final

Europol. (2017). *Defining Serious and Organised Crime*. SOCTA 2017. https://www.europol.europa.eu/socta/2017/defining-serious-and-organised-crime.html

Europol. (2018). *Internet Organised Crime*. Europol. doi:10.2813/858843

Express News Service. (2022, May 6). Child pornography content: Pimpri Chinchwad police file cases against 7 internet users. *The Indian Express*. https://indianexpress.com/article/cities/pune/child-pornography-content-pimpri-chinchwad-police-file-cases-against-7-internet-users-7902290/

Extra Judicial Execution Victim Families Association (EEVFAM) and Another. v. Union of India and Another Writ Petition (Criminal) No.129 of 2012

F.B.I. (2012). *About the NIBRS*. U.S. Department of Justice-Federal Burearu of Investigation. https://ucr.fbi.gov/nibrs/2012/resources/about-the-nibrs

Farooq, G. (2022). Old Conflicts in New Media Assemblages: India's Cow Vigilantism and YouTube. *Asiascape: Digital Asia*, *9*(1-2), 47–70. doi:10.1163/22142312-bja10027

FATF. (1996). *VII Annual Report (1995-1996).* NPLG. http://www.nplg.gov.ge/dlibrary/collect/0002/000828/Dis.Shashiashvili%20G.pdf

Fauna & Flora International (2021). *Using situational crime prevention to address illegal wildlife trade: A toolkit*. Flora & Fauna International.

Fazely, A. (2020). *Identity crimes in the UK: An examination of the strategies employed by front-line practitioners in the public and private sector to detect, prevent and mitigate against this crime* (Doctoral dissertation, Middlesex University).

Federal Bureau of Investigation (FBI). (2014). *Reports and publications*. FBI. https://www.fbi.gov/stats-services/publications

Felbab-Brown (2017). The extinction market: Wildlife trafficking and how to counter it. Oxford University Press.

Felbab-Brown, V. (2017). *The Extinction Market: Wildlife trafficking and how to counter it.* Oxford University Press.

Finckenauer, J. O. (2005). Problems of definition: What is organized crime? *Trends in Organized Crime*, *8*(3), 63–83. doi:10.1007/s12117-005-1038-4

Finklea, K. M. (2011, July). The interplay of borders, turf, cyberspace, and jurisdiction: Issues confronting US law enforcement. Congressional Research Service, Library of Congress.

First Information of Cognizable Crime Report under Section 154 Criminal Procedure Code at Police Station. (2023). Manipurpolice. https://www.manipurpolice.gov.in/wp-content/uploads/2023/10/FIR-NO.-60872023-IMPHAL-PS.pdf

Frangež, D., Klancnik, A. T., Karer, M., Ludvigsen, B.-E., Kończyk, J., Perez, F. R., Veijalainen, M., & Lewin, M. (2015). The importance of terminology related to child sexual exploitation. *Revija za Kriminalistiko in Kriminologijo*, *66*, 291–299.

Fraser, A., & Van Hellemont, E. (2020). Gangs and globalization. In Oxford Research Encyclopedia of Criminology and Criminal Justice.

Freitag, S. B. (1990). *Collective Action and Community: Public Arena and the Emergence of Communalism in North India*. Oxford University Press.

Fuller, R. C. (1942). Morals and the Criminal Law. *Journal of Criminal Law and Criminology (1931-1951)*, *32*(6), 624. doi:10.2307/1136815

Gallagher, A. T. (2015). Exploitation in migration: Unacceptable but inevitable. *Journal of International Affairs*, *68*(2), 55.

Gallen, J., & Mhuirthile, T. N. (Eds.). (2021). *Law, Responsibility and Vulnerability: State Accountability and Responsiveness*. Routledge.

Gambetta, D., & Hamill, H. (2005). *Streetwise: How taxi drivers establish customer's trustworthiness*. Russell Sage Foundation.

Garg, L. (2016, October 15). *Examining the Constituent Assembly Debates on Cow Protection*. The Wire. https://thewire.in/law/unveiling-indias-long-history-of-hypocrisy-on-cow-slaughter-laws

George, S., Fenn, J., & Robonderdeep, K. (2020). An Overview of Gambling in India. *Global Journal of Medical, Pharmaceutical, and Biomedical Update*, *15*(4), 4. doi:10.25259/GJMPBU_7_2020

Ghana Police Service. (n.d.). *Anti-Human Trafficking Unit*. Ghana Police Service. https://www.police.gov.gh/anti-human-trafficking-unit---ahtu.html on 29/12/2023.

Ghana Police Service. (n.d.). *drug law enforcement unit – narcotics*. Ghana Police Service. https://police.gov.gh/en/index.php/drug-law-enforcement-unit-narcotics/#:~:text=The%20Narcotics%20Unit%20is%20a,of%20the%20Ghana%20Police%20Service

Ghanaian Times. (2021). Ghana loses $19.8m through fraudulent activities. *Ghanaian Times.* https://www.ghanaiantimes.com.gh/ghana-loses-19-8m-through-fraudulent-activities/

Ghanaian Times. (2023). Prosecute persons culpable of embezzling COVID-19 funds – SEND Ghana. *Ghanaian Times.* https://www.ghanaiantimes.com.gh/prosecute-persons-culpable-of-embezzling-covid-19-funds-send-ghana/

Ghanaweb. (2022). *Abuga Pele speaks about jail time and how he was denied opportunity to confront accusers.* Ghanaweb. https://www.ghanaweb.com/GhanaHomePage/NewsArchive/Abuga-Pele-speaks-about-jail-time-and-how-he-was-denied-opportunity-to-confront-accusers-1587737 on 05/01/2024

Ghanaweb. (2023). Police arrest 12 members of organised crime syndicate involved in carjacking, robbery and murder. *GhanaWeb.* https://www.ghanaweb.com/GhanaHomePage/NewsArchive/Police-arrest-12-members-of-organised-crime-syndicate-involved-in-carjacking-robbery-and-murder-1706498 on 07/01/2024

Global Organised Crime Index. (2023). *Ghana*. GOCI. https://ocindex.net/country/ghana on 28/12/2023

Goga, K. (2014). *Responses to organized crime in a democratic South Africa*. Institute for Security Studies.

Goldstein, H. (1990). *Excellence in problem-oriented policing*. In New York NY: Police Executive Research Forum.

Goldstein, R., Sances, M. W., & You, H. Y. (2020). Exploitative revenues, law enforcement, and the quality of government service. *Urban Affairs Review*, *56*(1), 5–31.

Gore, M. L., Hilend, R., Prell, J. O., Griffin, E., Macdonald, J. R., Keskin, B. B., Ferber, A., & Dilkina, B. (2023). A data directory to facilitate investigations on worldwide wildlife trafficking. *Big Earth Data*, *7*(2), 1–11. doi:10.1080/20964471.2023.2193281

Government of India constitutes Peace Committee in Manipur under the Chairpersonship of Governor, Manipur. (n.d.). PIB. https://pib.gov.in/PressReleasePage.aspx?PRID=1931248

Government of India. (2015, December 9). Ministry of Home Affairs. Rajya Sabha. Unstarred Question No. 1198. https://sansad.in/getFile/annex/237/Au1198.pdf?source=pqars

Gowen, A. (2018, September 3). 'We Don't Have Any Fear': India's Angry Young Men and Its Lynch Mob Crisis. *Washington Post*. https://www. washingtonpost. com /world /asia pacific / we -dont -have -. . . - a0aa -11e8 -a3dd -2a1991f075d5 story. html? utm term =. 6a0084f604cd

Graphic Online. (2018). NACOB sets wee and khat worth GH¢600,000 on fire. *Graphic*. https://www.graphic.com.gh/news/general-news/nacob-partners-destroy-seized-narcotics.html

Green, J. (2021). Closing the accountability gap in corporate supply chains for violations of the Trafficking Victims Protection Act. *Business and Human Rights Journal*, *6*(3), 449–489.

Greyling, D. (2023). Transnet cable theft disaster. *Daily Investor.* https://dailyinvestor.com/south-africa/33912/transnet-cable-theft-disaster/

Gross, H. (2012). Crime, Harm, and Moral Wrong. In *Crime and Punishment: A Concise Moral Critique*. Academic. doi:10.1093/acprof:oso/9780199644711.003.0007

Guercke, L. (2021). State Responsibility for a Failure to Prevent Violations of the Right to Life by Organised Criminal Groups: Disappearances in Mexico. *Human Rights Law Review*, *21*(2), 329–357.

Guire, Mc. J., Reeves, P., & Brasted, H. (1996). Politics of Violence: From Ayodhya to Behrampada. New Delhi: Sage.

Guite, J., & Haokip, T. (2018). The Anglo-Kuki War, 1917–1919. *The Anglo-Kuki War, 1917–1919*. doi:10.4324/9780429431098

Haas, T. C., & Ferreira, S. M. (2016). Combating rhino horn trafficking: The need to disrupt criminal networks. *PLoS One*, *11*(11), e0167040. doi:10.1371/journal.pone.0167040 PMID:27870917

Hald, G. M., & Malamuth, N. M. (2014, April). Experimental Effects of Exposure to Pornography: The Moderating Effect of Personality and Mediating Effect of Sexual Arousal. *Archives of Sexual Behavior*, *44*(1), 99–109. doi:10.1007/s10508-014-0291-5 PMID:24729134

Hamer, R. (2022). Travelling though trauma: voices in partnership, 2020-2022-service evaluation.

Hampshire Safeguarding Children Partnership. (2020). HIPS Child Exploitation Strategy.

Hansen, T. B. (1999). *The Saffron Wave: Democracy and Hindu Nationalism in Modern India*. Princeton University Press. doi:10.1515/9781400823055

Haokip, T. (2020, November 30). *Anachronistic 'War on Drugs.'* https://papers.ssrn.com/sol3/papers.cfm?abstract_id=3739915

Hardouin, P. (2009). Banks governance and public-private partnership in preventing and confronting organized crime, corruption and terrorism financing. *Journal of Financial Crime*, *16*(3), 199–209.

Harré, T. (2022). Human traffickers' fair trial rights and transnational criminal law. *Anti-trafficking review*, (18), 159-173.

Harris, M. (1977). *Cannibals and Kings: The Origins of Cultures*. Vintage Books, a division of Random House, Inc.

Hart. (2010). Criminal infiltration of financial institutions: a penetration test case study – *Journal of Money Laundering Control, 13*(1).

Hasan, Z. K. (1982, February). Communalism and Communal Violence in India. *Social Scientist (New Delhi), 10*(2), 25–39. doi:10.2307/3516974

Hausing, K. K. S. (2009). *"Hills-valley divide as a site of conflict: Emerging dialogic space in Manipur," in Sanjib Baruah (ed.), Beyond counter-insurgency: Breaking the impasse in Northeast India (New Delhi: Oxford University Press, 2009), pp.263-89.* https://www.academia.edu/657205/_Hills_valley_divide_as_a_site_of_conflict_Emerging_dialogic_space_in_Manipur_in_Sanjib_Baruah_ed_Beyond_counter_insurgency_Breaking_the_impasse_in_Northeast_India_New_Delhi_Oxford_University_Press_2009_pp_263_89

Heerdt, D. (2021). *Blurred lines of responsibility and accountability: Human rights abuses at mega-sporting events*. Intersentia.

Hertfordhire Modern Slavery Partnership. (2022, October 28). Training and resources. Hertfordshire Modern Slavery Partnership. https://www.stopexploitationherts.org.uk/index.php/training-and-resources/

Herzog, S. (2005). The Relationship between Economic Hardship and Crime: The case of Israel and the Palestinians. *Sociological Perspectives*, *48*(2), 189–211. doi:10.1525/sop.2005.48.2.189

Higgins, K. C. (2022). *Realness, wrongness, justice exploring criminalization as a mediated politics of vulnerability* (Doctoral dissertation, London School of Economics and Political Science).

Hignett, K. (2021). Transnational organized crime and the global village. In *Routledge handbook of transnational organized crime* (pp. 305–317). Routledge.

Hills, A. (2000). *Policing Africa: internal security and the limits of liberalization*. Lynne Rienner Publishers.

Hingston, C. A., & Hingston, D. (2023). Human Trafficking: A Dark Side of the Cyberspace. In *Cybercrime and Challenges in South Africa* (pp. 177–192). Springer Nature Singapore.

Hirsch Ballin, E. (2022). Trust Beyond Borders: Selected Papers on the Significance of Human Rights and the Rule of Law.

Hobbs, S. (2023). From chains to chainsaws: Modern slavery and deforestation in the Brazilian Amazon. *Nature and Space,* 1-28.

Hodal, K. (2019). Illegal fishing by foreign trawlers costs Ghana $50m a year, researchers say. *The Guardian.* https://www.theguardian.com/environment/2019/jun/17/illegal-fishing-by-foreign-trawlers-costs-ghana-50-million-dollars-a-year-researchers-say on 18/01/2024

Hoggett, J., Redford, P., Toher, D., & White, P. (2019). Challenges for Police Leadership: Identity, Experience, Legitimacy, and Direct Entry. *Journal of Police and Criminal Psychology*, *34*(2), 145–155. doi:10.1007/s11896-018-9264-2

Home | Government of India. (n.d.). https://censusindia.gov.in/census.website/

Home Office. (March 2016). Modern Crime Prevention Strategy.

Hübschle, A. (2014). Of bogus hunters, queenpins and mules: The varied roles of women in transnational organized crime in Southern Africa. *Trends in Organized Crime*, *17*(1-2), 31–51. doi:10.1007/s12117-013-9202-8

Hughes, D. (2020). Differentiating the Corporation: Accountability and International Humanitarian Law. *Mich. J. Int'l L.*, *42*, 47.

Human Rights Watch. (2019, February 18). *Violent Cow Protection in India Vigilante Groups Attack Minorities*. Human Rights Watch. https://www.hrw.org/report/2019/02/19/violent-cow-protection-india/vigilante-groups-attack-minorities

Ibanga, D. A. (2017). *Patterns, trends, and issues of illicit wildlife hunting and trade: Analysis based on African environmental ethics*.

Ikejemba, E., & Schuur, P. (2018). Analyzing the impact of theft and vandalism in relation to the sustainability of renewable energy projects in Sub-Saharan Africa. *Sustainability (Basel)*, *10*(3), 814. doi:10.3390/su10030814

Immigration and Refugee Board of Canada. (2023, August 31). *National Documentation Packages*. IRB. https://irb.gc.ca/en/country-information/ndp/Pages/index.aspx?pid=12048

India-Myanmar - Bilateral Brief. (2020, May). MEA.

Institute of Licencing. (2018). Guidance on determining the suitability of applicants and licensees in the hackney and private hire trades.

Interagency Working Group. (2017). Annual Report. In International Centre For Missing and Exploited Children. IWG.

International Centre For Missing & Exploited Children. (2017). In Bulletin of the Marx Memorial Library (Vol. 133, Issue 1). doi:10.3828/bbml.2001.133.4

International Narcotics Control Board. (2014). *Report of the International Narcotics Control Board for 2013*. United Nations. https://www.incb.org/documents/Publications/AnnualReports/AR2013/English/AR_2013_E.pdf

Interpol. (2017). Annual Report 2017. In *INTERPOL* (*Vol. 5*). doi:10.7557/cage.6834

INTERPOL. (2022). *Stepping up the global fight against wildlife crime through a united response*. INTERPOL. https://www.interpol.int/en/News-and-Events/News/2022/Stepping-up-the-global-fight-against-wildlife-crime-through-a-united-response

IOL. (2022). *Illegal electricity connections and a spike in vandalism of electricity infrastructure in recent months across the city and the province is costing millions of rand*. IOL. https://www.iol.co.za/capeargus/news/vandalism-of-electricity-infrastructure-and-illegal-connections-costing-millions-of-rand-352c2318-03a3-4d53-8360-51cff7296a90

Ishikawa, T., & Kryvoi, Y. (Eds.). (2023). *Public and Private Governance of Cybersecurity: Challenges and Potential*. Cambridge University Press.

Islam, F. (2023). Human Trafficking Law Enforcement Over the Victims and Offenders: The Perspective of Anti-Trafficking Stakeholders. *Victims & Offenders*, 1–29.

IUCN. (2020). *"Operation Atacama", the recovery of trafficked threatened cacti*. International Union for Conservation of Nature. https://www.iucn.org/news/species-survival-commission/202012/operacion-atacama-recovery-trafficked-threatened-cacti

Jacob, C., & Kamath, M. (2023, March 9). 'Kill Two Million of Them': Institutionalised Hate Speech, Impunity and 21st Century Atrocities in India. *Global Responsibility to Protect*, *15*(2-3), 209–245. doi:10.1163/1875984X-20230002

Jacobs, M. H., Vaske, J. J., & Sijtsma, M. T. (2014). Predictive potential of wildlife value orientations for acceptability of management interventions. *Journal for Nature Conservation*, *22*(4), 377–383. doi:10.1016/j.jnc.2014.03.005

Jafferlot, C. (1998). *The Hindu Nationalist Movement in India.* New York: Columbia University Press.

Jafferlot, C. (2007). Hindu Nationalism: A Reader. Oxforsdshire: Princeton University Press. doi:10.1515/9781400828036

Jafferlot, C. (2019, April 4). *The Fate of Secularism in India*. Carnegie Endowment for International Peace. https://carnegieendowment.org/2019/04/04/fate-of-secularism-in-india-pub-78689

Jafferlot, C. (2021). *Modi's India Hindu Nationalism and the Rise of an Ethnic Democracy.* Princeton University Press.

Jain, B. (2023, May 17). Manipur official: No tribal bias in evictions or in war on drugs. *The Times of India.* https://timesofindia.indiatimes.com/india/manipur-official-no-tribal-bias-in-evictions-or-in-war-on-drugs/articleshow/100291179.cms?from=mdr

Jairath, V. K. (2005, September-December). Studying Communal Rights in India: Some Methodological Issues. *Sociological Bulletin*, *54*(3), 443–462. doi:10.1177/0038022920050309

Jakubiec, W., & Kuliński, M. (2023). The phenomenon of economic crime: Threats and contemporary trends. *Scientific Journal of Bielsko-Biala School of Finance and Law*, *27*(3), 55–58.

Janenova, S., & Knox, C. (2020). Combatting corruption in Kazakhstan: A role for ethics commissioners? *Public Administration and Development*, *40*(3), 186–195.

Jay, A. Independent Inquiry into Child Sexual Exploitation in Rotherham 1997–2013 (Rotherham

Jazeera, A. (2023, August 9). Why ethnic violence in India's Manipur has been going on for three months. *Al Jazeera.* https://www.aljazeera.com/news/2023/8/9/why-ethnic-violence-in-indias-manipur-has-been-going-on-for-three-months

Jenkins, J. P. (2019). *Pornography | sociology*. Encyclopædia Britannica. https://www.britannica.com/topic/pornography

Jha, D. (2009). *The Myth of the Holy Cow.* Navayana Publishing.

John, R. M., Sinha, P., Munish, V. G., & Tullu, F. T. (2021). Economic Costs of Diseases and Deaths Attributable to Tobacco Use in India, 2017-2018. *Nicotine & Tobacco Research: Official Journal of the Society for Research on Nicotine and Tobacco*, *23*(2), 294–301. doi:10.1093/ntr/ntaa154 PMID:32805055

Johnston, L. (1996). What is Vigilantism. *British Journal of Criminology*, *36*(2), 220–236. doi:10.1093/oxfordjournals.bjc.a014083

Jonathan, O. E., Olusola, A. J., Bernadin, T. C. A., & Inoussa, T. M. (2021). Impacts of crime on socio-economic development. *Mediterranean Journal of Social Sciences*, *12*(5), 71. doi:10.36941/mjss-2021-0045

Jones, J. (2020). Is It Time to Open a Conversation About a New United Nations Treaty to Fight Human Trafficking That Focuses on Victim Protection and Human Rights? The Palgrave International Handbook of Human Trafficking, 1803-1818.

Jones, N. P., Chindea, I. A., Argomedo, D. W., & Sullivan, J. P. (2022). A Social Network Analysis of Mexico's Dark Network Alliance Structure. *Journal of Strategic Security*, *15*(4), 76–105. doi:10.5038/1944-0472.15.4.2046

Joshi, N. R., & Phillips, R. W. (1953). *Zebu Cattle of India and Pakistan: A FAO Study*. Food and Agriculture Organization of the United Nations.

Kahler, J. S., Reynald, D. M., & Gore, M. L. (2023). "I let it go:" Quantifying residential guardianship intentions when witnessing wildlife poaching. *Biological Conservation*, *277*, 109829. doi:10.1016/j.biocon.2022.109829

Kannan, S. (2020, April 11). Pornography gets a pandemic boost, India reports 95 per cent rise in viewing. *India Today*. https://www.indiatoday.in/news-analysis/story/pornography-gets-a-pandemic-boost-india-reports-95-per-cent-rise-in-viewing-1665940-2020-04-11

Kansanga, M. M., Dinko, D. H., Nyantakyi-Frimpong, H., Arku, G., & Luginaah, I. (2021). Scalar politics and black markets: The political ecology of illegal rosewood logging in Ghana. *Geoforum*, *119*, 83–93. doi:10.1016/j.geoforum.2020.12.020

Kar, D., & Spanjers, J. (2017). Transnational crime and the developing world. *Global Financial Integrity*, 53-59.

Karenga, P. V. S. (2022). International Human Rights Laws and Trafficking in Persons. In *A West African Model to Address Human Trafficking* (pp. 199–210). Springer International Publishing.

Karenga, P. V. S. (2022). States' Obligations Under International Human Rights Law. In *A West African Model to Address Human Trafficking* (pp. 227–249). Springer International Publishing.

Kataria, G., & Gautam, M. (2022). Exploring Complex Dynamics Of Narcoterrorism And Its Impact On Human Rights In Indian Context. *Journal of Pharmaceutical Negative Results*, 4729–4740.

Kayode-Ajala, O. (2023). Applications of Cyber Threat Intelligence (CTI) in financial institutions and challenges in its adoption. *Applied Research in Artificial Intelligence and Cloud Computing*, *6*(8), 1–21.

Kemp, S. (2022, February 15). *Digital 2022: India — DataReportal – Global Digital Insights*. DataReportal. https://datareportal.com/reports/digital-2022-india

Kennedy, M. (2016). F*ake U.S. Embassy In Ghana Operated For A Decade, State Department Says*. NPR. https://www.npr.org/sections/thetwo-way/2016/12/05/504426012/state-department-says-fake-u-s-embassy-in-ghana-operated-for-a-decade on 05/01/2024

Kennert, M., & Eligh, J. (2019). *A militarized political weapon: The Philippines' war on drugs*. GI-TOC.

Kepuladze, N., & Sulamanidze, R. (2015). *Legalization of illegal income – money laundering*. NPLG. http://www.nplg.gov.ge/dlibrary/collect/0002/000828/Dis.Shashiashvili%20G.pdf

Kerner, X., & Dax, E. (1996). Money laundering. Guide to Current Legislation and Legal Practice. *International Relations*.

Keskin, B. B., Griffin, E. C., Prell, J. O., Dilkina, B., Ferber, A., MacDonald, J., & Gore, M. L. (2022). Quantitative investigation of wildlife trafficking supply chains: A review. *Omega*, 102780.

Khanna, V. (2017). The Holy Cow: Unravelling the Mystery of its Holiness. *Millenial Asia*, 217-233.

Killingray, D. (1986). The maintenance of law and order in British colonial Africa. *African Affairs*, *85*(340), 411–437. doi:10.1093/oxfordjournals.afraf.a097799

Kipgen, N. (2017). Land laws, ownership and tribal identity: the Manipur Experience. In Springer eBooks (pp. 111–126). doi:10.1007/978-981-10-5215-6_9

Kipgen, N., & Chowdhury, A. R. (2016). 'Contested state-craft' on the frontiers of the Indian nation: 'Hills Valley Divide' and the genealogy of Kuki ethnic nationalism in Manipur. *Studies in Ethnicity and Nationalism*, *16*(2), 283–303. doi:10.1111/sena.12184

Kiselev, I. (2009). *Dirty Money*. Jurisprudence.

Korom, F. J. (2000). Holy Cow! The Apotheosis of Zebu, or Why the Cow Is Sacred in Hinduism. *Asian Folklore Studies*, *59*(2), 181–203. doi:10.2307/1178915

Korystin, O. Y., Mihus, I. P., Svyrydiuk, N. P., Likhovitskyy, Y. O., & Mitina, O. M. (2020). Money laundering: macroeconomic assessment methods and current trend in Ukraine.

Kryszajtys, D. T., Hahmann, T. E., Schuler, A., Hamilton-Wright, S., Ziegler, C. P., & Matheson, F. I. (2018). Problem Gambling and Delinquent Behaviours Among Adolescents: A Scoping Review. *Journal of Gambling Studies*, *34*(3), 893–914. doi:10.1007/s10899-018-9754-2 PMID:29470759

Kuchalskis, K. (2020). Organised Crime: New Challenges and Response. *Eur. L. Enf't Rsch. Bull.*, *19*, 95.

Kumah, R. K. (2022). *Determinants and Implications of Chinese Involvement in Informal Artisanal and Small-scale Gold Mining in Ghana: Perspectives from the Grassroots* [Doctoral dissertation, Queen's University (Canada)].

Kumar Das, S. & East West Center Washington. (2007). Understanding Identity and Governance Crisis in Manipur. *Policy Studies*.

Kumar Sharma, S. & Vivekananda International Foundation. (2016). *Ethnic Conflict and Harmonization: A Study of Manipur*. Vif India. https://www.vifindia.org/

Kumar, S. (2022). The Deep Web and Children Cyber Exploitation. In *Research Anthology on Child and Domestic Abuse and Its Prevention* (pp. 621–638). IGI Global. doi:10.4018/978-1-6684-5598-2.ch035

Lakshman, A. (2023, July 18). Manipur violence I After Kuki Inpi hardens stance, signs of fissures among groups demanding separation. *The Hindu*. https://www.thehindu.com/news/national/other-states/manipur-after-kuki-inpi-hardens-stance-signs-of-fissures-among-groups-demanding-separation/article67091479.ece

Lallerstedt, K. (2022). Global Trade of "Illicit Goods" Its Scale, Consequences, and Addressing the Problem. In *Handbook of Security Science* (pp. 933–954). Springer International Publishing.

Lanning, K. (2018). The Evolution of Grooming: Concept and Term. *Journal of Interpersonal Violence*, *33*(1), 5–16. doi:10.1177/0886260517742046

Larkin, C., Pearce, N., & Shannon, N. (2022). Criminality and cryptocurrencies: Enforcement and policy responses – Part II. In S. Corbet (Ed.), *Understanding Cryptocurrency Fraud. The challenges and headwinds to regulate digital currencies*. De Gruyter. https://www.degruyter.com/document/doi/10.1515/9783110718485-010/html?lang=

Larry,, B. (1996). Underground Banking and National Security. *Journal of Contemporary Criminal Justice*.

Lautenbach, G. (2013). *The concept of the rule of law and the European Court of Human Rights*. OUP Oxford.

Lavorgna, A. (2020). Organized Crime and Cybercrime. The Palgrave Handbook of International Cybercrime and Cyberdeviance, 117-134.

Law Commission of India. (2018). *Legal Framework: Gambling and Sports Betting Including In Cricket In India, Report No. 276* (p. 105). Government of India.

Lazarus, L. (2012). Positive obligations and criminal justice: Duties to protect or coerce?.

Leavitt, K., Wodahl, E. J., & Schweitzer, K. (2020). Citizen willingness to report wildlife crime. *Deviant Behavior*. doi:10.1080/01639625.2020.1738643

Lefevre, M., Hickle, K., & Larkin, R. (2020). Child Criminal Exploitation in the South East of England: family experiences and professional responses.

Legal and Human Rights Centre. (2021). *Tanzania Human Rights Report 2021: Calls for Reform of Criminal Justice System to Safeguard Human Rights* (A. Henga, Ed.). Legal and Human Rights Centre.

Levi, M., & Maguire, M. (2004). Reducing and preventing organised crime: An evidence-based critique. *Crime, Law, and Social Change*, *41*, 397–469.

Levi, M., & Soudijn, M. (2020). Understanding the laundering of organized crime money. *Crime and Justice*, *49*(1), 579–631.

Lewis, F. B. (2015). Costly 'throw-ups': Electricity theft and power disruptions. *The Electricity Journal*, *28*(7), 118–135. doi:10.1016/j.tej.2015.07.009

Licensing Committee. (2019). Taxi & Private Hire Licensing – New Statutory Guidance from the Department of Transport.

Liddick, D. R. (2009). *An empirical, theoretical and historical overview of organised crime*. Edwin Mellen Press.

Liddick, D. R. Jr. (2020). *Transnational Organized Crime and Natural Resources Trafficking: Funding Conflict and Stealing from the World's Most Vulnerable Citizens*. Lexington Books.

Lillo Lobos, R. (2022). The Right to Access to Justice as a Key to Understand the Right to a Fair Trial in Civil Matters. In *Understanding Due Process in Non-Criminal Matters: How to Harmonize Procedural Guarantees with the Right to Access to Justice* (pp. 251–281). Springer International Publishing.

Lin, L. S. (2023). Asian Organized Crime in the United States: Perception, Institutions, and Policy Responses. In *Asian Organized Crime and the Anglosphere* (pp. 43–59). Springer International Publishing.

Lipner, J. (2016). Hindu Fundamentalism. In J. Dunn (Ed.), *Fundamentalisms: Threats and ideologies in the modern world* (pp. 93–116). I.B. Tauris and Co. Ltd.

Liu, J. H., & Khan, S. S. (2015). Nation building through historical narratives in pre-independence India: Gandhi, Nehru, Savarkar, and Golwalkar as entrepreneurs of identity. In M. Hanne, W. Crano, & J. Mio (Eds.), *Warring with words: Narrative and Metaphor in Politics* (pp. 211–237). Psychology Press.

Livey, F. R. (2017). *International legal framework for combating transnational organised crime* [Doctoral dissertation, University of Glasgow].

Local Government Association. (2015). Tackling serious and organised crime a local response.

Lopashenko, A. (1997). *Crimes in the Sphere of Economic Activity*. Aspect Press.

Lovelle, M. I., Yepes-Baldó, M., Romeo, M., & Soria, M. Á. (2017). Online Child Pornography: A Cultural Focus Literature Review [Pornografía infantil online: una revisión literaria de enfoque cultural]. *Para La Estructura*, *14*(2), 99.

Lucas, F. O. (2007). Criminal organizations and Judiciary Power. *Estudos Avançados, 21*, 107–117. doi:10.1590/S0103-40142007000300008

Lynch, M. J., & Pires, S. F. (Eds.). (2019). *Quantitative studies in green and conservation criminology: The measurement of environmental harm and crime*. Routledge. doi:10.4324/9780429453946

Macleod, C. (2016, August 25). *John Stuart Mill (Stanford Encyclopedia of Philosophy)*. Stanford.edu. https://plato.stanford.edu/entries/mill/

Madhusudhanan, K. (2023, June 9). Bridging the growing trust deficit in Manipur. *The Hindu*. https://www.thehindu.com/opinion/op-ed/bridging-the-growing-trust-deficit-in-manipur/article66947462.ece

Madinger, J. (2011). *Money Laundering: A Guide for Criminal Investigators* (3rd ed.). Shodh. http://shodh.inflibnet.ac.in/bitstream/123456789/3140/3/03_literature%20review.pdf doi:10.1201/b11845

Magnitude of Substance Use in India (p. 34). (2019). Ministry of Social Justice and Empowerment, Government of India and NDDTC, AIIMS. https://socialjustice.gov.in/writereaddata/UploadFile/Survey%20Report.pdf

Majumdar, R. (1957). *The Sepoy Mutiny and The Revolt of 1857*. Calcutta Oriental Press Private Limited.

Mallory, S. (2011). *Understanding organized crime*. Jones & Bartlett Publishers.

Manipur Tribal Forum Delhi vs The State of Manipur and Another WP (C) No 540 of 2023

Manukyan, Y., Stepanyan, A., & Ilyushina, M. (2023). METHODOLOGICAL FOUNDATIONS OF SOCIO-PHILOSOPHICAL AND LEGAL ANALYSIS OF CORRUPTION. *Wisdom*, (2 (26)), 212–222.

MarasM.-H. (2016). *Cybercriminology*.

Mareš, M., & Bjørgo, T. (2019). *Vigilantism against Migrants and Minorities: Concepts of Goals and Current Research*. Routledge.

Marteache, N., & Pires, S. F. (2020). Choice structuring properties of natural resource theft: An examination of redwood burl poaching. *Deviant Behavior, 41*(3), 311–328. doi:10.1080/01639625.2019.1565518

Martinez Cristaldo, C. E. (2023). The impact of institutional weakness on the presence of organised crime: A case study on Paraguay and organised crime in the Triple Frontier.

Maskara, S. (2021, May 3). *Cow Protection Legislation and Vigilante Violence in India*. ACLED Bringing Clarity to Crisis. https://acleddata.com/2021/05/03/cow-protection-legislation-and-vigilante-violence-in-india/

Maslen, H., & Paine, C. (2019). When should the police investigate cases of non-recent child sexual abuse? *Criminal Justice Ethics, 38*(2), 65–102.

Massari, M., & Monzini, P. (2004). Dirty business in Italy: Case study of illegal trafficking in hazardous waste. *Global Crime*, *6*(3), 285–304. doi:10.1080/17440570500273416

Matsne. (2021). *Law of Georgia - Regarding making changes to the Law of Georgia On Facilitating Prevention of Money Laundering and Financing of Terrorism*. MATSNE. https://matsne.gov.ge/ka/document/view/5137611?publication=0

Maxwell, N. J., & Artingstall, D. (2017). *The role of financial information-sharing partnerships in the disruption of crime*. Royal United Services Institute for Defence and Security Studies.

McCafferty, C. (2004). Only we can tackle porn. *Retrieved*, (March), 14.

McCarthy-Jones, A., Doyle, C., & Turner, M. (2020). From hierarchies to networks: The organizational evolution of the international drug trade. *International Journal of Law, Crime and Justice*, *63*, 100436.

McCurley, M. (2012). Operation: Game Over bans sex offenders from online games in New York. *Forbes*. https://www.engadget.com/2012-04-05-operation-game-over-bans-sex-offenders-from-online-games-in-new.html

McLean, R. (2019). *Gangs, drugs and (dis) organised crime*. Bristol University Press.

Meneses Falcón, M. D. C., Urío Rodríguez, S. J., & Uroz Olivares, J. (2019). Financing of trafficking in human beings in Spain.

Merem, E. C., Twumasi, Y., Wesley, J., Isokpehi, P., Fageir, S., Crisler, M., & Nwagboso, E. (2018). Assessing the menace of illegal wildlife trade in the sub-Saharan African region. *Advancements in Life Sciences*, *8*(1), 1–25. doi:10.5923/j.als.20180801.01

Metro News. (2019). *Facebook cracks down on sex predators*. Metro News. https://metro.co.uk/2008/05/09/facebook-cracks-down-on-sex-predators-129843/

Metropolitan Borough Council. Rotherham 2014)

Mill, J. & Lindsay, A. D. (2016). *On liberty and other essays*. Digireads.com Publishing.

Ministry of Defence. (n.d.). *Narcotics Control Commission*. Ministry of Defense. https://www.mint.gov.gh/agencies/narcotic-control-board/ on 29/12/2023.

Ministry of Gender, Children, and Social Protection. (2022). *National Plan of Action for the Elimination of Human Trafficking in Ghana, 2017-2021*. Ministry of Gender, Children, and Social Protection. https://www.unicef.org/ghana/media/1851/file/National%20Plan%20of%20Action%20for%20the%20Elimination%20of%20Human%20Trafficking%20in%20Ghana.pdf

Ministry of Home Affairs. (2021). *National Anti-Trafficking in Persons Plan of Action 2021 - 2024*. Ministry of Home Affairs.

Ministry of Road Transport and Highways (Transport Research Wing). (2022). *Road Accidents in India 2022*. Government of India. https://morth.nic.in/sites/default/files/RA_2022_30_Oct.pdf

Minority Rights Group International, & the Centre for Study of Society and Secularism. (2017, June). *A Narrowing Space: Violence and Discrimination against India's Religious Minorities.* Centre for Study of Society and Secularism and Minority Rights Group International. https://minorityrights.org/wp-content/uploads/2017/06/MRG_Rep_India_Jun17-2.pdf

Miraglia, P., Ochoa, R., & Briscoe, I. (2012). *Transnational organised crime and fragile states.*

Mishra, A. (1999). Savarkar and the Discourse on Islam in Pre-Independent India. *Journal of Asian History*, *33*(2), 142–184.

Mishra, S. (2023). The Fluidity of World Order and Break from Past: Opportunities and Challenges. *Social Development Issues*, *46*(1).

Missoni, E., & Alesani, D. (2023). *Management of International Institutions and NGOs: Insights for Global Leaders*. Taylor & Francis.

Mitsilegas, V. (1971). *Money laundering counter-measures in the European Union: a new paradigm of security governance versus fundamental legal principle*. Kluwer Law International. p.

Moeckli, D., Shah, S., Sivakumaran, S., & Harris, D. (Eds.). (2022). *International human rights law*. Oxford University Press.

Mohammad Hanif Quareshi v. State of Bihar (Supreme Court of India 1958).

Mohammed, M. A. L. L. A. M. (2022). Can Corruption and Organized Crime Affect Economic Growth in the ECOWAS Region? *Journal of Monetary Economics*, *17*(3), 411–436.

Monk, M. (2021). Emergent trends in the Chinese counterfeit pharmaceutical supply chain and opportunities for public-private reform.

Moodley, P. (2022). *Sabotage at power stations widespread.* Eskom CEO. https://www.sabcnews.com/sabcnews/sabotage-at-power-stations-widespread-eskom-ceo/

Moore, M. H. (1991). Drugs, the Criminal Law, and the Administration of Justice. *The Milbank Quarterly*, *69*(4), 529–560. doi:10.2307/3350227 PMID:1806801

Moreto, W. D., & Lemieux, A. M. (2015). From CRAVED to CAPTURED: Introducing a product-based framework to examine illegal wildlife markets. *European Journal on Criminal Policy and Research*, *21*(3), 303–320. doi:10.1007/s10610-014-9268-0

Moreto, W. D., & Pires, S. F. (2018). *Wildlife crime: An environmental criminology and crime science perspective*. Carolina Academic Press.

Morgan, A., Brown, R., Voce, I., & Cubitt, T. (2020). Organised and transnational crime. *Australian Policing: Critical Issues in 21st Century Police Practice*, 315.

Morgan, R. (1980). *Theory and Practice: Pornography and Rape, Take Back the Night: Women on Pornography*. William Morrow and Co.

Mthethwa, C. (2022). Cape Town taxi employee who burnt train so he could 'get paid more' sentenced to 20 years. *News24*. https://www.news24.com/news24/southafrica/news/cape-town-taxi-employee-who-burnt-train-so-he-could-get-paid-more-sentenced-to-20-years-20220423

Mukherjee, K. (2017). Insurgency and peace building in the northeast Indian state of Manipur. *Democracy and Security, 13*(3), 220–245. doi:10.1080/17419166.2017.1326308

Murphy, J., & De Vrieze, F. (2020). *Parliaments and independent oversight institutions. Global and countryspecific analysis of parliaments' relationships with Supreme Audit*. Anti-Corruption and Human Rights Institutions.

Murphy, S. D. (2020). Codifying the Obligations of States Relating to the Prevention of Atrocities. *Case W. Res. J. Int'l L., 52*, 27.

Mwalimu, H. (2016). Standard Operating Procedures for Protecting, Assisting and Referring Trafficked Children in Tanzania (p. 8). Research Gate.

Mweene, O. (2022). Construction of interpersonal helping behaviours exhibited among pirate taxi drivers in the city of Lusaka: an embedded mixed methods design (Doctoral dissertation, The University of Zambia).

MyGov Blogs. (n.d.). "Nisha Thadoklasi", Manipur Govt declares war on drugs. *MyGov Blog*. https://blog.mygov.in/nisha-thadoklasi-manipur-govt-declares-war-on-drugs/

MyGov.in | MyGov: A Platform for Citizen Engagement towards Good Governance in India. (n.d.). MyGov.in. https://www.mygov.in/

Nagle, L. E. (2013). How Conflict and Displacement Fuel Human Trafficking and Abuse of Vulnerable Groups. The Case of Colombia and Opportunities for Real Action and Innovative Solutions. *Groningen Journal of International Law, 1*(2).

Naim, M. (2010). *Illicit: How smugglers, traffickers and copycats are hijacking the global economy*. Random House.

Naím, M. (2022). *Ilícito: Cómo traficantes, contrabandistas y piratas están cambiando el mundo/ Illicit* (Vol. 18099). Debate.

Napolitano, G. (2020). The Rule of Law. The Oxford Handbook of Comparative Administrative Law, 421.

Natarajan, M. (Ed.). (2019). *International and transnational crime and justice*. Cambridge University Press.

National Council of Applied Economic Research. (2005). *Socio-Economic Impact of HIV and AIDS in Manipur*. UNDP. https://www.undp.org/sites/g/files/zskgke326/files/migration/in/socio_eco_impact_of_hiv_aids_in_manipur.pdf

National Crime Agency. (2015). Memorandum of Understanding Concerning Operation Stovewoos.

National Crime Records Bureau (NCRB), Indian Penal Code, Police Disposal of SLL Crime Cases (Crime Head-wise). (2020). Ministry of Home Affairs.

National Crime Records Bureau. (2021, September 9). *Untitled.* NCRB. https://ncrb.gov.in/sites/default/files/CII%202020%20Volume%201.pdf

National Research Council 2101 Constitution Ave Washington Dc 20418, & National Academies 500 Fifth Street Nw Washington Dc 20001. (1999). *Pathological Gambling: A Critical Review.* United States.

Navtej Singh Johar v. Union of India, (The Supreme Court of India, 2018). https://main.sci.gov.in/supremecourt/2016/14961/14961_2016_Judgement_06-Sep-2018.pdf

News24. (2020). Eskom workers 'held hostage', forced to restore illegal electricity connections. *News24.* https://www.news24.com/news24/southafrica/news/eskom-workers-held-hostage-forced-to-restore-illegal-electricity-connections-20200629

Neyroud, P. (2022). Policing "Landscapes" for the Rule of Law and Public Protection: The State of Evidence on Organisational Policies, Structures, and Human Resources. *Cambridge Journal of Evidence-Based Policing*, *6*(3-4), 140–161.

Ngo, N. (2021). Child sexual abuse violence against human dignity of children. *International Journal of Research*, *10*(15), 97–108.

Nicaso, A., & Danesi, M. (2021). *Organized crime: A cultural introduction.* Routledge.

Nilsson, S., & Ritzén, S. (2023). Maneuvering responsive, tactical, and preventive innovation in an innovation ecosystem to address the grand challenge of organized crime. *Creativity and Innovation Management.*

Nores, J. (2010). *War in the woods: Combating the marijuana cartels on America's public lands.* Lyons Press.

Nores, J. (2019). *Hidden War: How special operations game wardens are reclaiming America's wildland from the drug cartels.* Gun Digest Books.

Norwegian Ministry of Justice Legislation Department. (2006). *The General Civil Penal Code.* Wipolex. https://wipolex-res.wipo.int/edocs/lexdocs/laws/en/no/no122en.html

Ntuli, N. (2020). Eskom gives up on thieves. *News24.* https://www.news24.com/witness/news/eskom-gives-up-on-thieves-20200811

Nurse, A. (2015). *Policing wildlife: Perspectives on the enforcement of wildlife legislation.* Springer Publishing. doi:10.1057/9781137400017

Nuwer, R. L. (2021). Global cactus traffickers are cleaning out the deserts. *The New York Times.* https://www.nytimes.com/2021/05/20/science/cactus-trafficking-chile.html#:~:text="Just%20about%20every%20plant%20you,can%20take%20a%20serious%20toll.

Nuwer, R. L. (2018). *Poached: Inside the dark world of wildlife trafficking.* Scribe Publications.

O'Connell, R. (2003). *A TYPOLOGY OF CHILD CYBERSEXPLOITATION AND ONLINE GROOMING PRACTICES.* University of Central Lancashire. http://image.guardian.co.uk/sys-files/Society/documents/2003/07/17/Groomingreport.pdf

O'Neill, M. (2023). *The Transnational Crime of Human Trafficking: A Human Security Approach.* Taylor & Francis.

Obaga, A. (2021). *Illicit Financial Flows: a Legal Analysis of Tax Avoidance by Financial Institutions in Kenya* (Doctoral dissertation, University of Nairobi).

Obeng, A. S., & Yin, E. T. (2021). If I Die I Lose Everything: Understanding Poverty from the Perspective of Ankaful Residents in Ghana. *Asian Research Journal of Arts & Social Sciences, 15*(3), 32–44. doi:10.9734/arjass/2021/v15i330259

Ogunniyi, O. J., & Akpu, J. O. (2019). The Challenge of Drug Trafficking to Democratic Governance and Human Security in West Africa. *Africa Development. Afrique et Developpement, 44*(4), 29–50.

Oh, E. (2016). Mill on Paternalism. *Journal of Political Inquiry, 4.*

Oinam, A. (2022, November). *Revisiting Free Movement Regime (FMR): Challenges and Implications.* Claws. https://www.claws.in/static/IB-368_Revisiting-Free-Movement-Regime-FMR-Challenges-and-Implications.pdf

Okyere, S. (2017). 'Shock and Awe': A critique of the Ghana-centric child trafficking discourse. *Anti-Trafficking Review*, (9), 92–105. doi:10.14197/atr.20121797

Oliveira, A. P. (2023). *Organised crime is a human rights issue.* Global Initiative. https://globalinitiative.net/wp-content/uploads/2023/10/Ana-Paula-Oliveira-Four-reasons-why-organized-crime-is-a-human-rights-issue-GI-TOC-October-2023.pdf on 16/01/2024.

Olley, N. (2019). 207 Transnational policing and organised crime. *The Development of Transnational Policing: Past, Present and Future*, 207-238.

Oriolo, A. (2023). The rule of law, transnational crimes, and the human rights-based approach in the European Union: The Court of Justice as Ultimate Guardian of the 'Good' Laws. In *Solidarity and Rule of Law: The New Dimension of EU Security* (pp. 201–226). Springer International Publishing.

Ost, S., & Mooney, J.-L. (2013). *Group localised grooming:what is it and what challenges does it pose for society and law?* Semantic Scholar. https://api.semanticscholar.org/CorpusID:73615323

Ost, S. (2002). Children at Risk : Legal and Societal Perceptions of the Potential Threat That the Possession of Child Pornography Poses to Society. *Journal of Law and Society, 29*(3), 436–460. doi:10.1111/1467-6478.00227

Otusanya, O. J., & Adeyeye, G. B. (2022). The dark side of tax havens in money laundering, capital flight and corruption in developing countries: Some evidence from Nigeria. *Journal of Financial Crime, 29*(1), 62–100.

Overall, L. (2016). Abuse in Foster Care and Potential Liability for Local Authorities: Can liability be imposed through vicarious liability or a non-delegable duty?.

Overdevest, C., & Zeitlin, J. (2018). Experimentalism in transnational forest governance: Implementing European Union forest law enforcement, governance and trade (FLEGT) voluntary partnership agreements in Indonesia and Ghana. *Regulation & Governance*, *12*(1), 64–87. doi:10.1111/rego.12180

Owusu, G., Oteng-Ababio, M., Owusu, A. Y., & Wrigley-Asante, C. (2016). Can poor neighbourhoods be correlated with crime? Evidence from urban Ghana. *Ghana Journal of Geography*, *8*(1), 11–31.

Oxfordshire Safeguarding Adults Board. (2023, August 3). Other training. https://www.osab.co.uk/learning-zone/osab-core-adult-safeguarding-courses/traiing-hosted-by-osab/other-training/

Ozymy, J., & Jarrell, M. L. (2020). Of Sex Crimes and Fencelines: How Recognition of Environmental Justice Communities as Crime Victims Under State and Federal Law Can Help Secure Environmental Justice. *Pace Environmental Law Review*, *38*, 109.

Palermo, G. (2020). Transnational Organized Crime: The Branching of Mafias Into the Global Era. In Handbook of Research on Trends and Issues in Crime Prevention, Rehabilitation, and Victim Support (pp. 124-143). Igi Global.

Pandey, G. (1983). Rallying around the Cow. In R. Guha (Ed.), *Subaltern Studies* (Vol. 2, pp. 60–129). Oxford University Press.

Pandey, G. (1992). *The Construction of Communalism in Colonial North India*. Oxford University Press.

Pandey, G. (2001). *Remembering Partition: Violence, Nationalism, and History in India*. Cambridge University Press. doi:10.1017/CBO9780511613173

Paoli, L. (2008). *Mafia brotherhoods: Organized crime, Italian style*. Oxford University Press.

Parliamentlive.tv. (2019, March 27). Transport Committee Wednesday 27 March 2019. episode, London.

Pastor, R., Mignet, F., Mattes, T., Gurzawska, A., Nitsch, H., & Wright, D. (2021). COPKIT: Technology and Knowledge for Early Warning/Early Action-Led Policing in Fighting Organised Crime and Terrorism. In *Technology Development for Security Practitioners* (pp. 121–133). Springer International Publishing.

Patel, A. (2020, December 30). *The Dark Chronology Of India's Cow-Slaughter Laws*. Article 14. https://article-14.com/post/the-dark-chronology-of-india-s-cow-slaughter-laws

Pattanaik, D. (2022, February 15). *Who created the term Hinduism? And why did the British feel the need to defend Hinduism?* Scroll. https://scroll.in/article/1017342/who-created-the-term-hinduism-and-why-did-the-british-feel-the-need-to-defend-hinduism

Pavel, C. E. (2021). The international rule of law. In *Legitimacy Beyond the State* (pp. 52–71). Routledge.

Peach, D., Allen, D., Brown, P., Sanghera, K., Sharif, R., Lees, J., & Senior, J. (2015). Needs analysis report following the sexual exploitation of children in Rotherham.

Peprah, K. (2022). Drivers of Deforestation, Forest Degradation, and Management Responses in Ghana. In *Land Degradation Neutrality: Achieving SDG 15 by Forest Management* (pp. 61–79). Springer Nature Singapore. doi:10.1007/978-981-19-5478-8_4

Pereda, V. (2022). Why Global North criminology fails to explain organized crime in Mexico. *Theoretical Criminology*, *26*(4), 620–640.

Phale, M. O., & Kgosiemang, P. K. (2021). *Governance at a Glance: Botswana's APRM Experience*. Security Studies Collection.

Piemontese, L. (2023). Uncovering illegal and underground economies: The case of mafia extortion racketeering. *Journal of Public Economics*, *227*, 104997.

Pilling, D. (2023). *Scandal at South Africa's Eskom: the CEO and the cyanide-laced coffee*. AFR. https://www.afr.com/world/africa/scandal-at-south-africa-s-eskom-the-ceo-and-the-cyanide-laced-coffee-20230303

Pimentel, S. (2022). *Non-Traditional Collectors: Case Studies and Implications for the Private Sector* (Doctoral dissertation, San Diego State University).

Pires, S. F., Schneider, J. L., & Herrera, M. (2016). Organized crime or crime that is organized? The parrot trade in the neotropics. *Trends in Organized Crime*, *19*(1), 4–20. doi:10.1007/s12117-015-9259-7

Pires, S. F., Thomson, R. W., Petrossian, G. A., & Sosnowski, M. C. (2023). A Social Network Analysis of Large-Scale Wildlife Seizures Made at US Ports of Entry. *Deviant Behavior*, *44*(8), 1–14. doi:10.1080/01639625.2023.2169211

Pisillo Mazzeschi, R., & Pisillo Mazzeschi, R. (2021). Protection of Liberty and Security of the Person. *International Human Rights Law: Theory and Practice*, 329-341.

Pournara, M. (2020). *Strategic police decision-making in tackling organised crime* (Doctoral dissertation, Cardiff University).

Prakash, A. G. (2018). Role of Prohibitory Legislation in Preventing Online Sexual Abuse of Children: a Critical Socio-Legal Analysis. *Unitedworld Law Journal, 2*, 346–360. https://www.icmec.org/press/new-study-reveals-child-pornography-not-a-crime-in-most-countries/

Prenzler, T. (2021). *Ethics and accountability in criminal justice: Towards a universal standard.* Australian Academic Press.

Prescott, D. S., & Levenson, J. S. (2010). Sex offender treatment is not punishment. *Journal of Sexual Aggression*, *16*(3), 275–285.

Press Information Bureau, Government of India. (2020, January 25). *Press Information Bureau.* Press Information Bureau. https://pib.gov.in/PressReleseDetailm.aspx?PRID=1600505

Priyokumar Meitei, S. (2010). Migration and Social Tensions in Manipur. *International Journal of Scientific Research.*

Priyokumar Singh, T. (2022). A Critical Analysis of Narco-Politics In Manipur. *International Journal of Multidisciplinary Educational Research, 11*(1(5)).

PTI, & PTI. (2023, August 8). Drugs worth over Rs 1,610 crore seized by Assam Rifles in Manipur since July 2022. *Deccan Herald.* https://www.deccanherald.com/india/manipur/drugs-worth-over-rs-1610-crore-seized-by-assam-rifles-in-manipur-since-july-2022-2639227

Puia, R. (n.d.). *When boundaries matter: land, laws and territorial conflict in Manipur, Northeast India.* Academia. https://www.academia.edu/49356615/When_boundaries_matter_land_laws_and_territorial_conflict_in_Manipur_Northeast_India

Pūraitė, A. (2020). Economic impact of organised crime to state security. *Проблеми законності*, (149), 185-199.

Quiroz-Gutierrez, M. (2022). *A handful of NFT users are making big money off of a stealth scam. Here's how 'wash trading' works.* Fortune.

Rabkin, J. A., & Lerner, C. S. (2022). Criminal justice is local: Why states disregard universal jurisdiction for human rights abuses. *Vand. J. Transnat'l L., 55*, 375.

Rader, M. M. G. (2023). *Organized Crime: A Test of Durkheim's Theory of Punishment and Society* (Doctoral dissertation, University of South Alabama).

Raineri, L., & Strazzari, F. (2023). The data that we do (not) have: Studying drug trafficking and organised crime in Africa. *Trends in Organized Crime,* •••, 1–21.

Rajeshwari, B. (2004, March). *Communal Riots in India A Chronology (1947-2003).* Retrieved from Institute of Peace and Conflict Studies: http://www.nagarikmancha.org/images/1242-Documents-Communal_Riots_in_India.pdf

RAJYA SABHA UNSTARRED QUESTION NO. 1198. (2015, September 9). MHA. https://www.mha.gov.in/MHA1/Par2017/pdfs/par2015-pdfs/rs-091215/1198.pdf

Ramcharan, B. G. (2021). *The concept and present status of the international protection of human rights: forty years after the universal declaration* (Vol. 13). BRILL.

Ratner, S. R. (2001). Corporations and human rights: a theory of legal responsibility. *yale LJ, 111*, 443.

Reichl, J., Schmidthaler, M., & Schneider, F. (2013). Power Outage Cost Evaluation: Reasoning, Methods and an Application. *Journal of Scientific Research and Reports*, *2*(1), 249–276. doi:10.9734/JSRR/2013/3167

Remeikienė, R., & Gaspareniene, L. (2023). Effects of Economic and Financial Crime on the Government Budget and the Quality of Public Services. In *Economic and Financial Crime, Sustainability and Good Governance* (pp. 173–204). Springer International Publishing.

Reuter, P. (2014). Drug markets and organized crime. The Oxford handbook of organized crime, 359-381.

Richards, J. R. (1999). *Transnational criminal organizations, cybercrime and money laundering: A handbook for law enforcement officers, auditors, and financial investigators*. CRC Press.

Richie-Zavaleta, A. C., Baranik, S., Mersch, S., Ataiants, J., & Rhodes, S. M. (2021). From victimization to restoration: Multi-disciplinary collaborative approaches to care and support victims and survivors of human trafficking. *Journal of Human Trafficking*, *7*(3), 291–307.

Ripstein, A. (2006). Beyond the Harm Principle. *Philosophy & Public Affairs*, *34*(3), 215–245. doi:10.1111/j.1088-4963.2006.00066.x

Rizzuti, A. (2022). Organised food crime: An analysis of the involvements of organised crime groups in the food sector in England and Italy. *Crime, Law, and Social Change*, *78*(5), 463–482.

Robertson, P. (2022). Philippines undercounts recent 'drug war' deaths. *Human Rights Watch*. https:// www.hrw.org/news/2022/11/17/philippines-undercounts-recent-drug-war-deaths on 17/01/2024

Roelofse, C. J. (2009). *Organised Crime in South Africa. Urbanization, Policing and Security: Global Perspectives*. CRC Press.

Rolla, P. (2022). *The social consequences of organized crime groups* (Doctoral dissertation, University of Sussex).

Roth, M.P. (2010). *Organised Crime*. Upper Saddle River: prentice Hall.

Rotherham Metropolitan Borough Council. (2018) Commissioners' Timeline of key headlines / progress to the Ministry of Housing, Communities and Local Government February 2015 – February 2018 (3 Years)

Roth, M. P. (2017). *Global organized crime: A 21st century approach*. Taylor & Francis.

Rothstein, B. (2021). *Controlling corruption: The social contract approach*. Oxford University Press.

Rotman, E. F. (2017). A Qualitative Study of What US Parents Say and Do When Their Young Children See Pornography. *Academic Pediatrics*, *17*(8), 844–849. doi:10.1016/j.acap.2017.04.014 PMID:28450081

Rubio Grundell, L. (2022). The Intersection of Security and Neo-abolitionism in the EU's Anti-trafficking Policies. In *Security Meets Gender Equality in the EU: The Politics of Trafficking in Women for Sexual Exploitation* (pp. 119–163). Springer International Publishing.

Rutai, Z. (2020). *The Lanzarote Committee: protecting children from sexual violence in Europe and beyond.*

Ryder, N. (2012). *Title Money laundering – an endless cycle: a comparative analysis of the anti-money laundering policies in the United States of America, the United Kingdom, Australia, and Canada. London.* Routledge. doi:10.4324/9780203126783

Sage-Passant, L. (2023) *The security intelligence services of the private sector* (Doctoral dissertation, Loughborough University).

Sandor, A. (2016). *Assemblages of intervention: Politics, security, and drug trafficking in West Africa* [Doctoral dissertation, Université d'Ottawa/University of Ottawa].

Sanz-Levia, L., & Jiménez-Sánchez, F. (2021). Breaking democracy: Illegal political finance and organized crime in Guatemala. *Crime, Law, and Social Change*, *75*(1), 21–43.

Sasan, J. M. V. (2021). The Social Contract Theories of Thomas Hobbes and John Locke: Comparative Analysis.

Sauve, B., Woodley, J., Jones, N. J., & Akhtari, S. (2023). Methods of preventing corruption: a review and analysis of select approaches.

Savarkar, V. D. (1949). *Hindu Rashtra Darshan.*

Schell, B., Vargas Martin, M., Hung, P., & Rueda, L. (2007). Cyber child pornography: A review paper of the social and legal issues and remedies—and a proposed technological solution. *Aggression and Violent Behavior*, *12*(1), 45–63. doi:10.1016/j.avb.2006.03.003

Schoetz, A. N. (2023, August 4). When did Kukis reach Manipur and how the past is shaping the state's present. *India Today*. https://www.indiatoday.in/history-of-it/story/manipur-violence-when-did-kukis-reach-manipur-and-how-past-is-shaping-states-present-2416215-2023-08-04

Schönsteiner, J. (2022). Inter-American Elements for a Systemic Approach to State-Owned Enterprises' Human Rights Obligations. *Business and Human Rights Journal*, *7*(3), 397–417.

Schultze-Kraft, M. (2014). *Getting real about an illicit 'external stressor': Transnational cocaine trafficking through West Africa* (IDS Evidence Report 72). Brighton: IDS. http://opendocs.ids.ac.uk/opendocs/handle/123456789/3966

Schultze-Kraft, M. (2016). *Organised crime, violence and development: Topic guide*. GSDRC, University of Birmingham.

Scott, D. (1995). *Money Laundering and International Efforts to Fight It –The World Bank.* Public Policy for the Private Sector.

Scott, M. J., La Vigne, N. G., & Palmer, T. (2007). *Preventing Vandalism.* The Urban Institute Justice Policy Center.

Seabright, P., Stieglitz, J., & Van der Straeten, K. (2021). Evaluating social contract theory in the light of evolutionary social science. *Evolutionary Human Sciences*, *3*, e20.

Secretariat, U. N. (1975). *Economic and Social Consequences of Crime: New Challenges for Research and Planning*. OJP. https://www.ojp.gov/pdffiles1/Digitization/65619NCJRS.pdf

Seepma, A. P., de Blok, C., & Van Donk, D. P. (2021). Designing digital public service supply chains: Four country-based cases in criminal justice. *Supply Chain Management*, *26*(3), 418–446.

Seivold, G. (2023). What We've Learned: Lessons from the World's Leading Security Companies on Partnerships and Privatization. In *Handbook on Public and Private Security* (pp. 321–346). Springer International Publishing.

Sellin, T. (1963). Organized crime: A business enterprise. *The Annals of the American Academy of Political and Social Science*, *347*(1), 12–19. doi:10.1177/000271626334700103

Shabalala, Z. (2021). *How the illicit copper trade is sapping South Africa*. Reuters. https://www.reuters.com/world/africa/exclusive-how-illicit-copper-trade-is-sapping-south-africa-2021-10-15/

Sharma, N. (2023). EXAMINING THE LEGAL 'RELATIONSHIP'BETWEEN THE TAXI OWNER AND THE TAXI DRIVER IN FIJI: A CASE FOR REFORM. DRP Thesis.

Shashiashvili, T. (2015). *Legalization of illegal income as a criminal justice problem*. Grigol Robakidze University. http://www.nplg.gov.ge/dlibrary/collect/0002/000828/Dis.Shashiashvili%20G.pdf

Shashiashvili, B., & Taran, B. (2005). *World Economy and World Finance System*. International Finance Control.

Shaw, M. (1998). Organised crime in post-apartheid South Africa: Safety and governance programme (Occasional paper no 28). Institute for security studies.

Shelley, L. (2010). *Human trafficking: A global perspective*. Cambridge University Press.

Shelley, L. (2013). Human trafficking as a form of transnational crime. In *Human trafficking* (pp. 116–137). Willan.

Shulzhenko, N., & Romashkin, S. (2020). Internet fraud and transnational organized crime. *Juridical Tribune*, *10*(1), 162–172.

Sidebottom, A., Ashby, M., & Johnson, S. D. (2014). Copper cable theft: Revisiting the price-theft hypothesis. *Journal of Research in Crime and Delinquency*, *51*(5), 684–700. doi:10.1177/0022427814521216

Siegel, L. J. (2001). Criminology: theories, patterns, and typologies (7th edition.) Wadsworth/Thomson Learning.

Siegel, D. (2014). Women in transnational organized crime. *Trends in Organized Crime*, *17*(1), 52–65. doi:10.1007/s12117-013-9206-4

Silver, J. R., & Silver, E. (2020). The Nature and Role of Morality in Offending: A Moral Foundations Approach. *Journal of Research in Crime and Delinquency*, *58*(3), 343–380. doi:10.1177/0022427820960201

Simoons, F. J., Batra, S. M., Chakravarti, A. K., Diener, P., Ferro-Luzzi, G. E., Harris, M., Heston, A., Hoffpauir, R., Lodrick, D. O., Malik, S. L., Mey, W. E., Mishra, S. N., Palmieri, R. P., Pimentel, D., Robkin, E. E., Schwabe, C. W., Schwartzberg, J. E., Suryanarayana, M., & Wagner, P. L. (1979, September). Questions in the Sacred Cow Controversy. *Current Anthropology*, *20*(3), 467–493. doi:10.1086/202319

Simović, M., & Šikman, M. (2020), HUMAN RIGHTS AND ORGANISED CRIME-LIMITATION OF HUMAN RIGHTS V. PREVENTION OF ORGANISED CRIME. In *International Scientific Conference "Towards a Better Future: Human rights, Organized crime and Digital society"* (p. 129).

Singh, B. (2023, June 21). Over 2000 illegal immigrants took shelter in Manipur after military coup in Myanmar: CSC. *The Economic Times*. https://economictimes.indiatimes.com/news/india/over-2000-illegal-immigrants-took-shelter-in-manipur-after-military-coup-in-myanmar-csc/articleshow/101156422.cms

Singh, N., & Singh, K. (2023). The Poppy Menace in Manipur: Causes, Consequences and Responses. *European Chemical Bulletin*. doi: 10.48047/ecb/2023.12.si5a.073

Singh, P. (2023). Money Laundering and Abuse of the Financial System. *Issue 2 Indian JL & Legal Rsch., 5*, 1.

Singh, V. (2024, January 2). *Free Movement Regime to end at Myanmar border*. The Hindu. https://www.thehindu.com/news/national/centre-set-to-scrap-free-movement-regime-with-myanmar-people-in-border-areas-will-require-visas/article67698536.ece

Singh, D. (2022). The Causes of Police Corruption and Working towards Prevention in Conflict-Stricken States. *Laws*, *11*(5), 69. doi:10.3390/laws11050069

Singh, N., & Singh, K. (2023). The Poppy Menace in Manipur: Causes, Consequences and Responses. *European Chemical Bulletin*. doi:10.48047/ecb/2023.12.si5a.073

Singh, T. B. (2007). Poverty in Manipur. *Economic and Political Weekly*, *42*(3), 251–254. https://www.jstor.org/stable/4419165

Sitlhou, H. (2015). Confronting the State: Land rights discourse in the Hills of Manipur. *Economic and Political Weekly*, *50*(30), 70–77. https://www.jstor.org/stable/24481977

Sitompul, A., & Hasibuan, P. (2021). The Morality of Law Enforcement Agencies (Police, Prosecutor's Office, KPK) in Money Laundering With the Origin of the Corruption. *European Science Review*, (9-10), 55–63.

Skidmore, M. (2022). *Empirical Research to Contextualise Serious and Organised Crimes and Develop Perspectives on Effective Crime Control in the UK* (Doctoral dissertation, University of Portsmouth).

Slabbert, A. (2022). Cable thieves now armed with AK-47s. *News24*. https://www.news24.com/citypress/news/cable-thieves-now-armed-withak-47s-20220410

Slope, R. (2022). *Care in the Iron Cage: A Weberian Analysis of Failings in Care*. Taylor & Francis.

Small Arms Survey. (2023). *Out of Control: The Trafficking of Improvised Explosive Device Components and Commercial Explosives in West Africa*. Small Arm Survey. https://www.smallarmssurvey.org/sites/default/files/resources/SAS-Report-24-IEDs-WEB.pdf

Smith, S. L. & And Ericson D. (2008). *Money Laundering Monitor*. U.S. Department Of Justice, Criminal Division, Asset Forfeiture & Money Laundering Section.

Smith, R. B. (2020). CYBERCIME IN ASEAN: ANTI-CHILD PORNOGRAPHY LEGISLATION. *JOURNAL of INDONESIAN LEGAL STUDIES*, *5*(2), 277–292. doi:10.15294/jils.v5i2.37931

Smith, T. B. (2003). Electricity theft- comparative analysis. *Energy Policy*, *32*(18), 2067–2076. doi:10.1016/S0301-4215(03)00182-4

Smokov, S. M., Horoshko, V. V., Korniienko, M. V., & Medvedenko, S. V. (2022). Rule of Law as a Principle of Criminal Procedure (on materials of the European Court of Human Rights). *Pakistan Journal of Criminology*, *14*(3).

Snaphaan, T., & van Ruitenburg, T. (2024). Financial Crime Scripting: An Analytical Method to Generate, Organise and Systematise Knowledge on the Financial Aspects of Profit-Driven Crime. *European Journal on Criminal Policy and Research*, •••, 1–21.

Sollecito, A. (2023). *Honor behind Human Trafficking Absenteeism in Italian Mafias." A comparative study among Italian*. Nigerian and Albanian Mafias.

Solongo D. (2004). Russian Capitalism and Money-Laundering. *Global Program against Money Laundering.*

Sorochinsky, M. (2009). Prosecuting Torturers, Protecting Child Molesters: Toward a Power Balance Model of Criminal Process for International Human Rights Law. *Mich. J. Int'l L.*, *31*, 157.

Sotande, E. O. (2016). *Transnational organised crime and illicit financial flows: Nigeria, West Africa and the global North* [Doctoral dissertation, University of Leeds].

South Cambridgeshire District Council. (2022). South Cambridgeshire District Council Modern Slavery Statement 2022-23.

Spapens, A., Abraham, M., van Dijk, B., & Hofstra, D. (2021). 25 years of tackling large-scale drug crime in the Netherlands. *CIROC Newsletter*, (3), 2–3.

Spapens, T., White, R., Van Uhm, D., & Huisman, W. (Eds.). (2018). *Green crimes and dirty money*. Routledge.

Stadler, W. A., Jonson, C. L., & Gialopsos, B. M. (2023). Are we loving our national parks to death? A call for research on crime and law enforcement in the US national park system. *Criminal Justice Review*, *48*(1), 85–105. doi:10.1177/07340168211015726

State of Gujarat v. Mirzapur Moti Kureshi Kassab Jamat (Supreme Court of India 2006).

Steenkamp, C. (2024). Captagon and conflict: Drugs and war on the border between Jordan and Syria. *Mediterranean Politics*, •••, 1–25.

Stessens, G. (2000). *Money laundering: a new international law enforcement model*. Cambridge University. doi:10.1017/CBO9780511494567

Stewart, H. (1999). Legality and Morality in H.L.A. Hart's Theory of Criminal Law. *SMU Law Review*, *52*(1). https://scholar.smu.edu/cgi/viewcontent.cgi?article=1693&context=smulr

Strauss, D. P. (1980). Vicarious Municipal Liability: Creating a Consistent Remedial Policy for Local Government Violations of Civil Rights. *Cal. WL Rev.*, *16*, 58.

Strečanský, B. (2023). Dancing on a Thin Ice: Civil Society in Slovakia. *Contested Civic Spaces: A European Perspective, 22*, 193.

Strugała, R. (2021). The sharing economy as the contemporary challenge for the law of torts. In *Digital Technologies and the Law of Obligations* (pp. 45–53). Routledge.

Sumir Karmakar, D. H. N. S. Sumir Karmakar, & DHNS. (2023, July 29). Manipur starts collection of biometrics of "illegal migrants" from Myanmar amid massive rally by Meitei groups. *Deccan Herald*. https://www.deccanherald.com/india/manipur-starts-collection-of-biometrics-of-illegal-migrants-from-myanmar-amid-massive-rally-by-meitei-groups-1241977.html

Świątkowska, J. (2020). Tackling cybercrime to unleash developing countries' digital potential. *Pathways for Prosperity Commission Background Paper Series*, *33*, 2020–01.

Sylvie, G. (2010). *The construction of history and nationalism in India: Textbooks, controversies and politics*. Routledge.

Tagziria, L., & de Lugo, L. B. R. B. (2023) West Africa Organised Crime Resilience Framework.

Talbot, C. (1995). Inscribing the Other, Inscribing the Self: Hindu-Muslim Identities in Pre-Colonial India. *Comparative Studies in Society and History*, *37*(4), 692–722. doi:10.1017/S0010417500019927

Tankersley, J. (2021, November 25). Is pornography killing the economy? *Washington Post*. https://www.washingtonpost.com/news/wonk/wp/2013/09/06/is-pornography-killing-the-economy/

Targba, A. (2023). Illegal Transnational Migration And Illicit Drug Trafficking In Nigeria. *Wukari International Studies Journal*, *7*(3), 236–249.

Task and Finish Group on Taxi and Private Hire Vehicle Licensing. (2018). Taxi and Private Hire Vehicle Licensing Steps towards a safer and more robust system.

Tchakatumba, P. K., Gandiwa, E., Mwakiwa, E., Clegg, B., & Nyasha, S. (2019). Does the CAMPFIRE programme ensure economic benefits from wildlife to households in Zimbabwe? *Ecosystems and People (Abingdon, England)*, *15*(1), 119–135. doi:10.1080/26395916.2019.1599070

Thaimei, S. (2021). Intercultural business communication and Culture Identity: A case study of Manipur. *Global Media Journal*, *13*(1).

Thapar, R. (1989). Imagined Religious Communities? Ancient History and the Modern Search for a Hindu Identity. *Modern Asian Studies*, *23*(2), 209–231. doi:10.1017/S0026749X00001049

Thapar, R. (2014). *The Past as Present:Forging Contemporary Identities through History*. Aleph Book Company.

Tharoor, S. (2018). *Why I am a Hindu*. Aleph Book Company.

Thaver, M. (2020, December 15). Explained: How Maharashtra Police will use software to crack down on child porn. *The Indian Express*. https://indianexpress.com/article/explained/maharashtra-police-interpol-child-porn-software-7096513/

The Chanzo Reporter. (2022, April 12). LHRC: Option of fine as punishment obstructs efforts against trafficking in persons in Tanzania. *The Chanzo Reporter.* https://thechanzo.com/2022/04/11/lhrc-option-of-fine-as-punishment-obstructs-efforts-against-trafficking-in-persons-in-tanzania/

The Hindu Bureau & The Hindu Bureau. (2023, August 9). Manipur violence case, live updates | SC constitutes committee of 3 former women judges to oversee humanitarian measures. *The Hindu*. https://www.thehindu.com/news/national/manipur-violence-row-supreme-court-kuki-meity-clash-live-updates/article67167206.ece

The Narcotic Drugs and Psychotropic Substances Act. (1985). LD. https://lddashboard.legislative.gov.in/actsofparliamentfromtheyear/narcotic-drugs-and-psychotropic-substances-act-1985

The Protection of Children from Sexual offences Act 2012. (2012). *The Gazette of India*.

The Scroll. (2017, May 29). *Reading the law: government seems to be on thin ice as it bans trade on cattle for slaughter*. Scroll. https://scroll.in/article/838954/reading-the-law-government-is-on-thin-ice-as-it-imposes-de-facto-cattle-slaughter-ban#:~:text=The%20Rules%20have%20come%20in,for%20slaughter%20from%20animal%20fairs

The U.S. Department of Justice. (2010, August). *US Department of Justice*. Department of Justice. https://www.justice.gov/psc/docs/natstrategyreport.pdf

The White House. (2021). *The National Action Plan to Combat Human Trafficking*. The White House.

The Wire. (n.d.). Supreme Court slams claim that Manipur fake encounter probe will "Demoralise" Army. *The Wire*. https://thewire.in/law/supreme-court-army-manipur-fake-encounter

The Wire. (n.d.). What's Behind the Manipur Violence and Why Stopping It Poses a Test for Modi. *The Wire*. https://thewire.in/security/manipur-violence-reasons-failure-and-solution-q-and-a

Theron, A. (2018). *Copper theft remains a concern*. ESI Africa. https://www.esi-africa.com/southern-africa/copper-theftremains-a-serious-concern-eskom/

Thommandru, A., & Maratovich, F. F. (2024). Leveraging new emerging technologies to enhance the anticorruption arsenal: Assimilating India's experiential insights into Uzbekistan's criminoverse. *Multidisciplinary Reviews*, *7*(3), 2024058–2024058.

Thompson, L. J. (2013, December 23). *Paternalism | social science*. Encyclopedia Britannica. https://www.britannica.com/topic/paternalism

Thornberry, T. P. (Ed.). (2018). *Developmental theories of crime and delinquency*. Routledge.

Titeca, K. (2019). Illegal ivory trade as transnational organized crime? An empirical study into ivory traders in Uganda. *British Journal of Criminology*, *59*(1), 24–44. doi:10.1093/bjc/azy009

Tombs, S. (2018). For Pragmatism and Politics: Crime, Social Harm and Zemiology. In Zemiology: Reconnecting Crime and Social Harm (pp. 11–31). Palgrave Macmillan.

Torkelson, E. (2010). *Who profits from Copper Theft?* ISS. http://www.iss.co.za/iss_today.php?ID=1059

Transnet. (2021). *The impact of cable theft and vandalism of Transnet property*. Twitter. https://twitter.com/ReliableTFR/status/1458393093754036224

Trehan, J. (2004). *Crime and Money Laundering: The Indian Perspective*. Shodh. http://shodh.inflibnet.ac.in/bitstream/123456789/3140/3/03_literature%20review.pdf

Tretiakov, V. (2009). *Organized Crime and Legalization of Criminal Incomes*. Nekeri.

Tsuwa, J. T. (2023) The Impact of Migration and Transnational Organized Crime on Development in West Africa Rufus Aisedion.

Tyagi, A. (2021). *Early warning identity threat and mitigation system* (Doctoral dissertation).

U.S. Congress Office of Technology Assessment. (1995). Information Technologies for Control of Money Laundering. Washington, Dc: U.S. Government Printing Office.

U.S. Department of Justice. (2014). Dreamboard Member Sentenced to 45 Years in Prison for Participating in International Criminal Network Organized to Sexually Exploit Children. *Office of Public Affairs*. https://www.justice.gov/opa/pr/dreamboard-member-sentenced-45-years-prison-participating-international-criminal-network

U.S. Department of State. (2021). 2021 International Narcotics Control Strategy Report (INCSR). USDoS. https://www.state.gov/2021-international-narcotics-control-strategy-report/

U.S. Department of State. (2021). Tanzania 2021 Human Rights Report. U.S. Department of State.

U.S. Department of State. (2023, December 7). *Tanzania - United States Department of State*. US DoS. https://www.state.gov/reports/2023-trafficking-in-persons-report/tanzania/

U.S. Fish & Wildlife Service. (n.d.). *Office of Law Enforcement Training and Development Unit*. U.S. Fish & Wildlife Service. https://www.fws.gov/program/office-law-enforcement-training-and-development-unit/what-we-do

Uebel, M. (1999, January 1). *Toward a symptomatology of cyberporn*. YouTube. Retrieved July 14, 2022, from http://muse.jhu.edu/journals/theory_and_event/%20v003/3.4uebel.html

Uebel, M. (1999). Toward a Symptomatology of Cyberporn. *Theory & Event*, 3.

Uhl, A., Kučera, J., Hayrapetyan, L., Gartner, M., Leuven, K. U., & Stockreiter, S. (2020). Private Sector Engagement in the Prevention of Organized Crime.

UN General Assembly, *United Nations Convention against Transnational Organized Crime: resolution / adopted by the General Assembly*, 8 January 2001, A/RES/55/25

UN. (2023). *Our Common Agenda Policy Brief 9: A new agenda for peace*. UN. https://www.un.org/sites/un2.un.org/files/ our-common-agenda-policy-brief-new-agenda-for-peace-en.pdf on 17/01/2024.

Üngör, U. Ü. (2020). *Paramilitarism: Mass violence in the shadow of the state*. Oxford University Press.

UNICEF. (n.d.). *Protecting children online*. UNICEF. https://www.unicef.org/protection/violence-against-children-online

United Nations Office of Drug and Crime (UNODC). (2022). *World Drug Report 2022*. United Nations. https://www.unodc.org/unodc/en/data-and-analysis/world-drug-report-2022.html

United Nations Office of Drugs and Crime. (n.d.). Indian Ocean East. *Global Maritime Crime Programme*. UNDoC. https://www.unodc.org/unodc/en/piracy/indian-ocean-east.html

United Nations Office on Drugs and Crime. (2000, Novemeber 15). *United Nations Convention against Transnational Organized Crime and the Protocols Thereto*. United Nations Office on Drugs and Crime. https://www.unodc.org/documents/treaties/UNTOC/Publications/TOC%20 Convention/TOCebook-e.pdf

United Nations Office on Drugs and Crime. (2018, April). *Defining Organised Crime*. United nations Office on Drugs and Crime: https://www.unodc.org/e4j/zh/organized-crime/module-1/key-issues/defining-organized-crime.html

United Nations Office on Drugs and Crime. (2020). *Impact of the Covid-19 Pandemic on Trafficking in Persons: Preliminary Findings and Messaging Based on Rapid Stocktaking*. UN.

UNOC. (2023). *Money Laundering, Proceeds of Crime and the Financing of Terrorism*. UN. https://www.unodc.org/unodc/en/money-laundering/index.html

UNODC. (2009). *International Framework for Action To Implement the Trafficking in Persons Protocol*. UN.

UNODC. (2015a). *UNODC ANNUAL REPORT 2015*. UNDOC. www.unodc.org

UNODC. (2015b). *World Drug Report*. https://www.unodc.org/documents/wdr2015/World_Drug_Report_2015.pdf

UNODC. (2019). *Enhancing Criminal Justice Responses to Trafficking in Persons in Eastern Africa*. UN.

UNODC. (2019). Global study on homicide: Executive summary, Vienna. UNODC.

UNODC. (2020, April). Organized crime module 6 key issues: Ethical perspective - moral failure in decision-making. Organized Crime Module 6 Key Issues: Ethical Perspective - Moral Failure in Decision-Making. https://www.unodc.org/e4j/en/organized-crime/module-6/key-issues/ethical-perspective.html

UNTOC. (2000). *Protocol to Prevent*. Suppress and Punish Trafficking in Persons, Especially Women and Children.

US Attorney's Office. (2022). *Top Money Launderer For Ghana-Based Criminal Enterprise Sentenced To Nine Years*. USAO. https://www.justice.gov/usao-sdny/pr/top-money-launderer-ghana-based-criminal-enterprise-sentenced-nine-years on 07/01/2024

US Department of State. (2022). *Trafficking in Persons Report*.

Vaia, G., & Bisogno, M. (2020). Fighting organised crime and mafia-type firms: the role of public administrations. *Fighting organised crime and mafia-type firms*, 1-130.

Vaknin, S. (2000). The criminality of transition. In M. Pagon (Ed.), Policing in Central and Eastern Europe: Ethics, Integrity and Human Rights (pp. 61–70). Ljubljana, Slovenia: Fakulteta za policijsko-varnostne vede [College of Police and SecurityStudies].

van Diemen, D. (2023). Filthy seam of sabotage – how thieving cartels are plunging South Africa into darkness. *Daily Mavrick*. https://www.dailymaverick.co.za/article/2023-03-04-eskom-sabotage-cartels-power-cuts/

Van Niekerk, T., & Sebakamotse, J. K. T. (2020). A few critical observations of current oversight and accountability challenges of financial management of municipalities in the Free State province: An ethical dilemma. Journal for Christian Scholarship= Tydskrif vir Christelike Wetenskap, 56(3-4), 269-293.

Varese, F. (2011). *Mafias on the move: How organized crime conquers new territories*. Princeton University Press.

Varshney, A. (2002). *Ethnic Conflict and Civic Life: Hindus and Muslims in India*. Yale University Press.

Velasco, C. (2022, May). Cybercrime and Artificial Intelligence. An overview of the work of international organizations on criminal justice and the international applicable instruments. In *ERA Forum* (Vol. 23, No. 1, pp. 109-126). Berlin/Heidelberg: Springer Berlin Heidelberg.

Verdier, P. H., & Stephan, P. B. (2021). International Human Rights and Multinational Corporations: An FCPA Approach. *BUL Rev.*, *101*, 1359.

Verghese, A. (2018, 5 June). *Did Hindu-Muslim conflicts in India really start with British rule?* Scroll. https://scroll.in/article/880832/did-hindu-muslim-conflicts-in-india-really-start-with-british-rule

Villacampa, C., & Gómez, M. J. (2017). Online child sexual grooming: Empirical findings on victimisation and perspectives on legal requirements. *International Review of Victimology*, *23*(2), 105–121. doi:10.1177/0269758016682585

Villani, S. (2020). Fight Against Organized Crime and Resilience to Climate Change: A Relationship of Mutual Causality. The Palgrave Handbook of Climate Resilient Societies, 1-28.

Vinnakota, D., Arafat, S. M. Y., & Kabir, R. (2021). Pornography and Sexual Violence Against Women in India: A Scoping Review. *Journal of Psychosexual Health*, *3*(3), 216–221. doi:10.1177/26318318211023935

Viollaz, J., Long, B., Trung, C. T., Kempinski, J., Rawson, B. M., Quang, H. X., Hiền, N. N., Liên, N. T. B., Dũng, C. T., Huyền, H. T., McWhirter, R., Dung, N. T. T., & Gore, M. L. (2021). Using crime script analysis to understand wildlife poaching in Vietnam. *Ambio*, *50*(7), 1378–1393. doi:10.1007/s13280-020-01498-3 PMID:33738731

Von Ketelhodt, A., & Wöcke, A. (2008). The impact of electricity crises on the consumption behaviour of small and medium enterprises. *Journal of Energy in Southern Africa, 19(*1), 4-12. doi:10.17159/2413-3051/2008/v19i1a3321

von Lampe, K. (2016). *Organized Crime: Analyzing illegal activities, criminal structures, and extra-legal governance.* Sage. doi:10.4135/9781506305110

Waardenburg, M., Groenleer, M., & De Jong, J. (2020). Designing environments for experimentation, learning and innovation in public policy and governance. *Policy and Politics*, *48*(1), 67–87.

Waldron, J. (2021). The rule of law and the role of courts. *Global Constitutionalism*, *10*(1), 91–105.

Wannenburg, G. (2005). Organised Crime in West Africa. *African Security Review*, *14*(4), 5–16. doi:10.1080/10246029.2005.9627583

Ward, C. (1973). *Vandalism*. The Architecturel Press.

Ward, M. (2020). Walls and Cows: Social Media, Vigilante Vantage, and Political Discourse. *Political Discourse. Social Media + Society*, *6*(2). doi:10.1177/2056305120928513

Wasser, S. K., Torkelson, A., Winters, M., Horeaux, Y., Tucker, S., Otiende, M. Y., Sitam, F. A. T., Buckleton, J., & Weir, B. S. (2018). Combating transnational organized crime by linking multiple large ivory seizures to the same dealer. *Science Advances*, *4*(9), 1–10. doi:10.1126/sciadv.aat0625 PMID:30255141

Watson, D., Sousa-Santos, J. L., & Howes, L. (2021). Transnational and organised crime in Pacific Island countries and territories: Police capacity to respond to the emerging security threat.

Wayo, A. (2023). *The Role of Forensic Accounting in Combating Money Laundering in Ghana* [Doctoral dissertation, Northcentral University].

Wazambi, F., Komanya, J., & Henga, A. (2020). *Summary of the Tanzania Human Rights Report 2019: Tanzania Mainland.* Legal and Human Rights Centre.

Weale, A. (2020). MODERN SOCIAL CONTRACT THEORY C. Oxford University Press.

Webline Infosoft Pvt. Ltd., Dehradun. (n.d.). *Welcome to Forest Survey of India*. FSI. https://fsi.nic.in/isfr-volume-ii

Werleman, C. (2021). Rising Violence against Muslims in India Under Modi and BJP Rule. *Insight Turkey*, *23*(2), 39–50. doi:10.25253/99.2021232.3

What is child grooming? Here are the six steps a predator takes - Indiana Child Advocacy Centers and Chapter of NCA. (n.d.). Indiana Chapter of National Children's Alliance. https://incacs.org/what-is-child-grooming-here-are-the-six-steps-a-predator-takes/

Why are farmers in Manipur cultivating poppy ? (2019, November 23). Economic and Political Weekly. https://www.epw.in/engage/article/why-are-farmers-manipur-cultivating-poppy

Wilkinson, S. I. (2004). *Votes and Violence: Electoral Competition and Ethnic Riots in India*. Cambridge University Press. doi:10.1017/CBO9780511510458

Williams, B. (2023). *Policing Mental Health, Vulnerability and Risk*. Critical Publishing.

Williams, P. (2009). Illicit markets, weak states and violence: Iraq and Mexico. *Crime, Law, and Social Change*, *52*(3), 323–336. doi:10.1007/s10611-009-9194-0

Wilson, P. (1988). Preventing Vandalism and Graffiti. *Journal of Security Administration*, *11*(2), 28–35.

Windle, J., Moyle, L., & Coomber, R. (2020). 'Vulnerable'kids going country: Children and young People's involvement in county lines drug dealing. *Youth Justice*, *20*(1-2), 64–78.

Winters, G. M., & Jeglic, E. L. (2017). Stages of Sexual Grooming: Recognizing Potentially Predatory Behaviors of Child Molesters. *Deviant Behavior*, *38*(6), 724–733. doi:10.1080/01639625.2016.1197656

Wolf, B. (2011). 'Green-Collar Crime': Environmental Crime and Justice in the Sociological Perspective. *Sociology Compass*, *5*(7), 499–511. doi:10.1111/j.1751-9020.2011.00381.x

Wright, A. (2013). *Organised crime*. Routledge. doi:10.4324/9781843926450

Wright, J. P., Tibbetts, S. G., & Daigle, L. E. (2014). *Criminals in the making: Criminality across the life course*. Sage Publications.

Writer, S. (2021). Evidence of Eskom being destroyed from the inside: report. *Business Tech*. https://businesstech.co.za/news/energy/539754/evidence-of-eskom-being-destroyed-from-the-inside-report/

Wyatt, T. (2009). Exploring the organization of Russia Far East's illegal wildlife trade: Two case studies of the illegal fur and illegal falcon trades. *Global Crime*, *10*(1-2), 144–154. doi:10.1080/17440570902783947

Wyatt, T. (2014). The Russian Far East's illegal timber trade: An organized crime? *Crime, Law, and Social Change*, *61*(1), 15–35. doi:10.1007/s10611-013-9461-y

Wyatt, T., van Uhm, D., & Nurse, A. (2020). Differentiating criminal networks in the illegal wildlife trade: Organized, corporate and disorganized crime. *Trends in Organized Crime*, *23*, 350–366.

Xing, J. L. (2022). Driving as communities: Chinese taxi drivers' technology, job, and mobility choices under the pressure of e-hailing. *Mobilities*, *17*(5), 676–694.

Yar, M., & Steinmetz, K. F. (2019). *Cybercrime and society*. Sage Publications.

Yeebo, Y. (2017). The true story of the fake US embassy in Ghana. *The Guardian*. https://www.theguardian.com/world/2017/nov/28/the-true-story-of-the-fake-us-embassy-in-ghana on 05/01/2024

Yeh, S. S. (2022). *The End of Corruption and Impunity*. Rowman & Littlefield.

Yin, E. T. (2018). *Religion as an organizing principle in Ankaful maximum security prison, Ghana* [Doctoral dissertation, University of Cape Coast].

Yin, E. T. (2020). Religion, Rehabilitation, and Reintegration of Prison Inmates into Mainstream Society. Handbook of research on trends and issues in crime prevention, rehabilitation, and victim support, 398-414. IGI Global. doi:10.4018/978-1-7998-1286-9.ch023

Yin, E. T., & Seiwoh, B. M. (2021). Costs and delays in accessing justice: A comparative analysis of Ghana and Sierra Leone. In Advancing Civil Justice Reform and Conflict Resolution in Africa and Asia: Comparative Analyses and Case Studies (pp. 112-139). IGI Global. doi:10.4018/978-1-7998-7898-8.ch007

Yin, E. T., Atupare, P. A., Kofie, N., Owusu, L. P., & Botchway, T. P. (2021). Rights and religious belief in maintaining prison social order. *UCC Faculty of Law Journal*, *1*(1), 1–16. doi:10.47963/ucclj.v1i1.217

Yin, E. T., Boateng, W., & Kofie, N. (2022). Family acceptance, economic situation, and faith community: The lived experiences of ex-convicts in Ghana. *Social Sciences & Humanities Open*, *5*(1), 100240. doi:10.1016/j.ssaho.2021.100240

Yin, E. T., & Kofie, N. (2021). The informal prison economy in Ghana: Patterns, exchanges, and institutional contradictions. *Cogent Social Sciences*, *7*(1), 2004673. doi:10.1080/23311886.2021.2004673

Yorke-Smith, L. (2010). *Solving Copper Theft*. Hi-Tech Security Solutions. http://www.securitysa.com/article.aspx?pklarticleid=5905

Yousaf, F. N. (2018). Forced migration, human trafficking, and human security. *Current Sociology*, *66*(2), 209–225.

Yusuf, O. L., & Ojewale, O. R. (2023). Implications of urban violence on community security in Ibadan North Local Government Area of Oyo State, Nigeria. *Urban Crime. International Journal (Toronto, Ont.)*, *4*(1), 12–39.

Zabyelina, Y., & Thachuk, K. L. (Eds.). (2022). *The Private Sector and Organized Crime: Criminal Entrepreneurship, Illicit Profits, and Private Sector Security Governance*. Taylor & Francis.

Zafri, A. (2023, February 2023). *India's 'cow protectors' are getting away with murder*. Codastory. https://www.codastory.com/disinformation/india-cow-vigilantes/

Zatsepin, M. (1995). *Security of Entrepreneurship: Criminological and Criminal Law Issues*. Aspect Press.

Zavos, J. (1999, April). The Arya Samaj and the antecedents of Hindu nationalism. *International Journal of Hindu Studies*, *3*(1), 58–63. doi:10.1007/s11407-999-0008-x

Zomi Students Federation vs Union of India and Another WP (C) No 572 of 2023

About the Contributors

Alicia Danielsson, a distinguished academic and researcher, currently leads the Centre for Contemporary Coronial Law at the University of Bolton, a role she assumed in September 2022. In addition to this significant position, she also serves as the Director for the Centre for Trafficking, Exploitation and Modern Slavery Studies at the Hume Institute for Postgraduate Studies in Lausanne, Switzerland. This dual role underscores her commitment to addressing some of today's most pressing legal and humanitarian issues. Alicia's academic journey led her to earn her Ph.D. at Abertay University, Dundee, in 2021. Her thesis, titled 'Economic Activity or Public Order Limitations: The Interplay of the Regulation of Prostitution between National Law, EU Law and Efforts to Combat Human Trafficking,' reflects her deep expertise in EU law, employment law, criminal law, contract law, and human rights law. Her research interests are rooted in the intricate dynamics of legal frameworks, with a particular focus on the area of freedom, security, and justice, as well as EU labour law and human rights protection. In her role as an Assistant Teaching Professor in Law, Alicia is deeply involved in the academic and operational management of her centres, fostering a Teaching Intensive, Research Informed (TIRI) culture. She is known for her cross-disciplinary engagement and her ability to blend critical analysis with practical insights in her teachings.

***

Mohammed Kayed Abdel-Haq is currently the Founding Director of the Centre for Islamic Finance at the University of Bolton and serves as the Assistant Vice-Chancellor for Postgraduate Developments. He also holds the position of Executive Director of the Development Office at the same university. Additionally, Professor Abdel-Haq is the Principal of the Hume Institute for Postgraduate Studies in Lausanne, Switzerland, and a Professor in Banking. He fulfills the role of CEO at Oakstone Merchant Bank as well. His contributions to public service include chairing the UK Government's Advisory Task and Finish Group on Taxi and Private Hire Vehicle Licensing, with the report published in February 2019. Previously, he was a member of the Council of the Royal Institute for International Affairs (Chatham House) and, in 2011, was appointed Chairman of the UK Ministerial Advisory Group on Extremism in Universities and FE Colleges. Professor Abdel-Haq is affiliated with institutions such as King's College, London, where he is a Visiting Professor, and IDEAS at the London School of Economics, and he also serves as an Editor for the Middle East Element Series at Cambridge University Press.

Amit Anand is presently working as an Assistant Professor at School of Legal Studies, REVA University, Bengaluru. He has completed his PhD (Law) from Lancaster University, U.K. in 2022 on the topic 'Unheard and Unnoticed: Violence Against Women in India (A Study of Practice of Witch-hunting, Honour Killing and Devadasi System)'. He holds LL.M (Human Rights) from the University of Reading, U.K. (2015) and B.A.LL.B. (Honours.) from National Law School of India University, Bengaluru (2014). He has presented two oral statements to separate United Nations Treaty Bodies in 2023. The first statement was presented before the Committee on the Rights of Persons with Disabilities on the topic "Impacts and challenges faced by persons with disabilities in situations of risk & the role of state and non-state actors in addressing them" and the second statement was presented to the Committee on the Elimination of Discrimination against Women on "Equal and inclusive representation of women in decision-making systems". His joint submission on 'Measures to Prevent Sexual Abuse of Children in Residential Care Homes in India' to the United Nations Committee on the Rights of the Child (UNCRC), September 2021 has also been cited by the UNCRC in its Children's Rights and Alternative Care - Background Document. Dr. Amit has also submitted written evidence to the Women and Equalities Select Committee, House of Commons, UK Parliament on 'Women's reproductive health in the UK', October 2023. His submission has been accepted by the Select Committee and has been published on the Committee's website. He also has several paper publications in both national and international peer reviewed journals. His research interests lie in the area of International Human Rights Law (particularly on the issue of gender based violence, caste discrimination).

Himanshi Bhatia is an Assistant Professor at Symbiosis Law School, Nagpur. She is currently pursuing her Ph.D. from Maharashtra National Law University, Nagpur. She holds an LL.M in Criminal & Security Law from the National University of Juridical Sciences, Kolkata, and an LL.B (Hons) from the University of Delhi. Before joining academics, she worked at the High Court of Uttarakhand as Legal Researcher cum Judicial Clerk to the Hon'ble Chief Justice of the High Court. Her current research interest includes International Criminal Law for Environment, Criminology and Green Victimology

Junaid Khan is a dedicated and dynamic legal professional based in Burnley, England, United Kingdom, with a proven track record of academic and professional achievements in law. Graduating with a First Class LLB Law degree from the University of Bolton in April 2022, Junaid has consistently demonstrated academic excellence and a deep commitment to the legal field. Following his undergraduate studies, he pursued further specialization by enrolling in the Legal Practice Course (LPC) and Master of Laws (LLM) programmes at The Manchester Metropolitan University. Currently, Junaid is a Trainee Solicitor at ASK LEGAL SOLICITORS LTD in Bolton, England, a role he has held since November 2022.

Phathutshedzo Madumi serves as a Lecturer within the Department of Military Economics at Stellenbosch University in South Africa. An up-and-coming researcher with a strong commitment to advancing knowledge in the field, Phathutshedzo aspires to earn a Ph.D. in Economics. His professional endeavors center on a wide range of economic facets, encompassing Economic Development, Political Economy, Economic Growth, Economic Theory, International Economics, Public Economics, Income and Wage Inequality, Human Capital Development, and Labor Economics.

Jyothis Mary is a Teaching Scholar at the Centre for Trafficking, Exploitation, and Modern Slavery Studies at Hume Institute for Post-Graduate Studies, Lausanne, Switzerland. She is also a Legal Fellow, South Asia Team at the International Justice Mission. She holds a Master of Laws in Transnational Crime and Justice from the University for Peace and the United Nations Interregional Crime and Justice Research Institute, Italy. She worked as an Assistant Professor at reputed institutions in India from 2017 to 2022. She practiced in the District and Sessions Court, Calicut, India, and worked as a Paralegal Volunteer at Kerala Legal Services Authority, India.

Godfrey Mpandikizi is the Executive Director of Tanzania Anti Human Trafficking and Legal Initiatives (TATLI), an organization focusing on countering human trafficking in Tanzania. He is also an Advocate of the High Court of Tanzania and admitted Legal Counsel to the African Court on Human and Peoples Rights (AfCHPR). He holds an LLB and an LLM, majoring in Human Rights, Human Trafficking and Migration from the University of Dar Es Salaam. He is also a visiting scholar to Universities lecturing on African Human Rights Systems, Human Trafficking and Migration from the African Perspectives.

Baidya Nath Mukherjee, an Assistant Professor at the School of Law AURO University and a Research Scholar of Christ (Deemed to be University), combines academia with a knack for research, adorned with over 6 years of experience. His brilliance shines through 10+ papers in esteemed journals like the Manchester Journal of International Economic Law (ABDC Indexed), Journal of Liberty and International Affairs (Scopus Indexed), and Journal of Pharmaceutical Negative Results (Web of Science & Scopus indexed). He crafts knowledge in 10+ book chapters with prestigious publishers like Taylor and Francis, Springer, and more. A sought-after speaker in national constitutional rights programs, his expertise spans international law, human rights, and intellectual property. A radiant presence in international and national law conferences, he enriches discussions in workshops and round tables.

Joshua T. Shadwick is an Assistant Professor at Southeast Missouri State University in the Department of Criminal Justice, Social Work and Sociology. He teaches both undergraduate and graduate courses on topics ranging from research methods to gangs. His research interests include the justice system's response to social problems, police investigations, and wildlife crime. Dr. Shadwick's research has been published in peer-reviewed journals such as, Policing: An International Journal, Deviant Behavior, and Criminal Justice Policy Review. Prior to his current occupation, he served a total of seven years in law enforcement. These years of service were comprised of four years as a Sheriff Deputy for the Montgomery County Sheriff's Office and three years as a Conservation Agent for the Missouri Department of Conservation.

Prateek Sikchi is an Assistant Professor at Symbiosis Law School, Nagpur. He is currently pursuing his Ph.D. in Corporate Governance from National Law University, Jodhpur. He has pursued his LL.M. in Corporate and Commercial laws from National Academy for Legal Studies and Research University of Law, Hyderabad. He has done his B. Com. LL. B (Business Law Hons.) from Institute of Law, Nirma University, Ahmedabad.

Bodhisattwa Som, is working as an Assistant Professor in the School of Legal Studies, REVA University, Bangalore. He has graduated with a BA. LL.B (Hons.) degree from CHRIST (Deemed to be University), Bangalore and a LLM degree from the National Law School of India University, Bangalore. He is passionate about research and has presented papers in National and International conferences. He has recently contributed in a SCOPUS indexed book chapter, to be published by Routledge (Taylor and Francis). His research interests include International Law, Human Rights and International Criminal Law.

Elijah Tukwariba Yin is a senior lecturer at the Faculty of Law, where he teaches Legal Research, Jurisprudence, Philosophical Foundations of Law, Critical Thinking in Law, and Introduction to Sociology. Dr. Yin has a Bachelor of Arts degree from the University of Cape Coast (UCC) in Ghana, a Postgraduate Diploma in Law from the University of Law in the United Kingdom, and an International Master's in Sociology of Law from the Oñati International Institute for the Sociology of Law (IISL) of the Faculty of Law of the University of the Basque Country in Spain, in collaboration with the University of Milan in Italy. He earned his Master of Laws (LLM) degree from Unicaf University in Zambia and his Ph.D. from the UCC. Dr. Yin is an alumnus of the Institute for Global Law and Policy (IGLP) at Harvard Law School; a scholarship award recipient for the Scholars Writing Workshop in Bangkok, Thailand (2018), and the Global Scholars Academy in Geneva, Switzerland (2020). Dr. Yin is also a scholarship recipient for the Accra Socio-Legal Writing Workshop organised by Cardiff Law and Global Justice and the British Academy for the Humanities and Social Sciences at the Ghana Institute of Advanced Legal Studies in Accra, Ghana (2018). Dr. Yin has won research grants from notable research directorates and institutions, namely the Directorate of Research, Innovation and Consultancy of the UCC, the School of Law of the University of Ghana, etc. Dr. Yin's academic and research interests include criminology and criminal law, legal theory, comparative legal culture, international human rights law, sociology of law, civil justice and housing law, corporate law and governance, multicultural constitutionalism, environmental justice, and socio-legal research methods. Dr. Yin is a member of the Law and Society Association and the Institute for Global Law and Policy Network at Harvard Law School, all in the USA. He is also a member of the Onati Community in Spain.

Index

R

S

T

U

V

W

Z

www.ingramcontent.com/pod-product-compliance
Lightning Source LLC
LaVergne TN
LVHW081349300926
849161LV00008B/2106